Elisabetta Caminer Turra

SELECTED WRITINGS OF AN EIGHTEENTH-CENTURY VENETIAN WOMAN OF LETTERS

༄

Edited and Translated
by Catherine M. Sama

THE UNIVERSITY OF CHICAGO PRESS
Chicago & London

Elisabetta Caminer Turra, 1751–96

Catherine M. Sama is assistant professor of Italian at the University of Rhode Island.

The University of Chicago Press, Chicago 60637
The University of Chicago Press, Ltd., London
© 2003 by The University of Chicago
All rights reserved. Published 2003
Printed in the United States of America

12 11 10 09 08 07 06 05 04 03   1 2 3 4 5
ISBN: 0-226-81767-9 (cloth)
ISBN: 0-226-81768-7 (paper)

Library of Congress Cataloging-in-Publication Data

Caminer Turra, Elisabetta, 1751–1796.
   [Selections. English. 2003]
   Selected writings of an eighteenth-century Venetian woman of letters /
Elisabetta Caminer Turra ; edited and translated by Catherine M. Sama.
      p. cm. — (The other voice in early modern Europe)
   Includes bibliographical references and index.
   ISBN 0-226-81767-9 (alk. paper) — ISBN 0-226-81768-7 (pbk. : alk. paper)
      1. Caminer Turra, Elisabetta, 1751–1796—Correspondence. I. Sama,
   Catherine M. II. Title. III. Series.
   PQ4684.C44 A27 2003
   858'.609—dc21
   2003005006

To the memory of Elisabetta Caminer Turra, in appreciation of her intellect, courage, and persevering spirit

CONTENTS

Part II
Women and Society
The Intellectual Life

Fashion

Marriage or the Convent

ACKNOWLEDGMENTS

M any people have contributed to the research and writing of this book. I am deeply indebted to the foundations and institutions that so generously funded the extensive research phase in Italy and the writing phase as well: the Fiat Corporation, the Gladys Krieble Delmas Foundation, the Fulbright Commission, the University of Rhode Island, and the American Association of University Women. Without this financial support, I would never have been able to undertake or complete this project.

I would like to thank the Italian librarians and archivists who assisted me in my research, and I extend special thanks to the staff at the Biblioteca Nazionale Marciana di Venezia, the Museo Civico del Museo Correr, the Archivio di Stato di Venezia, the Biblioteca Civica della Bertoliana di Vicenza, the Archivio di Stato di Vicenza, the Biblioteca del Seminario di Padova, and the Archivio di Stato di Firenze.

I am indebted to Franco Fido, who first introduced me to Elisabetta Caminer Turra, and whose support over the course of a decade of research and writing has been immeasurably valuable. I extend deepest thanks to Mario Infelise, whose expert guidance and persistent prodding from across the Atlantic were fundamental in bringing this book to fruition. I cannot thank Angelo Colla enough for his generosity and creativity in exchanging ideas and information about Caminer with me. I am grateful for the guidance and intellectual companionship of Adriana Chemello, Antonia Arslan, and the Società delle Storiche Italiane. I cannot adequately express my gratitude to a special circle of colleagues and friends from the Veneto: Maria Teresa Sega and Guglielmo Fila, Maria Parrino and Mario Piccinini, Tiziana Plebani and Alberto Fiorin, Patrizia Bravetti and Piero Scarpa, Elena Bertagnolli, and Maria Magotti. Over the years, they have all given generously of their time, intelligence, hospitality, and sense of humor; as a group, they helped me make

Venice my home, and they keep me connected while I am away. I am indebted to the women in my writing group at the University of Rhode Island for carefully reading my manuscript and offering invaluable suggestions for its improvement. I extend special thanks to Wendy Wassyng Roworth, Franca Barricelli, Andrea Rusnock, Rebecca Messbarger, Paola Giuli, and Paula Findlen, who have supported and inspired me in my work on Caminer.

I am indebted to those who lent their expertise to improve my translation of Caminer's writing: Franco Fido for his help with some of the theatrical texts; Anthony Oldcorn for his assistance with the poetry; Maria Parrino and Mario Piccinini for their help with particularly obtuse passages; and especially Paschal Viglionese, who offered helpful suggestions for nearly every translation in the manuscript. I thank Erik Carlson for his meticulous editing and Randy Petilos for his help in bringing the manuscript to the publication stage. I am immeasurably indebted to Albert Rabil for his fine editorial eye, his wise counsel, and his unflagging encouragement. Heartfelt thanks go to my mother, Jane Isherwood Sama, for her help in the final stages of the book. Finally, I would like to express deep gratitude to my family and friends for their steadfast support and encouragement.

Catherine M. Sama

THE OTHER VOICE IN
EARLY MODERN EUROPE:
INTRODUCTION TO THE SERIES
Margaret L. King and Albert Rabil Jr.

THE OLD VOICE AND THE OTHER VOICE

In western Europe and the United States, women are nearing equality in the professions, in business, and in politics. Most enjoy access to education, reproductive rights, and autonomy in financial affairs. Issues vital to women are on the public agenda: equal pay, child care, domestic abuse, breast cancer research, and curricular revision with an eye to the inclusion of women.

These recent achievements have their origins in things women (and some male supporters) said for the first time about six hundred years ago. Theirs is the "other voice," in contradistinction to the "first voice," the voice of the educated men who created Western culture. Coincident with a general reshaping of European culture in the period 1300–1700 (called the Renaissance or early modern period), questions of female equality and opportunity were raised that still resound and are still unresolved.

The other voice emerged against the backdrop of a three-thousand-year history of the derogation of women rooted in the civilizations related to Western culture: Hebrew, Greek, Roman, and Christian. Negative attitudes toward women inherited from these traditions pervaded the intellectual, medical, legal, religious, and social systems that developed during the European Middle Ages.

The following pages describe the traditional, overwhelmingly male views of women's nature inherited by early modern Europeans and the new tradition that the "other voice" called into being to begin to challenge reigning assumptions. This review should serve as a framework for understanding the texts published in the series "The Other Voice in Early Modern Europe." Introductions specific to each text and author follow this essay in all the volumes of the series.

TRADITIONAL VIEWS OF WOMEN, 500 B.C.E.–1500 C.E.

Embedded in the philosophical and medical theories of the ancient Greeks were perceptions of the female as inferior to the male in both mind and body. Similarly, the structure of civil legislation inherited from the ancient Romans was biased against women, and the views on women developed by Christian thinkers out of the Hebrew Bible and the Christian New Testament were negative and disabling. Literary works composed in the vernacular of ordinary people, and widely recited or read, conveyed these negative assumptions. The social networks within which most women lived—those of the family and the institutions of the Roman Catholic Church—were shaped by this negative tradition and sharply limited the areas in which women might act in and upon the world.

GREEK PHILOSOPHY AND FEMALE NATURE. Greek biology assumed that women were inferior to men and defined them as merely childbearers and housekeepers. This view was authoritatively expressed in the works of the philosopher Aristotle.

Aristotle thought in dualities. He considered action superior to inaction, form (the inner design or structure of any object) superior to matter, completion to incompletion, possession to deprivation. In each of these dualities, he associated the male principle with the superior quality and the female with the inferior. "The male principle in nature," he argued, "is associated with active, formative and perfected characteristics, while the female is passive, material and deprived, desiring the male in order to become complete."[1] Men are always identified with virile qualities, such as judgment, courage, and stamina, and women with their opposites—irrationality, cowardice, and weakness.

The masculine principle was considered superior even in the womb. The man's semen, Aristotle believed, created the form of a new human creature, while the female body contributed only matter. (The existence of the ovum, and with it the other facts of human embryology, was not established until the seventeenth century.) Although the later Greek physician Galen believed there was a female component in generation, contributed by "female semen," the followers of both Aristotle and Galen saw the male role in human generation as more active and more important.

In the Aristotelian view, the male principle sought always to reproduce itself. The creation of a female was always a mistake, therefore, resulting from

---

1. Aristotle, *Physics* 1.9.192a20–24, in *The Complete Works of Aristotle*, ed. Jonathan Barnes, rev. Oxford trans., 2 vols. (Princeton, 1984), 1:328.

an imperfect act of generation. Every female born was considered a "defective" or "mutilated" male (as Aristotle's terminology has variously been translated), a "monstrosity" of nature.[2]

For Greek theorists, the biology of males and females was the key to their psychology. The female was softer and more docile, more apt to be despondent, querulous, and deceitful. Being incomplete, moreover, she craved sexual fulfillment in intercourse with a male. The male was intellectual, active, and in control of his passions.

These psychological polarities derived from the theory that the universe consisted of four elements (earth, fire, air, and water), expressed in human bodies as four "humors" (black bile, yellow bile, blood, and phlegm) considered respectively dry, hot, damp, and cold and corresponding to mental states ("melancholic," "choleric," "sanguine," "phlegmatic"). In this scheme the male, sharing the principles of earth and fire, was dry and hot; the female, sharing the principles of air and water, was cold and damp.

Female psychology was further affected by her dominant organ, the uterus (womb), *hystera* in Greek. The passions generated by the womb made women lustful, deceitful, talkative, irrational, indeed—when these affects were in excess—"hysterical."

Aristotle's biology also had social and political consequences. If the male principle was superior and the female inferior, then in the household, as in the state, men should rule and women must be subordinate. That hierarchy did not rule out the companionship of husband and wife, whose cooperation was necessary for the welfare of children and the preservation of property. Such mutuality supported male preeminence.

Aristotle's teacher Plato suggested a different possibility: that men and women might possess the same virtues. The setting for this proposal is the imaginary and ideal Republic that Plato sketches in a dialogue of that name. Here, for a privileged elite capable of leading wisely, all distinctions of class and wealth dissolve, as, consequently, do those of gender. Without households or property, as Plato constructs his ideal society, there is no need for the subordination of women. Women may therefore be educated to the same level as men to assume leadership. Plato's Republic remained imaginary, however. In real societies, the subordination of women remained the norm and the prescription.

The views of women inherited from the Greek philosophical tradition became the basis for medieval thought. In the thirteenth century, the supreme Scholastic philosopher Thomas Aquinas, among others, still echoed

---

2. Aristotle, *Generation of Animals* 2.3.737a27–28, in *The Complete Works*, 1:1144.

Aristotle's views of human reproduction, of male and female personalities, and of the preeminent male role in the social hierarchy.

ROMAN LAW AND THE FEMALE CONDITION.   Roman law, like Greek philosophy, underlay medieval thought and shaped medieval society. The ancient belief that adult property-owning men should administer households and make decisions affecting the community at large is the very fulcrum of Roman law.

About 450 B.C.E., during Rome's republican era, the community's customary law was recorded (legendarily) on twelve tablets erected in the city's central forum. It was later elaborated by professional jurists whose activity increased in the imperial era, when much new legislation was passed, especially on issues affecting family and inheritance.. This growing, changing body of laws was eventually codified in the *Corpus of Civil Law* under the direction of the emperor Justinian, generations after the empire ceased to be ruled from Rome. That *Corpus*, read and commented on by medieval scholars from the eleventh century on, inspired the legal systems of most of the cities and kingdoms of Europe.

Laws regarding dowries, divorce, and inheritance pertain primarily to women. Since those laws aimed to maintain and preserve property, the women concerned were those from the property-owning minority. Their subordination to male family members points to the even greater subordination of lower-class and slave women, about whom the laws speak little.

In the early republic, the *paterfamilias*, or "father of the family," possessed *patria potestas*, "paternal power." The term *pater*, "father," in both these cases does not necessarily mean biological father but denotes the head of a household. The father was the person who owned the household's property and, indeed, its human members. The *paterfamilias* had absolute power—including the power, rarely exercised, of life or death—over his wife, his children, and his slaves, as much as his cattle.

Male children could be "emancipated," an act that granted legal autonomy and the right to own property. Those over fourteen could be emancipated by a special grant from the father or automatically by their father's death. But females could never be emancipated; instead, they passed from the authority of their father to that of a husband or, if widowed or orphaned while still unmarried, to a guardian or tutor.

Marriage in its traditional form placed the woman under her husband's authority, or *manus*. He could divorce her on grounds of adultery, drinking wine, or stealing from the household, but she could not divorce him. She could neither possess property in her own right nor bequeath any to her children upon her death. When her husband died, the household property passed not to her but to his male heirs. And when her father died, she had no claim to any family inheritance, which was directed to her brothers or more remote male relatives. The effect of these laws was to exclude women from civil society, itself based on property ownership.

In the later republican and imperial periods, these rules were significantly modified. Women rarely married according to the traditional form. The practice of "free" marriage allowed a woman to remain under her father's authority, to possess property given her by her father (most frequently the "dowry," recoverable from the husband's household on his death), and to inherit from her father. She could also bequeath property to her own children and divorce her husband, just as he could divorce her.

Despite this greater freedom, women still suffered enormous disability under Roman law. Heirs could belong only to the father's side, never the mother's. Moreover, although she could bequeath her property to her children, she could not establish a line of succession in doing so. A woman was "the beginning and end of her own family," said the jurist Ulpian. Moreover, women could play no public role. They could not hold public office, represent anyone in a legal case, or even witness a will. Women had only a private existence and no public personality.

The dowry system, the guardian, women's limited ability to transmit wealth, and total political disability are all features of Roman law adopted by the medieval communities of western Europe, although modified according to local customary laws.

CHRISTIAN DOCTRINE AND WOMEN'S PLACE. The Hebrew Bible and the Christian New Testament authorized later writers to limit women to the realm of the family and to burden them with the guilt of original sin. The passages most fruitful for this purpose were the creation narratives in Genesis and sentences from the Epistles defining women's role within the Christian family and community.

Each of the first two chapters of Genesis contains a creation narrative. In the first "God created man in his own image, in the image of God he created him; male and female he created them" (Gen. 1:27). In the second, God created Eve from Adam's rib (2:21–23). Christian theologians relied principally on Genesis 2 for their understanding of the relation between man and woman, interpreting the creation of Eve from Adam as proof of her subordination to him.

The creation story in Genesis 2 leads to that of the temptations in Genesis 3: of Eve by the wily serpent and of Adam by Eve. As read by Christian theologians from Tertullian to Thomas Aquinas, the narrative made Eve responsible for the Fall and its consequences. She instigated the act; she deceived her husband; she suffered the greater punishment. Her disobedience made it necessary for Jesus to be incarnated and to die on the cross. From the pulpit, moralists and preachers for centuries conveyed to women the guilt that they bore for original sin.

The Epistles offered advice to early Christians on building communities of the faithful. Among the matters to be regulated was the place of women. Paul offered views favorable to women in Gal. 3:28: "There is neither Jew nor Greek, there is neither slave nor free, there is neither male nor female; for you are all one in Christ Jesus." Paul also referred to women as his coworkers and placed them on a par with himself and his male coworkers (Phil. 4:2–3; Rom. 16:1–3; 1 Cor. 16:19). Elsewhere Paul limited women's possibilities: "But I want you to understand that the head of every man is Christ, the head of a woman is her husband, and the head of Christ is God" (1 Cor. 11:3).

Biblical passages by later writers (though attributed to Paul) enjoined women to forgo jewels, expensive clothes, and elaborate coiffures; and they forbade women to "teach or have authority over men," telling them to "learn in silence with all submissiveness" as is proper for one responsible for sin, consoling them, however, with the thought that they will be saved through childbearing (1 Tim. 2:9–15). Other texts among the later Epistles defined women as the weaker sex and emphasized their subordination to their husbands (1 Pet. 3:7; Col. 3:18; Eph. 5:22–23).

These passages from the New Testament became the arsenal employed by theologians of the early church to transmit negative attitudes toward women to medieval Christian culture—above all, Tertullian (*On the Apparel of Women*), Jerome (*Against Jovinian*), and Augustine (*The Literal Meaning of Genesis*).

THE IMAGE OF WOMEN IN MEDIEVAL LITERATURE. The philosophical, legal, and religious traditions born in antiquity formed the basis of the medieval intellectual synthesis wrought by trained thinkers, mostly clerics, writing in Latin and based largely in universities. The vernacular literary tradition that developed alongside the learned tradition also spoke about female nature and women's roles. Medieval stories, poems, and epics also portrayed women negatively—as lustful and deceitful—while praising good housekeepers and loyal wives as replicas of the Virgin Mary or the female saints and martyrs.

There is an exception in the movement of "courtly love" that evolved in southern France from the twelfth century. Courtly love was the erotic love between a nobleman and noblewoman, the latter usually superior in social rank. It was always adulterous. From the conventions of courtly love derive modern Western notions of romantic love. The tradition has had an impact disproportionate to its size, for it affected only a tiny elite, and very few women. The exaltation of the female lover probably does not reflect a higher evaluation of women or a step toward their sexual liberation. More likely it gives expression to the social and sexual tensions besetting the knightly class at a specific historical juncture.

The literary fashion of courtly love was on the wane by the thirteenth century, when the widely read *Romance of the Rose* was composed in French by two authors of significantly different dispositions. Guillaume de Lorris composed the initial four thousand verses about 1235, and Jean de Meun added about seventeen thousand verses—more than four times the original—about 1265.

The fragment composed by Guillaume de Lorris stands squarely in the tradition of courtly love. Here the poet, in a dream, is admitted into a walled garden where he finds a magic fountain in which a rosebush is reflected. He longs to pick one rose, but the thorns prevent his doing so, even as he is wounded by arrows from the god of love, whose commands he agrees to obey. The rest of this part of the poem recounts the poet's unsuccessful efforts to pluck the rose.

The longer part of the *Romance* by Jean de Meun also describes a dream. But here allegorical characters give long didactic speeches, providing a social satire on a variety of themes, some pertaining to women. Love is an anxious and tormented state, the poem explains: women are greedy and manipulative, marriage is miserable, beautiful women are lustful, ugly ones cease to please, and a chaste woman is as rare as a black swan.

Shortly after Jean de Meun completed *The Romance of the Rose*, Mathéolus penned his *Lamentations*, a long Latin diatribe against marriage translated into French about a century later. The *Lamentations* sum up medieval attitudes toward women and provoked the important response by Christine de Pizan in her *Book of the City of Ladies*.

In 1355 Giovanni Boccaccio wrote *Il Corbaccio*, another antifeminist manifesto, though ironically by an author whose other works pioneered new directions in Renaissance thought. The former husband of his lover appears to Boccaccio, condemning his unmoderated lust and detailing the defects of women. Boccaccio concedes at the end "how much men naturally surpass women in nobility" and is cured of his desires.[3]

WOMEN'S ROLES: THE FAMILY. The negative perceptions of women expressed in the intellectual tradition are also implicit in the actual roles that women played in European society. Assigned to subordinate positions in the

---

3. Giovanni Boccaccio, *The Corbaccio, or The Labyrinth of Love*, trans. and ed. Anthony K. Cassell, rev. ed. (Binghamton, N.Y., 1993), 71.

household and the church, they were barred from significant participation in public life.

Medieval European households, like those in antiquity and in non-Western civilizations, were headed by males. It was the male serf (or peasant), feudal lord, town merchant, or citizen who was polled or taxed or succeeded to an inheritance or had any acknowledged public role, although his wife or widow could stand as a temporary surrogate. From about 1100, the position of property-holding males was further enhanced: inheritance was confined to the male, or agnate, line—with depressing consequences for women.

A wife never fully belonged to her husband's family, nor was she a daughter to her father's family. She left her father's house young to marry whomever her parents chose. Her dowry was managed by her husband, and at her death it normally passed to her children by him.

A married woman's life was occupied nearly constantly with cycles of pregnancy, childbearing, and lactation. Women bore children through all the years of their fertility, and many died in childbirth. They were also responsible for raising young children up to six or seven. In the propertied classes that responsibility was shared, since it was common for a wet nurse to take over breast-feeding and for servants to perform other chores.

Women trained their daughters in the household duties appropriate to their status, nearly always tasks associated with textiles: spinning, weaving, sewing, embroidering. Their sons were sent out of the house as apprentices or students, or their training was assumed by fathers in later childhood and adolescence. On the death of her husband, a woman's children became the responsibility of his family. She generally did not take "his" children with her to a new marriage or back to her father's house, except sometimes in the artisan classes.

Women also worked. Rural peasants performed farm chores, merchant wives often practiced their husbands' trades, the unmarried daughters of the urban poor worked as servants or prostitutes. All wives produced or embellished textiles and did the housekeeping, while wealthy ones managed servants. These labors were unpaid or poorly paid but often contributed substantially to family wealth.

WOMEN'S ROLES: THE CHURCH. Membership in a household, whether a father's or a husband's, meant for women a lifelong subordination to others. In western Europe, the Roman Catholic Church offered an alternative to the career of wife and mother. A woman could enter a convent, parallel in function to the monasteries for men that evolved in the early Christian centuries.

In the convent, a woman pledged herself to a celibate life, lived accord-

ing to strict community rules, and worshiped daily. Often the convent offered training in Latin, allowing some women to become considerable scholars and authors as well as scribes, artists, and musicians. For women who chose
the conventual life, the benefits could be enormous, but for numerous others placed in convents by paternal choice, the life could be restrictive and
burdensome.

The conventual life declined as an alternative for women as the modern
age approached. Reformed monastic institutions resisted responsibility for
related female orders. The church increasingly restricted female institutional
life by insisting on closer male supervision.

Women often sought other options. Some joined the communities of lay-
women that sprang up spontaneously in the thirteenth century in the urban
zones of western Europe, especially in Flanders and Italy. Some joined the
heretical movements that flourished in late medieval Christendom, whose anticlerical and often antifamily positions particularly appealed to women. In
these communities, some women were acclaimed as "holy women" or "saints,"
whereas others often were condemned as frauds or heretics.

In all, though the options offered to women by the church were sometimes less than satisfactory, they were sometimes richly rewarding. After 1520
the convent remained an option only in Roman Catholic territories. Protes-
tantism engendered an ideal of marriage as a heroic endeavor and appeared
to place husband and wife on a more equal footing. Sermons and treatises,
however, still called for female subordination and obedience.

THE OTHER VOICE, 1300–1700

When the modern era opened, European culture was so firmly structured by
a framework of negative attitudes toward women that to dismantle it was a
monumental labor. The process began as part of a larger cultural movement
that entailed the critical reexamination of ideas inherited from the ancient
and medieval past. The humanists launched that critical reexamination.

THE HUMANIST FOUNDATION. Originating in Italy in the fourteenth
century, humanism quickly became the dominant intellectual movement in
Europe. Spreading in the sixteenth century from Italy to the rest of Europe,
it fueled the literary, scientific, and philosophical movements of the era and
laid the basis for the eighteenth-century Enlightenment.

Humanists regarded the Scholastic philosophy of medieval universities
as out of touch with the realities of urban life. They found in the rhetorical
discourse of classical Rome a language adapted to civic life and public speech.

They learned to read, speak, and write classical Latin and, eventually, classical Greek. They founded schools to teach others to do so, establishing the pattern for elementary and secondary education for the next three hundred years.

In the service of complex government bureaucracies, humanists employed their skills to write eloquent letters, deliver public orations, and formulate public policy. They developed new scripts for copying manuscripts and used the new printing press to disseminate texts, for which they created methods of critical editing.

Humanism was a movement led by males who accepted the evaluation of women in ancient texts and generally shared the misogynist perceptions of their culture. (Female humanists, as we will see, did not.) Yet humanism also opened the door to a reevaluation of the nature and capacity of women. By calling authors, texts, and ideas into question, it made possible the fundamental rereading of the whole intellectual tradition that was required in order to free women from cultural prejudice and social subordination.

A DIFFERENT CITY.   The other voice first appeared when, after so many centuries, the accumulation of misogynist concepts evoked a response from a capable female defender: Christine de Pizan (1365–1431). Introducing her *Book of the City of Ladies* (1405), she described how she was affected by reading Mathéolus's *Lamentations:* "Just the sight of this book . . . made me wonder how it happened that so many different men . . . are so inclined to express both in speaking and in their treatises and writings so many wicked insults about women and their behavior."[4] These statements impelled her to detest herself "and the entire feminine sex, as though we were monstrosities in nature."[5]

The rest of *The Book of the City of Ladies* presents a justification of the female sex and a vision of an ideal community of women. A pioneer, she has received the message of female inferiority and rejected it. From the fourteenth to the seventeenth century, a huge body of literature accumulated that responded to the dominant tradition.

The result was a literary explosion consisting of works by both men and women, in Latin and in the vernaculars: works enumerating the achievements of notable women; works rebutting the main accusations made against women; works arguing for the equal education of men and women; work defining and redefining women's proper role in the family, at court, in public; works describing women's lives and experiences. Recent monographs and ar-

---

4. Christine de Pizan, *The Book of the City of Ladies,* trans. Earl Jeffrey Richards, foreword by Marina Warner (New York, 1982), 1.1.1, pp. 3–4.

5. Ibid., 1.1.1–2, p. 5.

ticles have begun to hint at the great range of this movement, involving probably several thousand titles. The protofeminism of these "other voices" constitutes a significant fraction of the literary product of the early modern era.

THE CATALOGS. About 1365 the same Boccaccio whose *Corbaccio* rehearses the usual charges against female nature wrote another work, *Concerning Famous Women*. A humanist treatise drawing on classical texts, it praised 106 notable women, ninety-eight of them from pagan Greek and Roman antiquity, one (Eve) from the Bible, and seven from the medieval religious and cultural tradition; his book helped make all readers aware of a sex normally condemned or forgotten. Boccaccio's outlook nevertheless was unfriendly to women, for it singled out for praise those women who possessed the traditional virtues of chastity, silence, and obedience. Women who were active in the public realm—for example, rulers and warriors—were depicted as usually being lascivious and as suffering terrible punishments for entering the masculine sphere. Women were his subject, but Boccaccio's standard remained male.

Christine de Pizan's *Book of the City of Ladies* contains a second catalog, one responding specifically to Boccaccio's. Whereas Boccaccio portrays female virtue as exceptional, she depicts it as universal. Many women in history were leaders, or remained chaste despite the lascivious approaches of men, or were visionaries and brave martyrs.

The work of Boccaccio inspired a series of catalogs of illustrious women of the biblical, classical, Christian, and local pasts, among them Filippo da Bergamo's *Of Illustrious Women*, Pierre de Brantôme's *Lives of Illustrious Women*, Pierre Le Moyne's *Gallerie of Heroic Women*, and Pietro Paolo de Ribera's *Immortal Triumphs and Heroic Enterprises of 845 Women*. Whatever their embedded prejudices, these works drove home to the public the possibility of female excellence.

THE DEBATE. At the same time, many questions remained: Could a woman be virtuous? Could she perform noteworthy deeds? Was she even, strictly speaking, of the same human species as men? These questions were debated over four centuries, in French, German, Italian, Spanish, and English, by authors male and female, among Catholics, Protestants, and Jews, in ponderous volumes and breezy pamphlets. The whole literary genre has been called the *querelle des femmes*, the "woman question."

The opening volley of this battle occurred in the first years of the fifteenth century, in a literary debate sparked by Christine de Pizan. She exchanged letters critical of Jean de Meun's contribution to *The Romance of the Rose* with two French royal secretaries, Jean de Montreuil and Gontier Col. When the matter became public, Jean Gerson, one of Europe's leading theologians, supported de Pizan's arguments against de Meun, for the moment silencing the opposition.

The debate resurfaced repeatedly over the next two hundred years. *The Triumph of Women* (1438) by Juan Rodríguez de la Camara (or Juan Rodríguez del Padron) struck a new note by presenting arguments for the superiority of women to men. *The Champion of Women* (1440–42) by Martin Le Franc addresses once again the negative views of women presented in *The Romance of the Rose* and offers counterevidence of female virtue and achievement.

A cameo of the debate on women is included in *The Courtier,* one of the most widely read books of the era, published by the Italian Baldassare Castiglione in 1528 and immediately translated into other European vernaculars. *The Courtier* depicts a series of evenings at the court of the duke of Urbino in which many men and some women of the highest social stratum amuse themselves by discussing a range of literary and social issues. The "woman question" is a pervasive theme throughout, and the third of its four books is devoted entirely to that issue.

In a verbal duel, Gasparo Pallavicino and Giuliano de' Medici present the main claims of the two traditions. Gasparo argues the innate inferiority of women and their inclination to vice. Only in bearing children do they profit the world. Giuliano counters that women share the same spiritual and mental capacities as men and may excel in wisdom and action. Men and women are of the same essence: just as no stone can be more perfectly a stone than another, so no human being can be more perfectly human than others, whether male or female. It was an astonishing assertion, boldly made to an audience as large as all Europe.

THE TREATISES. Humanism provided the materials for a positive counterconcept to the misogyny embedded in Scholastic philosophy and law and inherited from the Greek, Roman, and Christian pasts. A series of humanist treatises on marriage and family, on education and deportment, and on the nature of women helped construct these new perspectives.

The works by Francesco Barbaro and Leon Battista Alberti—*On Marriage* (1415) and *On the Family* (1434–37)—far from defending female equality, reasserted women's responsibility for rearing children and managing the housekeeping while being obedient, chaste, and silent. Nevertheless, they served the cause of reexamining the issue of women's nature by placing domestic issues at the center of scholarly concern and reopening the pertinent classical texts. In addition, Barbaro emphasized the companionate nature of marriage and the importance of a wife's spiritual and mental qualities for the well-being of the family.

These themes reappear in later humanist works on marriage and the education of women by Juan Luis Vives and Erasmus. Both were moderately sympathetic to the condition of women without reaching beyond the usual masculine prescriptions for female behavior.

An outlook more favorable to women characterizes the nearly unknown work *In Praise of Women* (ca. 1487) by the Italian humanist Bartolommeo Goggio. In addition to providing a catalog of illustrious women, Goggio argued that male and female are the same in essence, but that women (reworking the Adam and Eve narrative from quite a new angle) are actually superior. In the same vein, the Italian humanist Maria Equicola asserted the spiritual equality of men and women in *On Women* (1501). In 1525 Galeazzo Flavio Capra (or Capella) published his work *On the Excellence and Dignity of Women*. This humanist tradition of treatises defending the worthiness of women culminates in the work of Henricus Cornelius Agrippa *On the Nobility and Preeminence of the Female Sex*. No work by a male humanist more succinctly or explicitly presents the case for female dignity.

THE WITCH BOOKS. While humanists grappled with the issues pertaining to women and family, other learned men turned their attention to what they perceived as a very great problem: witches. Witch-hunting manuals, explorations of the witch phenomenon, and even defenses of witches are not at first glance pertinent to the tradition of the other voice. But they do relate in this way: most accused witches were women. The hostility aroused by supposed witch activity is comparable to the hostility aroused by women. The evil deeds the victims of the hunt were charged with were exaggerations of the vices to which, many believed, all women were prone.

The connection between the witch accusation and the hatred of women is explicit in the notorious witch-hunting manual *The Hammer of Witches* (1486) by two Dominican inquisitors, Heinrich Krämer and Jacob Sprenger. Here the inconstancy, deceitfulness, and lustfulness traditionally associated with women are depicted in exaggerated form as the core features of witch behavior. These traits inclined women to make a bargain with the devil—sealed by sexual intercourse—by which they acquired unholy powers. Such bizarre claims, far from being rejected by rational men, were broadcast by intellectuals. The German Ulrich Molitur, the Frenchman Nicolas Rémy, and the Italian Stefano Guazzo all coolly informed the public of sinister orgies and midnight pacts with the devil. The celebrated French jurist, historian, and political philosopher Jean Bodin argued that because women were especially prone to diabolism, regular legal procedures could properly be suspended in order to try those accused of this "exceptional crime."

A few experts such as the physician Johann Weyer, a student of Agrippa's, raised their voices in protest. In 1563 he explained the witch phenomenon thus, without discarding belief in diabolism: the devil deluded foolish old women afflicted by melancholia, causing them to believe they had magical powers. Weyer's rational skepticism, which had good credibility in the community of the learned, worked to revise the conventional views of women and witchcraft.

WOMEN'S WORKS. To the many categories of works produced on the question of women's worth must be added nearly all works written by women. A woman writing was in herself a statement of women's claim to dignity.

Only a few women wrote anything before the dawn of the modern era, for three reasons. First, they rarely received the education that would enable them to write. Second, they were not admitted to the public roles—as administrator, bureaucrat, lawyer or notary, or university professor—in which they might gain knowledge of the kinds of things the literate public thought worth writing about. Third, the culture imposed silence on women, considering speaking out a form of unchastity. Given these conditions, it is remarkable that any women wrote. Those who did before the fourteenth century were almost always nuns or religious women whose isolation made their pronouncements more acceptable.

From the fourteenth century on, the volume of women's writings rose. Women continued to write devotional literature, although not always as cloistered nuns. They also wrote diaries, often intended as keepsakes for their children; books of advice to their sons and daughters; letters to family members and friends; and family memoirs, in a few cases elaborate enough to be considered histories.

A few women wrote works directly concerning the "woman question," and some of these, such as the humanists Isotta Nogarola, Cassandra Fedele, Laura Cereta, and Olympia Morata, were highly trained. A few were professional writers, living by the income of their pens; the very first among them was Christine de Pizan, noteworthy in this context as in so many others. In addition to *The Book of the City of Ladies* and her critiques of *The Romance of the Rose*, she wrote *The Treasure of the City of Ladies* (a guide to social decorum for women), an advice book for her son, much courtly verse, and a full-scale history of the reign of King Charles V of France.

WOMEN PATRONS. Women who did not themselves write but encouraged others to do so boosted the development of an alternative tradition. Highly placed women patrons supported authors, artists, musicians, poets, and learned men. Such patrons, drawn mostly from the Italian elites and the courts of northern Europe, figure disproportionately as the dedicatees of the important works of early feminism.

For a start, it might be noted that the catalogs of Boccaccio and Alvaro de Luna were dedicated to the Florentine noblewoman Andrea Acciaiuoli and to Doña María, first wife of King Juan II of Castile, while the French translation of Boccaccio's work was commissioned by Anne of Brittany, wife of King Charles VIII of France. The humanist treatises of Goggio, Equicola, Vives, and Agrippa were dedicated, respectively, to Eleanora of Aragon, wife of Ercole I d'Este, duke of Ferrara; to Margherita Cantelma of Mantua; to Catherine of Aragon, wife of King Henry VIII of England; and to Margaret, duchess of Austria and regent of the Netherlands. As late as 1696, Mary Astell's *Serious Proposal to the Ladies, for the Advancement of Their True and Greatest Interest* was dedicated to Princess Anne of Denmark.

These authors presumed that their efforts would be welcome to female patrons, or they may have written at the bidding of those patrons. Silent themselves, perhaps even unresponsive, these loftily placed women helped shape the tradition of the other voice.

THE ISSUES. The literary forms and patterns in which the tradition of the other voice presented itself have now been sketched. It remains to highlight the major issues around which this tradition crystallizes. In brief, there are four problems to which our authors return again and again, in plays and catalogs, in verse and letters, in treatises and dialogues, in every language: the problem of chastity, the problem of power, the problem of speech, and the problem of knowledge. Of these the greatest, preconditioning the others, is the problem of chastity.

THE PROBLEM OF CHASTITY. In traditional European culture, as in those of antiquity and others around the globe, chastity was perceived as woman's quintessential virtue—in contrast to courage, or generosity, or leadership, or rationality, seen as virtues characteristic of men. Opponents of women charged them with insatiable lust. Women themselves and their defenders— without disputing the validity of the standard—responded that women were capable of chastity.

The requirement of chastity kept women at home, silenced them, isolated them, left them in ignorance. It was the source of all other impediments. Why was it so important to the society of men, of whom chastity was not required, and who more often than not considered it their right to violate the chastity of any woman they encountered?

Female chastity ensured the continuity of the male-headed household.

If a man's wife was not chaste, he could not be sure of the legitimacy of his offspring. If they were not his and they acquired his property, it was not his household, but some other man's, that had endured. If his daughter was not chaste, she could not be transferred to another man's household as his wife, and he was dishonored.

The whole system of the integrity of the household and the transmission of property was bound up in female chastity. Such a requirement pertained only to property-owning classes, of course. Poor women could not expect to maintain their chastity, least of all if they were in contact with high-status men to whom all women but those of their own household were prey.

In Catholic Europe, the requirement of chastity was further buttressed by moral and religious imperatives. Original sin was inextricably linked with the sexual act. Virginity was seen as heroic virtue, far more impressive than, say, the avoidance of idleness or greed. Monasticism, the cultural institution that dominated medieval Europe for centuries, was grounded in the renunciation of the flesh. The Catholic reform of the eleventh century imposed a similar standard on all the clergy and a heightened awareness of sexual requirements on all the laity. Although men were asked to be chaste, female unchastity was much worse: it led to the devil, as Eve had led mankind to sin.

To such requirements, women and their defenders protested their innocence. Furthermore, following the example of holy women who had escaped the requirements of family and sought the religious life, some women began to conceive of female communities as alternatives both to family and to the cloister. Christine de Pizan's city of ladies was such a community. Moderata Fonte and Mary Astell envisioned others. The luxurious salons of the French *précieuses* of the seventeenth century, or the comfortable English drawing rooms of the next, may have been born of the same impulse. Here women not only might escape, if briefly, the subordinate position that life in the family entailed but might also make claims to power, exercise their capacity for speech, and display their knowledge.

THE PROBLEM OF POWER. Women were excluded from power: the whole cultural tradition insisted on it. Only men were citizens, only men bore arms, only men could be chiefs or lords or kings. There were exceptions that did not disprove the rule, when wives or widows or mothers took the place of men, awaiting their return or the maturation of a male heir. A woman who attempted to rule in her own right was perceived as an anomaly, a monster, at once a deformed woman and an insufficient male, sexually confused and consequently unsafe.

The association of such images with women who held or sought power explains some otherwise odd features of early modern culture. Queen Elizabeth I of England, one of the few women to hold full regal authority in European history, played with such male/female images—positive ones, of course—in representing herself to her subjects. She was a prince, and manly, even though she was female. She was also (she claimed) virginal, a condition absolutely essential if she was to avoid the attacks of her opponents. Catherine de' Medici, who ruled France as widow and regent for her sons, also adopted such imagery in defining her position. She chose as one symbol the figure of Artemisia, an androgynous ancient warrior-heroine who combined a female persona with masculine powers.

Power in a woman, without such sexual imagery, seems to have been indigestible by the culture. A rare note was struck by the Englishman Sir Thomas Elyot in his *Defence of Good Women* (1540), justifying both women's participation in civic life and their prowess in arms. The old tune was sung by the Scots reformer John Knox in his *First Blast of the Trumpet against the Monstrous Regiment of Women* (1558); for him rule by women, defects in nature, was a hideous contradiction in terms.

The confused sexuality of the imagery of female potency was not reserved for rulers. Any woman who excelled was likely to be called an Amazon, recalling the self-mutilated warrior women of antiquity who repudiated all men, gave up their sons, and raised only their daughters. She was often said to have "exceeded her sex" or to have possessed "masculine virtue"—as the very fact of conspicuous excellence conferred masculinity even on the female subject. The catalogs of notable women often showed those female heroes dressed in armor, armed to the teeth, like men. Amazonian heroines romp through the epics of the age—Ariosto's *Orlando Furioso* (1532) and Spenser's *Faerie Queene* (1590–1609). Excellence in a woman was perceived as a claim for power, and power was reserved for the masculine realm. A woman who possessed either one was masculinized and lost title to her own female identity.

THE PROBLEM OF SPEECH. Just as power had a sexual dimension when it was claimed by women, so did speech. A good woman spoke little. Excessive speech was an indication of unchastity. By speech, women seduced men. Eve had lured Adam into sin by her speech. Accused witches were commonly accused of having spoken abusively, or irrationally, or simply too much. As enlightened a figure as Francesco Barbaro insisted on silence in a woman, which he linked to her perfect unanimity with her husband's will and her unblemished virtue (her chastity). Another Italian humanist, Leonardo Bruni, in advising a noblewoman on her studies, barred her not from speech but from public speaking. That was reserved for men.

Related to the problem of speech was that of costume—another, if silent, form of self-expression. Assigned the task of pleasing men as their primary occupation, elite women often tended toward elaborate costume, hairdressing, and the use of cosmetics. Clergy and secular moralists alike condemned these practices. The appropriate function of costume and adornment was to announce the status of a woman's husband or father. Any further indulgence in adornment was akin to unchastity.

THE PROBLEM OF KNOWLEDGE. When the Italian noblewoman Isotta Nogarola had begun to attain a reputation as a humanist, she was accused of incest—a telling instance of the association of learning in women with unchastity. That chilling association inclined any woman who was educated to deny that she was or to make exaggerated claims of heroic chastity.

If educated women were pursued with suspicions of sexual misconduct, women seeking an education faced an even more daunting obstacle: the assumption that women were by nature incapable of learning, that reasoning was a particularly masculine ability. Just as they proclaimed their chastity, women and their defenders insisted on their capacity for learning. The major work by a male writer on female education—that by Juan Luis Vives, *On the Education of a Christian Woman* (1523)—granted female capacity for intellection but still argued that a woman's whole education was to be shaped around the requirement of chastity and a future within the household. Female writers of the following generations—Marie de Gournay in France, Anna Maria van Schurman in Holland, Mary Astell in England—began to envision other possibilities.

The pioneers of female education were the Italian women humanists who managed to attain a literacy in Latin and a knowledge of classical and Christian literature equivalent to that of prominent men. Their works implicitly and explicitly raise questions about women's social roles, defining problems that beset women attempting to break out of the cultural limits that had bound them. Like Christine de Pizan, who achieved an advanced education through her father's tutoring and her own devices, their bold questioning makes clear the importance of training. Only when women were educated to the same standard as male leaders would they be able to raise that other voice and insist on their dignity as human beings morally, intellectually, and legally equal to men.

THE OTHER VOICE. The other voice, a voice of protest, was mostly female, but it was also male. It spoke in the vernaculars and in Latin, in treatises and dialogues, in plays and poetry, in letters and diaries, and in pamphlets. It battered at the wall of prejudice that encircled women and raised a banner announcing its claims. The female was equal (or even superior) to the male in essential nature—moral, spiritual, intellectual. Women were capable of higher education, of holding positions of power and influence in the public realm, and of speaking and writing persuasively. The last bastion of masculine supremacy, centered on the notions of a woman's primary domestic responsibility and the requirement of female chastity, was not as yet assaulted—although visions of productive female communities as alternatives to the family indicated an awareness of the problem.

During the period 1300–1700, the other voice remained only a voice, and one only dimly heard. It did not result—yet—in an alteration of social patterns. Indeed, to this day they have not entirely been altered. Yet the call for justice issued as long as six centuries ago by those writing in the tradition of the other voice must be recognized as the source and origin of the mature feminist tradition and of the realignment of social institutions accomplished in the modern age.

We thank the volume editors in this series, who responded with many suggestions to an earlier draft of this introduction, making it a collaborative enterprise. Many of their suggestions and criticisms have resulted in revisions of this introduction, though we remain responsible for the final product.

PROJECTED TITLES IN THE SERIES

Isabella Andreini, *Mirtilla*, edited and translated by Laura Stortoni

Tullia d'Aragona, *Complete Poems and Letters*, edited and translated by Julia Hairston

Tullia d'Aragona, *The Wretch, Otherwise Known as Guerrino*, edited and translated by Julia Hairston and John McLucas

Giuseppa Eleonora Barbapiccola and Diamante Medaglia Faini, *The Education of Women*, edited and translated by Rebecca Messbarger

Francesco Barbaro et al., *On Marriage and the Family*, edited and translated by Margaret L. King

Laura Battiferra, *Selected Poetry, Prose, and Letters*, edited and translated by Victoria Kirkham

Giulia Bigolina, *"Urania" and "Giulia,"* edited and translated by Valeria Finucci

Francesco Buoninsegni and Arcangela Tarabotti, *Menippean Satire: "Against Feminine Extravagance" and "Antisatire,"* edited and translated by Elissa Weaver

Maddalena Campiglia, *Flori, a Pastoral Drama: A Bilingual Edition*, edited and translated by Virginia Cox and Lisa Sampson

Rosalba Carriera, *Letters, Diaries, and Art*, edited and translated by Shearer West

Madame du Chatelet, *Selected Works*, edited by Judith Zinsser

Vittoria Colonna, *Sonnets for Michelangelo*, edited and translated by Abigail Brundin

Vittoria Colonna, Chiara Matraini, and Lucrezia Marinella, *Marian Writings*, edited and translated by Susan Haskins

Marie Dentière, *Epistle to Marguerite de Navarre and Preface to a Sermon by John Calvin*, edited and translated by Mary B. McKinley

Princess Elizabeth of Bohemia, *Correspondence with Descartes*, edited and translated by Lisa Shapiro

Isabella d'Este, *Selected Letters*, edited and translated by Deanna Shemek

Fairy-Tales by Seventeenth-Century French Women Writers, edited and translated by Lewis Seifert and Domna C. Stanton

Moderata Fonte, *Floridoro*, edited and translated by Valeria Finucci

Moderata Fonte and Lucrezia Marinella, *Religious Narratives*, edited and translated by Virginia Cox

Francisca de los Apostoles, *Visions on Trial: The Inquisitional Trial of Francisca de los Apostoles*, edited and translated by Gillian T. W. Ahlgren

Catharina Regina von Greiffenberg, *Meditations on the Life of Christ*, edited and translated by Lynne Tatlock

In Praise of Women: Italian Fifteenth-Century Defenses of Women, edited and translated by Daniel Bornstein

Louise Labé, *Complete Works*, edited and translated by Annie Finch and Deborah Baker

Madame de Maintenon, *Dialogues and Addresses*, edited and translated by John Conley, S.J.

Lucrezia Marinella, *L'Enrico, or Byzantium Conquered*, edited and translated by Virginia Cox

Lucrezia Marinella, *Happy Arcadia*, edited and translated by Susan Haskins and Letizia Panizza

Chiara Matraini, *Selected Poetry and Prose*, edited and translated by Elaine MacLachlan

Eleonora Petersen von Merlau, *Autobiography* (1718), edited and translated by Barbara Becker-Cantarino

Alessandro Piccolomini, *Rethinking Marriage in Sixteenth-Century Italy*, edited and translated by Letizia Panizza

Christine de Pizan et al., *Debate over the "Romance of the Rose,"* edited and translated by Tom Conley with Elisabeth Hodges

Christine de Pizan, *Life of Charles V*, edited and translated by Charity Cannon Willard

Christine de Pizan, *The Long Road of Learning*, edited and translated by Andrea Tarnowski

Madeleine and Catherine des Roches, *Selected Letters, Dialogues, and Poems*, edited and translated by Anne Larsen

Oliva Sabuco, *The New Philosophy: True Medicine*, edited and translated by Gianna Pomata

Margherita Sarrocchi, *La Scanderbeide*, edited and translated by Rinaldina Russell

Madeleine de Scudéry, *Selected Letters, Orations, and Rhetorical Dialogues*, edited and translated by Jane Donawerth with Julie Strongson

Justine Siegemund, *The Court Midwife of the Electorate of Brandenburg* (1690), edited and translated by Lynne Tatlock

Gabrielle Suchon, *"On Philosophy" and "On Morality,"* edited and translated by Domna Stanton with Rebecca Wilkin

Sara Copio Sullam, *Sara Copio Sullam: Jewish Poet and Intellectual in Early Seventeenth-Century Venice*, edited and translated by Don Harrán

Arcangela Tarabotti, *Convent Life as Inferno: A Report*, introduction and notes by Francesca Medioli, translated by Letizia Panizza

Laura Terracina, *Works*, edited and translated by Michael Sherberg

Madame de Villedieu (Marie-Catherine Desjardins), *Memoirs of the Life of Henriette-Sylvie de Molière: A Novel*, edited and translated by Donna Kuizenga

Katharina Schütz Zell, *Selected Writings*, edited and translated by Elsie McKee

ABBREVIATIONS

ASF	Archivio di Stato di Firenze
ASV	Archivio di Stato di Venezia
ASVic	Archivio di Stato di Vicenza
BCR	Biblioteca Civica di Rovereto
BEM	Biblioteca Estense di Modena
BSP	Biblioteca del Seminario di Padova

Elisabetta Caminer Turra (1751–96). Engraving by Marco Comirato.

VOLUME EDITOR'S
INTRODUCTION

1. THE OTHER VOICE

In the genre of her occupations Madame Caminer does honor to her sex, just as her way of translating extols her taste, her talents, and the elegance of her style.
—*Journal encyclopédique de Bouillon,* September 1772

Nature has bestowed upon the celebrated Elisabetta Caminer pleasing graces and endearing qualities of the mind and heart. She is young, beautiful, very spiritual, and extremely studious.
—*Mercure de France,* February 1773

[Y]ou do not lack studies, inclination or talent . . . so, remember only that by continuing in the career that you have chosen and by avoiding the obstacles that your sex and your merit will multiply for you during the course of your youth, I promise that you will have nothing to envy in Goldoni's glory, or in that more solid glory of other illustrious and rare Women.
—Giuseppe Pelli Bencivenni, *Europa letteraria,* June 1772

By the time Elisabetta Caminer (1751–96) reached the age of twenty-one, she had made a place for herself in the Republic of Letters with her remarkable accomplishments as a journalist, translator, and director of theatrical works. She was celebrated in the most prestigious French literary periodicals—both the *Journal encyclopédique de Bouillon* and the *Mercure de France*—as well as Italian literary periodicals outside the Veneto.[1] As one of the first

---

1. In *Novelle letterarie* (Firenze: Nella Stamperia Allegrini, Pisoni, e Compania, 1769–[83]) and in *Toelette o sia Raccolta galante di prose e versi toscani dedicata alle dame italiane* (Firenze: si vende in Allegrini, Pisoni e Compagnia), both edited by Giuseppe Pelli Bencivenni in Florence. See "Making of a Woman," texts 7, 8, 11, 12, 14, 15, 16, 18, 27, 28, and 30.

female journalist-publishers of the Italian Peninsula,[2] Caminer was an active participant in the Enlightenment discussions about civic, scientific, and religious authority, superstition and the power of human reason, the quest for individual and collective happiness, gender hierarchies in society, and the importance of public utility in devising methods of social, economic, and political reform. In her role as journalist, Caminer was part of a developing profession which played an important role in the Enlightenment project of educating the public by creating, maintaining, and expanding a community of readers and writers engaged in critical debate.[3]

As is evident from its title, her literary and philosophical periodical, the *Giornale enciclopedico (Encyclopedic Journal* [1777–82]),[4] was directly inspired by the French philosophes' project of gathering, organizing, and publishing the various branches of knowledge in one work, the *Encyclopédie*. In order to inform her readers of the latest publications and intellectual projects from across Europe, Caminer recruited the most renowned men of letters and science from the Italian Peninsula to contribute book reviews and essays to the *Giornale enciclopedico*. Under her direction, the periodical became the most progressive Enlightenment influence in the Veneto region of Italy. In her role as journalist and editor of the periodical, Caminer enjoyed the experience (rare for women) of participating in and monitoring contemporary debates on everything from the latest scientific experiments in regeneration,[5] to the status of the Italian language and literature, to the new fashion magazines for women.

2. Only two other women of the Italian Peninsula were professional journalists, Caterina Cracas and Elena Fonseca Pimentel. Caterina Cracas (1691–1771) inherited the journalistic trade from her father, the Hungarian-born Luca Antonio Cracas. After his death, she continued for forty years to publish the *Diario ordinario di Ungheria* in Rome, a political newspaper containing news of the war against the Turks. Between February and June 1799, Eleonora Fonseca Pimentel published the revolutionary paper of the Neapolitan Parthenopean Republic, *Il monitore*. On Pimentel, see Renzo De Felice, *I giornali giacobini italiani* (Milano: Feltrinelli, 1962); and Mario Battaglini, *Napoli 1799: I giornali giacobini* (Roma: Libreria Alfredo Borzi, 1988). On Cracas, see Giulio Natali, *Il Settecento*, vol. 8, bk. 1, of *Storia letteraria d'Italia* (Milano: Vallardi, 1936), 172; and Natalia Costa Zalessow, *Scrittrici italiane dal tredicesimo al ventesimo secolo: Testi e critica* (Ravenna: Longo Editore, 1982).

3. For more on journalism as a relatively new occupation during the eighteenth century, see section 4 ("Letters," "Journalistic Writing") of this introduction. For a concise analytical overview of the central debates of the Enlightenment, see Dorinda Outram, *The Enlightenment* (Cambridge: Cambridge University Press, 1995).

4. The *Giornale enciclopedico* was founded in 1774 by Caminer's father, Domenico. Elisabetta assumed direction of the periodical in 1777 and continued to publish it until her death in 1796, implementing two title changes over the years: *Nuovo giornale enciclopedico* (1782–89) and *Nuovo giornale enciclopedico d'Italia* (1790–97).

5. The term "regeneration" refers to the process by which animals and plants repair and regenerate their structure. In the eighteenth century natural philosophers like Caminer's friend and

Caminer's active participation in the intellectual life of the Veneto was furthered by her position (almost certainly unprecedented for a woman in Italy) as the editor-director of a printing press. At the age of twenty-nine, together with her husband, Antonio Turra, she opened the Stamperia Turra in Vicenza.[6] Over the course of fourteen years (1780–94) the Stamperia Turra was one of the most active publishing houses of the Veneto region (excluding Venice itself), producing over one hundred twenty literary, scientific, and pedagogical works.[7] Caminer used the press to publish some of the many volumes of literary, pedagogical, and historical works that she translated over the course of her life.[8]

In addition to her work as a journalist and publisher Caminer was an active presence in the theatrical life of post-Goldoni Venice. She translated over fifty plays from all over Europe and published them in three collections (1772, 1774, 1794).[9] The authors of the plays Caminer translated (from the French or from French versions) include, among others Baculard d'Arnaud, Beaumarchais, Calderon Della Barca, Robert Dodsley, Fenouillot de Falbaire, Madame de Genlis, the French Goldoni, Lessing, Molière, Bernard-Joseph Saurin, Voltaire, and—her playwright of choice—Louis-Sébastien Mercier. Many of her translations were not only published, but were also successfully performed

---

colleague Lazzaro Spallanzani were fascinated by the ability of certain organisms such as slugs, land snails, and salamanders to regrow amputated limbs or even heads. For Caminer's journalistic participation in these discussions, see "Making of a Woman," text 4.

6. See "Making of a Woman," texts 40 and 41.

7. Angelo Colla et al., "Tipografi, editori e librai," in *Storia di Vicenza*, vol. 3 of *L'età della Repubblica Veneta (1404–1797)* (Vicenza: Neri Pozza Editore, 1990), bk. 2:150.For more on the Stamperia Turra, see part 2 of this introduction, "Biography: The Making of a Woman of Letters."

8. Her translations include *Lettere di Milady Catesby* (c. 1772); *Il magazzino delle fanciulle, ovvero dialoghi tra una savia direttrice e parecchie sue allieve di grado illustre: Opera di Mad. di Beaumont* (Vicenza: Francesco Vendramini Mosca, 1774); *Quadro della storia moderna dalla caduta dell'Impero d'Occidente fino alla pace di Vestfalia, del Signor Cavaliere di Méhégan, tradotto dal francese* (Vicenza: Stamperia Turra, 1780); *Opere del Signor Salomone Gesnero tradotte con le due novelle morali del Signor D**** [Diderot] (Vicenza: Turra, 1781); *Del soggiorno dei Conti del Nord in Venezia nel gennaio 1782: Lettera di madama la Contessa vedova degli Orsini di Rosemberg al Signor Riccardo Wynne suo fratello a Londra* (Vicenza: Turra, 1782); *Le memorie di Massimiliano di Bettuna Ducca di Sully Ministro d'Enrico IV, tradotto dal Francese* (Vicenza: Turra, 1784–93); *Le nuove lettere inglesi, ovvero la storia del Cancelliere Grandisson di S. Richardson* (Venezia: Valvasense, 1786); *Nuova raccolta di novelle morali del Signor di Marmontel tradotte per le prima volta* (Vicenza, Turra, 1791–93); and *L'amico dei fanciulli, del Signor Arnaldo Berquin* (Vicenza: Turra, 1795–96).

9. *Composizioni teatrali moderne tradotte da Elisabetta Caminer* (Modern theatrical compositions in translation) (Venezia: Savioni, 1772; Savioni published a second edition of this collection in 1774); *Nuova raccolta di composizioni teatrali tradotte da Elisabetta Caminer Turra* (New collection of theatrical compositions translated by Elisabetta Caminer Turra) (Venezia: Savioni, 1774–76); and *Drammi trasportati dal francese idioma ad uso del teatro italiano da Elisabetta Caminer Turra: Per servire di proseguimento al corpo delle traduzioni teatrali pubblicato dalla medesima qualche anno fa* (Dramas translated from the French for the use of the Italian theater by Elisabetta Caminer Turra) (Venezia: Albrizzi, 1794).

in theaters in Venice, Padua, Bologna, and probably elsewhere in Italy. Perhaps even more significant, Caminer was one of the first Italian women to oversee stage productions of plays and to work directly with actors.[10] Her published translations and stage productions of the new French bourgeois dramas were responsible for popularizing the controversial genre in Italy and expanding upon Venetian playwright Carlo Goldoni's reform of the Italian theater.[11]

As one might expect from a woman whose own life transgressed the gender boundaries of her society, Caminer was fervently concerned about the status of women in society. She repeatedly disputed the popular notion of women's biological inferiority to men and stated that if women were less active participants in cultural and intellectual life than men, it was due to the injustice of not being granted a serious education. Caminer decried men's unjust treatment of women, but she was also quick to note that women should be aware of their own passive participation in the balance of power: as long as women willingly sacrificed the development of their minds to the false "empire" of superficial adulation offered to them by men, they would allow men to retain their superior position in the gender hierarchy of society. Caminer believed it was up to women—as individuals and as a collective group—to begin making changes to improve their lot in life.

Caminer's convictions about women's status in society and her determination to publish her thoughts on the matter were undoubtedly influenced by the heritage of Venetian women intellectuals before her, many of whom had participated in the *querelle des femmes*, the debate on the "woman question." Indeed, the Venetian Republic had been home to three centuries of celebrated women writers by the time Caminer was born. As early as the fifteenth century, the republic had produced the humanists Isotta Nogarola (1418–66), who wrote a dialogue on the relative responsibility of Adam and Eve for the fall of humankind,[12] and Cassandra Fedele (1465–1558), whose orations and letters made her the best-known female scholar in Europe during her life-

---

10. To my knowledge only Luisa Bergalli Gozzi preceded Caminer, when she was the manager of the S. Angelo Theater in Venice a quarter of a century earlier, during the 1747–48 theatrical season.

11. Carlo Goldoni's reform moved Italian theater away from the improvisational commedia dell'arte style (characterized by masked stock characters like Pantalone, Arlecchino, and others) toward a scripted theater with characters that represented contemporary middle-class society in everyday life. The French bourgeois dramas also focused on the everyday life of middle-class characters. See sections 2 and 4 of this introduction for more on the *drame bourgeois* and Caminer's role in popularizing it in Italy.

12. "Of the equal or unequal sin of Adam and Eve," written in 1451. See, in this series, Isotta Nogarola, *Complete Writings*, ed. and trans. Margaret King and Diana Robin (Chicago: University of Chicago Press, forthcoming).

time.[13] During the sixteenth century, the Venetian Republic was home to Veronica Franco (1546–92), the most famous "honorable courtesan," whose renowned poetry earned her an international reputation, and Moderata Fonte (1555–92), who became famous for an epic poem and a literary dialogue that claimed women's superiority to men.[14] During the seventeenth century, the Veneto produced the first woman ever to earn a doctorate, Elena Piscopia Cornaro (1646–84), the epic poet Lucrezia Marinella (1571–1653) who published a treatise on the excellence of women, and the nun Arcangela Tarabotti (1604–52), who wrote scathing criticisms of the practice of forced monachization.[15] All of these women, and others, contributed to the debate on the condition of women in society even as they transgressed traditional gender boundaries by writing and publishing their work.

As a woman of the eighteenth century, Elisabetta Caminer occupied a new position among such illustrious women, or *donne illustri*, of the Veneto. Unlike nearly all of the renowned women writers and intellectuals before her. Caminer was not an aristocrat, a courtesan, or a woman of the cloth. She did not publish treatises, dialogues, epistolary essays, or collections of poetry to be circulated primarily among the upper classes or among readers who were literate in Latin. Rather, Caminer forged new ground as a woman of letters from the middle class who earned her living with her pen and wrote in a medium—a biweekly periodical in the vernacular[16]—which was easily accessible and affordable to the burgeoning readership from her own class.

13. See, in this series, Cassandra Fedele, *Letters and Orations*, ed. and trans. Diana Robin (Chicago: University of Chicago Press, 2000).

14. See, in this series, Veronica Franco, *Poems and Selected Letters*, ed. and trans. Ann Rosalind Jones and Margaret F. Rosenthal (Chicago: University of Chicago Press, 1998); and Moderata Fonte, *The Worth of Women: Wherein Is Clearly Revealed Their Nobility and Their Superiority to Men*, ed. and trans. Virginia Cox (Chicago: University of Chicago Press, 1997). See also Moderata Fonte, *Tredici canti del Floridoro*, ed. Valeria Finucci, trans. Julia Kisacky (Chicago: University of Chicago Press, forthcoming).

15. The term "forced monachization" refers to the commonplace practice during the early modern era of families' forcing young girls to become nuns, either because they could not afford an appropriate dowry or out of a desire for financial or political gain. On Piscopia, see Paul Kristeller, "Learned Women of Early Modern Italy," in *Beyond Their Sex: Learned Women of the European Past*, ed. Patricia LaBalme (New York: New York University Press, 1984), 97–106; and Lodovico Maschietto, *Elena Lucrezia Cornaro Piscopia (1646–1684): Prima donna laureata nel mondo* (Padova: Antenore, 1978). On Marinelli see, in this series, Lucrezia Marinelli, *The Nobility and Excellence of Women, and the Defects and Vices of Men*, ed. and trans. Anne Dunhill (Chicago: University of Chicago Press, 1999); on Tarabotti see, in this series, Arcangela Tarabotti, *Paternal Tyranny*, ed. and trans. Letizia Panizza (Chicago: University of Chicago Press, forthcoming).

16. In other words, Caminer did not write in Latin, but in Italian, which was accessible to a much greater number of readers. Of course, she was writing for individuals with some degree of formal or informal education, but those readers further popularized information from periodicals by reading aloud to others.

In her multifaceted professional life Caminer wore the hats of journalist, editor, translator, publisher, correspondent, poet, and *salonnière*. In these diverse roles, she represents not only an "other voice," but many "other" voices; it is imperative, therefore, that we hear her speak through the various genres in which she wrote. This anthology includes seventy texts drawn from Caminer's letters, prefaces, poems, and journalistic writing. The texts represent both the exceptional and the quotidian aspects of her personal and her professional life, and they allow the reader to gain a sense of the range of topics that interested Caminer as well as the variety of genres in which she published.

The first part of the anthology—entitled "The Making of a Woman of Letters in the Eighteenth-Century Veneto"—is designed to illustrate two aspects of Caminer's life and work. First, the texts provide evidence of the strategies Caminer used to successfully make a place for herself in male-dominated professions, in part by building and maintaining a network of influential male colleagues. Second, the collection of texts provides detailed information about the daily business of Caminer's work as a journalist, critic, translator, and publisher—offering the reader a rare "behind-the-scenes" glimpse into the world of these professions in eighteenth-century Italy.

The forty-nine texts in this part of the anthology—primarily letters, but also poems, journalistic writing, a preface, and a fly sheet—are organized chronologically, so as to follow the progress of Caminer's career over the course of her life. The chronological order offers the reader a sense of Caminer's development both as a woman in her society and as an Enlightenment woman of letters. In addition, the letters serve as "miniportraits" of Venice and Vicenza during the second half of the eighteenth century, at times inviting the reader inside a Venetian theater or out to the countryside, where Caminer and her friends gathered for holidays. The letters bring the reader face to face with the individuals populating these spaces, whether they be anonymous theatergoing crowds or renowned public figures such as Giacomo Casanova. Thus, the first part of the anthology provides the biographical, cultural, and historical base from which to read and interpret the selection of Caminer's writing included in the second part of the book.

Entitled "Women and Society," the second part of the anthology contains a selection of twenty-one texts that in various ways reflect Caminer's convictions, perplexities, hopes, and disillusionments about the condition of women in her society. The texts are organized into three thematic sections: "The Intellectual Life," "Fashion," and "Marriage or the Convent." Together with the texts in the first part of the anthology, these reviews, poems, and letters reveal much about how Caminer perceived her own place in her society, both as an exceptional woman and as an advocate for women generally. Most important, they constitute the core of Caminer's contributions to the centuries-old debate on the "woman question," in which she participated from the age of seventeen until her death at age forty-four.[17]

2. BIOGRAPHY: THE MAKING OF A WOMAN OF LETTERS

I am at an age and in a situation that do not allow me to hope for mediocre knowledge, to say nothing of great learning, and yet I am full of desire to cultivate my mind. This is, if not the only, at least the most useful and constant inner disposition to which I have abandoned myself with joy.

—Elisabetta Caminer, letter to Giuseppe Pelli Bencivenni, 1770

Elisabetta Caminer penned these lines at the age of nineteen in a letter to her new colleague and mentor, the Florentine journalist Giuseppe Pelli Bencivenni.[18] They bear witness to the driving force that led Caminer to dedicate herself to an intellectual life, despite her society's overwhelming prejudices against formal education for women. The words Caminer used to describe her intellectual leanings are significant. Defining her desire for knowledge as an

17. See "Series Editors' Introduction" for a general history of the debate and section 3 of this introduction for the eighteenth-century context of the debate.

18. Giuseppe Pelli Bencivenni (1729–1808) was born in Florence and studied law in Pisa. For many years he held various administrative governmental posts in Florence. From 1775 to 1793 he was the director of the Royal Gallery in Florence (Real Galleria di Firenze). Pelli's real interests lay not with bureaucratic work, however, and throughout his life he participated in the intellectual life of the Republic of Letters through his correspondence, his journalistic work, and his academic endeavors. He enjoyed a vast correspondence with celebrated men of letters and science of his day, including (briefly) Cesare Beccaria, whom he admired greatly. He was a member of the Accademia de' Georgofili and participated in its debates about agricultural reform. Pelli published one of the first scholarly appraisals of biographical sources on Dante, *Memorie per servire alla vita di Dante ed alla storia della sua famiglia* (Venezia, 1759), and he also published a history of the collections at the Royal Gallery, *Saggio istorico delle Real Galleria di Firenze* (Firenze, 1779). He is perhaps best known for his manuscript diary, the *Efemeridi*, which is a rich source of information about the literary, artistic, philosophical, and scientific individuals, publications, and events that Pelli observed or interacted with. Pelli was an avid reader of French and Italian periodicals, and he amassed a considerable collection of them during his lifetime. During the period in which he corresponded with Caminer, he was directing the literary periodical the *Novelle letterarie* (from 1770 to 1777) (thus continuing the work of Giovanni Lami after the latter's death) and the *Toelette* (1770–71), a Tuscan literary periodical for women. His fascination for journalistic publications—and of course his own work as a journalist—were undoubtedly what led to his interest in Elisabetta Caminer. His correspondence with his compatriot Giulio Perini—who was living in Venice during this period and occasionally collaborating on the *Europa letteraria*—further insured an eventual contact between Pelli and Caminer. On Pelli, see: R. Zapperi, "Bencivenni Pelli, Giuseppe," in *Dizionario biografico degli italiani* (hereafter *DBI*), 8:219–22; Maria Augusta Morelli Timpanaro, *Autori, stampatori, librai: Per una storia dell'editoria in Firenze nel secolo XVIII* (Firenze: Olschki, 1999), 192–206; and Morelli Timpanaro's inventory of Pelli's correspondence, *Lettere a Giuseppe Pelli Bencivenni, 1747–1808* (Roma: Pubblicazioni degli Archivi di Stato, 1976).

"inner disposition" implied that it was a natural or innate condition: a notion that directly contradicted prevalent contemporary beliefs about women's physical constitutions and mental abilities. Caminer was also careful to describe her desire to develop her mind as "useful" and "constant." In doing so, she reinforced the legitimacy of her desire within the Enlightenment ethic of social utility, and she distinguished herself (through her constancy) from commonplace stereotypes of feminine inconstancy or superficiality. Perhaps most significant of all, Caminer described her desire to cultivate her mind in terms of a joyful, personal satisfaction—a need or right that was very rarely recognized for women (or even voiced by them) at that time.

The passage above is also marked by modesty—perhaps somewhat excessively—since by the time Caminer wrote this letter she had already earned a reputation as an accomplished journalist and enjoyed successful performances of her theatrical translations on the Venetian stage. A certain amount of formulaic self-deprecation was a typical eighteenth-century trope for men of letters as well as for women. But for women it had special meaning—and function—as a strategic move, as they were beginning to "invade" and take part in the public, professional sphere, which was still considered men's territory. Throughout her late teens and early twenties Caminer often adopted this combined discourse of ambition and modesty in order to soften the boldness with which she presented herself, or in response to criticism of her work. This brief passage is emblematic of currents that run through Caminer's writing especially during the early part of her career: the pleasure she took in learning, her ambition tempered by modesty or by reason, and her agility at constructing a network of male patrons who would foster her career. These were crucial strategies she employed to confront and defy, in her words, the "prejudice [that] would have women confined within unreasonable limits."[19]

Elisabetta Caminer was born in Venice on 29 July 1751 to Anna Maldini and Domenico Caminer,[20] and she was baptized in the S. Benedetto church

---

19. From Caminer's first letter to Pelli, dated 20 October 1770. See "Making of a Woman," text 7. All translations from French and Italian are mine unless otherwise noted.

20. The interesting life and multifaceted career of Domenico Caminer (1731–95) have yet to be thoroughly researched. We know that this extremely prolific writer was a gazetteer, journalist, theatrical impresario, political chronicler, contemporary historian, and perhaps even book dealer. Scholars believe that—in addition to the literary periodicals, the *Europa letteraria* (1768–73), and the *Giornale enciclopedico* in its early years (1774–76)—Caminer also compiled the weekly manuscript paper and political gazette *Europa* (c. 1761–80), the biweekly urban gazette the *Nuova gazzetta veneta* (1762), and the daily newspaper the *Diario Veneto*(1765). He also compiled, in collaboration with his son Antonio, the weekly gazette the *Nuovo postiglione* (from 1780 to his death in 1795). Although today Caminer is best known for his journalistic work, he may have thought of himself as primarily a contemporary historian; in the April 1770 issue of the *Europa*

five days later. Aside from these facts, little is known about her early years. As a young girl she may have been placed in a milliner's shop to learn the trade of bonnet making, but she soon began working for her journalist father, probably in her early teens.[21] Caminer had at least four siblings, and her status as the oldest daughter—and perhaps the oldest child—may have been influential in her father's decision to invite her to work with him.[22]

Domenico's profession afforded his daughter unusual access to a constant flow of letters, books, and periodicals from across Europe—the very tools necessary for anyone aspiring to become an active member of the intellectual community of the Republic of Letters.[23] His work also provided her with the training and connections for establishing herself as a professional journalist and theater critic.[24] Caminer probably began her training in the journalistic

---

letteraria, his "principal exercise for over twenty years" was described as "strictly that of the history of our times" (105). For many years (from 1776 perhaps until his death) Caminer published an annual historical chronicle, *La storia dell'anno,* and he also authored several historical and political books including the *Saggio storico del regno di Corsica dalla sollevazione del 1729 sino all metà del 1768* (Venezia, 1768) and *Vita di Federigo II il Grande* (Venezia, 1787). Caminer's most extensive publication was his monumental eighteen- or twenty-volume history of contemporary European diplomacy and warfare (with a focus on the Russo-Turkish hostilities and the struggles between Russia and Prussia over the partition of Poland), *Storia della guerra presente* (Venezia, 1770– c. 1793). Domenico's publications were reveiwed over the years in his and his daughter's periodicals, from the *Europa letteraria* to the *Nuovo giornale enciclopedico.* On Domenico Caminer, see Cesare De Michelis, "Caminer, Domenico," in *DBI,* 17:234–36; and Mario Infelise, "'Europa': Una gazzetta manoscritta del Settecento," in *Non uno itinere: Studi Storici offerti dagli allievi a Federico Seneca* (Venezia: Stamperia di Venezia, 1993), 221–29. See also Larry Wolff, *Venice and the Slavs: The Discovery of Dalmatia in the Age of Enlightenment* (Stanford, Calif.: Stanford University Press, 2001).

21. This was the way many British women had gotten into the journalistic profession in the first half of the eighteenth century—through their fathers, husbands, or brothers.

22. Caminer's four known siblings were Antonio (b. 1756 or 1757), who was five or six years her junior, and three much younger siblings: a brother, Angelo (b. 1771 or 1772), and two sisters, Carlotta (b. 1772 or 1773) and Antonia (b. 1774 or 1775). Like his older sister Elisabetta, Antonio followed in his father's footsteps. He collaborated with his father on the periodical the *Nuovo postiglione* and continued to direct it after his father's death, until 1816. Antonio also occasionally contributed articles to the *Europa letteraria.* Little is known about Caminer's other siblings; since they were born at least twenty years after Elisabetta, they essentially belonged to a different generation. We know that Angelo was a legal consultant (*interveniente*), and that he was twice admonished for Jacobinism in the 1790s. Caminer's sisters Carlotta and Antonia appear in an 1805 population register as involved in some way with a school (*facenti scuola*) when they were in their thirties. I am indebted to Elena Bertagnolli for sharing the information on Caminer's sisters (Archivio Comunale di Venezia, 1805 Registro anagrafe generale) and to Mario Infelise for sharing the information on Angelo Caminer (Archivio di Stato di Venezia [hereafter ASV], Inquisitori di Stato, busta 1243, busta 526).

23. For more on the concept of the Republic of Letters see "Letters" in section 4 of this introduction.

24. Domenico Caminer dabbled in other aspects of the publishing world besides journalism. While he may not have officially worked as a bookseller or a publisher, he supplied books to

profession by working as a copyist for her father, thus gaining constant practice in reading and transcribing letters and book reviews, probably to some extent reading and writing in French. Between the ages of eleven and fourteen,
Caminer most likely assisted her father with three journalistic endeavors: the
manuscript gazette *Europa*, the literary periodical *Nuova gazzetta veneta*, and the
daily, "local" newspaper, the *Diario Veneto*.[25] In doing so she would have had the
opportunity to learn the business end of the trade, as well as to become familiar with the international language of the day. Caminer may even have begun
to learn English in her teens.[26] By the age of seventeen, Caminer was a primary
member of her father's journalistic team (along with the naturalist Alberto Fortis) for the literary and philosophical periodical the *Europa letteraria* (*Literary Europe*) which Domenico founded in 1768.[27] Two of her very first contributions
to the periodical were translations of Voltaire's writing, both taken from recent issues of the French periodical the *Mercure de France*. The first was her
translation of Voltaire's tale *La princesse de Babilonie* (*The Princess of Babylonia*), and
the second was her translation of a letter the French philosophe had recently
(22 April 1768) written about smallpox.[28]

Domenico Caminer's open-mindedness and his ability to recognize and
encourage the personal drive and talents of his daughter were fundamental
in opening the doors to her education and training. But his financial concerns
were also important factors: as he testified in an official petition in 1770, the
financial burden of supporting his family made his daughter's assistance with
his work important.[29] It is worth noting that this door was open to Elisabetta

---

individuals who requested them. In letters to Charles Bonnet, Lazzaro Spallanzani actually refers
to Caminer as a "Venetian bookseller" (*Libraire vénitien*). See Lazzaro Spallanzani, *Epistolario*, ed.
Benedetto Biagi (Firenze: Sansoni Antiquariato, 1958), 1:340. The *Mercure de France* also described Domenico as a "Libraire de Venise" (February 1773, 88).

25. See Mario Infelise, "L'utile e il piacevole: Alla ricerca dei lettori italiani del Secondo Settecento," in *Lo spazio del libro nell'Europa del XVIII secolo*, ed. M. G. Tavoni and F. Waquet (Bologna: Patron, 1997), 113–26, and "'Europa': Una gazzetta manoscritta del Settecento," 221–29.

26. Caminer's correspondence indicates that her godfather bought her an English dictionary
when she was eighteen years old, and that Francesco Albergati at least intended to give her lessons in English during this same period.

27. The *Europa letteraria* was published in Venice between 1768 and 1773 by printers Carlo Palese
(September 1768–September 1769) and Modesto Fenzo (October 1769–May 1773). It was sold
in bookshops in Bologna, Florence, Milan, Naples, Padua, Udine, and Venice.

28. These contributions appeared in the first and second issues of the *Europa letteraria* (September 1768, 3–19; October 1768, 30–33). Caminer indicated in her heading that she had translated both pieces from the *Mercure de France*. On the commonplace practice of borrowing other
journalists' work, see "Journalistic Writing" in section 4 of this introduction.

29. In a formal petition (1770) to the Riformatori dello Studio di Padova, Domenico described
the nature of Elisabetta's collaboration with him: "with an incredible assiduousness in the study

precisely because she had *not* been born into an aristocratic family, where working for money might have been deemed inappropriate or shameful. Economic concerns undoubtedly contributed to furthering Caminer's education in another way as well. In order to supplement the income from his journalistic work, her father rented out rooms in the Caminer home. When Elisabetta was eight years old, a native French speaker and French tutor was residing with the family and almost certainly offered her and her siblings instruction in French. This helps explain why, at the young age of seventeen, Caminer was already a proficient translator of Voltaire.[30]

It is impossible to overstate the importance of Caminer's being born in Venice during the eighteenth century, when the Lagoon City was the principal center of journalistic activity in all of Italy.[31] One Venetian historian has described the cultural world in the Veneto region during this period as a "multicolored emporium of ideas and debates," whose exceptionally rich book market and extremely active publishing houses inspired "a crowd of literati" to participate in the intellectual life of the region and of its capital city, Venice.[32] Indeed, the city of Caminer's apprenticeship was unique in the ways it fostered intellectuals striving to make a living with pen and press. According to another Venetian historian, "there existed no other city on the [Italian] peninsula where it was possible to earn a living from intellectual work, translating from the French, editing books, revising proofs, compiling newspapers."[33]

While Caminer's personal drive and talent are not to be underestimated,

---

of the sciences and letters and with admirable filial affection, she assists her unhappy father in earning a living for a large family of twelve people." The document is located in the ASV, Riformatori dello Studio di Padova, filza 37, carta 87.

30. According to the scholar Chantal Dumas, Caminer signed 130 articles (primarily reviews of works that had been published within twelve months prior to her writing) in the first fifteen months of the periodical. Ninety-four of these were translations, mostly from the *Mercure de France* and the *Journal encyclopédique de Bouillon*, usually appearing in the *Europa letteraria* with only one to two months' lag time. Generally speaking about 70 percent of Caminer's translations were literal, and about 30 percent underwent modifications in the form of cuts, additions of personal commentary, or restructuring of the original texts. All testify to Caminer's excellent knowledge of the French language. See Chantal Dumas, "Le traduzioni giornalistiche di Elisabetta Caminer nell'*Europa letteraria* dall sua creazione all'anno 1769," directed by Gérard Loubinoux (thesis, Université Blaise Pascal, Clermont II, Lettres et Sciences Humaines, 1996), 53, 56–57, 59.

31. A. Postigliola and N. Boccara, eds., *Periodici italiani d'antico regime* (Roma: Società Italiana di Studi sul secolo XVIII, 1986).

32. Gianfranco Torcellan, "Giornalismo e cultura illuministica nel Settecento veneto," in *Settecento veneto e altri scritti storici* (Torino: Giappichelli, 1969), 177.

33. Mario Infelise, "Gazzette e lettori nella Repubblica veneta dopo l'ottantanove," in *L'eredità dell'Ottantanove e l'Italia*, ed. Renzo Zorzi (Firenze: Olschki Editore, 1992), 310.

her Venetian birth and her middle-class status also helped "set the stage," so to speak, for the development of her interest and activity in the theatrical world. At the beginning of the eighteenth century Venice boasted eight public theaters, which was more than either London or Paris could claim.[34] Caminer's father's interests and his financial struggles further ensured her exposure to the theatrical world.[35] In order to supplement the income from his journalistic work, Domenico became one of the most active private investors involved in the financial management of theaters, especially for productions of musical theater. He was among the many impresarios who managed the S. Moisè Theater.[36] Thus, the young Elisabetta's first encounters with the theatrical life of Venice probably occurred because of her father's direct involvment in it.

As early as 1769—from the age of eighteen—she began publishing her translations of the most recent French plays for Venetian theater companies who wished to perform them. She made her public debut on the theatrical scene with the publication and the performance of her translation of Fenouillot de Falbaire's play *The Honest Criminal; or, Filial Love* at the S. Salvatore Theater in Venice.[37] Remarkaby, Caminer enjoyed the privilege (extremely rare for a woman) of directing the performances of some of her translations between 1769 and 1771 at the S. Angelo Theater. With these performances, Caminer's public extended beyond the *Europa letteraria*'s literate or intellectual audience to include a more "popular" crowd whose tastes often contrasted

34. Marvin Carlson, *The Italian Stage: From Goldoni to D'Annunzio* (Jefferson, N.C.: McFarland and Co., 1981), esp. 2, 13.

35. Domenico had written at least one comedy himself; De Michelis mentions a comedy entitled *Fattor galantuomo*, published in 1757 (De Michelis, "Caminer, Domenico," 235).

36. N. Mangini, *I teatri di Venezia* (Milano: Mursia, 1974), 109, 119. Impresarios like Domenico Caminer organized and or financed (at their own risk) performances of theatrical works, and they hired musicians and actors for specific theaters in return for a share of the profits. Impresarios thus exerted a notable economic and cultural influence on the theatrical life of the cities where they worked. Caminer must have known that Luisa Bergalli Gozzi was the first female manager of the S. Angelo Theater in 1747–48. Perhaps this knowledge informed her own decision to act as a resident director in the same theater some twenty-five years later.

37. *L'onesto colpevole e sia l'Amore filiale dramma in cinque atti in prosa di Charles Georges Fenouillot de Falbaire de Quincey* (The honest criminal; or, Filial love) (Venezia: Graziosi, 1769). In the same year (1769) Caminer also published her translations of Baculard d'Arnaud's *Eufemia* (Venezia: Colombani), and Bernard-Joseph Saurin's *Beverlei* (Venezia: Pavini). It is worth noting that Caminer's *Onesto colpevole* and *Eufemia* were performed in public theaters in Italy long before the French originals were performed publicly in France (1790 and 1789, respectively). Charles George Fenouillot de Falbaire's *Honnête criminel ou l'Amour filial* was written in 1767 and performed in 1768 in a private theater, but not until 1790 was it performed at the Théâtre Français. Baculard d'Arnaud's play was originally published in 1768, but it was not performed in Paris until 1789, because of its antiecclesiastical tone.

with those of established men of letters.[38] Through the theater—perhaps to a greater extent than through her initial collaboration on the family periodical—Elisabetta Caminer became a visible presence in the public sphere.

Were it not for her fortuitous circumstances—her Venetian birth, her middle-class status, her father's involvement in journalism and the theater, and Domenico's devotion to her—Caminer would very likely not have gained access to an education, much less to a profession in letters. There was no official system of public schooling available for girls in eighteenth-century Italy. If girls did get an education—and those who did usually held aristocratic status—they typically did so through a convent, through relatives, or through their brothers' tutors. As the scholar Madile Gambier has noted, the Venetian Republic never instituted a system of public education for girls, not even after the reforms of 1774;[39] it was not until 1792 that schools for girls were opened.[40]

In contrast to the many positive influences in the young Caminer's life, evidence of a restricting influence that helped shape the direction of her professional development is revealed in a letter she wrote before her eighteenth birthday to the renowned naturalist (and contributor to the *Europa letteraria*) Lazzaro Spallanzani.[41] In the letter she expressed her indignation that as a young woman "the Sciences [would] be forbidden to [her] forever" and that

38. See "Making of a Woman," text 25.

39. Madile Gambier, "Destini di donna nel Settecento veneziano," in *La donna galante ed erudita: Giornale dedicato al bel sesso* (1786–88), ed. Cesare De Michelis (Venezia: Marsilio, 1983), 313–28, esp. 323. For more on Venetian scholastic reforms see G. Gullino, *La politica scolastica veneziana nell'età delle riforme* (Padova: Deputazione di Storia Patria per le Venezie, 1973). For a broader discussion of the debate about women's education, see section 3 of this introduction.

40. Pompeo G. Molmenti, *La storia di Venezia nella vita privata*, vol. 3 of *Il decadimento*, 7th ed. (1927–29; reprint, Trieste, Edizioni Lint, 1973), 342.

41. Lazzaro Spallanzani (1729–99) would be a friend and correspondent for all of Caminer's life. Although there are not many extant letters, their correspondence was quite extensive, beginning in January 1769 (or earlier) and lasting at least into 1793. Spallanzani originally came to know Caminer because he was a friend of Alberto Fortis and an early collaborator on the *Europa letteraria*. Spallanzani was born in Scandiano and studied rhetoric and philosophy in Reggio. Although he went to the University of Bologna to study law (in accordance with his father's wishes), his cousin Laura Bassi—with whom he studied mathematics—encouraged him to pursue his interest in the natural sciences. In 1769 Spallanzani was offered the professorship of natural history at Pavia, which he held for the rest of his life. He became one of the most renowned Italian naturalists, one who embodied the eighteenth-century ideal of rejecting scholasticism and preconceived notions in favor of drawing conclusions from unbiased experiments and observations. His careful approach to scientific research brought him international fame, and Voltaire dubbed him "le meilleur observateur de l'Europe." He published original works on digestion, circulation, and various experiments in the animal and vegetable world. He had an extensive correspondence with Charles Bonnet, and in 1769–70 he published the translation *Contemplazione della natura del sig. Carlo Bonnet*, which had second and third editions in 1773 and

she would be constrained to "translation, or at the most, to writing bits of poetry," despite what she felt to be her "aptitude" for the sciences.[42] Perhaps at a young age Caminer gave up on the idea of following her inclination for scientific study because she recognized that the gender boundaries of her society would not readily allow her such a possibility. This private revelation challenges the traditional image of Caminer and the scholarly assumptions about her "natural love" for literature and theater.

As these glimpses of her correspondence with the celebrated naturalist (Spallanzani) and journalist (Pelli) indicate, Caminer began developing a correspondence network with the most renowned male intellectuals of her day during the early years of her career. In her role as journalist, she wrote letters to colleagues in and beyond the Veneto in order to solicit articles, reviews, and extracts for the periodical, to discuss borrowing books or purchasing volumes of the periodical, and to request help in expanding the list of subscribers to the periodical.[43] Correspondences that began as strictly work-oriented exchanges in many cases grew into friendships which lasted for years, and some for the whole of Caminer's life. This circle of erudite friends and colleagues expanded rapidly, and some of her earliest correspondents played key roles in publicly supporting her through some of the polemics during the first years of her career.

By the age of eighteen, Caminer had begun to develop a reputation for herself as a journalist and as a theater critic, translator, and director. Her professional life had brought her into the public sphere, where she attracted the attention—both supportive and hostile—of the Veneto reading public and theatergoers. One of her greatest admirers at this stage of her career was the

---

1781. On Spallanzani, see Claude E. Dolman, "Spallanzani, Lazzaro," in *Dictionary of Scientific Biography*, ed. Charles Coudson Gillispie (New York: Charles Scribner's Sons, 1975), 12:553–67; and Spallanzani, *Epistolario*.

42. See "Making of a Woman," text 4. In the same year (1769), Caminer published lavish praises for eighteenth-century women who were accomplished in the sciences. Her descripton of Madame du Châtelet, "who cultivated her own talents so well!" is particularly wistful. See "Women and Society," text 2. Caminer's interest in scientific developments is also evident in the fact that between 1768 and 1769 the number of reviews of scientific works she signed was second only to the number of literary works she reviewed (and greater than the number of historical, philosophical, or economic works) (Dumas, "Le traduzioni giornalistiche di Elisabetta Caminer," 53).

43. For more detailed information about Caminer's correspondence, see section 3 of this introduction. Dena Goodman underscores the importance of correspondence networks in the eighteenth century, describing this "reciprocal exchange" as "crucial to the Republic of Letters from its inception" and "the means of expanding a scholarly republic into what Habermas has called a 'critically debating public,' a 'public engaged in rational-critical debate.'" See Dena Goodman, *The Republic of Letters: A Cultural History of the French Enlightenment* (Ithaca: Cornell University Press, 1994), 138.

playwright and dilettante actor from Bologna the marquis Francesco Albergati Capacelli.[44] The earliest extant letters suggest that both Elisabetta and her father had written to Albergati regarding the forthcoming publication of some of his translations of French theatrical works, which they wanted to review in the *Europa letteraria*. Almost immediately after this initial contact had been made, Francesco engaged Elisabetta in a secret courtship correspondence, which, as extant letters indicate, was passionately pursued on both sides.[45] Albergati promised a life together that would be dedicated to books, theatrical rehearsals, and productions, a house in the country, tranquility, and excitement, all guided by a shared Enlightenment philosophy. Undoubtedly this image of a life with the aristocratic playwright—a marriage that would constitute a move up the social ladder as well as a companionship of shared interests—was enticing to the young Caminer.

Although she was clearly taken with the older, more experienced Albergati, the correspondence reveals that she did not trust him completely. Albergati quoted her as saying she "did not want to be played" or toyed with,[46] and he responded many times throughout the correspondence to her doubts

---

44. Francesco Albergati Capacelli (1728–1804), aristocratic playwright, translator, and dilettante actor from Bologna, was an avid supporter of Goldoni's reform of the Italian theater and an admirer of contemporary French bourgeois dramas. As his original works for the theater and his correspondence reveal, Albergati used his work to critique the social customs of his day, most notably the practice of forced monachization and the struggle between "old" and "new" nobility. Among his most well known plays are *Il sofà* (1770), *Il saggio amico* (pt. 1, 1770; pt. 2, 1773), and *Il prigioniero* (1774). His most ambitious work, *Il Nuovo teatro comico* (1774–78), is a collection of his original theatrical compositions as well as some of his translations. Albergati's notable translations of French theatrical works include Racine's *Phèdre* and *Iphigénie* and Voltaire's *Don Pèdre*, *Sophonisbe*, and *Les guères ou la tolérance*. Albergati was the proprietor of a large theater, the Teatro Zola, in his sumptuous villa near Bologna, where he and other dilettante actors performed French and Italian comedies and tragedies, including those he had translated. For more on Albergati in this introduction, see notes 48, 52, and 53 below. See also Ernesto Masi, *La vita, i tempi, gli amici di Francesco Albergati: Commediografo del secolo XVIII* (Bologna: Zanichelli, 1878); Alberto Asor-Rosa, "Albergati Capacelli, Francesco," in *DBI*, 1:624–27; and Enrico Mattioda, *Il dilettante "per mestiere": Francesco Albergati Capacelli commediografo* (Bologna: Società editrice il Mulino, 1993), which contains a rich bibliography on Albergati.

45. Unfortunately, we have only one side of the story from this correspondence, because all the extant letters are Albergati's. The first letter dates from November 1768, and the last from November 1771; the letters peak in frequency and intensity in the year 1769. Roberto Trovato published the correspondence in "Lettere di Francesco Albergati Capacelli alla Bettina (Nov. 1768–Nov. 1771)," ed. Roberto Trovato, *Studi e Problemi di Critica Testuale* 28 (1984): 99–173.

46. "As for the rest, Mademoiselle, you have found a very sure and rigorous way to impose silence upon me about certain points. The more I examine some of your sentences, the more I know I should keep quiet. *I carry bantering too far. You do not want to be played with. Let us bring our exchange back to Literature.*" The letter is dated 27 January 1769 ("Lettere di Francesco Albergati Capacelli alla Bettina," 108).

about his constancy. Some of her hesitation was almost certainly due to his reputation as something of a "ladies' man." But her caution probably also stemmed from self-consciousness and a certain amount of disbelief that such a well-known playwright and nobleman would court her. Ultimately, their class difference did emerge as a potential obstacle to their marriage.[47] Although Albergati claimed he "did not care a fig" for the laws stating that a chevalier who married a nonnoble woman forfeited aristocratic status for himself and for all his descendants,[48] he said he could not abide the familial resistance and gossip that would surely result from an interclass marriage. He claimed that it was in order to avoid such "violent obstacles" that he was forced to insist upon the greatest secrecy and prudence in all matters concerning the personal nature of their correspondence and marriage plans.[49] At one point, he pointed out to Caminer that since "people know that you write to me from time to time" regarding theatrical matters, it would be a good idea for her to write him an impersonal and "brief little letter" containing her opinion about a recent play since "no one would believe you would not have written to me about it."[50] This way, should anyone inquire about their correspondence, he could show the "professional" letter as a cover for the more intimate missives they were sending each other. In fact, not only did Albergati want to arrange a clandestine marriage, but he also wanted the two of them to remain secluded from society until they had been married for some time.[51]

Caminer appears to have been willing to accept Albergati's proposal of a clandestine marriage, but she was put off by her suitor's intense need for secrecy, which bordered at times on paranoia. Her doubts were compounded when Albergati disclosed that he had already been married once and had had the union annulled.[52] He repeatedly had to reassure Caminer that he would

47. Ibid., 124–25.

48. Ibid., 125. Albergati was worried that if he married Caminer he would risk losing the honorary titles granted him by the king of Poland. In 1767, King Stanislaus II granted Albergati the title of chamberlain to the king. In 1768, at Albergati's insistence, the king has also granted him an honoray military title as a general aide (*Generale aiutante di campo di servizio*). According to his biographer Ernesto Masi, Albergati was extremely covetous of these titles. See Masi, *La vita, i tempi, gli amici di Francesco Albergati*, 181–85. For more on Albergati's complex and shifting position on the issue of class, especially as it manifests itself in his theatrical writing, see Mattioda, *Il dilettante "per mestiere*," esp. 18–20, 30–32.

49. "Lettere di Francesco Albergati Capacelli alla Bettina," 122–25.

50. Ibid., 117.

51. Ibid., 125.

52. Albergati married three times during the course of his life. His first marriage—to the contessina Teresa Orsi—was arranged by his parents in 1748. It was annulled in 1751, the year Caminer was born. Albergati told Caminer about the marriage in a letter dated 2 May 1769.

not change his mind after marrying her and decide to annul their marriage as well. The correspondence indicates that she was frustrated by the contradiction in his constant declarations of love and his equally constant deferral of their meeting in person, which he insisted was necessary before any official engagement could be made. It is conceivable that Caminer's suspicions regarding Albergati's forthrightness may have been correct: his biographer Ernesto Masi posits that, at the time of his courtship correspondence with Caminer, he was already involved with the woman who would become his wife, Caterina Boccadabati, who may already have been pregnant with their future son. Certainly, if this was true, it suggests yet another motive behind Albergati's great need for secrecy.[53] It is equally conceivable that, against Albergati's wishes, Caminer confided in her parents about the secret correspondence and had been pressured into refusing Albergati. Or she may simply have concluded that despite his idealistic words the Bolognese marquis would not follow through on his promises if the secret courtship were to become public.

In any case, upon their first meeting in person sometime in the late summer of 1769, it appears that Caminer refused Albergati's proposal of marriage. He agreed grudgingly to continue their relationship as friends and colleagues, saying, "So, dear Bettina, our friendship and our tender correspondence must remain intact, if you enjoy such an innocent pastime."[54] Undoubtedly there was disapointment on both sides—her idealistic hopes deflated, his quest unfulfilled—but Caminer and Albergati maintained a friendly and collegial relationship.[55] She continued to review his publications positively in the family periodical, and he fostered her career as well, asking her to direct a performance of one of his plays and writing supportively of her in his correspondence with others.

Although this mutually passionate courtship seems to have been unique in Caminer's life, it was not the last time she found herself in a position to set boundaries—diplomatically, without causing offense—between herself and

---

53. In 1772, Albergati married Caterina Boccadabati. That Albergati and Boccadabati might have been involved even as he was talking of marrying Caminer is suggested by the timing, since the Caminer-Albergati marriage plan was called off in September of 1769, and Albergati's and Boccadabati's first son was probably born in 1770. In 1787, Boccadabati allegedly committed suicide. Although the details of what actually happened remain somewhat murky, Albergati was accused and acquitted of her murder. In 1789, he married the twenty-five-year-old dancer and actress Teresa Checchi Zampieri. See Masi, *La vita, i tempi, gli amici di Francesco Albergati.*

54. "Lettere di Francesco Albergati Capacelli alla Bettina," 163.

55. For a more detailed analysis of this episode in Caminer's life see Catherine M. Sama, "Becoming Visible: A Biography of Elisabetta Caminer Turra (1751–1796) during Her Formative Years," *Studi veneziani*, n.s., 43 (2002): 349–88.

admiring male colleagues. Her reputation as an intelligent, spirited, and attractive young woman both enhanced and complicated her efforts to build and maintain the network of male patrons so essential for her burgeoning career. Two of her most avid supporters and mentors influenced the course of her professional career as well as her personal life in this way: the Paduan naturalist Alberto Fortis[56] and the Florentine man of letters Giulio Perini.[57]

56. Alberto Fortis (1741–1803), was exposed from his youth to the company of the most renowned Paduan men of letters and science, who frequented the salon of his mother, Francesca Maria Capodilista (remarried after Fortis's father's death), herself a woman of letters. Having studied at the Seminario vescovile in Padua, Fortis entered the Order of the Eremitani di S. Agostino (Hermits of St. Augustine) in 1757. He pursued studies in theology, but his real interest lay in natural history, and he broke with the Augustinian order in 1767 in order to pursue his scientific studies more freely (though he was not able officially to leave the order until 1771). He moved to Venice, began working as a journalist for the *Magazzino italiano*, and established contact with two internationally celebrated naturalists whose work was featured in the periodical, Lazzaro Spallanzani and Charles Bonnet. In 1768 he began working for Domenico Caminer on the *Europa letteraria*—perhaps meeting Elisabetta for the first time in this capacity—and he continued to collaborate with her (on and off) throughout her journalistic career. Fortis undertook a series of geological, archeological, and anthropological expeditions during his lifetime. He made repeated travels to Dalmatia, and he also traveled extensively in southern Italy, where he lived for some years in the service of the court of Naples. Fortis's discovery of a source of saltpeter—essential for making gunpowder—near Molfetta led to his attempts to reform mining and production systems there. He published two controversial works on the topic, *Del nitro minerale* (Napoli, 1783) and *Lettera a Melchiorrre Delfico* (Napoli, 1783). After returning to the Veneto, Fortis pursued his interest in paleontology, collaborating with G. Olivi on *Zoologica adriatica* (1792) and undertaking excursions in search of fossils with Giambattista Brocchi. Perhaps Fortis's greatest work was his *Viaggio in Dalmazia* (Venezia, 1774), the account of his travels and explorations in Dalmatia. His sympathetic portrait of the Morlacchi people and his investigations of the province's natural resources and economic potential helped change preconceptions about this geographical and cultural area of the Venetian Republic. Fortis's book was rapidly translated into the principal European languages and helped inspire a rediscovery of the culture of Baltic Europe. On Fortis, see Luca Ciancio, "Fortis, Alberto," in *DBI*, 49:205–10; Gianfranco Torcellan, "Alberto Fortis," in *Riformatori delle antiche repubbliche, dei ducati, dello stato pontificio e delle isole*, vol. 7 of *Illuministi italiani*, ed. Giuseppe Giarrizzo, Gianfranco Torcellan, and Franco Venturi (Milano: Ricciardi, 1965), 281–390; Luca Ciancio, *Autopsie della terra: Illuminismo e geologia in Alberto Fortis (1741–1803)* (Firenze: Olschki, 1995); and Larry Wolff, *Venice and the Slavs*.

57. The life and work of Giulio Perini (c. 1740–1801), an erudite Florentine man of letters, has yet to be thoroughly researched. He was an avid translator of French and German literary works and a collaborator on the *Encyclopédie méthodique* (for the entry on Tuscany). Perini was an active member of the Accademia dei Georgofili and a librarian at the Magliabechiana Library (from 1783). He corresponded with many French and Italian literati, and he counted among his friends Andrea Memmo, Alberto Fortis, Francesco Albergati, Giuseppe Pelli Bencivenni, and the Caminers. Perini resided in Venice for at least part of the 1760s and 1770s, and during this period he collaborated on the *Europa letteraria*. His translations include *Il primo navigatore, e Selim e Selima poemi tradotti dal Tedesco dall'Abbate Giulio Perini Nobile Fiorentino* (Venezia: Palese, 1771), *La felicità* (Helvétius) ([Firenze, with false imprint of Berna], 1781), and *Saggi* (Montaigne) (Amsterdam: Filandro, 1785). On the first of these translations, see "Making of a Woman," text 26. On Perini, see Leo Neppi Modona, "Per la storia della *Encyclopédie* in Italia: L'abate Giulio Perini collabora-

As primary members of the editorial team of the newly established *Europa letteraria*, Fortis and Caminer became close friends as well as working partners. Scholars have often described the spiritual and intellectual bond the two shared over the course of their lives.[58] Indeed, as a mentor, friend, and business partner over the years, Fortis was probably one of the single most influential people in Caminer's life. Nevertheless, Fortis's relationship with both Caminers—especially with Domenico—was a conflicted one. Indeed, after less than a year of collaboration on the *Europa letteraria*, he wrote a letter in which he broke with the Caminer team and refused to contribute further to the periodical.[59] Despite the vehemence of Fortis's letter, he returned to the *Europa letteraria* within a couple of months. But the following spring (1770), he separated once again from the Caminers, and this time his absence from the *Europa letteraria* lasted into 1772.[60] As evidence from Elisabetta Caminer's correspondence reveals, she was upset at Fortis's leave-taking. In response to a friend's condolences about the turn of events, she penned the following rather bitter comment: "I am more sorry than anyone else about Fortis's alienation; but I know that good things rarely last, and it was useless to hope that they would."[61] For his part, Fortis wrote to Perini that he might never reconcile with Domenico but that he was shocked that Elisabetta was no longer writing to him.[62] Perhaps their relationship was strained because she had felt

---

tore della *Encyclopédie méthodique*," *Revue des études italiennes* 10 (1964): 81–91; "Andrea Memmo," in Giarrizzo, Torcellan, and Venturi, *Riformatori delle antiche repubbliche*, 269–70; and Morelli Timpanaro, *Autori*.

58. Referring to Fortis as a member of the *Europa letteraria*'s editorial team, Marino Berengo writes (my translations): "Elisabetta could not have found a better ally for transforming the diligent newspaper of extracts into a combative journal" (Berengo, *Giornali veneziani del Settecento: Linea di sviluppo della stampa periodica veneta* (Milano: Feltrinelli, 1962), liii). Gianfranco Torcellan describes the bond between Caminer and Fortis as "a mixture of sentiment and spiritual attraction" (Torcellan, "Alberto Fortis," 285); and Angelo Colla refers to Fortis as "Elisabetta's teacher and ideal friend" (Colla, "Elisabetta Caminer Turra e il giornalismo 'enciclopedico,'" in *Varietà settecentesche: Saggi di cultura veneta tra rivoluzione e restaurazione*, vol. 3 of Filologia Veneta [Padova: Editoriale Programma, 1991], 87).

59. Fortis did not sign any reviews in the May or June 1769 issues of the *Europa letteraria*. In a 17 June 1769 letter to Domenico Caminer, Fortis vented his anger at the unfair treatment he believed he had received at the hands of Domenico and warned him to act more respectfully or he might retaliate. The letter is located in the Archivio di Stato di Firenze (hereafter ASF), Acquisti e doni, 93, inserto 77.

60. Fortis's second period of absence (aside from a few occasional reviews) began with the March 1770 issue (thus April 1770) and lasted into mid-1772. See Dino Benacchio, "Alberto Fortis e i giornali dei Caminer," directed by Gilberto Pizzamiglio (thesis, University of Venice, 1985–86).

61. From Caminer's 24 April 1770 letter to Giuseppe Gennari. The letter is located in the Biblioteca del Seminario di Padova, codice 620, carta 201r.

62. This undated letter is located in the ASF, Acquisti e doni, 93, inserto 77.

compelled to defend her father rather than taking Fortis's side in their disagreement.

Not only did Fortis leave, but he seems to have carried out a vague threat of retaliation that he had made earlier to Domenico. Although the primary target of his anger may have been her father, the person he attacked was Elisabetta. He published something negative—perhaps a satirical poem—about her. This text has not been found, but Giulio Perini's correspondence offers us evidence of the publication and of Fortis's possible motives for writing it. According to Perini, Fortis was "although he does not say so, enamored of the girl," who was "most wise, and [who] felt much gratitude and friendship for him, and nothing of love."[63] After a series of conflicts with Domenico, Perini explained, Fortis "published an unworthy text [*un foglio indegno*]" against Elisabetta, of which "fortunately only a few copies circulated because of some threats made to him . . . and finally the friendship and his collaboration on the *Journal* were ended."[64] In fact, Fortis's public criticism of Caminer was used as evidence against her in an attack by a rival journalist later that summer. Ultimately, the conflict between the two men closest to Caminer—Domenico and Alberto—cost her a mentor and friend in Fortis and risked damaging her good reputation at an early point in her career.

Although Fortis and Elisabetta Caminer eventually resumed their friendship and remained close for their whole lives, over the years their relationship was marked by conflict. It seems that they had fluctuating periods of collaboration or contact through the years, in part as a result of Fortis's travels to Dalmatia and southern Italy, as his phases of collaboration on and distance from the periodical reflect. Some comments in their few extant letters reflect phases of affectionate and frequent communication, while others suggest frustration and attenuated contact.

Giulio Perini's position as mediator in the conflicts between Alberto Fortis and Domenico Caminer was complicated as well. His correspondence attests to the fact that he too was suffering from the frustrations of unrequited love for Elisabetta.[65] Although he initially hid his amorous feelings, sometime during 1771 Perini wrote four letters to her in which he revealed his feelings and asked whether she might not return them.[66] Apparently Caminer was

63. From Giuseppe Perini's 18 August 1770 letter to Giuseppe Pelli, located in the ASF, Carteggi Pelli Bencivenni, fascio 15.

64. Ibid.

65. In a letter to their mutual friend and colleague, Giuseppe Pelli, he asked the Florentine journalist to convince Caminer to let him serve her "with both of his pens." The letter, dated 28 December 1770, is located in the ASF, Carteggi Pelli Bencivenni, fascio 16.

66. These letters are undated, but they were probably written sometime in 1771: between the fall of 1770 and Caminer's June 1772 marriage and subsequent move to Vicenza, because the let-

emotionally attached to someone else at this point, since Perini metaphorically alluded to the fact that the "pathway" to her heart was already occupied.[67] His use of the S. Angelo Theater's narrow doorway—which allowed only one person in at a time—as a metaphor for the human heart was particularly clever. It would have been quite meaningful to Caminer, since at that time she was working at the S. Angelo Theater, translating plays for the actors there and supervising their performances.

Caminer responded to Perini's letter and explained the nature of her feelings for him. We must rely on Perini's comments, of course, to infer what the content of her letter must have been, but it is clear that Caminer, in her direct and diplomatic fashion, had told him that she viewed him as a friend, not a suitor.[68] In his subsequent letter Perini began by expressing his gratitude for her honesty. He asked her forgiveness for having been somewhat bold with the "most discreet and honest girl I have ever met." He begged her to "put him to the test," to allow him to show her how he would restrain the violence of his instinct and show her "all the esteem and respect" she deserved from men. It appears that Perini accepted this arrangement gracefully, and he resolved to quell his passion for her. Managing a collegial rapport with Perini earned Caminer a lifelong friend, but it also worked to her advantage professionally, because Perini proved to be an important ally in the midst of a vicious attack against her reputation.

For, as Francesco Albergati had warned her, Caminer had to pay a price for her newly acquired visibility in the public sphere. In a remarkably prescient letter (May 1769), he had presented the seventeen-year-old Caminer with a list of her personal and professional transgressions: "I will speak very clearly: the increase in your beauty, vivaciousness, knowledge; the fact that you have made a well-deserved name for yourself . . . in the Republic of Letters; the fact that you have a vast circle of learned people who admire and approach you . . . all this is a body of crimes, and grave crimes, that will not be easily pardoned."[69] Indeed, Caminer's early professional success did bring her into conflict with other journalists, translators, and playwrights.

---

ters are addressed to "Bettina Caminer" in Venice. The letters are located in the ASF, Acquisti e doni, 97, inserto 1. Since they are not numbered in any way and are not identifiable by date, I shall simply refer to them as "Perini to Caminer, ASF" in the notes here.

67. "[V]edo già occupato l'andito che conduce alla platea del vostro cuore." Perhaps Perini was referring to Caminer's future husband, Antonio Turra.

68. Perini had written: "Now that you have been so good as to tell me that you only want to be my friend, wait until you see what kind of dam I shall construct against the impetus of [my] emotions; I will regard you as an image of virtue and wisdom, and I shall suffocate every desire of mine." Perini to Caminer, ASF, Acquisti e doni, 97, inserto 1.

69. "Lettere di Francesco Albergati Capacelli alla Bettina," 137.

Two of the most significant episodes of conflict involved a rival journalist named Cristoforo Venier[70] and Carlo Gozzi[71] who was the most established playwright in Venice at the time. Both men criticized Caminer because she had dared to assume the position of literary critic, despite her sex and her lack of education. Venier, the more extreme of the two men, pushed his attack of Caminer to the point of sexual slander, and Domenico Caminer took legal action against him in order to defend his daughter's (and his family's) honor. Venier claimed that even Elisabetta's mentor, Alberto Fortis, had publicly criticized her intellectual limits, and that the Paduan abbé—barely cloaked as "Padre A. F."—knew her "inside and out" (*intus & in cute*). With this assertion, Venier called into question the nineteen-year-old's sexual mores and clearly insinuated that she was not only intellectually arrogant, but also sexually promiscuous.[72] An attack on Caminer's moral reputation jeopardized her

70. Very little is known about Cristoforo Venier. Originally from Istria, the abbé Venier moved to Venice around 1739. By 1771 he had already established an infamous reputation for making sacrilegous comments in public, and between 1763 and 1771 he was officially accused by the Sant'Uffizio of atheism. Venier worked at some point for the Baglioni publishing house, and he was recognized by some as a talented editor or "correttore di stampe." He compiled the literary periodical the *Nuovo corrier letterario*, about which little is known. I presume it is the continuation of Francesco Griselini's *Corrier letterario*, a Venetian periodical that was issued weekly between December 1765 and December 1768. The surviving pages from a few 1770 issues of the *Nuovo corrier letterario* indicate that it was issued every Saturday, that subscription cost eight *lire* per semester, and that Giammaria Bassaglia was the bookseller who handled subscriptions as well as the collection of any articles or information submitted by readers. I am indebted to both Federico Barbierato and Mario Infelise for sharing their knowledge of Venier with me and for directing my attention to the two archival sources of information about him and his periodical at the ASV: Sant'Uffizio, busta 148; and Riformatori dello Studio di Padova, filza 37, carte 86, 87, 90, 94, and 97.

71. Carlo Gozzi (1720–1806), aristocratic Venetian playwright and chief rival to fellow Venetian playwright Carlo Goldoni (1707–93), came to prominence as a playwright in the 1760s with his extremely popular *Fiabe*. These "fables for the theatre"—in direct opposition to Goldoni's reality-based comedies of the 1750s—featured traditional commedia dell'arte masks engaged in magical adventures and supernatural transformations. The first of these theatrical fables, *L'amore delle tre melarance*, directly mocked playwrights Goldoni and Pietro Chiari. In collaboration with the famous Antonio Sacchi and his company of actors, Gozzi produced a series of these works on the Venetian stage between 1761 and 1765, including *Il Corvo, Re Cervo, Turandot, La donna serpente*, and *L'augellino Belverde*. Gozzi did not decide to publish his theatrical works until 1772, when his rivalry with Elisabetta Caminer (and her translations of French bourgeois dramas) was intensifying. It was in this year that both Caminer and Gozzi began publishing the first collections of their theatrical works—his originals (*Opere* [Venezia: Colombani]) and her translations (*Composizioni teatrali moderne tradotte*)—in direct competition with each other. On Gozzi, see Carlo Gozzi, *Five Tales for the Theatre*, ed. and trans. Albert Bermel and Ted Emery (Chicago: University of Chicago Press, 1989), and *Opere: Teatro e polemiche teatrali*, ed. Giuseppe Petronio (Milano: Rizzoli, 1962); and Gerard Luciani, *Carlo Gozzi (1720–1806): L'homme et l'oeuvre* (thesis, Université de Dijon, 1974; Lille: Atelier; Paris: Librairie Honoré Champion, 1977).

72. *Nuovo corrier letterario*, 4 August 1770, 233. Such conflation of public life with sexual activity dates back at least to Renaissance debates about women's education and public activity. In the

prospects for social acceptance as well as the future of her respectable career. Fortunately, her father's petition to vindicate her reputation was successful: thereafter Venier was prohibited from working as an editor (*correttore*) for the Venetian Republic or for any bookellers or printers.[73]

Even after the magistrate's official sentence had been passed, the show of support for Caminer was not over. In Florence about one month later, the journalist Giuseppe Pelli Bencivenni (whom Caminer did not know) responded to Venier's attack, thus extending the publicity of the episode into Tuscany. When Caminer wrote to Pelli to thank him for publicly coming to her defense, she used the opportunity to boldly insist that he must act as a mentor for her, especially in matters of translation.[74] Thus, in gaining an instructor as well as a supporter, Caminer was able to turn an ugly episode into an opportunity to build her network of male patrons and further her education.[75]

Her conflict with the playwright Carlo Gozzi was not so quickly or neatly resolved. Gozzi's contention with Caminer was born of her successful introduction into Italy of the new bourgeois dramas from France.[76] The protagonists of bourgeois dramas were members of the middle classes—not kings and lofty heroes—and the subject of these plays was the events of the characters' daily lives.[77] The bourgeois drama was a theater of sentiment with a decisive pedagogical and moralistic goal: its purpose was to instill moral behavior in the public by providing examples of virtuous and vice-ridden char-

---

eighteenth century, this type of reaction reflected a culture in which women's sexuality was often used as a metaphor for all that was dissolute in society—reaching a peak in the pornographic portrayals of the woman in the (symbolically) highest position of power in France—Queen Marie Antoinette. See Lynn Hunt, *The Family Romance of the French Revolution* (Berkeley: University of California Press, 1992).

73. ASV, Sant'Uffizio, busta 148. The Riformatori decided in favor of the Caminers, and they sent a copy of their 14 September 1770 decision to the head of the publishing guild so that he would communicate the news to the parties involved and also oversee its execution.

74. See "Making of a Woman," texts 7 and 8.

75. Other male colleagues with whom Caminer corresponded also came to her defense. Giulio Perini even tried to influence the outcome of the magistrate's decision in favor of suppressing the publication of Venier's periodical altogether.

76. The *drame bourgeois* is a theatrical form whose definition originated in the writings of Diderot. Building on the work of authors such as Lillo and his *London Merchant* (1731), Moore and his *Gamester* (1753), and Nivelle de la Chaussée and the genre of the *comédie larmoyante* (so dubbed by its enemies), Diderot theorized about a theatrical spectrum at the center of which lay the "serious genre" (*genre sérieux*), itself containing two branches: the "serious comedy" (*la comédie du genre sérieux*) and the "domestic or bourgeois tragedy" (*la tragédie domestique ou bourgeoise*). Diderot's most important theoretical writings on the genre are *Entretiens sur le fils naturel* (1757), *De la poésie dramatique* (1758), and *Paradoxe sur le comédien* (written c. 1770–78; published 1830). His first efforts to put his theories into practice are embodied in *Le fils naturel* and *Le père de famille*.

77. In Caminer's words, "princes or heroes" do not appear on the stage. See "Making of a Woman," text 25.

acters with whom the audience could identify. Emotional involvement or *commozione* with the characters and the events onstage were designed to inspire the audience to acts of virtue, in part through exposure to the horrors of vice. Caminer fully embraced the pedagogical goal and the emotional power of the bourgeois drama, and she was optimistic that the new genre could educate a broad spectrum of the public, since people from all social classes attended the theater regularly.[78] In the preface to her first volume of theatrical translations,[79] Caminer openly stated that these French plays could serve as a model for Italian theater.

Carlo Gozzi viewed the performances of the new bourgeois dramas as an unwelcome challenge to his position of preeminence on Venetian stages. He also believed that the public went to the theater to be entertained, not educated, and, above all, he found the "morality" fostered by the dramas to be reprehensible. As an aristocrat and as a man deeply attached to the traditional authorities of church and state, he reacted viscerally against the bourgeois dramas' celebration of the values of the commercial class. He vehemently objected to the way the plays exposed the public to ideas and situations such as the plights of an aristocrat who wants to marry a woman of a lower class, a married woman who falls in love with another man, or a deserter from the army who is painted as a victim of unjust laws rather than as a traitor to his prince.[80]

The Caminer-Gozzi polemic lasted for years both onstage and in the pages of a variety of texts including letters, periodicals, and prefaces and footnotes to translations.[81] Between 1769 and 1771, while Caminer was overseeing the performances of her translations at the S. Angelo Theater with the Lapy-Bresciani-Martelli troupe, Gozzi was directing productions of his plays with Antonio Sacchi's troupe at the S. Salvatore Theater. In 1771 their competitive battle for the theatergoing public's favor even led Gozzi to direct the

---

78. This was especially true in Venice, where the price of entry into theaters was very low.

79. *Composizioni teatrali moderne tradotte* (1772). See "The Making of a Woman," text 25.

80. In fact, Gozzi's major objection to the genre was based on its power to miseducate rather than on any literary grounds.

81. On the Caminer side the texts include letters from Elisabetta's correspondence with Albergati and Pelli Benicivenni (1768–73), reviews or comments by Elisabetta and Domenico in the *Europa letteraria* and the *Giornale enciclopedico* (1770–74), Elisabetta's collections of translations (the 1772 collection, its second edition, and the 1774–76 collection), and especially Elisabetta's prefaces to these two theatrical collections. As for Gozzi, there are several texts to consider: the preface to his translation, "Prefazione del Traduttore," in *Il fajel* (Venezia: Colombani, 1772), the *Manifesto* (Venezia: Colombani, 1772), the eight-volume Colombani edition of his *Opere* (1772–74), the letter to Giuseppe Baretti (1776), and the 1802 *Più lunga lettera* in the 1801–2 Zanardi edition of his works.

performance of a bourgeois drama which he translated for the occasion, claiming that this would "persuade their respected Public that they [the actors in the Sacchi troupe at S. Salvatore] too were capable of performing a tragic play with decorum."[82] Gozzi dedicated the entire preface to the published version of his translation to a comparison (in his favor) of the two plays and the two performances. In this way he successfully created a forum in which he could publicly criticize both Caminer and the theatrical genre she favored.

As her letter to a colleague makes clear, Caminer wrote the preface to the first volume of her collection of theatrical translations as a direct response to Gozzi's criticisms: "I am too exposed to the indiscretion of malicious or envious people who want to believe me culpable for even the most innocent actions. If you have read the preface to *Fayel,* which occasioned the one in my first volume, you will be convinced of this truth."[83] Caminer rather slyly painted her Enlightenment project to instruct the masses and to continue a reform of the Italian theater as nothing more than the "innocent action" of translating a handful of French plays. At the same time, by claiming that Gozzi's criticisms had demanded a response (in the form of her own provocative preface) she placed all culpability back upon the shoulders of her critic. Although she did not name him directly in her preface, Caminer addressed Gozzi implicity and quoted directly from his *Fayel* preface. Thus, Caminer's preface was at once a history of the Italian theater, an apology for the bourgeois drama, and a skillful essay in self-defense.[84]

Perhaps the series of conflicts so early on in Caminer's career—and especially the sexual slander case—influenced Caminer's decision to marry and leave Venice not long afterward. Marriage was the primary option available to a young woman seeking social protection and public approval, and Caminer (or her parents) might have concluded that it would lend a degree of "normalcy" to her otherwise exceptional life. At the same time, however, Caminer would have sought a husband who would not deny her the freedom to pursue her intellectual development, her network of male colleagues, and her profes-

---

82. C. Gozzi, "Prefazione del Traduttore," 15. Gozzi chose the play by Baculard d'Arnaud— *Fayel, or, Gabrielle de Vergy*—because Caminer and her troupe had just performed her translation of another version of the same play written by Pierre Laurent Buyrette de Belloy, entitled *Gabrielle de Vergy.* For a detailed analysis of the Caminer-Gozzi polemic, see Catherine M. Sama, "Verso un teatro moderno: La polemica tra Elisabetta Caminer e Carlo Gozzi," in *Elisabetta Caminer Turra (1751–1796): Una letterata veneta verso l'Europa,* ed. Rita Unfer-Lukoschik (Verona: Essedue Edizioni, 1998), 63–79.

83. See "Making of a Woman," text 30.

84. See "Making of a Woman," text 25.

sional career. She might have viewed Antonio Turra[85]—a well-established man of her own social class who was also a well-regarded member of the Republic of Letters—as just such an individual. Indeed, some months after her marriage to Turra, the Parisian literary periodical the *Mercure de France* described him as "a renowned doctor in Padua who loves Letters and who will support [Caminer] in her taste for literature."[86]

Evidence about Caminer's relationship with the Vicentine physician and botanist is scarce. The two may have met sometime in late 1770 or early 1771, possibly through Caminer's friend Andrea Corner,[87] who was the brother of the Bishop Marco Corner whose botanical garden Antonio Turra cultivated.[88] Elisabetta and Antonio may also have met because of his occasional collaboration on the Caminer family periodical: beginning in the fall of 1770, Turra began to contribute reviews to the *Europa letteraria*.[89] By December 1771, they were officially engaged and Caminer announced the news formally in letters to friends and colleagues. During this period she described her fiancé to a colleague: "Doctor Turra is in fact an expert botanist and a fine naturalist, but what must be most appreciated in him is his good soul."[90] If we may rely upon the evidence in her correspondence with Albergati, "an honest soul" was in fact one of the qualities she desired in a companion (in addition to a heart that belonged totally to her, and an attractive appearance).[91]

---

85. Antonio Turra (1736–97) was born in Vicenza to a well-off middle-class family. He earned a degree in medicine at the University of Padua and practiced medicine in Vicenza. Turra helped found Vicenza's Agrarian Academy and was its lifetime secretary from 1773 until his death in 1797. His most famous publication was *Florae italicae prodromus*, a catalog of seventeen hundred species of Italian plants. In 1780 he published this catalog with the printing press he and Caminer had recently opened in their home. Turra's work earned him awards and membership in many scientific academies both in Italy and abroad. Ironically, Turra's contributions in medicine, agriculture, and botany have been perpetually overshadowed by Caminer's fame. For a scholarly profile of Turra, see Anna Bellesia, "L'accademia di agricoltura," in *Storia di Vicenza*, vol. 2 of *L'età della Repubblica veneta (1404–1797)*, (Vicenza: Neri Pozza Editore, 1990), 367–77.

86. *Mercure de France*, February 1773, 88.

87. See Caminer's poem to Corner, "Making of a Woman," text 6.

88. The link between Bishop Corner, Antonio Turra, and Elisabetta Caminer was first posited by Angelo Colla. Colla interprets the nature of Caminer's marriage to Turra in "Elisabetta Caminer e Antonio Turra," in *Il vicentino tra rivoluzione giacobina ed età napoleonica 1797–1813*, ed. Renato Zironda (Vicenza: Biblioteca civica Bertoliana, 1989), 24–28. I doubt Caminer was involved with Turra much earlier than 1771. As late as October 1770—as we see in the poem she wrote at that time to Andrea Corner—she was dissillusioned in love and not in a frame of mind to be open to new suitors, despite Corner's advice to that effect.

89. According to the scholar Chantal Dumas, Turra contributed one to three signed articles a year during this period. See Dumas, "Le traduzioni giornalistiche di Elisabetta Caminer," 59.

90. See "Making of a Woman," text 26.

91. It is possible to reconstruct Caminer's words through Albergati's response in his letters. See "Lettere di Francesco Albergati Capacelli alla Bettina," 131.

The qualities that the sober, steady Doctor Antonio Turra might offer Caminer could hardly have been more different from those offered by the passionate, excitable marquis Francesco Albergati. Perhaps the disappointing end to Caminer's secret courtship with Albergati—and to her apparent willingness to accept his demands for a clandestine marriage—further influenced her subsequent decision to accept a more conventional match with a financially stable man from her own class. Turra's expertise in science may also have been attractive to Caminer, since a life with him guaranteed her at least a vicarious connection to a field she felt had been denied to her. Most important, Elisabetta must have been certain that Antonio would not object to her continuing her professional life. Indeed, when she shared her engagement news with her friends and colleagues, she consistently made a point of telling them that her marriage and her move would not interfere in any way with her work or her correspondence.[92] In one letter she explained that her writing would "complement [her] husband's mind" in the same way that it had done her father's.[93]

On 20 June 1772 Elisabetta Caminer and Antonio Turra were married in Venice, and they left later that day for Padua and then Vicenza. Shortly after the move to Vicenza, Caminer described her husband as "the most respectable man, the most adorned with solid qualities, and the most affectionate I could possibly find. I have in him a tender spouse and a sincere and admirable friend."[94] Their marriage remained childless, and one can only speculate on whether this was a conscious choice or not. Caminer obviously had great affection and concern for children, as evidenced by the series of pedagogical works for children she translated and published over the course of her life, and by the youth theater she established for some years in Vicenza. It is possible, of course, that physical problems (in either spouse) determined the outcome of things, but it may be that Elisabetta (or Antonio) preferred not to have children. In fact, the only evidence to date suggests that the latter scenario is more likely.

In response to her friend Giuseppe Pelli's queries about potential pregnancy, Caminer wrote, "I am healthy, nor is there any appearance that I am about to give my spouse the testimony of which you speak, even though my marriage is fourteen months old today. As far as letters are concerned, whether it is for better or for worse that I occupy myself with them, and despite my small success, I will certainly never abandon them. I now have it in mind to

---

92. See "Making of a Woman," texts 24, 26, 31, and 33.

93. From a 6 June 1772 letter to an unidentified recipient. The letter is located in the Biblioteca Comunale Archiginnasio di Bologna, Aut. Pallotti VI, 365.

94. See "Making of a Woman," text 30.

write a comedy."[95] In the same breath Caminer declared her healthy state, her lack of pregnancy, and her absolute commitment to her intellectual life. Clearly, she did not consider the duties of motherhood unrelated to the demands of a professional career. She had only to look to the example of her compatriot Luisa Bergalli Gozzi to see that even an "exceptional" woman like her was unable to continue a life of the pen when she had a family to raise.[96] Perhaps, despite her affection for children, Caminer consciously decided that she would not risk sacrificing her career for the pleasures and responsibilities of motherhood. Indeed, the passage from the letter cited here contains the first indication of Caminer's plans to move beyond translation to composing original theatrical works, thus indicating her desire to expand the avenues of her creativity through her life of the mind.[97]

Caminer's move from the cosmopolitan city of Venice to the provincial town of Vicenza proved to be difficult for her, as her correspondence indicates very clearly: she missed her family, her friends, and her home. She struggled to adapt to "the shift from a free, relaxed, and good city to a silly, malicious one full of prejudices."[98] She described a rather solitary existence in which she avoided intimate contact with anyone in order to "forget that I am in the beautiful and delightful but lazy and stolid Vicenza, whose very kind but deep down evil inhabitants would render it hateful to me if I paid much

95. See "Making of a Woman," text 33.

96. Luisa Bergalli (1703–79) published most of her original theatrical works, including *Agide, re di Sparta* (1725), a drama set to music by Giovanni Porta; *Le avventure del poeta* (Roma: Vecchiarelli, 1730), a comedy satirizing the nobility and writers' dependence on them for patronage, and *Elenia* (1730), a melodrama set to music by Albinoni, in her twenties. Bergalli enjoyed this success well before her marriage in 1738, when, at age thirty-five, she married her longtime companion, Gasparo Gozzi. This marriage to a financially unstable man of higher social standing proved disastrous to Bergalli's reputation and career. She was sharply criticized for marrying a younger man of higher social status, and familial duties constrained her literary ambitions. She had five children with Gozzi, and she took on the impossible task of the financial management of the impoverished Gozzi household. For some years Bergalli was the sole bread earner for the extended Gozzi family. Her brother-in-law Carlo Gozzi publicly accused her of bringing the family to financial ruin because of her obsession with poetry and writing. Eventually, Bergalli's own career was eclipsed by those of her husband and brother-in-law. One wonders if Caminer had this history in mind when considering her own options. For more on Bergalli, see Adriana Chemello, "Le ricerche erudite di Luisa Bergalli Gozzi," in *Geografie e genealogie letterarie: Erudite, biografe, croniste, narratrici, "épistolières," utopiste tra Settecento e Ottocento*, ed. Adriana Chemello and Luisa Ricaldone (Padova: Il Poligrafo, 2000), 49–88; Luisa Ricaldone, *La scrittura nascosta: Donne di lettere e loro immagini tra Arcadia e Restaurazione* (Paris: Honoré Champion; Firenze: Edizioni Cadmo, 1996),esp. 183–202; and L. Bergalli, *Le avventure del poeta*. See also Pamela Stewart, "Eroine della dissimulazione: Il teatro di Lusia Bergalli Gozzi," *Quaderni veneti* 19 (1994): 73–92.

97. In her subsequent letter to Pelli, Caminer described the type of play she intended to write: "As far as my comedy is concerned, the subject I have chosen is pathetic without being tragic." See "Making of a Woman," text 35.

98. See "Making of a Woman," text 30.

attention to them!" In this new and stifling environment, the company of her husband, she wrote to a friend, "is the only recompense I have for my losses, at least up to a certain point."[99] Elisabetta and Antonio probably enjoyed an amicable marriage for several years, although it is almost certain that they eventually separated. Caminer may have been disillusioned in her first love, and she may have settled for a practical marital match, but it is undeniable that this decision was crucial in freeing her to develop and maintain a career that lasted for the whole of her life.

Shortly after her move to Vicenza, Caminer assured her colleagues once again of her intentions to continue her work as a journalist. "I need to write to you," she wrote to Giuseppe Gennari,[100] "so that you will know that my change in status and in home must not interrupt our correspondence."[101] She urged him to continue sending articles for publication in "my father's periodical, which will continue to be mine as well, given that I will never stop working on it."[102] Perhaps Caminer's insistence on this matter in letters to her friends during the months prior to and following her marriage belies some anxiety on her part that familial duties and the move away from Venice—center of publishing in the Veneto and home to past generations of successful women writers—might in fact constrain her literary ambitions.

Nevertheless, she continued working with her father and other colleagues

99. Ibid. Even five years after her move to Vicenza Caminer was still not accepted by some in the community, as is evident in a polemic with a reader of her periodical in 1777. See "Making of a Woman," text 39.

100. Giuseppe Gennari (1721–1800), Paduan abbé, was an erudite man of letters and an avid local historian. From a young age he showed an inclination for the ecclesiastic state and a passion for letters. Once he became a cleric, he dedicated himself to religious studies and earned a doctorate. He was a leader in the Academy of the Orditi in Padua. Despite offers from the bishops of Feltre and Bergamo of professorships in their seminaries, Gennari decided to remain in his beloved Padua. He maintained a vast correspondence with literary and scientific intellectuals of his day and collaborated on various journalistic enterprises, including Girolamo Zanetti's *Nuove Memorie per servire alla Storia Letteraria* and the Caminers' *Europa letteraria*. He was a member of the Accademia de' Granelleschi, and for many years he was the secretary of the Accademia di Scienze, Lettere ed Arti in Padua. His many and varied publications include *Antico corso de' fiumi in Padova* (1776), *Informazione storica della città di Padova* (written around 1776; published in 1796), *Orazioni in lode della Veneta Repubblica* (1782), *Annali della città di Padova* (1804), *Dissertazione sopra il rinnovamento e i progressi delle umane lettere nell'Italia* (1821) and *Del commercio e della navigazione de' Veneziani* (1823). The first letters in the Caminer-Gennari correspondence reveal that in 1769 Gennari had asked her to write a sonnet for the collection of occasional poetry he was organizing in memory of the Contessa Antonia Dondi-Orologio Borromeo; she included the sonnet in her 2 September 1769 letter to him, and it was published that same year. On Gennari, see Bartolomeo Gamba, "Gennari, Giuseppe," in *Biografia degli italiani illustri nelle scienze, lettere ed arti del secolo XVIII, e de' contemporanei*, ed. Emilio De Tipaldo, 10 vols. (vols. 1–8, Venezia: Alvisopoli, 1834–41; vols. 9–10, Tipografia Gio. Cecchini, 1844–45), 2:123–27.

101. See "Making of a Woman," text 31.

102. Ibid.

on the *Europa letteraria* through 1773, when the Caminers restructured the periodical and gave it a new name, the *Giornale enciclopedico* (*Encyclopedic Journal*). The transition marked the beginning of significant changes for the periodical. Although Domenico Caminer was still officially the head of the journalistic team and although the format remained largely the same, fewer of the reviews were translated, and there were more original contributions to the journal. Given the success of the *Europa letteraria*, the Caminers were actually able to lower the price of the periodical—from twenty-four *lire* to twenty-two *lire*—even as they simultaneously increased the number of pages in a single issue and changed its periodicity from monthly to biweekly.[103] The Caminers were very successful in gauging the public's interest, as indicated by the increasing number of cities in which the periodical was sold over the years. The *Giornale enciclopedico* was sold in nineteen cities across the Italian Peninsula and in Lugano—a vast increase over the seven cities in which the *Europa letteraria* had been sold.[104]

When Elisabetta assumed direction of the *Giornale enciclopedico* in 1777, she moved the periodical's publication site to Vicenza and instituted editorial changes that were clearly modeled on Enlightenment values as expressed by the French philosophes. In a letter to her colleague and friend Lazzaro Spallanzani she described the changes and asked him to continue contributing news and extracts to the periodical. Although she couched the significance of such an important professional transition in practical terms, she also promised a more sophisticated periodical under her direction: "Because my father's many affairs do not allow him to make it his principle occupation, he has agreed to allow me to take on the responsibility, whereby this periodical might perchance become more refined and more exact."[105]

In the fly sheet announcing the new phase of the *Giornale enciclopedico*, Caminer sometimes used the same phrases that d'Alembert used in his *Preliminary Discourse* to the first volume of the *Encyclopédie*. She introduced her periodical by way of its title, defining the word "encyclopedia" as a "concatenation of cognitions."[106] She explained that the *Giornale enciclopedico*'s goal was to

---

103. Subscribers could purchase the *Giornale enciclopedico* either in loose sheets (as individual issues) or bound in volumes (with four months of issues in each volume). This information is found on the frontispieces of the periodicals. Giuseppe Ricuperati also describes these changes in detail in *La stampa italiana dal '500 al '800* (Roma: Edizioni Laterza, 1976), 301.

104. The January 1777 issue of the *Giornale enciclopedico* listed the following cities where local booksellers distributed the periodical: Bergamo, Bologna, Brescia, Firenze, Fogliano, Lugano, Mantova, Milano, Modena, Napoli, Padova, Parma, Pesaro, Treviso, Turino, Udine, Venezia, Vercelli, Verona, and Vicenza.

105. See "Making of a Woman," text 37.

106. See "Making of a Woman," text 38.

"gather and present together diverse cognitions which, remaining scattered, would be largely unknown," and she underscored her belief that if "knowledge contributes to happiness," then her periodical, "a repertory of such cognitions . . . a union of the diverse thoughts of cultured peoples," would be both useful and pleasureable to readers.[107] She declared that she would often call on experts in various fields to contribute to her journal, because "an encyclopedic journal can be produced, but an encyclopedic head cannot be found."[108]

Under Caminer's direction the periodical became the primary filter through which most Transalpine ideas flowed into the Veneto. Whereas the periodical under her father's direction had been primarily a journal of extracts designed to inform readers about new publications and to consolidate material from other literary and foreign journals, under her direction it became a "combative journal" that challenged "the principle of authority . . . on all fronts . . . from theology to law, from literature to economy, from the slavish politics of the colonial powers to the arrogance of feudal lords and big landowners in the Veneto."[109]

During the first phase of the *Giornale enciclopedico* under her direction (1777–82), Caminer's principal collaborator was the legal scholar Giovanni Scola.[110] Some historians contend that the periodical experienced its finest, most progressive years in the hands of these two. In the very first year of their collaboration, they published original reviews of works by Helvétius, one of the most censored writers in the Veneto region (second only to Rousseau).[111] The *Giornale enciclopedico's* favorable published response to the Enlightenment

---

107. Ibid.

108. Ibid.

109. Berengo, *Giornali veneziani del Settecento*, lvi. For a detailed history of the Caminer periodicals, see Berengo, *Giornali veneziani del Settecento*, li–lviii, 343–515; and Angelo Colla's two essays, Colla et al., "Tipografi, editori e librai" (esp. 149–59); and Colla, "Elisabetta Caminer Turra e il giornalismo 'enciclopedico.'"

110. The life and work of the Enlightenment intellectual Giovanni Scola (1736–1820) have yet to be thoroughly researched. Scola was a lawyer, a journalist, a Freemason, and a representative of the municipal government in Vicenza after the fall of the Venetian Republic. An admirer of the philosophy of d'Alembert, Giambattista Vico, Pietro Verri, and Francesco Antonio Grimaldi, Scola was himself an active participant in the Republic of Letters, especially through his collaboration (1777–81) with Elisabetta Caminer Turra on the *Giornale enciclopedico*. As Scola's contributions to the periodical reveal, he was particularly interested in educational and agricultural reform and in geographical and historical influences on the possibilities for socioeconomic reform. On Scola, see Giovanni Mantese, *Dal primo Settecento all'annessione del Veneto al regno d'Italia (1700–1866)*, vol. 5 of *Memorie storiche della chiesa vicentina* (Vicenza: Accademia Olimpica, 1982); and Franco Venturi, *L'Italia dei lumi: La Repubblica di Venezia*, vol. 5, bk. 2, of *Settecento riformatore* (Torino: Einaudi, 1990), 237–52.

111. Scola published a favorable review of *On Man (De l'homme*, 1773) which he claimed was the first published in Italy (*Giornale enciclopedico*, April 1777, 97–106). The *Giornale enciclopedico* also reviewed Helvétius's poem *Happiness (Le Bonheur*, 1772) and translated into Italian his *Fragment d'une*

philosopher was the exception to the rule in the Veneto region.[112] The historian Franco Piva describes Caminer's skillful handling of this provocative material as evidence of her place as a "consummate journalist who was in conflict with the Veneto censorship."[113]

These were turbulent years for the periodical: Caminer encountered problems with censors and with conservative readers.[114] In a letter to her colleague Clemente Vannetti, she described her frustration at seeing "bizarre censors" send back to her "the most harmless things," which she sarcastically claimed did nothing "but demonstrate their intelligence."[115] She despaired that the Italian presses were subject to the judgment of such "ignorant" censors and declared that "as long as the press is not free, Italy will be inferior in matters of literature."[116] An anonymous critical booklet about the *Giornale enciclopedico* was published in 1779, and Caminer responded in the pages of her periodical with a scathing twenty-nine-point rebuttal.[117] One of the complaints made against her was her opposition to the death penalty. The anonymous writer, she responded, "praises the gallows and condemns journalists because they hope that education will make gallows less necessary. Ergo: The person who desires to see his neighbor hanged is a good Christian!"[118] Caminer's objections to the death penalty in her periodical echo those she had expressed seven years earlier when defending her decision to change the ending of Mercier's play *The Deserter*.[119]

During this more mature period of her career, Caminer was less depend-

---

épitre sur le superstition (1773) (*Giornale enciclopedico*, March 1777, 88–93). Although there was no signature appended to this review and translation, Franco Piva claims that Caminer was the author. See Franco Piva, "Contributo all fortuna di Helvétius nel Veneto del secondo Settecento," pt. 2, *Aevum* 45 (1971): 430–63.

112. Piva, "Contributo all fortuna di Helvétius," 460.

113. Ibid., 454.

114. See Colla et al., "Tipografi, editori, e librai," 155–56. See also "Making of a Woman," text 39.

115. This letter, dated both 1 and 6 August 1778, is located at the Biblioteca Civica di Rovereto, MS.7.1 (145, 145b, 146, 146b).

116. Ibid.

117. Ludovico Barbieri, *Riflessi giusti e necessari sul Giornale enciclopedico* (Just and necessary reflections on the *Giornale enciclopedico*) (Venezia: Valvasense, 1779). Caminer's response, published in the April 1779 issue of the *Giornale enciclopedico*, 113–32, was entitled "Ricerche sommesse intorno ad alcuni dei riflessi giusti e necessari (che qualcuno oserà forse di non credere necessari né giusti) sul Giornale enciclopedico" (Humble researches about some of the just and necessary reflections (that some will perhaps dare to believe are neither necessary nor just) on the *Encyclopedic Journal*).

118. Berengo published Caminer's entire, lengthy response to the *Riflessi giusti* in *Giornali veneziani del Settecento*, 415–24.

119. See "Making of a Woman," texts 21, 22, and 25.

ent upon mentors and in fact assumed the role of mentor and patron herself, as her correspondence with the classicist Clemente Vannetti reveals.[120] She edited and published some of his works ("I am your *manager*," she wrote to him in one letter), and she admonished him for preferring Latin to Italian ("It is the great delirium of all you Latinists that you do not want to do a little honor to your own language, and that you prefer to it a dead language that very few people consider anymore").[121] In 1779 Caminer became a member of the literary Academy of the Agiati in Rovereto, originally founded by Vannetti's parents in 1750.[122]

In 1782 Caminer again instituted important editorial changes in the periodical. As she wrote in a letter to a colleague, "The business of my journal has become very serious; decisive changes, a partnership formed, a much more extensive correspondence, all of this together with my infinite other occupations are enslaving me."[123] Although scholars have assumed that this new partnership was exclusively formed with her old colleague Alberto Fortis, the manifesto for the new phase of the periodical—now entitled *Nuovo giornale enciclopedico* (*New Encyclopedic Journal*)—indicates that Caminer at least

---

120. See "Making of a Woman," texts 40, 42, 43, and 46. The classicist Clemente Vannetti (1754–95) was born in Rovereto to two literary-minded parents, Giuseppe Valeriano Vannetti and Bianca Laura Saibanti. By age eleven Vannetti was extremely proficient in Latin, and at age fourteen he wrote a comedy in Latin (*Lampadaria*) in the style of Plautus and Terence. He was a member of the conservative Accademia della Crusca in Florence and collaborated on the direction of the *Vocabolario della Crusca* (published posthumously in Verona, 1806). Despite Vannetti's and Caminer's differing opinions about the status of the Italian language, Vannetti was an avid collaborator on the *Giornale enciclopedico*, and for some years he compiled for Caminer the *Lazzaretto letterario*, a series of "reviews" of imaginary books that were humorous or sarcastic critiques of contemporary society. He authored many essays and poetic works and was the lifetime secretary of Rovereto's literary academy, the Accademia degli Agiati. His major work was *Osservazioni sopra Orazio* (Rovereto, 1794). On Vannetti, see Giuseppe Talani, "Vannetti, Clemente," in De Tipaldo, *Biografia degli italiani illustri*, 1:438–40.

121. See "Making of a Woman," texts 40 and 43.

122. By September 1778 she had received the official diploma with her academic name of Critonilla. See her 26 September 1778 letter to Vannetti, which is located in the Biblioteca Civica di Rovereto, MS.7.1 (150, 150b). Other celebrated women admitted to the academy included Bianca Laura Saibante, Laura Bassi, Luisa Bergalli Gozzi, Catterina Gualtieri Boschi, Cristina Roccati, and Paola Soardi Grismondi. See *Memorie dell'I. R. Accademia di Scienze Lettere ed Arti degli Agiati in Rovereto pubblicate per commemorare il suo 150esimo anno di vita: Aggiunte e correzioni alle biografie dei soci* (Rovereto: Tipografia U. Grandi & Col., 1905). A posthumous publication of four of Caminer's poems indicates that she was also admitted to one of the academies in Este, probably the Accademia degli Eccitati d'Este. See *Per le faustissime nozze del Conte Pietro Dalle-Ore colla Marchesa Giulia Buzzaccarini* (For the most propitious wedding of Count Pietro Dalle-Ore with the marquise Giulia Buzzaccarini) (Padova: Cartellier e Sicca, 1839).

123. The letter to Urbano Pagani Cesa—dated 24 May 1782—is located at the Biblioteca del Museo Civico di Bassano, Epistolario Gamba, no. 2480.

intended it to consist of a number of individuals officially known as the Literary Society of Vicenza. In the manifesto, Caminer alerted her readers that her many literary obligations were too demanding for her to continue acting as the sole director of the periodical, and that she had decided to "form a partnership of erudite minds, each of whom would be in a position to contribute materials in his area of competence" to the periodical.[124] She also indicated that she would "share with them the precious responsibility of choosing the extracts, the original articles, and the announcements" to be published in the *Nuovo giornale enciclopedico*.[125]

These years marked another important shift in Caminer's career: she and her husband opened a publishing house, and Caminer began her career as a publisher-editor. Her correspondence indicates that Antonio Turra made the financial investments to open the press between March and April of 1779 and that the Vicentine bookseller Antonio Veronese oversaw the printing, while she made the editorial decisions for the press. Turra obtained an official license for the publishing house and the name Stamperia Turra the following year, in 1780.[126] Together, Caminer and Turra used the press, which they set up in their own home on contrà Canove, to publish a variety of works including her periodical, her translations, and her collections of occasional poetry, and a series of botanical and agricultural works that Turra wrote, edited, or published in his role as lifetime secretary of the Agrarian Academy of Vicenza. The Stamperia Turra was one of the most active presses in the Veneto region until it closed in 1794.[127] In her role as publisher, Caminer collaborated closely with the owners of the most important bookshops in Vicenza: Domenico Bardella (in whose shop Caminer and colleagues often met), Francesco Modena (who published her periodical in 1777 and 1778), Francesco Vendramini Mosca (who published the periodical in 1778), and Antonio Veronese (who sold subscriptions to her periodical).[128]

Above and beyond her work as journalist, editor, and now publisher, Caminer continued to produce volumes of translations (from French or French versions) of epistolary novels, poetry, dialogues, memoirs, and histories—in

---

124. A copy of the manifesto, which appears to have been a fly sheet, is bound into the March 1782 issue of the *Giornale enciclopedico* located in the Marciana Library in Venice.

125. Perhaps this new collective business partnership explains why the collaboration between Scola and Caminer ended: if he preferred working within a smaller directorial group, he may have decided to leave rather than try to adapt to the new system.

126. For this and all detailed information about the Caminer-Turra publishing house see Colla et al., "Tipografi, editori e librai," 149–59.

127. Ibid.

128. Ibid., 148.

addition to original works she translated regularly in the extracts of her peri-
odical. The authors of these literary, historical, and pedagogical works include
Marie-Jeanne Riccoboni, Guillaume-Alexandre Méhégan, Diderot, Justine
Rosenberg-Orsini Wynne, Maximilien de Béthune (duke of Sully), and Samuel
Richardson.[129] She published a series of translations of pedagogical works for
children, including works by Jeanne-Marie Le Prince de Beaumont, Jean
François Marmontel, and Arnaud Berquin. Some of Caminer's most successful publications were completed in these years and bear the imprint of the
family publishing house, including the deluxe edition of her translation of
the complete works of the poet Salomon Gessner, which she published together with her translation of two moral tales by Diderot,[130] and a collection
of poetry by written by divers hands that Caminer organized in which the
renowned poet Giuseppe Parini participated.[131]

Despite what must have been a frenetic work pace, Caminer made time
in her life for yet another enterprise: sometime between 1787 and the early
1790s, she established and directed a theater in Vicenza where she taught
children and young adults the art of acting.[132] Evidence from her periodical
reveals that she supervised performances of plays by Louis-Sébastien Mercier
(undoubtedly using her own translations of his works) and Carlo Goldoni.

The fourth decade of Caminer's life came to a close with a period of tur-
moil. In July of 1789 Caminer described "extremely serious revolutions" oc-

129. Caminer, *Quadro della storia moderna dalla caduta dell'Impero d'Occidente fino alla pace di Vestfalia, del Signor Cavaliere di Méhégan, tradotto dal francese* (1780), *Opere del Signor Salomone Gesnero tradotte con le due novelle morali del Signor D**** [Diderot] (1781), *Del soggiorno dei Conti del Nord in Venezia nel gennaio 1782: Lettera di Madama la Contessa vedova degli Orsini di Rosenberg al Signor Riccardo Winne suo fratello a Londra* (1782), *Le memorie di Massimiliano di Bettuna Ducca di Sully Ministro d'Enrico IV, tradotto dal francese* (1784), *Le nuove lettere inglesi, ovvero la storia del Cancelliere Grandisson di S. Richardson* (1786), *Nuova Raccolta di novelle morali del Signor di Marmontel tradotte per le prima volta* (Vicenza: Turra, 1791–93), and *L'amico dei fanciulli, del Signor Arnaldo Berquin* (Vicenza: Turra, 1795–96).

130. Caminer, *Opere del Sig. Salomone Gesnero* 1781. The two tales by Diderot that Caminer translated were *I due amici di Borbona* and *Conversazioni d'un padre co' suoi figluoli ovvero Del pericolo di volersi rendere superiori alle Leggi.*

131. Caminer, "Versi a Camillo Gritti," in *Tributo alla verità* (Vicenza: Turra, 1788). Parini described Caminer in the following lines: "E penetrante al cor voce arguta di donna, / Che vaga e bella, in gonna / Dell'altro sesso anco le glorie ottiene, / Fra le Muse immortali / Con fortunato ardir spiegando l'ali" (Giuseppe Parini, *Poesie e prose*, ed. L. Caretti [Milano: Ricciardi, 1951], 231–38).

132. Orietta Renzi discusses Caminer's "teatrino" in her thesis and corrects erroneous information in Renato Zironda's "Il teatro a Vicenza in età napoleonica." See O. Renzi, "Elisabetta Caminer e la diffusione del dramma borghese nella seconda metà del Settecento," directed by Nicola Mangini, (thesis, University of Padua, 1989–90), 85–99; and R. Zironda, "Il teatro a Vicenza in età napoleonica," in *Il Vicentino tra rivoluzione giacobina ed età napoleonica, 1797–1813,* ed. R. Zironda (Vicenza: Biblioteca Civica Bertoliana, 1989), 183. See also Unfer-Lukoschik, *Elisabetta Caminer Turra (1751–1796),* 56.

curring in her home, which caused her to debate whether or not she should take "the most decisive steps possible in the life of a woman."[133] She explained to her lifelong friend Lazzaro Spallanzani that the crisis had drastically affected her work, her health, and her very sense of self, but that it had recently been happily resolved. We can only speculate about what she may have been referring to, but the drastic language suggests some kind of conflict with or separation from her husband.[134] Perhaps the situation was "resolved" by an agreement to occupy different parts of their house, as the inventory of Caminer's belongings at her death indicates they did do.[135]

According to the scholar Angelo Colla, Caminer's business partnerhsip with Fortis was officially dissolved in 1789, perhaps due in part to his distance from Vicenza, as he spent a great deal of time traveling in southern Italy.[136] The last phase of the periodical (1790–96) brought significant editorial changes. Caminer renamed the peridocial for the last time, calling it the *Nuovo giornale enciclopedico d'Italia* (*New Encyclopedic Journal of Italy*). She no longer published the periodical in Vicenza but had it published in Venice by Giacomo Storti. Fortis and other colleagues continued to contribute reviews and essays to her periodical, but it appears that she managed the editing, publication, and financial accounts of the periodical single-handedly for the remaining six years of her life. Despite its ambitious title, the periodical in this phase was less combative and lively than in earlier phases, and historian Marino Berengo describes the *Nuovo giornale enciclopedico* as a "cold, erudite bulletin."[137]

This was undoubtedly due to the fact that the final years of Caminer's life were marked by struggle, in terms of both her finances and her health. In 1791, she may have experienced the first symptoms of the cancer which would end her life five years later. Nonetheless, she continued to work assiduously, producing volumes of translations and poetry in addition to managing the periodical—even when she was forced to work from her bed for months. However, she could no longer direct the operations of the Stampe-

---

133. The letter, dated 6 July 1789, is located at the Biblioteca Estense di Modena, Raccolta Campori. See "Making of a Woman," text 47.

134. Another indication of a separation from Turra may be that at her death Caminer left the bulk of her possessions to her brother Antonio and nothing to her husband. This information is found in her testament of 3 May 1796 (Archivio di Stato di Vicenza [hereafter ASVic], Notarile Vicentino, notaio Ottavio Borizio, busta 3821). Caminer's testament was published in Mantese, *Dal primo Settecento*, 774.

135. The inventory is located at the ASVic, *Notarile Vicentino* (notary Ottavio Borizio), busta 3827, carte 38–44.

136. Colla et al., "Tipografi, editori, e librai," 156.

137. Berengo, *Giornali veneziani del Settecento*, lviii.

ria Turra, and her husband sold it in 1794. She was forced to go into debt with friends and to pawn silver and table linens at the Monte di Pietà of Vicenza.[138] By this time it appears that all financial as well as intellectual collaboration between husband and wife had ceased. According to Caminer's final will and testament, because her husband had not given her "the minimum advancement" to help her with the upkeep of the house for six to seven years—a period which corresponds to that of their speculated separation—she had been forced to go into debt.

By 1795, she knew her breast cancer would probably be terminal. As she wrote to a friend in February: "I have been seriously ill for four months; it is destined to prove fatal. My problem is a tumor in my breast."[139] Letters from her physician friends during the winter and spring of 1795 poignantly reveal the intense pain and anxiety she experienced as the cancer progressed. She contemplated various methods of treatment and finally agreed to have an operation, which was performed in Venice, probably in June of that year.[140] Still, Caminer's letters continued to abound with details of the daily business of managing her periodical: the exchange of books, subscriptions, articles, delinquent payments, and tardy mail. Three and a half months before she died, she wrote a brief letter (to an unidentified correspondent) from her bed: "For nearly two months now I have been unable to get out of bed. Daily fever, pains, etc. . . . in the meantime, for goodness sake, [send me] the extract of the book you promised me."[141]

Elisabetta Caminer Turra died at the age of forty-four on 7 June 1796, in her home in via contrà Canove in Vicenza.[142] It appears that her sister Carlota was with her. Within twenty-four hours of her death, there was controversy surrounding an alleged apology she had made for her life's work. Two local chroniclers' accounts offer contrasting opinions on the truth of the matter, but they both describe talk of Caminer in her last days having asked her parish priest to publicly proclaim that she was deeply pained for having mis-

---

138. Colla et al., "Tipografi, editori, e librai," 158.

139. Ibid., 158.

140. According to Giambattista Baseggio, Caminer was examined by a surgeon named Baldini and operated on by a Doctor Paiola. See Baseggio, "Caminer Turra, Elisabetta," in De Tipaldo, *Biografia degli italiani illustri*, 5:461–64. For more on the medical treatments Caminer sought, see Rita Unfer-Lukoschik, "Elisabetta Caminer Turra (1751–1796): Una letterata veneta verso l'Europa," in Unfer-Lukoschik, *Elisabetta Caminer Turra (1751–1796)*, 54–55.

141. From Caminer's 21 February 1796 letter to an unidentified recipient. See "Making of a Woman," text 49.

142. Contrary to current scholary assumptions that Caminer died in her friend Giovanni Battista Fracanzani's villa in Orgiano, the inventory of her belongings cataloged just after her death clearly indicates that she died in her home in Vicenza.

led or upset anyone with her unorthodox lifestyle and her controversial periodicals and translations.[143] It is entirely conceivable that the local clergy
would have made such a claim in an attempt to clear the reputation of their
beloved city, "tarnished" by its association with a woman who began her career translating Voltaire and continued to publish positive reviews of books
with anticlerical leanings from her deathbed. On the other hand, it is unlikely that Caminer would have renounced a lifetime of convictions through
a member of the clergy. Indeed, a circle of her friends and supporters rushed
to deny this claim and dispersed a written statement defending her reputation. In the midst of this final polemic, Caminer was buried at the Santo Stefano Church in Vicenza, where today there stands no marker of her extraordinary life.

3. CAMINER'S WRITING ON WOMEN AND SOCIETY

The nature of women and their role in society was hotly debated across Europe over the course of the eighteenth century. Although the debate on the
"woman question" was not new,[144] there are some characteristics that were
particular to the century in which Caminer lived. In contrast to the more
rhetorical debates of earlier centuries, the eighteenth-century discussion was
marked by a new pragmatism or seriousness, undoubtedly driven by the Enlightenment's ethic of social utility and the demand to determine what was in
the public interest.[145] The growing number of middle- and upper-class urban
women who were becoming regular attendees of the theater, salons, parties,
public strolls, and even cafés brought the question vividly into focus. The
polemic was further fueled by the growing number of exceptional women
who were making professional careers for themselves in areas that typically
excluded women: art, literature, journalism, and the sciences. In eighteenth-
century Italy, there was a notable female presence in academies and even in

---

143. The two chronicles are located in the Biblioteca Bertoliana di Vicenza: "Memorie di Vicenza del Co. Arnaldo I° Tornieri che cominciano dall'anno 1767. 18 Giugno e terminano nel
1822" (Gonzati.20.10.10 [3018], carta 228 bis); and "Descrizione delle cose seguite nel convento di S. Corona dopo la morte del P. Tommaso Ricciardi. Cronaca continuata da F. Gio: Tommaso Faccioli" (Gonzati 22.10.14).

144. See "Series Editors' Introduction" for a history of the debate in earlier centuries.

145. Scholars have posited that prior to the eighteenth century the *querelle des femmes* (debate on
women) was often tied to the word games or intellectual diversion of male academics who were
reworking theoretical arguments about the nature of women. See Linda Woodbridge, *Women
and the English Renaissance: Literature and the Nature of Womankind, 1540–1620* (Urbana: University of
Illinois Press, 1984); and Rebecca Messbarger, *The Century of Women: Representations of Women in
Eighteenth-Century Italian Public Discourse* (Toronto: Toronto University Press, 2002), introduction.

universities.[146] This increasing presence of women in the public sphere heightened societal anxiety over shifting notions of femininity and masculinity and influenced the course of the debate.

The eighteenth-century debate shaped and was shaped by the explosion of new texts written by, for, and about women, especially during the second half of the century.[147] The number of female readers from the middle and upper classes increased dramatically enough that a new and widely disdained female caricature emerged: the dilettante female intellectual.[148] A woman only superficially educated in letters or philosophy (*letteratuccia, critichessa, filosofessa, sacentuccia*), she tried to appear more knowledgeable and sophisticated than she really was and succeeded only in revealing her ignorance. This stereotypical figure appeared publicly with book in hand and made a show of spouting maxims, but she understood little or nothing of substance.[149] Ironically, women of society were on the one hand expected to live up to this superficial show of education, and on the other hand mocked for it.

One of the most important catalysts for renewed discussion on the nature and role of women in society was the Enlightenment's universalist claims about the human right to liberty and equality. The exclusion of women (as well as the lower classes and nonwhite races) from this claim led to attempts to rationalize the coexistence of "universal equality" and separate social roles defined according to sexual difference.[150] Many of these arguments were based on "natural" or scientific "fact" rather than on traditional scriptural au-

---

146. For women's presence in Italian universities and academies, see Marta Cavazza, "Dottrici e lettrici dell'Università di Bologna nel Settecento," in *Annali di storia delle università italiane* (Bologna: CLUEB, 1997), 1:109–25, which contains a rich bibliography on the topic. See also Paula Findlen, "Translating the New Science: Women and the Circulation of Knowledge in Enlightenment Italy," *Configurations* 2 (1995): 167–206; and R. Messbarger, "Waxing Poetic: Anna Morandi Manzolini's Anatomical Sculptures," *Configurations* 91 (2001): 65–97.

147. Elena Bertagnolli, "Letture e pubblico femminile a Venezia nella seconda metà del Settecento," directed by Mario Infelise (thesis, Dipartimento di Studi Storici, Università di Venezia, 1989–90).

148. Although the critical stereotype of affected female intellectuals was not new—we have only to think of Molière's enormously successful comedy on the subject, *Le précieuses ridicules* (1659)—it took on new meaning in the eighteenth century as the number of female readers increased dramatically and as the phenomenon cut across social classes.

149. Caminer described this phenomenon as "the cultured lunacy that appreciates only / Those who have books in their hands and glib maxims on their lips" ("Women and Society: Marriage or the Convent," text 7). Caminer also lamented "those women today who pretend to become cultivated, to study, and who spout pretensions and unfortunately serve as fodder for the wits' laughter" ("Women and Society: Intellectual Life," text 2).

150. Geneviève Fraisse, *Reason's Muse: Sexual Difference and the Birth of Democracy*, trans. Jane Marie Todd (Chicago: University of Chicago Press, 1994).

thority (although the latter voice was also strong throughout the century), and the century witnessed a new reliance upon secular rather than strictly religious authorities to explain and justify the gender hierarchy of the day.[151] Thus, the eighteenth century added much mention of women's fibers, fluids, humors, and nerves to the debate, even as it echoed traditional discussions about female virtues of modesty, reticence, chastity, and obedience. It focused on women's role as procreators as well as women's supposed propensities to irrationality, sensitivity, instability, licentiousness, and frivolity.[152]

The body of Caminer's writing on women and society reflects many of the issues fueling this broad and often contradictory debate. As the selection of texts in this anthology illustrates, critiquing and working to improve the condition of women was one of Caminer's most passionate endeavors. Throughout the twenty-eight years of her career she published reviews and announcements of events or books by, for, and about women in her periodical. She commented on a wide range of issues: women and literature (as object and as author), childcare issues (whether or not mothers should nurse, or whether or not they should follow Lady Mary Montague's suggestion of inoculating children against smallpox), religious issues (forced vow taking, power hierarchies within the clergy), matrimonial issues (dowries, the health and duties of women about to marry), social issues (houses established by women to care for poor or orphaned children), women in history, women in Eastern or New World cultures as compared to those of Italy or Europe, women and education, and fashion publications for women.

Caminer was particularly interested in three areas of this debate: the question of women's right to an intellectual life, the effect of fashion periodicals on women, and the implications for women of their choice between marriage and the convent. While each of these themes may be studied separately, it is more informative to consider Caminer's writing on the three subjects as intertwined with each other. It is equally important to study these texts in connection with what Caminer wrote about her life experiences, because her writing on women is consistently informed by her personal struggle with the gendered boundaries of her society as she stepped across them to make a professional life for herself as an Enlightenment woman of letters.

151. Thomas Laqueur, *Making Sex: Body and Gender from the Greeks to Freud* (Cambridge, Mass.: Harvard University Press, 1990), 149–207.

152. On the debate in eighteenth-century Italy, I refer to the following works by Rebecca Messbarger: "Voice of Dissent: A Woman's Response to the Eighteenth-Century Debate on the Education of Women," *Cincinatti Romance Review* 13 (1994): 69–80, *The Century of Women*, and her introduction to the forthcoming volume in this series, *The Contest for Knowledge: Debates over Women's Education in Eighteenth-Century Italy*, ed. and trans. Paula Findlen and Rebecca Messbarger, with Rachel Scarlett-Trotter.

Women and the Intellectual Life

Woman's intellect is very fine,
But to study, wary man won't give her time.
If woman were to study, then wretched man
Would be left with spindle and distaff in hand.
And if woman should her intellect adopt,
Man would be beneath, and she on top.
—Carlo Goldoni, *The Clever Woman,* 1743

Women's abilities to learn, to imagine, and to think abstractly were much debated over the course of the eighteenth century. As the quotation above illustrates, the debate raised centuries-old fears about the world turning "upside down" if women were given access to a serious education.[153] One of the novelties of the debate over women's intellectual abilities in eighteenth-century Italy was the institutionalization of the debate, as it entered the hallowed walls of elite male literary and scientific academies.[154] In Italy, the renowned Academia de' Ricovrati in Padua held a public debate in 1723 on the question of whether or not women should be educated in the sciences and liberal arts. The debate was monitored by the president of the academy (Antonio Vallisneri), and the two opposing sides were represented by two members of the academy (Guglielmo Camposanpiero and Giovan Antonio Volpi). Significantly, women were present among the audience, and, as Rebecca Messbarger points out, they undoubtedly influenced the content and the course of the debate by their very presence.[155] The official answer to the academic query was that only aristocratic, exceptionally gifted women should be given formal instruction. But that was hardly the end of the discussion. From the moment the academy published its proceedings in 1729[156]—appending several texts to the document, including a defense of women written by a woman—the debate flourished throughout the century.

In many forms of public discourse—treatises, poems, essays, and journalistic commentaries—Italian men and women of letters discussed the question of why women should study and which areas of study were appropriate for them.[157] A whole spectrum of opinions emerged, from the most conser-

---

153. See "Series Editors' Introduction" for a history of the debate from earlier centuries.

154. Messbarger, *The Century of Women,* chap. 1.

155. For a detailed analysis of the debate and the publication of the proceedings, see ibid.

156. *Discorsi academici di vari autori viventi intorno agli studii delle donne, la maggior parte recitati nell'Accademia de' Ricovrati di Padova* (Padova: Stamperia del Seminario, 1729).

157. See Luciano Guerci, *La discussione sulla donna nell'Italia del Settecento: Aspetti e problemi* (Torino: Tirrenia Stampatori, 1987); L. Guerci, *La sposa obbediente: Donna e matrimonio nella discussione dell'Italia del Settecento* (Torino: Tirrenia Stampatori, 1988); and A. M. Rao, "Il sapere velato: L'educazione

vative voices forbidding women access to intellectual development to those progressive voices arguing in favor of women's education as useful to society as a whole. Often the essays themselves were contradictory, making it difficult to easily categorize any individual's stance as for or against women's right to a life of the mind. Broadly speaking, however, a general set of tenets was often repeated and argued by moderate or progressive thinkers in favor of some degree of study for women, within certain restrictive guidelines.

Perhaps the fundamental reason given for why a woman should study was so that she would become capable of fulfilling her familial duties in life: she should know how to read, write, and do enough arithmetic to enable her to run a household efficiently and to keep a precise account of household expenses. Women should study and become enlightened mothers in order to properly educate their children, but also in order to participate in conversation and to avoid appearing ignorant in social situations. Women should become somewhat "enlightened" in order to protect themselves from modern frivolities and prejudices. Some degree of study was seen as an antidote to boredom—which could lead women into trouble—and to the potential emptiness of old age, once women had lost their youth and beauty. Finally, women who were morally well-instructed had the responsibility to exert a positive influence on men by setting a good example and by monitoring their behavior. It is important to note, however, that education under these restrictions contributed to maintaining women's subordinate and domestic role rather than opening doors to new careers or social freedoms.[158]

Women's right to a life of the mind was one of Caminer's most passionate concerns. The texts included in the anthology under "The Intellectual Life" offer a broad panorama of Caminer's thoughts about the complex issues surrounding women and the intellectual life. They reveal her deepest convictions, her personal investment, and occasionally her contradictory points of view on the matter. Collectively they provide a general picture of the development of her opinions over the course of her life, from a confident call for change to a bitter resignation that she would not see this change in her lifetime.

As was the case with many of her contemporaries participating in the debate about women and education, Caminer did not outline a precise plan for the schooling of girls and women. Rather, she advocated the right—and more unusually, she emphasized the need—women had to develop their minds.

---

delle donne nel dibattito italiano di fine Settecento," in *Misoginia: La donna vista e malvista nella cultura occidentale,* ed. Andrea Milano (Roma: Edizioni Dehoniane, 1992), 243–310. See also Messbarger *The Century of Women.*

158. Guerci, *La sposa,* 238–51.

Significantly, Caminer argued that a woman should develop her intellect not only to "make herself useful to her nation" but also to "bring her[self] real advantages or pleasures."[159] There was no question in Caminer's mind that women were men's intellectual equals. The problem lay rather in societal restrictions that prevented most women from becoming and acting as fully developed human beings: as she said at age eighteen, "I am much put out by the fact that my situtation will not permit me to aspire to the exercise of reason."[160] If women were ever to improve their status in society, Caminer believed, their right to develop their minds had to be recognized.

Caminer's conviction that society, not nature, had been—and would be—responsible for shaping women's destiny led her to dismiss almost entirely the prevalent discussions of anatomical differences between the sexes as an approach to the question. On a rare occasion when she did publish a book review with such an approach, she translated the review directly from a French periodical and indicated as much in the heading of the review. When the topic turned from anatomy to the effects of formal education on men, however, Caminer added a few lines of her own to the review. After translating the French journalist's comment that women worked from the heart and men from the head, Caminer turned the usual conclusion on its head. Rather than stating that men were therefore more rational, productive members of society, Caminer claimed that this difference between the sexes made women more honest human beings and more natural writers than men: "This is why deception comes more easily to men . . . and [why] . . . it requires greater effort for a man to write one page than it does for a woman to write ten."[161] Clearly, Caminer was not above using an argument that she did not usually support in order to express her indignation at men's injustice and her pride in women's abilities.

More typical of Caminer's approach to the question were her efforts to vindicate the intellectual accomplishments of women from all epochs in history. Repeatedly in her periodical, Caminer publicly recognized the achievements that women had made in the past, giving special attention to their contributions to the sciences, literature, and philosophy. As women writers like Luisa Bergalli had done before her,[162] Caminer constructed a genealogy of

159. See "Making of a Woman," text 39.

160. See "Making of a Woman," text 4.

161. Caminer's comments did not go unchallenged by her male peers. See "Women and Society: Intellectual Life," text 1, for the reaction of her suitor, Francesco Albergati, to her accusations of men's dishonesty.

162. Luisa Bergalli Gozzi published a two-volume anthology of Italian women poets entitled *Componimenti Poetici delle più illustri Rimatrici d'ogni secolo* (Poetic compositions by the most illustrious

female heroines (biblical, mythical, and historical) that served both as proof of women's capabilities and as a model for contemporary women—including herself.

One element of Caminer's vindication of women's reputations was her insistence on distinguishing between famous women (virtuous or accomplished women worthy of praise) and infamous women (whose salacious stories served to titillate readers rather than instruct them). She criticized catalogs of illustrious women because they often included women known for their vices alongside those known for their virtues, thus equating the spectacular aspects of some women's stories with the substantial contributions to culture made by other women. Caminer found this practice to be "a solemn injustice" to "that respectable number of women who distinguished themselves in the virtues, in letters, in the sciences, in the arts, and even in arms, many of whom deserve to be better known to the world than they are presently."[163]

Another of Caminer's campaigns was to redress the fact that even well-meaning authors who praised exceptional French and British women often ignored or were unaware of the achievements of Italian women, especially contemporary Italian women. In her review of a French historical dictionary of illustrious women, Caminer claimed that the author could have "improve[d] his *Dictionary* greatly" if he had "made sure it was complete, and not overlooked many others among our Italian women."[164] Indeed, Caminer used her review to correct this omission, and she proudly described the merits of her compatriots, including "Laura Cereti [*sic*]. . . and Cassandra Fedele . . . for her profound knowledge and for the eloquence of her Latin orations . . . . the famous Madame Agnesi of Milan. . . the deservingly celebrated Madame Laura Bassi . . . the learned and most notable Venetian Countess [Luisa] Bergalli Gozzi, who honors letters, and particularly fine poetry, with her excellent compositions."[165] In her review of a defense of women written in response to one of the most popular misogynist works of the century, Caminer reiterated her concern that even publications designed to pay tribute to women were guilty of not recognizing enough of the many Italian women who were "worthy of standing alongside great men."[166]

As these comments illustrate, Caminer viewed her Italian contempo-

---

female poets from every century) (Venezia: Marino Rossetti, 1726) and a modern edition of Gaspara Stampa's poetry which made her writing available to readers for the first time in nearly two hundred years. On Bergalli's efforts at textual recovery, see Chemello, "Le ricerche erudite di Luisa Bergalli Gozzi," 49–88.

163. See "Women and Society: Intellectual Life," text 2.

164. Ibid.

165. Ibid.

166. See "Women and Society: Intellectual Life," text 4.

raries (as well as women from past centuries) as part of a historical network of European women shaping culture.[167] By publicizing their accomplishments in her periodical or in her occasional poetry, Caminer helped foster the reputations or careers of many contemporary European women of science and letters, including (in addition to those mentioned above) Madame du Châtelet, Anne (Lefèvre) Dacier, Lady Mary (Wortley) Montagu, Mary Wollstonecraft, Teresa Bandettini, Paolina Grismondi, Isabella Teotochi, and numerous others.[168] In the case of publications by anonymous female writers, Caminer made a point of praising the women and either commending or chastising their modesty in hiding their names.[169]

Similarly, in her poem to Caterina Dolfin Tron, Caminer held the Venetian patrician up as proof of "how much noble intelligence / And knowledge nature has bestowed upon our sex."[170] Slyly couched amid the requisite lavish praise for Dolfin Tron's noble family and the civic virtues of her politically prominent spouse, Caminer countered the argument of women's biological inferiority by claiming that nature herself granted women intellectual ability and access to learning. Subtle and lyrical as this call to nature's authority is, the context of its publication heightens its significance. Caminer composed the poem for a collection of verse entitled *Rhymes of Illustrious Women*, which was organized by Luisa Bergalli, the most renowned Venetian female poet and

---

167. Caminer's campaign to publicize Italian women's accomplishments was also part of her conviction that Italian intellectual contributions generally were an important part of the European Enlightenment.

168. Lady Mary [Wortley] Montagu (1689–1762), English autodidact, poet, essayist, and letter writer, is best known today for her travels to Constantinople and her description of the everyday lives of Turkish women in *Turkish Embassy Letters*, published posthumously in 1763. Mary Wollstonecraft (1759–97), Enlightenment philosopher, novelist, and journalist, was deeply committed to improving the condition of women in society. She is best known for her *Vindication of the Rights of Woman* (1792; reprint, Cambridge: Cambridge University Press, 1995), an analysis of the injustices and disadvantages women suffered because of social, economic, political, and educational inequality; see "Women and Society: Intellectual Life," text 6. Teresa Bandettini (1763–1837), known as Amarilli Etrusca in the Arcadia Academy, was one of the most famous female poet-improvisers of the eighteenth century, along with Maddalena Moretti Fernandez (in Arcadia, Corilla Olimpica) and Fortunata Sulgher Fantastici (in Arcadia, Temira Parasside). The Contessa Paolina Secco Suardi Grismondi (1746–1801) (in Arcadia, Lesbia Cidonia) was another renowned female poet of the Arcadia Academy. On Châtelet and Dacier, see "Women and Society: Intellectual Life," text 2,notes 76 and 78. On Teotochi, see "Women and Society: Intellectual Life," text 7.

169. On women's modesty, see "Women and Society: Intellectual Life," text 8, and "Making of a Woman," texts 19 and 39.

170. See "Women and Society: Intellectual Life," text 3. Caterina Dolfin (1736–93) was born in Venice to an impoverished patrician family. After her first (arranged) marriage was annulled in 1772, she married the influential patrician and government official Andrea Tron. Dolfin Tron is best known for her gracious poetry, her rich library of Enlightenment texts, and her salon, which was frequented by erudite men of letters and politics.

playwright of the day. The twenty-two-year-old Caminer was thus invited to join the ranks of the more established female intellectuals who contributed to the collection, including the professor of physics from Rovigo, Cristina Roccati.[171] Consequently, Caminer's "proof" of her sex's natural intelligence was published in a collection which itself constituted a living network of women joining together in the life of the pen.

Yet Caminer's own position as an exceptional woman complicated her vindication of a network of illustrious women. The public recognition she received from her male contemporaries—including letters published in numerous periodicals that described her as an example for women to follow—made Caminer well aware of her own position as a "model" for her sex and of her own place in this historical tradition of accomplished women. She could not avoid addressing these questions. Did she consider herself another exception to her sex that proved the general rule of women's inferiority? Were only some women intellectually gifted, or did all women have the ability and the right to develop their intellects? Learned women had always been caught in this bind, but Caminer's visibility in the public sphere—both to the learned individuals who read her periodical and to the broader crowds of theatergoers who flocked to performances of her translations—heightened the intensity of the dilemma.

Certainly, in order to be taken seriously as a professional writer Caminer was constrained to pay lip service to the notion of the "exceptional" woman and to lead her extraordinary life in part by distancing herself from the rest of her sex. On rare occasions, her concession to this distinction seeped into her published commentary, especially during the most vulnerable period of her career, when she was trying to establish herself. In one review, for example, Caminer inveighed against men's injustice in wanting to "claim exclusively for themselves the right to teach in universities," despite the "good number of women who held posts and taught classes at the most celebrated universities."[172] She proudly described her exceptional compatriots from Bologna, highlighting in particular Laura Bassi[173] "who counts among her dis-

---

171. On Cristina Roccati (1732–97), see Paula Findlen, "A Forgotten Newtonian: Women and Science in the Italian Provinces," in *The Sciences in Enlightened Europe*, ed. William Clark, Jan Golinski, and Simon Schaffer (Chicago: University of Chicago Press, 1999), 331–49.

172. See "Women and Society: Intellectual Life," text 2.

173. Caminer was well aware that her colleague Lazzaro Spallanzani—an internationally renowned naturalist—had studied under Laura Bassi. On Bassi, a famous experimental philosopher in Bologna, see "Women and Society," text 2, n. 64. For scholarship on Bassi, see Gabriella Berti Logan, "The Desire to Contribute: An Eighteenth-Century Italian Woman of Science," *American Historical Review* 99, no. 3 (1994): 785–812; Paula Findlen, "Science as a Career in Enlightenment Italy: The Strategies of Laura Bassi," *Isis* 84 (1993): 441–69; and Marta Cavazza,

ciples many of the most renowned professors, who came out of her school and joined the ranks of the most illustrious academies of Italy."[174] Immediately on the heels of such a provocative criticism, however, Caminer backpedaled, acquiescing to the commonplace assumption that "it would not be a useful thing if a great number of women were to succeed so well, because then we would see things turn upside down, and men . . . would be reduced to spinning in order to survive."[175]

In fact, although endorsing the exceptional woman paradigm might have helped make her own position more secure (by rendering her less threatening to the male majority), ultimately Caminer did not see herself—or did not wish to see herself—as an isolated figure. In the same review, she insisted that "[w]hat must not be neglected in the education of women . . . is a sufficient cultivation of the mind, which, if it became less rare, would bring no small number of advantages to civil society."[176] She claimed that education need not threaten women's domestic duties, and, significantly, she asserted that it would spare women the embarassment of feeling ignorant in social situations. One of Caminer's unique contributions to the debate was her argument that women had a right to intellectual development for their own personal sense of pride and accomplishment. She proclaimed openly that there was "no reason for us [women] to hide ourselves," that it was "most reasonable that women [found] satisfaction in seeing themselves as good as men at everything."[177] At least in the early years of her career, Caminer could imagine a future in which the exception might become the rule, a future in which women would no longer "[have] to blush upon hearing the wonderment people express when a woman is a little less uneducated than usual."[178]

As the years passed, however, Caminer grew disillusioned, and not least with the members of her own sex who were not living up to her expectations. She began to focus more on women's passive participation in the unequal balance of power between the sexes. She warned her peers that as long as women willingly forfeited the development of their minds—or even the use of their common sense—in return for "a frivolous exchange of apparent homages, ill-founded praises, dangerous adulations, and futile bonds, which

---

"Laura Bassi 'maestra' di Spallanzani," in *Il cerchio della vita: Materiali di ricerca del Centro Studi Lazzaro Spallanzani di Scandiano sulla storia della Scienza del Settecento,* ed. W. Bernardi and P. Manzini (Firenze: Olschki, 1999), 185–202.

174. See "Women and Society: Intellectual Life," text 2.

175. Ibid.

176. Ibid.

177. Ibid.

178. Ibid.

keep us ever more bound in slavery even as we believe ourselves to be receiving tributes and as we go along proud of our empire,"[179] they would allow men to retain their superior position in the gender hierarchy of society. Caminer was disillusioned at so many women's susceptibility to "apparent homages" and "dangerous adulations," but, still, she wrote in a marriage poem for a friend, "I do not wish to believe that right-thinking women / Find pleasing these dangerous ways."[180]

Sadly, by the last decade of Caminer's life, her faith in the potential for the improvement of women's status in society had diminished. During the mid-1780s, when she launched an attack against the new fashion periodicals and their claims to educate women, she was forced to recognize that her voice represented a minority, even—and perhaps especially—among women.[181] In the 1790s, her comments about women and the intellectual life were primarily sarcastic, bitter, or inscrutable. Her reviews of Mary Wollstonecraft's *Vindication of the Rights of Woman* (1792) are especially revealing. Caminer concurred with the spirit and the content of Wollstonecraft's treatise, but she was not optimistic about the feasibility of putting the ideas into practice. She praised her English contemporary for trying to bring the female sex "up out of the void in which some would leave it," and she affirmed Wollstonecraft's belief that as long as women's influence continued to depend upon their youth and beauty rather than "on a better education, on the development of their intellectual abilities," women would never gain real power in society.[182] Indeed, these beliefs had formed the core of Caminer's own writing on the condition of women during the previous quarter of a century.

But the Venetian journalist's acrid conclusion that Wollstonecraft's *Vindication* "proves for the millionth time that women might deserve the honor of being considered part of the human race" reveals the extent to which the simplest notion—that women are full-fledged human beings—was still the most radical one for her society.[183] Even more personal was Caminer's comment about the uselessness of fighting for change: "This woman is the champion of her sex. But what will she gain? Revolutions are not so easy or frequent in all genres."[184] After having heard a lifetime of rhetoric without witnessing concrete change, Caminer implied that the French Revolution had been more

179. See "Making of a Woman," text 39.
180. See "Women and Society: Marriage or the Convent," text 7.
181. For Caminer's writing on fashion, see the next section of this introduction.
182. See "Women and Society: Intellectual Life," text 6.
183. Ibid.
184. Ibid.

easily instigated than a revolution for women's rights ever would be—and not least because of women's own complicity in their lot. Ultimately, despite her passionate writing and the example of her boundary-breaking life, Caminer remained isolated as an exceptional woman rather than having been—as she would have wished—part of a changing tide bringing greater intellectual freedom to a majority of women.

Fashion

> Thirty Things (*Preferably Joined Together*) That Make a Woman Perfect
> Now scientific academies are not the only ones proposing queries: Fash-
> ion has this right as well. . . . How many things are needed to make a
> woman perfect? Thirty. Whatever might these be? Three black; three
> white; three red; three long; three short; three large; three big; three
> fine; three narrow; three small. What are the three black? Hair, eye-
> lashes, and eyelids. The three white? Skin, teeth, and hands. The three
> red? Lips, cheeks, and nails. The three long? Body, hair, and hands. The
> three short? Teeth, ears, and feet. The three large? Chest, forehead, and
> eyebrows. The three big? Arms, thighs, calves. The three fine? Fingers,
> hair, and lips. The three narrow? Mouth, nostrils, and size. And the
> three small? Teeth, nose, and head.
> —The Venetian fashion periodical *The Gallant and Erudite Woman*, 1776

During the final quarter of the eighteenth century fashion periodicals came into their own for the first time, with Italy following England's and especially France's lead.[185] As a woman and as an editor of a periodical herself, Elisabetta Caminer Turra was in a unique position to evaluate and critique their growing popularity. She published a series of reviews during the 1770s and 1780s deal-ing specifically with fashion periodicals or with published satirical critiques of fashion trends. Her thoughts about fashion's influence on women also ap-pear as isolated comments or digressions in her reviews of literary works and advice books, in her occasional poetry, and in her correspondence.[186]

Growing up in Venice undoubtedly contributed to Caminer's interest in

185. See Grazietta Butazzi, "Mode e modelli culturali nell'ultimo ventennio del secolo XVIII at-torno a un'iniziativa editoriale milanese," in *Giornale delle nuove mode di Francia e d'Inghilterra,* ed. G. Butazzi (Torino: Umberto Allemandi & C., 1988), cxiii–cxliii.

186. For more of Caminer's comments on fashion (not inluded in the "Women and Society: Fashion" section of the anthology), see "Making of a Woman," text 39, and "Women and Soci-ety: Marriage and the Convent," texts 6 and 8. For a detailed analysis of Caminer's position on fashion, see Catherine M. Sama, "Liberty, Equalty, Frivolity! The *Nuovo giornale enciclopedico's* Cri-tique of Fashion Periodicals in Italy," *Eighteenth-Century Studies* 37, no. 3 (spring 2004).

the fashion phenomenon, because since at least the sixteenth century Venice had been a center of clothing consumption in both aristocratic and popular circles. During Caminer's lifetime the fashion trade was flourishing in Venice, as evidenced by a tremendous increase in the number of guild-registered tailors and seamstresses during the second half of the eighteenth century.[187] As a writer who earned a living in the difficult business of producing a periodical, Caminer might have been inclined to sympathize with the new fashion periodicals. But her role as a woman of letters working to counteract anything that celebrated female frivolity ultimately placed her in direct opposition to them.

Caminer was not opposed to the fashion industry per se, however. As a middle-class businesswoman herself, she saw fashion (*la moda*) as a "futile matter in itself, but which is an essential part of luxury and of interest to commerce."[188] Like other supporters of the industry, she almost certainly viewed it as good for the economy because it promoted international trade and encouraged innovation on the part of manufacturers. She seems not to have shared the concerns that many of her contemporaries voiced about fashion. She did not fear that it would lead irrevocably to licentiousness and greed, or that it represented a threat to social order.[189] Nor did she worry that women's obsession with fashion trends would cause them to neglect their domestic duties. Rather, her concern was that women's preoccupation with their outward appearance led them to neglect the development of their minds. In her view, this meant that women would never be considered the intellectual equals of men. Further, it exposed women's complicity in helping to maintain the gendered hierarchy of their society.

187. See Patricia Allerston, "Clothing and Early Modern Venetian Society," *Continuity and Change* 15, no. 3 (2000): 371; and G. Butazzi, "The Scandalous Licentiousness of Tailors and Seamstresses," in *I Mestieri della Moda a Venezia: The Arts and Crafts of Fashion in Venice, from the Thirteenth to the Eighteenth Century*, ed. Doretta Davanzo Poli (1988; rev. ed., London: European Academy and Accademia Italiana, 1997), 47.

188. See "Women and Society: Fashion," text 3.

189. One of the most noted criticisms lodged against the fashion industry was that it threatened to undermine the visible (sartorial) distinctions between classes. As the middle classes began to imitate the dress and manners of the upper classes, and servants their masters, it became difficult to determine the social status of individuals simply by their appearance. The blurring of visual distinctions based on social emulation also worked in the other direction. In the last decades of the century, aristocrat and bourgeois alike began to adopt simpler styles of clothing—often made of cotton prints rather than fine silks—that recalled pastoral or peasant wear. See Butazzi, "Mode e modelli culturali," cxxviii–xxvii, cxx. The origin of this trend is often attributed to Queen Marie Antoinette, and it was made famous—and infamous—by the 1783 portrait of her by Elisabeth Vigée Lebrun. See Aileen Ribeiro, *Dress in Eighteenth-Century Europe* (New York: Holmes and Meier Publishers, 1984), 153.

Caminer's early comments on fashion trends—during 1777 and 1778—
reveal that she was primarily amused by the fashion plates[190] that encouraged
both women and men to strive to keep up with the ever-quickening pace of
changing French fashions. She even seems to have been amused that her role
as a journalist—with the duty of informing her readers of the latest publications—required her to "participate" in the business of fashion periodicals to
some extent. When she wrote a review of a new fashion supplement to the
Tuscan Gazette (*Gazzetta toscana*), for example, she sent an advance copy of her
piece to a colleague, indicating that she had written it expressly "to provoke
laughter."[191] In the same review, her playful handling of a long list of the latest
trimmings, bonnets, cravats, collars, and hoops that the supplement advertised to readers hinted at Caminer's own fascination with *la moda*. Caminer's
only serious objection in this review was that a suprisingly large number of
her compatriots—both men and women—eagerly subjugated themselves to
France's leadership in this matter.

The sole surviving portrait of Caminer further indicates that she was not
immune to the draw, demands, or pleasures of the fashion industry (frontis-
piece).[192] The portrait depicts her in a Turkish-style dress with a pleated
double ruffle—the height of fashionable wear for women in the late 1770s
and early 1780s. In accordance with current practices, she had undoubtedly
placed a toupee or hair pad under her own hair in order to create a more voluminous effect.[193] Her reputation as a beautiful woman could only have been
affirmed by a show of her "literacy" in the latest fashion trends. The fashionable, "feminine" portrait may also have served to mitigate contemporaries'
uneasiness about her usurpation of the intellectual, "masculine" position of
journalist and literary critic.

190. Fashion plates were typically small, hand-painted engravings of male and female figures
sporting the latest clothing, accessories, and hairstyles. They were usually accompanied by
short captions which described the items featured and the situations appropriate for wearing
them. Fashion plates were sometimes produced by renowned artists and were often printed in
series. An exemplary model of a fashion plate series was the *Galeries des modes*, published in Paris
between 1778 and 1787.

191. See "Women and Society: Fashion," texts 1 and 2.

192. We do not know when the original portrait of Caminer was painted (the status of its sur-
vival and location are unknown), or when the two surviving etchings of it were made. However,
given Caminer's appearance in terms of age, we may surmise that she would have been in her late
twenties or early thirties at the time this portrait was made, thereby dating the portrait to the
late 1770s or early 1780s, when the Turkish-style dress was fashionable.

193. Of course, we cannot know whether these styles represent what she really wore from day
to day or whether it was the painter's decision to portray her this way, as was often the custom
for portraitists. But whether or not these were her own clothes or her usual coiffure, the fact that
she wanted to or agreed to have herself portrayed this way is significant.

Caminer's reputation as a beautiful woman and an intellectual exception to her sex made her the source of much curiosity on the part of her male colleagues. If, as she said, she was "pleased" that her beauty could "be an advantage," she was also careful to articulate an important distinction regarding where her own toilette fit into her life priorities.[194] In a letter to a male colleague, she claimed that she did not sacrifice time for writing to friends for "time for adorning [herself]."[195] It is essential to note that in her case, "writing to friends" meant participating in the critical debates of the day with the most prominent Italian men of letters and science.

Although initially Caminer acknowledged her own moderate participation in the pleasures of fashion, over the course of the next ten years she became a vehement critic of fashion's influence on women. Perhaps the most important reason for this change was that fashion plates developed into full-fledged fashion periodicals. Fashion periodicals incorporated the plates into a publication specifically dedicated to light reading for women. The reading material was intentionally insipid and superficial, and it highlighted beauty remedies, moral tales, and instructions on deportment and proper manners for women in society. This combination of the written word and iconographic fashion images was a powerful new force in promulgating ideas about gender roles in society.[196] As fashion periodicals became more focused on women as their primary audience, their goal went beyond that of advertising luxury items to that of constructing a new forum for the "education" of women. Caminer became wary of the fashion periodical's power to proscribe—rather than just describe—the interests of a female audience, and she became an ardent critic of the genre.

By 1786 when she published reviews of two new Italian fashion periodicals, Caminer understood that the genre was becoming a new forum for defining and redefining women's place in society—indeed for manipulating the notion of "femininity" itself.[197] When she announced the imminent pub-

194. See "Making of a Woman," text 14.

195. Ibid.

196. Daniel Roche, *La culture des apparences: Une histoire du vêtement XVIIe au XVIIIe siècle* (Paris: Fayard, 1989), 452. One of the earliest and most successful fashion periodicals was the *Cabinet des Modes*, compiled by Jean Antoine Lebrun in Paris. It was founded in 1785 and continued with two title changes until it ceased publication in 1792. One testament to the widespread popularity of *Cabinet des modes* is that it was copied in England, Germany, and Italy.

197. The two Italian periodicals—the Milanese *Giornale delle Dame e delle Mode di Francia* (Journal of the ladies and fashions of France) and the Venetian *La donna galante ed erudita: Giornale dedicato al bel sesso* (The gallant and learned woman: Journal dedicated to the fair sex)—were essentially copies of the the immensely popular French fashion periodical compiled by Jean Antoine Lebrun in Paris, *Cabinet des modes* (The fashion cabinet), adapted for a Italian audiences. For modern

lication of the Milanese *Journal of the Ladies and Fashions of France*, she protested the implication that "ladies" and "fashions" were "objects" of equal status.[198] She was alarmed by the new fashion periodical's explicit goal of educating women and attending to their "moral well-being." She inundated her readers with the silly and superficial subjects which the fashion periodical proposed for "straightening out women's heads."[199] Recalling the poor state of women's education and sarcastically relating the fashion periodical's promises to ameliorate it, she reminded her readers that the publishers of the periodical would actually have them pay to provide their daughters with such a form of "miseducation."

The hardest blow for Caminer, however, was the idea that the author of this fashion periodical was a woman. She lamented to her female readers, "Were we not treated with enough disdain by men without reducing ourselves to the humiliation of showing ourselves to be contemptible?"[200] From her point of view, women's leadership role in publishing fashion periodicals helped to legitimize such stereotypically "feminine" behavior in a powerful way. Caminer's open expression of indignation and humiliation clearly reflects her anxiety about fashion's ability to undermine intellectual accomplishments women were making, or might make in the future.[201] To make matters worse, the Milanese editor of the *Journal of the Ladies and Fashions of France* may have been the first *Italian* woman to edit a fashion periodical, thereby bringing the treacherous phenomenon ever closer to home for Caminer.

One can only imagine her distress some months later when faced with the delicate situation of reviewing *The Gallant and Erudite Woman: Journal Dedicated to the Fair Sex*, a Venetian fashion periodical that was compiled by her own sister-in-law, Gioseffa Cornoldi Caminer.[202] Caminer published without commentary a list of articles that would appear in the first issues of *The Gallant and Erudite Woman* (including the "Thirty Things (*Preferably Joined Together*) That Make a Woman Perfect," quoted as the epigraph of this section). The brevity and the rather cryptic tone of the review were undoubtedly Caminer's way of

reprints of the Italian periodicals, see Grazietta Butazzi, ed., *Giornale delle nuove mode di Francia e d'Inghilterra* (Torino: Umberto Allemandi & C., 1988); and De Michelis, *La donna galante ed erudita*.

198. See "Women and Society: Fashion," text 4.

199. Ibid.

200. Ibid.

201. Of course, this reveals Caminer's bias regarding the kinds of accomplishments she deemed positive for women. As her review of the Venetian periodical reveals (see below), other women were beginning to view the fashion periodical as a new model for female empowerment.

202. Gioseffa Cornoldi Caminer (b. ca. 1758) was married to Elisabetta Caminer's younger brother, Antonio.

critiquing the periodical without damaging her family's reputation. Perhaps the most striking aspect of the review is her concluding remark, which acknowledged that women would rush to subscribe to this periodical: "Ladies will so easily find what they need in this periodical," she wrote, "that it will be hard for them not to compete at increasing the number of its subscribers."[203] The comment reflects the realization on her part that fashion periodicals had already conquered the market of female readers. She knew women would subscribe in great numbers because by then women readers—and even women writers—were entirely implicated in this cultural construction of femininity. By the time Caminer published this review, she had gone from viewing fashion as a "futile matter . . . of interest to commerce" to recognizing it as an overwhelmingly powerful force in shaping the gendered boundaries of her society.[204]

In her role as the editor of a fashion periodical for women, Gioseffa Cornoldi Caminer was not a woman rejecting a career at the writing table in favor of endless hours at her toilette. Rather, she was merging the two things and helping to create a new model of femininity. The contrast between the two sisters-in-law embodies two very different models of women readers and writers coming to the fore in the last decades of the eighteenth century. Caminer's goal was to prove that women were as capable as men of intellectual development: if they were allowed a proper education, women could read and write the same erudite material as could men. In contrast, Cornoldi preferred to embrace a genre that was explicitly for women: frivolous as fashion periodicals might be, they could also be promoted as exclusively written—and controlled—by women.[205] If Cornoldi believed she was helping to promote a genre that was "separate but equal" to other genres that were more suitable for men, Caminer was convinced that this conclusion would only help solidify the "separate and unequal" balance of power between men and women.[206]

---

203. See "Women and Society: Fashion," text 5.

204. Caminer's comment also raises the question of competition between fashion periodicals and her own journal. Caminer almost certainly asked herself whether she (and others like her) could successfully compete with such a popular source of diversion for women and undoubtedly surmised that this new model of light, entertaining fare for women would prevail over her model of providing instructive reading material for all who sought to develop their minds.

205. On Gioseffa Cornoldi Caminer's role as editor of the *Donna galante ed erudita*, see Messbarger, *The Century of Women*, chap. 5.

206. Put in today's terms, the differences between Caminer's and her sister-in-law's periodicals parallel almost exactly the differences in ideology and format of *Ms.* and *Cosmopolitan* magazines.

Marriage or the Convent

Should we poor women either subject ourselves to a husband we don't like, or go off and shut ourselves inside four walls? . . . A miserable young girl is asked: Do you want a husband? No, sir. Then you want to withdraw from the world? No, sir, not that either."
—Francesco Albergati, *The Wise Friend*, 1770

The Italian phrase *maritar o monacar* (to marry or to become a nun) aptly describes the two essential choices women in eighteenth-century Europe faced for their adult life. As the above quotation from a contemporary play suggests, young girls were often miserably caught between the two. Elisabetta Caminer Turra's thoughts about marriage and the convent emerge at times in her correspondence, and more clearly in her occasional poetry and in her journalistic writing. The texts included under "Marriage or the Convent" range from her review of a controversial French play, to her poetry for weddings and veil-taking ceremonies, to her review of an advice book for new wives and mothers. Collectively, the texts may be read as a series of Caminer's social commentaries on the balance of power in her society (along class lines, between men and women, within clerical hierarchies), the concept of what constitutes a "useful" life for women (in terms of religious contemplation, familial and civic duties, and the demands of fashion), and the dangers of the world (slander, duplicity, abuse of power, vanity) that penetrate both the cloister and the family home.

Caminer used the review of a play as a forum for commenting on the lack of power young women had even in their freedom to choose which of the two conditions—marriage or the convent—they might prefer.[207] Significantly, she published her thoughts on the matter while aligning herself with two renowned men of letters (Gaspard Dubois-Fontanelle and Francesco Albergati, the author and translator, respectively, of the play) and while praising a theatrical work that had been publicly burned in France for its inherent critique of forced monachization.[208] Caminer extended Fontanelle's critique by draw-

---

207. Caminer published the review, of Francesco Albergati's *The Wise Friend*, in *Europa letteraria*, April 1770, 73–77, and almost certainly supervised the staging of the play at the S. Salvatore Theater in Venice during carnival of 1769. See "Lettere di Francesco Albergati Capacelli alla Bettina," 106–7.

208. The protagonist of Fontanelle's play, Éricie, is a Vestal virgin, chosen against her will for a life of chastity and ultimate self-sacrifice to the goddess Vesta. She falls in love with a young man (Osmide) who tries to convince her to flee with him. In the desperation of not being able to reconcile her desires and her duties, Éricie contemplates suicide. Although the play is set in ancient Rome and in the context of the pagan tradition of sacrificing young girls to a life of devotion to the goddess Vesta and to keeping watch over her eternal flame, there is an inherent

ing a direct parallel between forced monachization and forced marriages: "If Éricie had been forced into marriage, would she not have been equally unhappy? Would she not have declaimed equally against her condition?"[209]

The distinction between forced decisions and voluntary choices for women also runs through Caminer's review of a book of sermons for nuns. While respectfully acknowledging those women who chose to take the veil out of true religious inspiration, Caminer highlighted the tragic condition of women who entered the convent under coercion or with misguided illusions. She described the convent as a "tranquil place of repose" for women called to a religious vocation but as a "painful prison" for women who where forced into such a life.[210] She closed her review by expressing her sincere desire that the number of women in the latter category would not increase.

Caminer's writing on marriage and the convent is also marked by another recurring theme: the importance of women leading useful lives. In their roles as wives and mothers, Caminer contended, women could be useful members of society by obtaining a good education for themselves and for their children as well as by fulfilling their duties to their nation. On the other hand, she questioned whether the concept of usefulness could even be applied to the religious life: when comparing the duties of mothers with those of cloistered nuns, for example, she noted rather forcefully that nuns' lives cannot be viewed "in any possible way" as "useful to the human race."[211] In another review Caminer described nuns' primary obligation as that of "doing nothing for the whole course of their lives."[212] In the sonnet Caminer wrote on the occasion of a veil-taking ceremony, she expressed bewilderment that the young woman would be willing to renounce "the sacred duties of the useful life."[213] Neither contemporary clerics nor colleagues with anticlerical leanings would have missed Caminer's rather provocative use of the term "sacred" to describe the value of a secular life.

---

critique of the contemporary practice of forced Christian monachization and perhaps even implications of a critique against superstition. As Albergati had written to Caminer in response to her comments on the play, "I was very sure that we were in agreement on the subject of the convent. You are too reasonable, Mademoiselle, to sacrifice yourself to the despair of Vestals. And should that somehow happen, there would be too many Osmides who whould steal you from Vesta, and I myself would be the first to race to extinguish the superstitious flame" ("Lettere di Francesco Albergati Capacelli alla Bettina," 106.) In fact, Caminer had introduced Albergati to the play in 1768, the year it was first published.

209. See "Women and Society: Marriage or the Convent," text 1.

210. See "Women and Society: Marriage or the Convent," text 2.

211. Ibid.

212. See "Women and Society: Marriage or the Convent," text 4.

213. See "Women and Society: Marriage or the Convent," text 5.

If Caminer considered the lives of mothers inherently useful to society, she considered their duty to properly educate their children an especially important responsibility.[214] In one of the poems she wrote for a marriage ceremony, Caminer ascribed to the aristocratic couple the responsibility of teaching their children that virtue, not noble lineage, determined the worth of a person;[215] clearly, she considered her Enlightenment code of ethics applicable to her aristocratic acquaintances. In a review of an advice book for new mothers, Caminer stressed the importance of setting a good example for children. She concurred with the anonymous female author of the book that Rousseau's theory of keeping the first part of a child's education "negative"— in other words, avoiding the development of a child's intellect before age twelve—was untenable and ill-advised, because children's natural curiosity would lead them to seek out anyone who would answer their questions.[216] In critiquing Rousseau's enormously influential book, *Emile; or, On Education* (1762), Caminer placed the authority of common sense over that of the Genevan philosopher.[217]

Caminer's concern for the education of young girls in particular is evident in her discussion of mothers' responsibilities to their daughters. In one of her marriage poems, she dedicated a stanza to advising the bride that she must teach her daughters that "Fate allows women, too, / To rise up glorious beyond the stars."[218] In directing this duty to the bride (and not to the couple, as in other stanzas) Caminer implied that the outside world (or men) would certainly not teach young girls this lesson. Women would have to rely upon each other if they wanted to improve conditions for themselves or for their daughters. In the same poem, she also warned the young bride that women bore some responsibility for their "lowly position" in life because they made the mistake of subjecting themselves to the demands of fashion and thus "[i]t is we who make of ourselves a weak sex."[219]

Caminer lamented this fact again in her review of the advice book for

---

214. Caminer's passionate interest in the education of children is also evident in the numerous pedagogical volumes she translated and published. See section 2 of this introduction.

215. See "Women and Society: Marriage or the Convent," text 3

216. See "Women and Society: Marriage or the Convent," text 6.

217. Caminer had earlier pitted the "common sense" of the theatergoing public against the literary expertise of the playwright Carlo Gozzi in her conflict with him over the value of the bourgeois drama. See "Making of a Woman," text 25. For more on the figure of Rousseau (and Voltaire) in the *Giornale enciclopedico*, see Franco Piva, "Gli echi della morte di Voltaire e di Rousseau nel *Giornale enciclopedico* di Venezia," *Aevum* 53 (1979): 498–518, esp. 511.

218. See "Women and Society: Marriage or the Convent," text 3.

219. Ibid.

new wives and mothers, in which she critiqued mothers who failed to warn their daughters against the dangers of submitting to the whims of fashion. She described the pitiful sight of women striving to ape the latest fashions, noting that the women's "misguided delight in making themselves seen blinds them to the point that they cannot read the derision" on the faces of all those who look upon and judge them.[220]

Interestingly, when discussing women on the marriage path of life, Caminer did not focus on their duties to husbands. On a rare occasion when she did directly discuss women's spousal duties, she adopted a sarcastic tone. In her review of the advice book for new wives and mothers, she mocked the British author's maxim that a woman could never strive enough to please her husband. Caminer believed such advice to be so far removed from contemporary reality that it would "sound like Arabic to young women of fashionable society in Italy or France."[221] Ultimately, Caminer dismissed this part of the advice book with her own rather humorous maxim that "in some circumstances it is quite desirable to exercise moderation even when administering good doctrines."[222]

Despite the many differences between a secular life for women and a religious one, Caminer believed that women were not immune to the dangers of the world in either state. Caminer's marriage poem to her young friend Francesca Ceroni is replete with warnings on the subject.[223] In the course of the long poem, Caminer presented herself as a link between the world of men and that of the young bride, as a mentor sharing her knowledge of the world on the occasion of her friend's "passage" into it through marriage.

On the one hand, even though the opening stanzas addressed the male colleagues Caminer had asked to contribute poems to the collection, they issued a warning against men's insincere flattery or dishonorable intentions of seduction, which kept women under the oppression of the male sex. On the other hand, Caminer used the opening stanzas to hold up her relationship with these male colleagues as a model for the bride: sincere, honest and respectful frienships between women and men were possible if one avoided the common traps of insidious male flattery or frivolous feminine caprice. Caminer dedicated a large portion of this lengthy poem to preparing her young

---

220. See "Women and Society: Marriage or the Convent," text 6. Caminer stressed the theme of women's complicity in their subjugation to men nearly every time the topic of fashion arose.
221. Ibid.
222. Ibid.
223. See "Women and Society: Marriage or the Convent," text 7.

friend for life's "immense army of deceits," exhorting Fortune and Destiny to protect her from duplicitous friends, slanderous gossip, and the general cruelty of the world.[224]

Caminer's tongue-in-cheek review of a satirical poem offering advice to new nuns exposed the worldly dangers that could penetrate the cloister. Indeed, the parlatory, or *parlatorio*, of eighteenth-century convents was a kind of salon for visiting family members, dignitaries, and even lovers, where the latest gossip could be heard and the latest styles of clothing seen through the nuns' large, iron-grilled windows.[225] The poem Caminer reviewed posited—albeit in a humorous vein—that nuns were still subject to the temptations of the flesh, vanity, and power. The poet mocked the proclivity of abbesses to relish power within the convent; Caminer described it as "the self-love, the vanity, and the taste for supremacy that an abbess can have in common with a queen."[226] Clearly, Caminer's less-than-positive view of convent life was a factor in her decision to publish this satire, despite the fact that, as she said herself, "one reads few compositions for nuns that are written in this tenor."[227] Not surprisingly, Caminer's writing on the convent received scathing criticism from local clerics, including (by her own account) one friar who claimed that anyone who read her periodical jeapordized his or her salvation: "Priests furiously formed a league . . . to no longer give me their hand when meeting me in the street . . . and a friar as much as declared from the pulpit that anyone reading a journal compiled by a little woman placed his salvation in doubt."[228]

In her writing on marriage and the convent, Caminer clearly demonstrated the value she placed on the secular life over the religious life. But she also warned her readers of the duplicity and the imbalance of power that was present in each state. In writing about the two choices women faced—to marry or to withdraw from the world—Caminer also lamented the prevalent models of male-female relationships of her day. Perhaps her focus on the education of children, both in her journalistic writing and in her translations of pedagogical works signaled her hopes for future generations.

224. Ibid.
225. Guardi's painting entitled *Il Parlatorio* (*The Parlatory*) (c. 1745–58) is a valuable illustration of convent social life. For a review in which Caminer presented her readers with a satirical image of a young nun arranging her veil before a mirror in in an attempt to imitate the latest fashions, see "Woman and Society: Fashion," text 3.
226. See "Women and Society: Marriage or the Convent," text 8.
227. Ibid.
228. From Caminer's 2 July 1778 letter to Clemente Vannetti. The letter is located in the Biblioteca Civica di Rovereto, MS.7.1 (138, 138b, 139, 139b).

4. READING CAMINER'S WRITING:
THE ANTHOLOGY FORMAT

This anthology includes a selection of Caminer's letters, prefaces to her translations, occasional verse, and journalistic writing. Individually and as an integrated whole, these texts offer a testimony of Caminer's personal and professional life, as well as her convictions about Venice, journalism and the press, the theater, and the condition of women in her society.

The Genres

This section of the introduction is designed to provide historical context and analytical guidance for reading Caminer's writing in the anthology format. What Caminer wrote and the way she wrote it—how freely or guardedly she expressed her opinions, for example, or how much she tempered her ambition with shows of modesty—varied according to her audience and to the genre in which she was writing. The letter, the literary periodical, the preface to a translation, occasional verse—each genre presented different constraints and freedoms and each belonged to a precise social and cultural context. These are important factors for understanding and interpreting Caminer's writing about herself and her society.

Letters

Perhaps the singlemost revealing source of information about Caminer is her correspondence. There are roughly four hundred known letters—about half written by Caminer and half by her many correspondents—and there are undoubtedly more to be discovered.[229] Many of the letters survived because the Italian men of letters and science with whom Caminer corresponded (and their descendants) deemed the men's correspondence to be of some historical importance.[230] Other extant letters, particularly those preserved in Vicenza, have survived because of Caminer's own reputation as an exceptional woman. However, because women's correspondence was generally not preserved (or less carefully preserved than that of men), we may never have evidence of whether Caminer enjoyed an extensive correspondence with other women, although she may likely have done so.

229. The letters—dating from 1768 through 1796—are scattered across libraries and archives in northern and central Italy and Monaco.
230. See section 2 of this introduction for a partial list of some of these correspondents.

The letter has been called "the dominant form of writing in the eighteenth century."[231] One of the reasons for this is that personal correspondence was not necessarily intended to be private, and people wrote letters knowing they might be made public. Colleagues shared letters that they received, read them aloud, circulated them, and published them in periodicals. Caminer published letters from her friend Alberto Fortis, for example, when he wrote to her during his travels in Dalmatia and southern Italy.[232] Letters provided a means to create, maintain, and expand scholarly communities dedicated to the spread of knowledge and critical debate. Correspondence networks created and were created by what one historian has described as an "active and interactive reading public."[233] This international community of critical thinkers, readers, and writers—often referred to as the Republic of Letters—is in many ways comparable to the "information superhighway" of the twenty-first century.

As was the case for anyone aspiring to become a member of the Republic of Letters, Caminer's network of correspondents was of the utmost importance to her role as journalist, editor, and publisher. The colleagues with whom she corresponded (among many others) included the naturalists Lazzaro Spallanzani and Alberto Fortis, the journalist Giuseppe Pelli Bencivenni, the playwrights Louis-Sébastien Mercier, Francesco Albergati Capacelli, and Alessandro Pepoli, the poets Vincenzo Monti and Francesco Carcano, the physicians Francesco Aglietti, Michele Vincenzo Malacarne, and Michele Rosa, the publisher Giuseppe Remondini, and the literary and historical scholars Giuseppe Gennari, Clemente Vannetti, Aurelio De' Giorgi Bertòla, and Melchiorre Cesarotti.

Caminer's role as journalist, editor, and publisher required her to produce and receive a constant stream of letters. She probably wrote a dozen letters a day in order to solicit reviews and extracts for her periodical, to participate in the exchange of books, to request assistance in procuring subscribers for her translations and for her periodical, and to obtain critical evaluations of her writing and to provide the same for her colleagues. As was the case for her male colleagues, her correspondence was a somewhat private, somewhat public forum for developing a public persona, and it was a primary means for her to participate in the contemporary debates of the Republic of Letters.

But Caminer's sex made her correspondence crucial in other ways as

---

231. Goodman, *The Republic of Letters*, 138.

232. Among others, Caminer published Fortis's letter to her from Puglia in the April 1789 issue of the *Nuovo giornale enciclopedico*, 98–114.

233. Goodman, *The Republic of Letters*, 137.

well. Because as a woman she did not have access to a formal education, Caminer relied upon her correspondence in a way that her male contemporaries did not need to do: as the primary means by which she furthered her education, especially during the early years of her career. The first letters of her correspondence with the Florentine man of letters Giuseppe Pelli are excellent examples of the way Caminer consciously used her correspondence as an educational tool.[234] Similarly, Caminer's subjection to the cultural imperatives of marriage and motherhood heightened the importance of her ties with these mentors and colleagues: her correspondence with them represented a lifeline to her professional life when she married and assumed the duties of a wife (and potential mother). Indeed, Caminer's anxiety over the possibility that marriage might impinge upon her professional life—and her determination to avoid such an outcome—are evident in the fact that she even dashed off a note to Pelli on her wedding day, between the ceremony and the trip from Venice to Vicenza.[235]

Journalistic Writing

As mentioned above, Caminer's letter writing was closely intertwined with her journalistic work. Indeed, eighteenth-century newspapers and journals were essentially an outgrowth of the epistolary genre. With the advantage of being printed and thus more widespread (but with the disadvantage of being subject to religious and state censorship), published periodicals were an essential means of communication within and across the monarchies, principalities, republics, and duchies of Europe. By extending the Republic of Letters to include readers and subscribers, journalists were important agents in the Enlightenment project of shaping a critical reading public.[236] In Italy, the number and variety of periodicals increased dramatically during Caminer's lifetime, and the greatest number of them were produced in Venice.[237] Caminer was born at midcentury, during a period of transition in the Veneto from the tradition of purely erudite periodicals (designed to provide uncritical information to readers) to a new tradition of journalism with a political-cultural agenda. Indeed, she would be among the leaders in bringing this change to fruition.[238]

234. See "Making of a Woman," texts 7 and 8.

235. See "Making of a Woman," text 29.

236. Goodman, *The Republic of Letters*, 177.

237. For a history of journalism in Italy see V. Castronovo, G. Ricuperati, and C. Capra, eds., *La stampa italiana dal '500 al '800* (Roma: Edizioni Laterza, 1976); Berengo, *Giornali veneziani del Settecento* , and Postigliola and Boccara, *Periodici italiani d'antico regime.*

238. Berengo, *Giornali veneziani del Settecento*, xvi, xxiv, li–lviii.

Literary and philosophical periodicals like Caminer's typically consisted of reviews, extracts,[239] or announcements of the latest or forthcoming literary, scientific, historical, or philosophical publications from across Europe. They also provided information about the activities of scientific and literary academies. Journalists' appraisals could influence the success of books and the reputations of writers. They also affected the livelihood of the printers (*stampatori*) or booksellers (*librai*) whose recent and forthcoming publications were often advertised in the periodical.[240] For those privileged readers who could invest in buying books, the periodical's reviews and extracts and its information about where to obtain the books helped them to make informed choices. This was particularly pertinent in the Veneto region of Italy, which during the eighteenth century boasted one of the richest book markets in Europe and suffered no lack of erudite readers.[241]

For the majority of readers, however, ownership of books was not feasible, because books were costly. There were few public libraries,[242] and while private libraries were much more common, they belonged to the most elite (aristocratic or wealthy) members of society, and most people did not have access to them. In contrast, journals were affordable and easily accessible from local booksellers and sometimes in cafés. Thus, journals were the principal means by which most readers obtained access to new ideas.

Even journalists themselves often did not have access to the books (usually foreign) they wanted to review. On these occasions, they relied on the work of other journalists—often reprinting their reviews word for word or in a slightly adapted form. Italian journalists frequently relied on French periodicals for their information about the most recent French publications. Caminer was no exception: as mentioned earlier, her earliest contributions to the *Europa letteraria* were her translations of Voltaire's writing, which she had taken from French periodicals.[243] Journalists were free to decide whether to sign their reviews or remain anonymous, whether to indicate when they were

239. An extract republished sections of books directly in the periodical.

240. The periodical reviewed books printed by the same firm that printed the periodical or by the same (Venetian) booksellers who sold it. Ricuperati uses an apt phrase when he describes the periodical's function as a "book trade bulletin for merchants" (*La stampa italiana*, 271). For the collaboration between journalists and booksellers in eighteenth-century Venice, see Mario Infelise, *L'editoria veneziana del settecento* (Milano: Franco Angeli, 1989).

241. Berengo, *Giornali veneziani del Settecento*, x.

242. Caminer mentions a public library in her appraisal of the availability of books in Vicenza. See "Making of a Woman," text 39.

243. See section 2 of this introduction. See also "Women and Society: Intellectual Life," text 2, where Caminer laments the way Italian journalists were often forced to rely on French journals for information.

borrowing from another journal or not. This borrowing, adapting, translating, and republishing was commonplace and an essential factor in the working of the Republic of Letters.

Although this system of shared authorship was commonplace, it is important that whether reviews were original or borrowed, signed or unsigned, the journalist publishing them in his or her periodical held the ultimate authority and responsibility for them. In other words, if readers objected to these reviews, they took it up with the journalist of the periodical they read. The reactions of the reading public to reviews published in the periodical played an important role in editorial decisions. Rival journalists replied in the pages of their own periodicals, while authors whose works were under review in a periodical used the manifestos or the prefaces to their own books as a forum for provocation or response. Authors could damage the reputation of journalists, often by calling into question their honesty and intelligence. As Venier's attack of Caminer indicates, a female journalist was also subject to being dismissed because of her sex and her lack of a formal education.[244] Thus, assuming the role of cultural conduit and monitor placed the journalist in a position that was both powerful and precarious. Domenico Caminer claimed that adopting such a profession required "a brazen soul" (*un'anima di bronzo*).[245]

To locate a journalist's personal opinion in the context of a literary periodical like Caminer's it is essential to look in the margins of the reviews or extracts. Often, for example, Caminer opened or closed a review with a personal comment, even if she had translated the body of the review from a French periodical. Or—as in the case of her comment about women's superior capacities as "natural" writers mentioned earlier in this introduction—Caminer sometimes inserted her personal opinion in the midst of a translated review.[246] One of the most powerful ways in which Caminer's "voice" surfaces in her journalistic writing is in her digressions from the publication under review. Inside her appraisal of a compendium on the New Testament, for example, Caminer published a fervent plea to women, urging them to recognize that their own willingess to believe men's "dangerous adulations" kept them "ever more bound in slavery."[247] As this example vividly illustrates, the title of the book under review does not always provide a reliable guide for anticipating the contents of a review (or for finding the most original or provocative comments of the journalist). Caminer often used the "cover" of one

---

244. For the Venier scandal, see section 2 of this introduction.

245. *Europa letteraria*, January 1771, 21.

246. See section 3 of this introduction, and "Women and Society: Intellectual Life," text 1.

247. See "Making of a Woman," text 39.

title to surreptitiously introduce a different—perhaps more radical—subject to her readers.

At times, in order to avoid censorship, Caminer skirted any discussion of the more risky sections of a work. In these cases she focused instead on inspiring her subscribers to procure the book, she revealed the name of the author (if anonymous) and, significantly, she informed her readers which local booksellers could make the work in question available to them.[248] When journalists did make openly provocative statements—as when Caminer insisted that women should have the right to teach at universities, for example—they were sometimes constrained to backpedal, offering a more conventional modification of their statement—as when Caminer stated that it would not be wise if a great number of women rose to such intellectual heights.[249] Nevertheless, this was a strategy that allowed her to print what otherwise might not have passed through the censors.

In selecting the journalistic writing to include in this anthology I have given primacy to texts (reviews and notices) that were original works by Caminer. I avoided including her translations from French periodicals and I excluded entirely those articles written (and signed) by her colleagues, despite her role as editor in approving them for publication.[250] Since Caminer did not always sign her articles, I have included a number of unsigned texts in the anthology when they either clearly reflect Caminer's point of view, or because in some way her "voice" comes through either as writer or editor.

The Preface

The preface was (and still is) an important locus for a writer to elucidate her goals in publishing a work. But in the eighteenth century it was also a fundamental place in which authors responded to criticism, challenged other authors, or continued polemical debates. This was perhaps especially true if the work in question was a translation—as in Caminer's volumes of theatrical translations—since it was the only area (besides footnotes) in which the author could speak directly to readers.

As mentioned above, this function of the preface extended the relationship between books and periodicals. One of the earliest polemics in Caminer's career illustrates this relationship perfectly. The *Europa letteraria* published an

248. See "Women and Society: Marriage and the Convent," texts 1 and 8.

249. See section 3 of this introduction and "Women and Society: Intellectual Life," text 2.

250. An exception to this policy is "Women and Society: Intellectual Life," text 1, which is a translated review, except for a few original lines by Caminer. For a discussion of this exception, see section 3 of this introduction.

unflattering (and unsigned) review of a translation, indicating that the information for the review had been taken directly from a Florentine periodical. The journalist from the *Europa letteraria* even invited the translator to respond to such criticism. In the preface of his next volume of translations, the author defended himself quite ably and, in addition, he specifically attacked Elisabetta Caminer for having republished the criticisms from the Florentine periodical, and for even reading such a journal in the first place.[251]

Similarly, Caminer used the prefaces to her volumes of theatrical translations to defend herself against criticisms that had been published against her. Her conflict with the playwright Carlo Gozzi over the status of the Italian theater and her introduction into Italy of the new and controversial bourgeois drama from France is a case in point. Caminer's preface offers readers an analysis of the history of Italian literature and a defense of the contemporary bourgeois drama, but it is also, and essentially, Caminer's response to Gozzi's criticims in the preface to his translation of the play *Fayel*.[252] As such, the preface is a document of Caminer's view of herself as an active participant in helping to shape the future of the dramatic art in Italy.

The preface is also an excellent example of the strategies Caminer often employed to promote her work and at the same time preserve her good reputation: she called upon the authority of a supportive and renowned male colleague (the playwright Louis-Sébastien Mercier) as well as the favor of the general public (Venetian theatergoers), and she confronted her critic (Carlo Gozzi) by quoting him directly and wielding his own accusations against him. For example, in response to criticism for having changed the ending of Mercier's play *The Deserter* (in her translation of it), Caminer published a passage from a letter she had received from Mercier in which he thanked her for having saved the life of the protagonist who had been put to death in the original: "As in Italy, this death was not well received in France. I wanted to make a political point with my play, to enlighten my nation about the horror of this inhumane law [of capital punishment] . . . I thought I would encourage her [France] to reject the law by offering her this tableau. She could not tolerate in painting that which she permits in reality. I owe you renewed thanks for having changed this bloody catastrophe."[253] Thus, Caminer used her preface to assert her theatrical expertise, but also to affirm her stance against capital punishment and to publicize her correspondence with a renowned member of the Republic of Letters.

---

251. It is not clear whether Caminer had indeed been responsible for including the review in the family periodical. For details of this polemic, see Sama, "Becoming Visible," 349–88.

252. See section 2 of this introduction for details about the Caminer-Gozzi polemic.

253. See "Making of a Woman," text 25.

In writing about the positive response to the bourgeois drama and to her involvement in its dissemination, Caminer used her preface to highlight the theatergoing public's overwhelmingly favorable reaction: "The uneducated multitude, guided solely by its own common sense," whose "insistence of applause proved demonstratively to the disapproving scholars that sharpness of mind is fallacious whenever and however it wrongs the rectitude of the heart."[254] In this way, Caminer effectively pitted the public's opinion against the literary experts like Gozzi.

Caminer frequently used irony as a weapon against her critics, and the preface is no exception. Here, she used the very accusations previously wielded against her to justify her right to defend herself and the bourgeois drama: "The right that I might have acquired [to defend bourgeois dramas] by transporting some of them from the French idiom into our own would not be sufficient to permit me to enter into discussions were it not for the fact that I have been rudely provoked by aggressors in spite of my sex and my young age, my weakness of mind, and the respect that I have forever shown and nurtured toward everyone."[255] Behind a mask of compulsory feminine modesty and innocence—at once sweetening and sharpening her counterattack—Caminer transformed her critics' barbs into a vehicle for expressing her ideas.

Poetry

As did most men and women of letters during the eighteenth century, Caminer wrote poetry for inclusion in published collections of occasional verse. Occasional verse—poetry written to commemorate social or political events usually involving aristocratic or politically prominent individuals—was common during the sixteenth and seventeenth centuries, but published collections of this type of verse experienced a boom in Italy during the eighteenth century.[256] Typical occasions for organizing these collections or *raccolte* included weddings, births, deaths, graduations, veil takings, and promotions to governmental posts. The verse collections provided a public forum in which to display one's poetic agility and bravura, but the social context of the poetry was often more important than the style and, eventually, even the content of the poems.[257] So overwhelming did the quantity of such *raccolte* become that satires of these collections appeared by midcentury, and by the

254. Ibid.

255. Ibid.

256. Natali, *Il Settecento*, 36.

257. It became commonplace in these *raccolte* to include poems that addressed topics entirely unrelated to the social event at hand (ibid., 36).

last quarter of the century they were beginning to be viewed as insipid exercises of formality and supercilious panegyrics. Nevertheless, the *raccolte* served as an important tool in building patronage networks, and participation in them was still often felt to be obligatory.

Caminer's occasional verse sometimes reflects her frustration with the social obligation attached to the *raccolte*: "For nothing in common with the holy name / Of beautiful Pure Truth have poetic exertions," she wrote in a 1774 marriage poem, "Or the many insipid collections / By now no longer read."[258] Nevertheless, she participated in at least ten collections during her lifetime and published poetry for marriages, promotions to governmental posts, and veil-taking ceremonies. In fact, the first text Caminer ever published was an occasional poem. Although the ostensible subject of the poem was the dedicatee (the noblewoman Paolina Gambara Pisani), the first half of the poem and the footnote Caminer attached to it indicating that "the author of this sonnet is twelve years of age" served to introduce herself, the aspiring twelve-year-old poet.[259] Other examples of Caminer's occasional verse illustrate the way Caminer used public occasions to express her opinions on social issues such as one's duties to children, class differences, monachization, and the worldly dangers of slander and dishonesty. Together these poems offer the reader a window into Caminer's critique of the social customs of her day.

To be considered somewhat separately are the three informal poems I have included in the anthology that Caminer wrote to her friends.[260] She composed them primarily to amuse her friends and almost certainly never intended them for public consumption. These poems (and a fourth poem not included in this anthology) were published together almost fifty years after Caminer's death as a short collection of poetry on the occasion of a marriage.[261] The editor of the collection dedicated them to the bride, prefacing them with a short biography of Caminer; he assured her that these poems had never been published before, and that he was doing so in her honor.[262] Clearly, Caminer's reputation as a remarkable women of letters was still flourishing a half century after her death. I have included the poems here as an index into Caminer's private side: the rapport she shared with some of her male colleagues, her sense of humor, and, in one case, shades of her disappointments in love.

---

258. See "Women and Society: Marriage or the Convent," text 3.

259. See "Making of a Woman," text 1.

260. "Making of a Woman," texts 2, 7, and 34.

261. Lodovico Falco compiled this collection, entitled *Per le faustissime nozze del Conte Pietro Dalle-Ore colla Marchesa Giulia Buzzaccarini.*

262. By the end of the eighteenth century it had become common practice to include unpublished manuscripts in collections of occasion verse (Natali, *Il Settecento*, 38).

In order to fully appreciate Caminer's writing in each of these genres—the letter, the journalistic review, the preface, and occasional verse—it is important to read them intertextually. As themes—and even turns of phrase—reoccur within and across genres and within and across the different sections of the anthology, increasingly nuanced levels of meaning emerge, as do the breadth and complexity of Caminer's thought.

5. FROM THE SPOTLIGHT INTO THE VOID AND BACK

During her life Elisabetta Caminer Turra was perceived as an exceptional woman whose cultural presence influenced those around her. Her work as a journalist, theatrical director, translator, editor, and publisher placed her in the spotlight of eighteenth-century Italian intellectual life. Since her death, Caminer's fame and influence has traveled a somewhat wavelike trajectory, moving from her initial renown to near oblivion and, recently, back into the spotlight of international scholarly attention.

During the first seventy years after her death, the tradition of biographical writing on Caminer began with the work of Venetian and especially Vicentine scholars, who preserved Caminer's memory almost religiously; sometime prior to 1868, the local Vicentine historian Giovanni Da Schio wrote that Elisabetta's life story was so well chronicled as to be common knowledge for his readers.[263] It must be noted, however, that such familiarity with Caminer's life and work was almost certainly restricted to a small circle of academic or local historians. Only ten years later, in his 1878 biography of Francesco Albergati Capacelli, the literary historian Ernesto Masi claimed that the Venetian woman of letters had already been forgotten: "not even the translation of Gessner's *Idylls*, with which she hoped to acquire great fame, was able to outswim the sepulchral waters of oblivion."[264] Broadly speaking, about fifty years after her death, the figure of Caminer slipped into a historical void and, with a few notable exceptons, did not receive serious scholarly attention for another century.

Caminer's accomplishments did not go completely unrecognized during this period, however. Throughout the nineteenth century and into the first

263. Giovanni Da Schio (1798–1868) compiled an unpublished history of famous Vicentine families. The multivolumed manuscript, entitled "Memorabili," is located in the Biblioteca Bertoliana di Vicenza. The entry on Caminer is found under the call number Ms. 3399, on pages 21–22.

264. Ernesto Masi, *La vita, i tempi, gli amici di Francesco Albergati*, 209. The subscribers to Caminer's translation of Gessner's works hailed from sixty-two cities, including Paris, Zurich, and Vienna. Subscribers included Gessner himself and a good number of celebrated women, including the duchess of Modena, Caterina Dolfin Tron, Maria Pellegrina Amoretti, Francesca Maria Capodilista, Francesca Roberti Franco, and Elisabetta Contarini Mosconi.

half of the twentieth century, brief notices of Caminer's accomplishments appeared sporadially in almanacs, literary histories, and especially dictionaries of notable Italians or Italian women. These descriptions typically consist of no more than paragraph- or page-length entries, and the information about Caminer is limited, repetitive, and nearly entirely undocumented.[265] Almost without exception, these accounts offer fanciful descriptions of Elisabetta's early years: they describe her neglecting her work as a bonnet maker (*crestaia*) in order to read novels and poetry on the sly and to flirt perilously with young boys. When appraising her work, the authors of these "biographies" usually place Caminer in one specific (and limiting) professional category: she is usually defined as a journalist, or a poet, or a writer of theatrical works, but not as a woman of letters with a multifaceted profession. Much of the information in these sources is erroneous or purely speculative. All of these characteristics are commonplace in the catalog genre, which typically portrays individual women as symbols of virtuous womanhood or examples of infamous sinners. Indeed, the dictionary of famous women tends to create a symbolic, ahistorical, and generalized figure that ultimately destroys the reality of the individual woman.[266]

There are a few notable exceptions to this group of early catalog publications. Between 1891 and 1920, three authors published articles in the *Nuovo Archivio Veneto* which were devoted entirely to the figure of Elisabetta Caminer: Vittorio Malamani, Laura Lattes, and Sebastiano Stocchiero.[267] Each of the authors consulted Caminer's letters, poetry, and other publications directly, even publishing some of them in the body of their articles. Lattes's article is especially commendable for dispelling or at least questioning some of the legendary aspects of Caminer's life story. Malamani, on the other hand, continued the exaggerated, yarn-spinning approach to recounting Caminer's life story, and he added a decidedly misogynist twist to the tradition— one which subsequent writers, including those contributing to the catalog genre—adopted. One of the most striking contributions of the nineteenth-

265. A careful analysis of this body of literature reveals that the authors of these accounts tended to take their information directly from previous 'biographers,'' even lifting whole paragraphs without citing their sources.

266. Caminer, for example, is sometimes described as "the Luisa Bergalli of Vicenza," and occasionally she is even confused with Bergalli directly. For general analysis of the catalog genre, see Fiorenza Taricone and Susanna Bucci, *La condizione della donna nel XVII e XVIII secolo* (Roma: Carucci, 1983), 146.

267. Vittorio Malamani, "Una giornalista veneziana del secolo XVIII," *Nuovo Archivio veneto* 2 (1891): 251–75; Laura Lattes, "Una letterata veneziana del secolo XVIII (Elisabetta Caminer Turra)," *Nuovo Archivio veneto*, n.s., 27 (1914): 158–90; and Sebastiano Stocchiero, "La redazione di un giornale settecentesco," *Nuovo Archivio veneto*, n.s., 40 (1920): 173–81.

and early-twentieth-century literature on Caminer is its portrayal of her as an iconic figure of seduction: she is either the dangerous seductress or the "amiable sinner" who bewitches every male colleague she encounters. Despite these authors' misogynist and patriarchal approaches, however, they were correct in considering Caminer's sex as a primary factor when analyzing this exceptional woman's life.

By contrast—perhaps intentionally so—the second category of publications about Elisabetta Caminer excluded any consideration of her sex from its analysis. In this body of scholarly literature—produced between the 1960s and the mid-1980s—the focus is on Caminer's career as a professional journalist, rather than on her biography (or on any other aspect of her professional life). The authors of these publications are the most important historians of journalism and the Enlightenment movement in the Veneto, and their work brought Caminer's career into the public eye for the first time in nearly a century.[268] If the first category of texts presents Caminer in a roster of accomplished women, these studies portray her as one journalist among many other (male) journalists. These scholars view Caminer as an agent in the history of Italian or Venetian journalism, and they single her out for her role in spreading Enlightenment ideas in Italy. Caminer's name becomes practically synonymous with that of her periodical because, rather than the figure of Caminer herself, the authentic subject of this scholarship is the history of journalism or the Enlightenment movement in the Veneto.

The most important contributors to this useful body of scholarship are Italian historians. Marino Berengo published a critical analysis of the Caminer periodicals as part of a history of eighteenth-century Venetian journalism, and his anthology includes a selection of reviews from the periodicals. Gianfranco Torcellan shed light on Caminer's journalistic career most notably through his portrait of her colleague, Alberto Fortis. Franco Piva's description of French culture in the libraries of Vicenza and his analysis of the presence of the French philosophes within the Caminer periodicals are important tools for an assessment of Caminer's life and work. Giuseppe Ricuperati's extensive history of the press in Italy and his shorter essays which focus on the Caminers are invaluable; Ricuperati is also the first scholar to begin to question how Caminer's sex might have influenced her career. Mario

---

268. See the following standard works: Berengo, *Giornali veneziani del Settecento;* Torcellan, "Giornalismo e cultura illuministica nel Settecento veneto," 177–202; Castronovo, Ricuperati, and Capra, *La siampa italiana dal '500 al '800;* Piva, "Gli echi della morte di Voltaire e Rousseau nel *Giornale enciclopedico* di Venezia," 498–518; and especially Giuseppe Ricuperati, "I giornalisti fra poteri e cultura dalle origini all'Unità,"in *Storia d'Italia: Annali 4: Intellettuali e potere,* ed. Corrado Vivanti (Torino: Einaudi, 1981), 1085–1132.

Infelise's work on gazetteers, journalists, and the press in eigtheenth-century Venice has illuminated the context in which Caminer worked, and his research on the figure of her father, Domenico, is fundamental to an understanding of her life and work.[269] Finally, the detailed information which Cesare de Michelis provided in his bio-bibliographical entry on Caminer for the *Dizionario biografico italiano* was crucial for opening up possibilities of new studies of Caminer.[270]

The first wave of scholarly literature that focused specifically on Elisabetta Caminer—and secondarily on her periodical and on her colleagues—began with the work of the editor and scholar Angelo Colla.[271] He was the first to explore the multifaceted nature of Caminer's professional life, considering her as journalist, editor, publisher, translator, and correspondent. In doing so, he utilized a variety of archival records—many for the first time—in order to reconstruct aspects of Caminer's life. Colla's knowledge of Caminer's contemporaries from Vicenza has helped flesh out our knowledge of Caminer's life after she married and moved to that city.

More recently, Rita Unfer-Lukoschik has brought the figure of Caminer further into the international scholarly spotlight.[272] She organized the first roundtable discussion ever dedicated specifically to Caminer, in which scholars from Italy, Germany, and the United States participated. Her scholarly contributions are commendable for their meticulous use of archival records to reconstruct Caminer's participation in literary debates in eighteenth-

269. See Infelise, *L'editoria veneziana nel settecento*, "'Europa': Una gazzetta manoscritta del settecento," 221–29, and "L'utile e il piacevole: Alla ricerca dei lettori italiani del Secondo Settecento," 113–26.

270. De Michelis, "Caminer, Elisabetta," 236–41.

271. See Colla et al., "Tipografi, editori e librai," 109–62; and Colla, "Elisabetta Caminer e Antonio Turra," 24–28, "Elisabetta Caminer Turra e il 'giornalismo enciclopedico,'" 83–111, and "Elisabetta Caminer Turra," in *Le stanze ritrovate: Antologia di scrittrici venete dal Quattrocento al Novecento* (Venezia: Eïdos, 1991), 140–50.

272. See the volume Unfer-Lukoschik edited, *Elisabetta Caminer Turra (1751–1796)*, esp. 9–61, which contains a reprint of her article "Elisabetta Caminer Turra (1751–1796)," originally published in *Atti dell'Accademica degli Agiati di Rovereto*, ser. 7, vol. VII.A, anno 247 (1997): 215–52. See also her essays "L'educatrice delle donne: Elisabetta Caminer Turra (1751–1796) e la 'Querelle des Femmes' negli spazi veneti di fine '700," *Memorie dell'Accademia delle scienze di Torino*, 5th ser., 24 (2000): 249–63, "Salomon Gessner fra Aurelio de' Giorgi Bertola ed Elisabetta Caminer Turra," in *Un europeo del Settecento: Aurelio de' Giorgi Bertola*, ed. A. Battistini (Ravenna: Longo 2000), 401–24, and "Das Familienunternehmen der Caminer: Zur Zirkulation europäischen Gedankengutes der Aufklärung im Italien des ausgehenden 18. Jahrhunderts," *Das Achtzehnte Jahrhundert*, Jahrgang 24, Heft 1 (2000): 25–36. For Caminer's circle of Veronese colleagues, see Calogero Farinella's essay "'Nel giornale di Bettina': Elisabetta Caminer Turra e alcuni amici veronesi," in Unfer-Lukoschik, *Elisabetta Caminer Turra (1751–1796)*, 81–114.

century Europe, and for their focus on Italo-German relations in the literary world. Franco Fido has contributed to the recent discussion of Caminer with an essay on contemporary literary portraits of Caminer.[273] The wave of studies on Elisabetta Caminer continues to gain momentum. Most recently, Mariagabriella di Giacomo has published a selection of extracts from the Caminer periodicals which highlights the way Caminer, as a female journalist, implemented the Enlightenment ethic of instruction and delight in her reviews and extracts over the course of her twenty-eight-year career.[274]

My own research combines a focus on gender and the use of a wide variety of archival materials in order to reconstruct Caminer's life and work and to place it in the context of women intellectuals in early modern Europe. To understand how Caminer made a place for herself in professional arenas usually reserved for men, I pay close attention to the ways in which her professional life influenced her personal life and, in turn, the ways in which her personal life informed her professional life. I have focused on the strategies she employed—especially in the first half of her career—to make a place for herself as a journalist, theater director, and literary critic. Throughout, I have considered Caminer's complex and nuanced writing on the condition of women in society in the context of her own experience as a woman successfully crossing the gender boundaries of her society.[275] With this volume, I hope to truly return Caminer to the spotlight by making her writing—in the form of an annotated anthology of both private letters and published texts—available to modern readers for the first time. In doing so, I consciously place the figure of Caminer in the current scholarly discussion of the ways women were actively shaping literary, artistic, and scientific culture in eighteenth-century Italy and Europe.

---

273. See Franco Fido, "Bettina in bianco e in nero: Ritratti letterari di Elisabetta Caminer," in *Miscellanea di Studi in Onore di Claudio Varese*, ed. Giorgio Cerboni Gaiardi (Roma: Vecchiarelli, 2001), 391–97.

274. Mariagabriella di Giacomo, *Illuminismo e le donne: Gli scritti di Elisabetta Caminer: "Utilità e Piacere"*, *ovvero la coscienza di essere letterata* (Roma: Università degli Studi di Roma la Sapienza, Dipartimento di studi filologici linguistici letterari, 2002). See also di Giacomo's essay "La Signora dell'erudizione leggera," *Tuttestorie* 6 (September–November 2000): 91–94.

275. See Catherine M. Sama, "Women's History in Italian Studies: Elisabetta Caminer and 'The Woman Question,'" *La Fusta: Journal of Italian Literature and Culture* 10 (fall 93–spring 94): 119–36, "Caminer, Elisabetta" in *Feminist Encyclopedia of Italian Literature*, ed. Rinaldina Russell (Westport, Conn.: Greenwood Press, 1997), 37–39, "Verso un teatro moderno," 63–79, "Becoming Visible," and "Liberty, Equality, Frivolity! The *Nuovo giornale enciclopedico*'s Critique of Fashion Periodicals in Italy." I am currently completing an edited anthology of Caminer's writing in the original Italian, to be published by *Eïdos* of Venice.

6. NOTE ON THE TRANSLATION

My guiding principle in translating Caminer's writing has been to preserve the original tenor of her voice as much as possible. In order that my translation might reflect as accurately as possible eighteenth-century denotation and con- notation of words and idiomatic expressions, I have relied upon the Italian- English dictionary published by Caminer's contemporary Giuseppe Baretti (1719–89) for direction.[276] Caminer's writing exhibits typical eighteenth- century style in its elaborate syntax and formality, and most of the time I of- fer a fairly literal rendering of it. When necessary, however, I have broken up and reorganized sentences in order to enhance comprehension. Words within brackets serve to clarify subjects of sentences or phrases. Abbreviations have been written out in full. In her published writing, Caminer sometimes itali- cized words and phrases, either for emphasis or, more often, to indicate that she was quoting from another text. Because it is at times unclear which pur- pose the italics serve, I have maintained her italics throughout. In her letters, Caminer underlined words or phrases when quoting another source, when indicating titles of published works (though she did not underline titles con- sistently), and, rarely, for emphasis. In most respects, I have reproduced texts exactly—italicizing where she underlined—but in the name of consistency book and periodical names are italicized even when Caminer did not under- line them herself, and capitalization is made to conform to modern English standards. I have not attempted to reproduce rhyme schemes in Caminer's po- etry. I have published all texts—letters, poems, preface, fly sheets, and other journalistic writings—in their entirety.[277] For the convenience of readers I have assigned a title to each text published here. These titles are not Caminer's and do not appear in her original writing.

276. Specifically, I consulted the *Dizionario italiano ed inglese di Giuseppe Baretti: Ultima edizione italiana corretta ed ampliata* (Bologna: Francesco Cardinali, 1830), and the *English and Italian Dictionary by Joseph Baretti: New edition modelled after that of Leghorn, and augmented with numerous additions and improve- ments* (Florence: Cardinal Printing Office, 1832). The first edition of Baretti's dictionary was pub- lished in 1760.

277. I made two exceptions to this rule in order to adhere to the thematic content of part 2 of the anthology: "Marriage or the Convent," texts 7 and 8.

VOLUME EDITOR'S
BIBLIOGRAPHY

CHRONOLOGICAL BIBLIOGRAPHY OF WORKS
BY ELISABETTA CAMINER (TURRA)

1763

"Sonetto all'Eccellentissima Signora Procuratessa Paolina Gambara Pisani Cognata Dignissima dell'Ecc. Signor Procuratore." In *Poetici Componimenti per l'ingresso solenne alla dignità di Procurator di S. Marco per merito dell'Eccellentissimo Signor Gian-Francesco Pisani: Raccolti da Giambatista Lusa Nobile di Feltre* (Poetic compositions for the solemn entry to the dignified post of procurator of San Marco by the Most Excellent Gian-Francesco Pisani), xv. Venezia: Guglielmo Zerletti, 1763.

1769

Beverlei: Tragedia urbana in cinque atti in versi di Bernard-Joseph Saurin (Beverley: An urban tragedy). Venezia: n.p., 1769.

Eufemia, ovvero il Trionfo della religione: Dramma in tre atti ed in versi da François Thomas Marie Baculard d'Arnaud (Euphemia; or, The triumph of religion). Venezia: Colombani, 1769.

L'onesto colpevole e sia l'Amore filiale: Dramma in cinque atti in prosa di Charles Georges Fenouillot de Falbaire de Quincey (The honest criminal; or, Filial love). Venezia: Graziosi, 1769.

"Rime." In *Poesie di diversi autori in morte della Contessa Antonia Dondi Orologio-Borromeo*, lv. Padova: Stamperia Gonzati, 1769.

1770

L'onesto colpevole e sia l'Amore filiale: Dramma in cinque atti in prosa di Charles Georges Fenouillot de Falbaire de Quincey (The honest criminal; or, Filial love). Venezia: Fenzo, 1770.

1771

Il disertore: Dramma in cinque atti in prosa di Louis-Sébastien Mercier. Venezia: Colombani, 1771.

Gabriella di Vergy: Tragedia in cinque atti in versi di Pierre Laurent Buyrette de Belloy. Venezia: 1771.

L'indigente: Dramma in quattro atti in prosa di Louis-Sébastien Mercier. Venezia, n.p., 1771.

1772

Composizioni teatrali moderne tradotte da Elisabetta Caminer (Modern theatrical compositions in translation). 4 vols. Venezia: Savioni (and distributed by Paolo Colombani), 1772; 2d ed., 1774.

Il disertore: Dramma in cinqu'atti e in prosa del Sig. Mercier. Venezia, n.p., 1772.

1773

"Stanze." In *Rime di donne illustri a Sua Eccellenza Caterina Dolfina cavaliera e procuratessa Tron nel gloriosissimo ingresso alla dignità di procurator per merito di San Marco di sua eccellenza cavaliere Andrea Tron* (Rhymes of illustrious women to Her Excellency Caterina Dolfin Chevalière and Procuratress Tron on the occasion of His Excellency Chevalier Andrea Tron's most glorious entrance to the post of meritorious procurator of San Marco), 20–21. Venezia: Pietro Valvasense, 1773.

1774

Composizioni teatrali moderne tradotte da Elisabetta Caminer (Modern theatrical compositions in translation). 2d ed. 4 vols. Venezia: Savioni (and distributed by Paolo Colombani), 1774.

Il magazzino delle fanciulle, ovvero dialoghi tra una savia direttrice e parecchie sue allieve di grado illustre: Opera di Madama di Beaumont: Prima traduzione italiana. 4 vols. Vicenza: Francesco Vendramini Mosca, 1774.

Nuova raccolta di composizioni teatrali tradotte da Elisabetta Caminer Turra (New collection of theatrical compositions translated by Elisabetta Caminer Turra). 6 vols. Venezia: Pietro Savioni, 1774–76.

"Stanze." In *Poesie per le faustissime nozze del Signor Conte Niccolò Nievo con la Signora Contessa Bernardina Ghellini nobili vicentini* (Poems for the most propitious wedding of Count Niccolò Nievo with Countess Bernardina Ghellini, Vicentine nobles), xix–xxii. Vicenza: Vendramini Mosca, 1774.

1780

Eufemia, ovvero il Trionfo della religione: Dramma in tre atti ed in versi da François Thomas Marie Baculard d'Arnaud. Venezia, n.p., 1780.

Quadro della storia moderna dalla caduta dell'Impero d'Occidente fino alla pace di Vestfalia, del Signor Cavaliere di Méhégan, tradotto dal francese. 3 vols. [Vicenza, with false imprint of Parigi: Stamperia Turra], 1780.

1781

Il magazzino delle adulte, ovvero dialoghi tra una savia direttrice e parecchie sue allieve di grado illustre che serve di continuazione al Magazzino delle fanciulle: Opera di Madama Le Prince di Beaumont: Prima traduzione italiana. 4 vols. Vicenza: Francesco Vendramini Mosca, 1781.

Opere del Signor Salomone Gesnero tradotte con le due novelle morali del Signor D*** [Diderot]. 3 vols.Vicenza: Turra, 1781; 3d ed., 2 vols., Vicenza, c. 1790.

"Sonetto a sua eccellenza Polo Querini cugino della sacra sposa." In *Poesie nell'occasione che veste l'abito di S. Benedetto nel Nobilissmo monastero di S. Zaccaria di Venezia la nobil donna Foscarina Garzoni che prende il nome di Maria Pisana*, xxviii. Venezia: Stamperia Fenzo, 1781.

1782

Del soggiorno dei Conti del Nord in Venezia nel gennaio 1782: Lettera di Madama la Contessa vedova degli Orsini di Rosemberg al Signor Riccardo Wynne suo fratello a Londra. Vicenza: Turra, 1782.

Istruzioni per le giovani dame ch' entrano nel mondo, e si maritano, loro doveri in questo stato, e verso i loro figliuoli, per servire di continuazione e di compimento al Magazzino delle fanciulle, e a quello delle adulte: Opera di Madama di Beaumont: Prima traduzione italiana. 4 vols. Vicenza: Francesco Vendramini Mosca, 1782.

1784

Le memorie di Massimiliano di Bettuna Ducca di Sully Ministro d'Enrico IV, tradotto dal Francese. 9 vols. Vicenza: Turra, 1784–93.

1785

"Ottave." In *Ottave per le felici nozze dei Signori Francesca Ceroni e Giuseppe Dottor Disconzi,* 3–10. Vicenza: Turra, 1785.

1786

Idillio per il felicissimo ingresso di Sua Eccellenza Reverendissima Mons. Marco Zaguri alla Chiesa Vescovile di Vicenza. Vicenza: Turra, 1786.
Le nuove lettere inglesi, ovvero la storia del Cancelliere Grandisson di S. Richardson. Venezia: Valvasense, 1786–?

1787

Idilli del Signor Salomone Gessner Tradotti. 2 vols. Livorno: C. Giorgi, 1787.
Idillio per il felicissimo ingresso alla dignità di Procurator di S. Marco di Sua Eccellenza il Signor Cav. Andrea Memmo. Vicenza: Turra, 1787. P. 10. Republished in *Anno poetico* (1796), 25–31.
Il primo navigatore: Poemetto del sig. Salomone Gessner, tradotto dalla signora Elisabetta Caminer Turra. Livorno: C. Giorgi, 1787.

1788

"Versi a Camillo Gritti." In *Tributo alla verità,* 3–18, 101–6. Vicenza: Turra, 1788.

1790

"Versi." In *Raccolta di sentimenti ingenui presentati al Reverendissimo Signor D. Bartolomeo Fiorese nel suo solenne ingresso alla Pieve di S. Angelo da Antonio Caminer,* 58–63, 83–84. Vicenza: Turra, 1790.

1791

"Idillio nel solenne ingresso del Rev. Signor Abate Antonio Gobbetti alla Chiesa Parrocchiale di S. Stefano di Vicenza." In *Giornale Poetico, ossia Poesie inedite d'Italiani viventi.* Venezia: Giacomo Storti, 1791.
Nuova Raccolta di novelle morali del Signor di Marmontel tradotte per la prima volta. 5 vols. Vicenza: Turra, 1791–93.
Il Serto: Alla nobile Signora Contessa Lucietta Porto, 16. Vicenza: Turra, 1791; 2d ed., 1793.

1793

"L'ammalato immaginario, commedia con prologhi e intermezzi di Moliere, traduzione." In *Biblioteca teatrale della nazione francese, ossia raccolta de' più scelti componimenti teatrali d'Europa,* 9:1–194. Venezia: Stella, 1793.

"Lettera a S. E. il senatore Pietro Zaguri P.V. sopra le prime Tragedie di Vittorio Alfieri." In *Saggi dell'Accademia degli Unanimi*, 1:77. Torino: Stamperia di Giacomo Fea, 1793.

1794

Drammi trasportati dal francese idioma ad uso del teatro italiano da Elisabetta Caminer Turra: Per servire di proseguimento al corpo delle traduzioni teatrali pubblicato dalla medesima qualche anno fa (Dramas translated from the French for the use of the Italian theater by Elisabetta Caminer Turra). 2 vols. Venezia: Albrizzi, 1794.

1795

L'amico dei fanciulli, del Signor Arnaldo Berquin. 4 vols. Vols. 1–3, Vicenza: Turra, 1795; vol. 4, Vicenza: Rossi, 1796–99. Caminer translated through p. 184 of vol. 4.

1796

"Rime." In *Anno Poetico, ossia Raccolta Annuale di Poesie Inedite di Autori Viventi*, 4:25–36. Venezia: Tip. Pepoliana, 1796.

1839

Poems for Alberto Fortis (1768), Andrea Corner (1770), and Giuseppe Giupponi (1773). In *Per le faustissime nozze del Conte Pietro Dalle-Ore colla Marchesa Giulia Buzzaccarini* (For the most propitious wedding of Count Pietro Dalle-Ore with the Marquise Giulia Buzzaccarini). Padova: Cartellier e Sicca, 1839.

MANUSCRIPT SOURCES

Archivio di Stato di Venezia (ASV)

Riformatori dello Studio di Padova, filza 37, carte 86, 87, 90, 94, and 97. The filza contains four items: Domenico Caminer's petition to the Riformatori against Cristoforo Venier's slanderous attack on Elisabetta Caminer in the periodical *Nuovo corrier letterario;* two pages from the 28 July 1770 issue of *Nuovo corrier letterario;* four pages from the 4 August 1770 issue; and the decision on the case by the Riformatori.

Inquisitori di Stato, busta 1238 (142), carte 3–4, 13 May 1785. Elisabetta Caminer listed as one of two female Freemasons in Vicenza.

Inquisitori di Stato, busta 372, 28 January 1794. Describes package of thirty-five books and pamphlets directed to Elisabetta Caminer (Turra) from the bookseller Lorenzo Manini of Cremona that was stopped by censors.

Archivio Comunale di Venezia (ACV)

Registro anagrafe generale, 1805 (under Antonio Caminer fu Domenico). Description of Caminer family.

Archivio di Stato di Vicenza (ASVic)

Notarile Vicentino (notary Ottavio Borizio), busta 3821, testamento, 3 May 1796. Envelope containing E. Caminer (Turra)'s secret testament.

Notarile Vicentino (notary Ottavio Borizio), busta 3827, carte 38–44, Tordi 542, 14, inventario dei beni, June 1796. Inventory of Elisabetta Caminer (Turra)'s possessions.

Biblioteca Bertoliana di Vicenza

MS. Gonzati 22.10.14 (3191), "Descrizione delle cose seguite nel Convento di
S. Corona dopo la morte del P. Tommaso Ricciardi: Cronaca continuata da F. Gio:
T. Faccioli," 8 June 1796. Entry recording Elisabetta Caminer's death.
MS. Gonzati 20.10.10 (3018), carta 228 bis, "Memorie di Vicenza del Conte Arnaldo
I° Tornieri che cominciano dall'anno 1767, 18 giugno e terminano nel 1822." En-
try on Elisabetta Caminer (Turra).
MS. Gonzati 26.5.18, "Notizie Biografiche di alcuni Scrittori Vicentini del Secolo
XVIII estese dal Conte Arnaldo Arnaldi I Tornieri." Entry on Elisabetta Caminer
(Turra).
MS 3399, 21–22, Giovanni Da Schio, "Memorabili." Entry on Elisabetta Caminer.
MS. Gonzati 27.5.13 (1855), Vincenzo Gonzati, "Tipografia vicentina del Secolo
XVIII."

Biblioteca Nazionale di Firenze (BNF)

Giuseppe Pelli Bencivenni, *Efemeridi*, Nuovi acquisti 1050, vol. 26, carta 177, and vol.
29, carta 120. References to beginning of correspondence between G. Pelli Bencivenni and E. Caminer, and date of E. Caminer's marriage to A. Turra.

CORRESPONDENCE CITED IN THIS ANTHOLOGY

Letters by Elisabetta Caminer (Turra)

Fifty-one letters to Giuseppe Pelli Bencivenni, 1770–77. Archivio di Stato di Firenze
(ASF), carteggi Giuseppe Pelli Bencivenni.
Four letters to Aurelio de' Giorgi Bertòla, 1780–82. Three at Biblioteca Comunale di
Forlì, raccolta Piancastelli; one at Biblioteca Comunale di Bassano, Epistolario
Gamba.
One letter to Alberto Fortis, 1780. Biblioteca Bertoliana, carteggi Trissino, MS
G.1.1.3 (15), coll. E.105.
Thirty-three letters to Giuseppe Gennari, 1769–90. Biblioteca del Seminario Vesc-
ovile di Padova (BSP), codice 620, vols. 10, 13, 18.
One letter to Michele Sorgo (Miho Sorkočević), 1777. Archivio Storico dell'Istituto
dell'Acc. Iugoslavia di Zagubria, fondo Kaznacic, XV 21/A.IV, 45.
Ten letters to Lazzaro Spallanzani, 1769–92. Biblioteca Estense di Modena (BEM),
raccolta Campori, raccolta Paradisi.
Fifty-six letters to Clemente Vannetti, 1777–86. Fifty-four at Biblioteca Civica di
Rovereto (BCR); one at Biblioteca Comunale dell'Archiginnasio di Bologna, coll.
autografi XIII, 3827; one at Biblioteca Comunale di Forlì, raccolta Piancastelli.
One letter to an unidentifiable recipient, 1796. Biblioteca Comunale di Forlì, raccolta
Piancastelli.

Letters to Elisabetta Caminer (Turra) or Mentioning Her

Albergati Capacelli, Francesco. Sixty-five letters to E. Caminer, 1768–71. Archivio di
Stato di Bologna, fondo Albergati, serie IX, carteggi, busta 264.

Fortis, Alberto. Letter to Domenico Caminer, 1769. Archivio di Stato di Firenze, Acquisti e doni, 93, inserto 77.

———. Letter to Giulio Perini, 1769. Archivio di Stato di Firenze, Acquisti e doni, 93, inserto 77.

Gennari, Giuseppe. Twenty-six letters to E. Caminer, 1769–90. Biblioteca del Seminario Vescovile di Padova, codice 621, vols. 3 and 4.

Perini, Giulio. Five letters to E. Caminer, c. 1771–95. Archivio di Stato di Firenze, Acquisti e doni, 97, inserto 1; Biblioteca Bertoliana di Vicenza, MS G.44.8 (coll. Le 1).

PUBLISHED PRIMARY SOURCES

Albergati Capacelli, Francesco. *Nuovo teatro comico*. Venezia: Pasquali, 1774.

———. *Opere drammatiche complete e scelte prose*. Bologna: Emidio Dall'Olmo, 1828.

Baretti, Giuseppe. *Dizionario italiano ed inglese di Giuseppe Baretti, ultima edizione italiana corretta ed ampliata*. 1760; reprint, Bologna: Francesco Cardinali, 1830.

———. *English and Italian Dictionary by Joseph Baretti: New edition modelled after that of Leghorn, and augmented with numerous additions and improvements*. Florence: Cardinal Printing Office, 1832.

Bergalli (Gozzi), Luisa. *Le avventure del poeta*. Edited by Louisa Ricaldone. 1730; reprint, Roma: Vecchiarelli Editore, 1997.

———. *Componimenti Poetici delle più illustri Rimatrici d'ogni secolo* (Poetic compositions by the most illustrious female poets from every century). Venezia: Marino Rossetti, 1726.

———, ed. *Rime di donne illustri a sua eccellenza Caterina Dolfina cavaliera e procuratessa Tron nel gloriosissimo ingresso alla dignità di procurator per merito di San Marco di sua eccellenza cavaliere Andrea Tron* (Rhymes of illustrious women to Her Excellency Caterina Dolfin Chevalière and Procuratess Tron on the occasion of His Excellency Chevalier Andrea Tron's most glorious entrance to the post of meritorious procurator of San Marco). Venezia: Pietro Valvasense, 1773.

Blum, Stella, ed. *Eighteenth-Century French Fashion Plates in Full Color: Sixty-four Engravings from the "Galerie des Modes," 1778–1787*. New York: Dover Publications, 1982.

Capacelli, Albergati. "Il Carteggio di Albergati Capacelli con Elisabetta Caminer." Edited by Roberto Trovato. *La Bottega del Teatro: Periodico di vita teatrale* 5, no. 1 (January–March 1983): 116–41.

———. "Lettere di Francesco Albergati Capacelli alla Bettina (Nov. 1768–Nov. 1771)." Edited by Roberto Trovato. *Studi e Problemi di Critica Testuale* 28 (1984): 99–173.

Casanova, Giacomo. *The Story of My Life*. Selected and introduced by Gilberto Pizzamiglio. Translated by Stephen Sartarelli and Sophie Hawkes. New York: Penguin Books, 2000.

Cereta, Laura. *The Collected Letters of a Renaissance Feminist*. Translated and edited by Diana Robin. Chicago: University of Chicago Press, 1997.

D'Alembert, Jean Le Rond. *Discours préliminaire de l'Encyclopédie*. Edited by F. Picavet. Paris: Gonthier, 1966.

De Lacroix, Jean François. *Dictionnaire historique portatif des femmes célèbres* (Portable historical dictionary of celebrated women). Paris: L. Cellot, 1769.

De Lacroix, Jean François, and Joseph de La Porte. *Histoire littéraire des femmes françoises, ou Lettres historiques et critiques, contenant un précis de la vie et une analyse raisonnée des ouvrages des femmes qui se sont distinguées dans la littérature française* (Literary history of French women). Paris: Lacombe, 1769.

Diderot, Denis. *Le dramme bourgeois.* Vol. 10 of *Oeuvres complètes,* edited by Herbert Dieckmann, Jean Fabre, and Jacques Proust. Paris: Hermann, 1975– ?

Diderot, Denis, et al. *The "Encyclopédie."* Edited by John Lough. 1971; reprint, Genève: Editions Slatkin, 1989.

Discorsi academici di vari autori viventi intorno agli studii delle donne, la maggior parte recitati nell'Accademia de' Ricovrati di Padova. Padova: Stamperia del Seminario, 1729.

La donna galante ed erudita: Giornale dedicato al bel sesso (The gallant and learned woman: Journal dedicated to the fair sex) (1786–87). Edited by Gioseffa Cornoldi (Caminer). Venezia: Albrizzi, 1786–88.

Europa letteraria (1768–73). Venezia: Stamperia Palese, September 1768–September 1769; Venezia: Stamperia Fenziana, October 1769–May 1773.

Fedele, Cassandra. *Letters and Orations.* Edited and translated by Diana Robin. Chicago: University of Chicago Press, 2000.

Ferrazzi, Cecilia. *Autobiography of an Aspiring Saint.* Edited and translated by Anne Schutte. Chicago: University of Chicago Press, 1996.

Fonte, Moderata (Modesta Pozzo). *Tredici canti del Floridoro.* Edited by Valeria Finucci. Translated by Julia Kisacky. Chicago: University of Chicago Press (forthcoming).

———. *The Worth of Women Wherein Is Clearly Revealed Their Nobility and Their Superiority to Men.* Edited and translated by Virginia Cox. Chicago: University of Chicago Press, 1997.

Franco, Veronica. *Poems and Selected Letters.* Edited and translated by Ann Rosalind Jones and Margaret F. Rosenthal. Chicago: University of Chicago Press, 1998.

Gazzetta Veneta. Venezia: Pietro Marcuzzi, 1760–62.

Giornale enciclopedico. (1774–82). Venezia: Stamperia Fenziana January 1774–January 1777; Vicenza: Stamperia Modena, February 1777–January 1778; Vicenza: Stamperia Mosca, February–December 1778. Vicenza: Stamperia Turra, January 1779–June 1782. See also *Nuovo giornale enciclopedico.*

Goldoni, Carlo. *Tutte le opere* Edited by Giuseppe Ortolani. 1935; 4th ed., Milano: Mondadori, 1959.

Gozzi, Carlo. "Prefazione del Traduttore." In *Il fajel: Tragedia del Sig. Baculard d'Arnaud, tradotta in versi sciolti dal Co: Carlo Gozzi.* Venezia: Colombani, 1772 (but possibly end of 1771).

———. *Fiabe teatrali.* Edited by Paolo Bosisio. Roma: Bulzoni, 1984.

———. *Manifesto del Co: Carlo Gozzi dedicato a' magnifici Signori Giornalisti, Prefattori, Romanzieri, Pubblicatori di Manifesti, e Foglivolantisti dell'Adria.* Venezia: Colombani, [1772].

———. *Memorie inutili.* Edited by Giuseppe Prezzolini. 2 vols. Bari: Laterza & Figli, 1910.

———. *Opere.* 8 vols. Venezia: Colombani, 1772–74.

———. *Opere: Teatro e polemiche teatrali.* Edited by Giuseppe Petronio. Milano: Rizzoli, 1962.

———. *Opere edite ed inedite.* 14 vols. Venezia: Zanardi, 1801–2.

———. *Il ragionamento ingenuo.* Edited by Alberto Beniscelli. Genova: Costa & Nolan, 1983.

———. "Scritti inediti di Carlo Gozzi." *Atti del Reale Istituto Veneto delle Scienze, Lettere ed Arti,* 6th ser., 4 (November 1885–October 1886): 1201–25, 1319–46.

————. *Useless Memoirs*. Translated by John Addington Symonds. Edited by Philip Horne. London: Oxford University Press, 1962.

Marinelli, Lucrezia. *The Nobility and Excellence of Women, and the Defects and Vices of Men*. Edited and translated by Anne Dunhill. Chicago: University of Chicago Press, 1999.

Monti, Vincenzo. *Epistolario*. Vol. 1. Edited by A. Bertoldi. Firenze: Le Monnier, 1927.

Napoli-Signorelli, D. Pietro. *Storia critica de' teatri antichi e moderni*. Vol. 3. Napoli: Stamperia Simoniana, 1777.

Novelle letterarie. Edited by Giuseppe Pelli Bencivenni. Firenze: Nella Stamperia Allegrini, Pisoni, e Compania, 1769–[83].

Nuovo giornale enciclopedico (1782–89). Vicenza: Stamperia Turra, July 1782–December 1789.

Nuovo giornale enciclopedico d'Italia (1790–97). Venezia: Giacomo Storti, 1790–97.

Parini, Giuseppe. *La magistratura*. Edited by Bernardo Morsolin. Venezia: G. Antonelli, 1884.

————. *Poesie e prose*. Edited by Lanfranco Caretti. Milano: Ricciardi, 1951.

Pluquet, F. A. *Dizionario dell'eresie, degli errori, e degli scismi, osia Memorie per servire all'Istoria degli Sviamenti dello spirito umano, rapporto alla Religione Cristiana: Opera tradotta dal Francese, ed accresciuta di nuovi Articoli, Note, ed Illustrazioni*. Translated by T. A. Contin. 2d ed. Venezia, G.G. Garbo, 1772.

Rousseau, Jean-Jacques. *Emile; or, On Education*. Edited and translated by Allan Bloom. New York: Basic Books, 1979.

Spallanzani, Lazzaro. *Epistolario*. Edited by Benedetto Biagi. Firenze: Sansoni antiquariato, 1958–64.

Tarabotti, Arcangela. *Paternal Tyranny*. Edited and translated by Letizia Panizza. Chicago: University of Chicago Press (forthcoming).

Toelette o sia Raccolta galante di prose e versi toscani dedicata alle dame italiane (Toilette; or, Gallant collection of Tuscan prose and verse dedicated to Italian ladies). Edited by Giuseppe Pelli Bencivenni. Firenze: si vende in Allegrini, Pisoni e Compagnia, 1772–72.

Wollstonecraft, Mary. *"A Vindication of the Rights of Men" and "A Vindication of the Rights of Woman."* Edited by Sylvana Tomaselli. Cambridge: Cambridge University Press, 1995.

SECONDARY SOURCES

Aggiunti e correzioni alle biografie dei soci. Rovereto: Tipografia U. Grandi & Co., 1905.

Alic, Margaret. *Hypatia's Heritage: A History of Women in Science from Antiquity through the Nineteenth Century*. Boston: Beacon Press, 1986.

Allerston, Patricia. "Clothing and Early Modern Venetian Society." *Continuity and Change* 15, no. 3 (2000): 367–90.

Alpern, Sara, Joyce Antler, Elisabeth Israels Perry, and Ingrid Winther Scobie, eds. *The Challenge of Feminist Biography*. Urbana: University of Illinois Press, 1992.

Amari, Rosalia. "Elisabetta Caminer Turra." *Berico: Giornale di agricoltura, arti industriali, letteratura, e varietà* (Vicenza?) 10 aprile 1859, 309–10.

Anderson, Bonnie S., and Judith P. Zinsser. *A History of Their Own. Women in Europe from Prehistory to the Present*. 2 vols. New York: Harper and Row, 1988.

Angelini, Franca. "Teatri moderni (Intermezzo lagrimoso)." In *Letteratura italiana*, edited by Alberto Asor Rosa, 6:117–20. Torino: Einaudi, 1986.

Ariès, Phillipe, and Georges Duby, eds. *De la Renaissance aux Lumières*. Vol. 3 of *Histoire de la vie privée*. Paris: Editions du Seuil, 1986.

Arnaldi, Girolamo, and M. Pastore Stocchi, eds. *Storia della cultura veneta*. 6 vols. Vicenza: Neri Pozza, 1985.

Arslan, Antonia, Adriana Chemello, and Gilberto Pizzamiglio, eds. *Le stanze ritrovate: Antologia di scrittrici venete dal '400 al '900*. Venezia: Eïdos, 1991.

Badinter, Elisabeth. *Emilie, Emilie: L'ambition féminine au XVIIIe siècle*. Paris: Flammarion 1983.

Ros Ballaster, Margaret Beetham, Elizabeth Fraser, and Sandra Hebron, eds. *Women's Worlds: Ideology, Femininity and the Woman's Magazine*. Basingstoke: Macmillan, 1991.

Bandini Buti, Maria, ed. *Poetesse e scrittrici*. 6th ser. of *Enciclopedia biografica e bibliografica "italiana."* Roma: Istituto editoriale italiano, 1942.

Barbieri, Franco. *Illuministi e neoclassici a Vicenza*. Vicenza: Accademia Olimpica, 1972.

Baron, Samuel, and Carl Pletsch, eds. *Introspection in Biography: The Biographer's Quest for Self-Awareness*. Hillsdale, N.J.: Analytic Press, 1985.

Baseggio, Giambattista. "Elisabetta Caminer Turra." In *Biografia degli italiani illustri nelle scienze, lettere ed arti del secolo XVIII, e de' contemporanei compilata da professore Emilio De Tipaldo*, edited by Emilio De Tipaldo, 5:461–64. Venezia: Alvisopoli, 1837.

Battaglini, Mario. *Napoli 1799: I giornali giacobini*. Roma: Libreria Alfredo Borzi, 1988.

Belfanti, Carlo Marco, and Fabio Giusberti. "Clothing and Social Inequality in Early Modern Europe: Introductory Remarks." *Continuity and Change* 15, no. 3 (2000): 359–65.

Bellavitis, Anna. "L'histoire des femmes en Italie: Bilan de quinze années de débats." *Cahiers du Centre de recherches historiques* (Ecole des Hautes Etudes en Sciences Sociales Centre National de la Recherche Scientifique) 5 (1990): 61–72.

Bellesia, Anna. "L'accademia di agricoltura." In *L'età della Repubblica veneta (1404–1797)*, vol. 3 of *Storia di Vicenza*, edited by Franco Barbieri and Paolo Preto, bk. 2:367–77. Vicenza: Neri Pozza Editore, 1990.

Benacchio, Dino. "Alberto Fortis e i giornali dei Caminer." Directed by Gilberto Pizzamiglio. Thesis, Università di Venezia. 1985–86.

Berengo, Marino. "La crisi dell'arte della stampa veneziana alla fine del diciottesimo secolo." In *Studi in onore di Armando Sapori*. 2:1319–38. Milano: Istituto editoriale cisalpino, 1957.

———. *Giornali veneziani del Settecento: Linea di sviluppo della stampa periodica veneta*. Milano: Feltrinelli, 1962.

———. "Il salotto di Elisabetta Turra Caminer." In *Vicenza illustrata*, edited by Loredana Olivato, 363–64. Vicenza: Neri Pozza 1982.

———. *La società veneta alla fine del Settecento: Ricerche storiche*. Firenze: Sansoni, 1956.

Bertagnolli, Elena. "Letture e pubblico femminile a Venezia nella seconda metà del Settecento." Directed by Mario Infelise. Thesis, Dipartimento de Studi Storici, Università di Venezia, 1989–90.

Bock, Gisela. *Storia, storia delle donne, storia di genere*. Firenze: Estro Editrice, 1988.

———. "Women's History and Gender History: Aspects of an International Debate." *Gender and History* 1 (1989): 7–30.

Bonatti, Maria Ines. "L'educazione femminile nel pensiero degli Illuministi e nei romanzi di Chiari." *Annali d'Italianistica* 7 (1989): 226–41.

Bonora, Ettore. *Letterati, memorialisti, e viaggiatori del Settecento.* Milano: Ricciardi, 1951.

Branca, Vittorio, ed. *Dall'età barocca all'Italia contemporanea.* Vol. 3 of *Storia della civiltà veneziana.* Firenze: Sansoni, 1979.

Bridenthal, Renate, Claudia Koonz, and Susan Stuard, eds. *Becoming Visible: Women in European History.* 2d ed. Boston: Houghton Mifflin, 1987.

Browne, Alice. *The Eighteenth Century Feminist Mind.* Brighton: Harvester Press, 1987.

Brunelli, Bruno. "La cultura della donna veneziana nel settecento." *Archivio Veneto,* 5th ser., 12 (1932): 40–64.

Butazzi, Grazietta ed., *Giornale delle nuove mode di Francia e d'Inghilterra.* Torino: Umberto Allemandi & C., 1988.

———. "Mode e modelli culturali nell'ultimo ventennio del secolo XVIII attorno a un'iniziativa editoriale milanese." In *Giornale delle nuove mode di Francia e d'Inghilterra,* edited by Grazietta Butazzi, cxiii–cxliii. Torino: Umberto Allemandi & C., 1988.

———. " 'The Scandalous Licentiousnes of Tailors and Seamstresses': Considerations on the Profession of the Tailor in the Republic of Venice." In *I Mestieri della Moda a Venezia: The Arts and Crafts of Fashion in Venice, from the Thirteenth to the Eighteenth Century,* edited by Doretta Davanzo Poli, 46–49. 1988, rev. ed., London: European Academy and Accademia Italiana, 1997. A different revised edition was published in Venice in 1995.

Carlson, Marvin. *The Italian Stage: From Goldoni to D'Annunzio.* Jefferson, N.C.: McFarland and Co., 1981.

Carroll, Berenice A., ed. *Liberating Women's History: Theoretical and Critical Essays.* Urbana: University of Illinois Press, 1976.

Casati, Giovanni. *Dizionario degli scrittori d'Italia (dalle origini ai viventi).* 3 vols. Milano: Ghirlanda, [1925?].

Castronovo, Valerio, Giuseppe Ricuperati, and Carlo Capra, eds. *La stampa italiana dal '500 al '800.* Roma: Edizioni Laterza, 1976; 2d ed., 1986.

Cavazza, Marta. "Dottrici e lettrici dell'Università di Bologna nel Settecento." In *Annali di storia delle università italiane,* edited by Gian Paolo Brizzi, 1:109–25. Bologna: CLUEB, 1997.

Ceppa, Leonardo. "Dialettica dell'Illuminismo e opinione pubblica: i modelli di Habermas e Koselleck." *Studi Storici* 25, no. 2 (1984): 343–52.

Cerruti, Marco, ed. *Il genio muliebre: Percorsi di donne intellettuali fra '700 e '900 nel Piemonte.* Alissandria: Ed. dell'Orso, 1990.

Cessi, Roberto. *Storia della Repubblica di Venezia.* 1946; reprint, Firenze: Giunti Martello, 1981.

Chemello, Adriana. "Le ricerche erudite di Luisa Bergalli Gozzi." In *Geografie e genealogie letterarie: Erudite, biografe, croniste, narratrici, "épistolières," utopiste tra Settecento e Ottocento,* edited by Adriana Chemello and Luisa Ricaldone, 49–88. Padova: Il Poligrafo, 2000.

Chemello, Adriana, and Luisa Ricaldone. *Geografie e genealogie letterarie: Erudite, biografe, croniste, narratrici, "épistolières," utopiste tra Settecento e Ottocento.* Padova: Il Poligrafo, 2000.

Ciancio, Luca. *Autopsie della terra: Illuminismo e geologia in Alberto Fortis (1741–1803).* Firenze: Olschki, 1995.

Cicogna, Emanuele Antonio. *Saggio di Bibliografia veneziana.* Venezia: Tipografia di G.B. Merio, 1847; reprint, Bologna: Forni Editore, 1967.

Colla, Angelo. "Elisabetta Caminer e Antonio Turra." In *Il vicentino tra rivoluzione giacobina ed età napoleonica 1797–1813,* edited by Renato Zironda, 24–28. Vicenza: Biblioteca Civica Bertoliana, 1989.

———. "Elisabetta Caminer Turra." In *Le stanze ritrovate: Antologia di scrittrici venete dal Quattrocento al Novecento,* 140–50. Venezia: Eïdos, 1991.

———. "Elisabetta Caminer Turra e il giornalismo 'enciclopedico.'" In *Varietà settecentesche: Saggi di cultura veneta tra rivoluzione e restaurazione,* vol. 3 of Filologia Veneta, 83–111. Padova: Editoriale Programma, 1991

Colla, Angelo, et al. "Tipografi, editori e librai." In *L'età della Repubblica veneta (1404–1797),* vol. 3 of *Storia di Vicenza,* edited by Franco Barbieri and Paolo Preto, bk. 2:109–62. Vicenza: Neri Pozza Editore, 1990.

Colombo, Rosa Maria. *Lo "Spectator" e i giornali veneziani del Settecento.* Bari: Adriatica Editrice, 1966.

Concari, Tullio, ed. *Storia letteraria d'Italia: Scritta da una società di professori: Il Settecento.* Milano: Vallardi, n.d. [after 1888].

Costa Zalessow, Natalia. *Scrittrici italiane dal XIII al XX secolo: Testi e critica.* Ravenna: Longo Editore, 1982.

Covato, Carmela. *Sapere e pregiudizio: L'educazione delle donne fra '700 e '800.* Roma: Archivio Guido Izzi, 1991.

Cuaz, Mario. "Giornali e Gazzette." In *Storia della cultura veneta,* edited by Girolamo Arnaldi and M. Pastore Stocchi, vol. 5, bk. 1:113–29. Vicenza: Neri Pozza, 1985.

Cutrufelli, Maria Rosa. "Elisabetta Caminer nel '700." In *Una donna un secolo,* edited by Sandra Petrignani, 26–31. Roma: Il Ventaglio, 1986.

Dandolo, Girolamo. *La caduta della Repubblica di Venezia ed i suoi ultimi cinquanti anni: Studi storici di Girolamo Dandolo.* 2 vols. Venezia: P. Naratovich, 1855.

Daniele, Antonio. "Attività letteraria." In *L'età della Repubblica veneta (1404–1797),* vol. 3 of *Storia di Vicenza,* edited by Franco Barbieri and Paolo Preto, bk. 2:67–68. Vicenza: Neri Pozza Editore, 1990.

Darnton, Robert. *The Business of Enlightenment: A Publishing History of the "Encyclopédie," 1775–1800.* Cambridge, Mass.: Harvard University Press, 1979.

———. "The Forbidden Books of Pre-revolutionary France." In *Rewriting the French Revolution: The Andrew Browning Lectures, 1989,* edited by Colin Lucas, 1–32. Oxford: Clarendon Press, 1991.

Davanzo Poli, Doretta. "The Fashion Trades in Venice." In *I Mestieri della Moda a Venezia. The Arts and Crafts of Fashion in Venice, from the Thirteenth to the Eighteenth Century,* edited by Doretta Davanzo Poli, 7–23. 1988; rev. ed., London: European Academy and Accademia Italiana, 1997. A different revised edition was published in Venice in 1995.

———. "La moda nella Venezia del Settecento." In *La donna galante ed erudita: Giornale dedicato al bel sesso,* edited by Gioseffa Cornoldi Caminer, edited (1983) by Cesare De Michelis, 329–39. Venezia: Marsilio Editore, 1983.

———, ed. *I Mestieri della Moda a Venezia. The Arts and Crafts of Fashion in Venice, from the Thirteenth to the Eighteenth Century.* 1988; rev. ed., London: European Academy and Accademia Italiana, 1997. A different revised edition was published in Venice in 1995.

De Blasi, Jolanda. *Antologia delle scrittrici italiane dalle origini al 1800.* Firenze: Nemi, 1930.

———. *Le scrittrici italiane dalle origini al 1800.* Firenze: Nemi, 1930.

De Goncourt, Edmond, and Jules De Goncourt. *La femme au 18e siècle.* Paris: G. Charpentier Editeur, 1882.

De Felice, Renzo. *I giornali giacobini italiani.* Milano: Feltrinelli, 1962.

Delpierre, Madeleine. *Dress in France in the Eighteenth Century.* Translated by Caroline Beamish. New Haven, Conn.: Yale University. Press, 1997.

De Michelis, Cesare. "Un giornale dedicato al bel sesso." In *La donna galante ed erudita: Giornale dedicato al bel sesso,* edited by Gioseffa Cornoldi Caminer, edited (1983) by Cesare De Michelis, vii–xxi. Venezia: Marsilio Editore, 1983.

———, ed. *La donna galante ed erudita: Giornale dedicato al bel sesso,* edited by Gioseffa Cornoldi Caminer. Venezia: Marsilio Editore, 1983.

De Stefanis Ciccone, Stefania. "Per una lettura del *Giornale delle dame e delle mode di Francia.*" In *Giornale delle nuove mode di Francia e d'Inghilterra,* edited by Grazietta Butazzi, lvii–cx. Torino: Umberto Allemandi & C., 1988.

De Tipaldo, Emilio, ed. *Biografia degli italiani illustri nelle scienze, lettere ed arti del secolo XVIII, e de' contemporanei.* 10 vols. Vols. 1–8, Venezia: Alvisopoli, 1834–41; vols. 9–10, (Tipografia Gio. Cecchini, 1844–45).

Di Giacomo, Mariagabriella. *Illuminismo e le donne: Gli scritti di Elisabetta Caminer: "Utilità e Piacere": Ovvero la coscienza di essere letterata.* Roma: Università degli Studi di Roma la Sapienza, Dipartimento di studi filologici linguistici letterari, 2002.

———. "La Signora dell'erudizione leggera." *Tuttestorie* 6 (settembre–novembre 2000): 91–94.

Dizionario biografico degli italiani (DBI). Edited by Alberto M. Ghisalberti, Massimiliano Pavan, Fiorella Bartoccini, and Mario Caravale. Roma: Società Grafica Romana, 1960–.

Dolfin, Bortolo Giovanni. *Caterina Dolfin Tron ed i Gozzi.* Milano: Tipografia Selvatico, 1926.

Dolman, Claude E. "Lazzaro Spallanzani." In *Dictionary of Scientific Biography,* edited by Charles Coudston Gillispie, 12:553–67. New York: Charles Scribner's Sons, 1975.

Delle donne illustri italiane dal XIII al XIX secolo. Roma, n.d.

Le donne più illustri del regno lombardo-veneto. Milano: P. e G. Vallardi, [1800s?].

Dumas, Chantal. "Le traduzioni giornalistiche di Elisabetta Caminer nell'*Europa letteraria* dall sua creazione all'anno 1769." Directed by Gérard Loubinoux. Thesis, Lettres et Sciences Humaines, Université Blaise Pascal, Clermont II, 1996.

Ehlstain, Jean. *Public Man, Private Woman: Women in Social and Political Thought.* Princeton, N.J.: Princeton University Press, 1987.

L'età dei lumi: Studi storici sul Settecento europeo in onore di F. Venturi. Edited by R. Ajello, E. Cortese, and V. Piano Mortari. Napoli: Jovene, 1985.

Ezell, Margaret J. M. *Writing Women's Literary History.* Baltimore: Johns Hopkins University Press, 1993.

F. P. [Pietro Ferri?]. *Le donne illustri d'Italia: Almanacco per l'anno 1827.* Milano: Fratelli Ubicini, 1827.

Fachini, Ginevra Canonici. *Prospetto biografico delle donne italiane in letteratura dal secolo decimoquarto fino a' giorni nostri.* Venezia: Alvisopoli, 1824.

Fairchilds, Cissie. "Fashion and Freedom in the French Revolution." *Continuity and Change* 15, no. 3 (2000). 419–33.

Farina, Lorenza. "Carteggi di Elisabetta Caminer Turra." Directed by Marco Pecoraro. Thesis, Università di Padova, 1978–79.

Farina, Rachele, and Maria Teresa Sillano. "La pastorella d'Arcadia contesta . . . Il Settecento femminista in Italia." In *Esistere come donna: Catalogo della mostra a Palazzo Reale, Milano 1983*, edited by Rachele Farina, 10–15, 27–35. Milano: Mazzotta, 1983.

Farinella, Calogero. "'Nel giornale di Bettina': Elisabetta Caminer Turra e alcuni amici veronesi." In *Elisabetta Caminer Turra (1751–1796): Una letterata veneta verso l'Europa*, edited by Rita Unfer-Lukoschik, 81–114. Verona: Essedue Edizioni, 1998.

Fattorello, Francesco. "Giornali e riviste." In *Problemi ed orientamenti di lingua e di letteratura italiana*, edited by Attilio Momigliano, 1, bk. 3:37–156. Milano: Casa Editrice Marzorati, 1948.

———. *Il giornalismo veneto nel Settecento*. Vol. 2. 2d ed. Udine: Istituto delle edizioni accademiche, 1933.

Ferri, Pietro Leopoldo. *Biblioteca femminile italiana*. Padova: Tipografia Crescini, 1842.

Fido, Franco. "Bettina in bianco e in nero: Ritratti letterari di Elisabetta Caminer." In *Miscellanea di studi in onore di Claudio Varese*, edited by Giorgio Cerboni Gaiardi, 391–98. Roma: Vecchiarelli, 2001.

———. *Da Venezia all'Europea: Prospettive sull'ultimo Goldoni*. Roma: Bulzoni, 1984.

———. "I drammi spagnoleschi di Carlo Gozzi." In *Atti dei Convegni Lincei: Convegno internazionale sul tema Italia e Spagna nella cultura del Settecento: Roma, 3–5 dicembre 1990*, 63–85. Roma: Accademia Nazionale dei Lincei, 1992.

———. "Italian Contributions to the Eighteenth-Century Debate on Women." *Annali d'Italianistica* 7 (1989): 217–25.

———. *Le muse perdute e ritrovate: Il divenire dei generi letterari fra Sette e Ottocento*. Firenze: Vallecchi, 1989.

———. *Il paradiso dei buoni compagni: Capitoli di storia letteraria veneta*. Padova: Ed. Antenone, 1988.

Findlen, Paula. "A Forgotten Newtonian: Women and Science in the Italian Provinces." In *The Sciences in Enlightened Europe*, edited by William Clark, Jan Golinski, and Simon Schaffer, 331–49. Chicago: University of Chicago Press, 1999.

———. "Science as a Career in Enlightenment Italy: The Strategies of Laura Bassi." *Isis* 84 (1993): 441–69.

———. "Translating the New Science: Women and the Circulation of Knowledge in Enlightenment Italy." *Configurations* 2 (1995): 167–206.

Formenton, Francesco. *Memorie storiche della città di Vicenza dalla sua origine fino all'anno 1867*. Vicenza: Staider, 1867.

Fox-Genovese, Elizabeth. "Culture and Consciousness in the Intellectual History of European Women." *Signs* 12, no. 3 (1987): 528–39.

Fraisse, Geneviève. *Reason's Muse: Sexual Difference and the Birth of Democracy*. Translated by Jane Marie Todd. Chicago: University of Chicago Press, 1994.

Franceschini, Giovanni. "Elisabetta Caminer." *Conversazioni della Domenica* (Milano), 18 December 1887, 403–4.

Franzina, Emilio. *Vicenza: Storia di una città, 1404–1866*. Vicenza: Neri Pozza, 1980.

Gamba, Bartolomeo. *Alcuni ritratti di donne illustri delle provincie veneziane*. Venezia: Alvisopoli, 1826.

Gambier, Madile. "Destini di donna nel settecento veneziano." In *La donna galante ed erudita: Giornale dedicato al bel sesso*, edited by Gioseffa Cornoldi Caminer, edited (1983) by Cesare De Michelis, 313–28. Venezia: Marsilio Editore, 1983.

Giarrizzo, Giuseppe, Gianfranco Torcellan, and Franco Venturi, eds. *Illuministi italiani.* Milano: Ricciardi, 1965

Goldgar, Anne. *Impolite Learning: Conduct and Community in the Republic of Letters (1680–1750).* New Haven, Conn.: Yale University Press, 1995.

Goldsmith, Elizabeth, and Dena Goodman eds. *Going Public: Women and Publishing in Early Modern France.* Ithaca, N.Y.: Cornell University Press, 1995.

Goodman, Dena. *The Republic of Letters: A Cultural History of the French Enlightenment.* Ithaca, N.Y.: Cornell University Press, 1994.

Gottardi, Michele. *L'Austria a Venezia: Società e istituzioni nella prima dominazione austriaca, 1798–1806.* Milano: Franco Angeli, 1993.

Green, F.C. *Diderot's Writings on the Theatre.* Cambridge: Cambridge University Press, 1936.

Groag Bell, Susan, and Marilyn Yalom, eds. *Revealing Lives: Autobiography, Biography, and Gender.* Albany, N.Y.: SUNY Press, 1990.

Guerci, Luciano. *La discussione sulla donna nell'Italia del Settecento: Aspetti e problemi.* Torino: Tirrenia Stampatori, 1987.

———. *La sposa obbediente: Donna e matrimonio nella discussione dell'Italia del Settecento.* Torino: Tirrenia Stampatori, 1988.

Gugenheim, S. "Drammi e teorie drammatiche di Diderot." *Etudes italiennes* 3 (1921): 166.

Gullino, G. *La politica scolastica veneziana nell'età delle riforme.* Padova: Deputazione di Storia Patria per le Venezie, 1973.

Hazard, Paul. *La révolution française et les lettres italiennes.* Paris: Librairie Hachette, 1910.

Hazard, Paul, and Henri Bedarida. *L'influence française en Italie au dix-huitième siècle.* Paris: Les Belles Lettres, 1934.

Hoffmann, P. *La femme dans la pensée des lumières.* Paris: Editions Ophrys, 1977.

Holland, Vyvyan B. *Hand Coloured Fashion Plates, 1770–1899.* London: Batsford, 1955.

Hunt, Alan. *Governance of the Consuming Passions: A History of Sumptuary Law.* New York: St. Martin's Press, 1996.

Hunt, Lynn. *The Family Romance of the French Revolution.* Berkeley: University of California Press, 1992.

———. *Politics, Culture and Class in the French Revolution.* Berkeley: University of California Press, 1984.

———, ed. *The New Cultural History.* Berkeley: University of California Press, 1989.

Hunt, Margaret, et al. *Women and the Enlightenment.* New York: Haworth Press, 1984.

Infelise, Mario. "Appunti su Giovanni Francesco Scottoni illuminista veneto." *Archivio veneto,* 5th ser., 119 (1982): 39–73.

———. *L'editoria veneziana nel Settecento.* Milano: Franco Angeli, 1989.

———. "'Europa': Una gazzetta manoscritta del settecento." In *Non uno itinere: Studi Storici offerti dagli allievi a Federico Seneca,* 221–39. Venezia: Stamperia di Venezia, 1993.

———. "Gazzette e lettori nella Repubblica veneta dopo l'ottantanove." In *L'eredità dell'Ottantanove e l'Italia,* edited by Renzo Zorzi, 307–50. Firenze: Olschki Editore, 1992.

———. "L'utile e il piacevole: Alla ricerca dei lettori italiani del Secondo Settecento." In *Lo spazio del libro nell'Europa del XVIII secolo,* proceedings of a conference in Ravenna, 15–16 December 1995, edited by M. G. Tavoni and F. Waquet, 113–26. Bologna: Patron, 1997.

Jones, Vivien, ed. *Women in the Eighteenth Century: Constructions of femininity.* London: Routledge, 1990.

Kelly, Joan. "Early Feminist Theory and the 'Querelle des Femmes', 1400–1789." *Signs* 8, no. 1 (1982): 4–28.

Kelly Gadol, Joan. "The Social Relation of the Sexes: Methodological Implications of Women's History." *Signs* 1, no. 4 (1976): 809–23.

King, Margaret L. "Book-Lined Cells: Women and Humanism in the Early Italian Renaissance." In *Beyond Their Sex: Learned Women of the European Past*, edited by Patricia Labalme. New York: New York University Press, 1980. 66–90.

————. "Thwarted Ambitions: Six Learned Women of the Italian Renaissance." *Soundings. An Interdisciplinary Journal* 59 (1976): 280–304.

————. *Women of the Renaissance*. Chicago: University of Chicago Press, 1991. Originally published as *Le Donne nel Rinascimento* (Roma-Bari: Laterza & Figli, 1991).

A King's Purchase: King George III and the Collection of Consul Smith. Catalog of an exhibition at the Queen's Gallery, March–December 1993. London: Queen's Gallery, 1993.

Kinnear, Mary. *Daughters of Time: Women in the Western Tradition*. Ann Arbor: University of Michigan Press, 1982.

Kleinert. Annemarie. "La presse de mode." In *Le journalisme d'Ancien Régime*, 187–95. Lyon: Presses Universitaires de Lyon, 1982.

Kristeller, Paul. "Learned Women of Early Modern Italy." In *Beyond Their Sex: Learned Women of the European Past*, edited by Patricia Labalme, 97–106. New York: New York University Press, 1984.

Labalme, Patricia. "Women in Early Modern Venice: An Exceptional Case." In *Beyond Their Sex. Learned Women of the European Past*, edited by Patricia LaBalme. New York: New York University Press, 1980. 129–52.

————, ed. *Beyond Their Sex: Learned Women of the European Past*. New York: New York University Press, 1980.

Landes, Joan B. *Women and the Public Sphere in the Age of the French Revolution*. Ithaca, N.Y.: Cornell University Press, 1988.

Lane, Frederic. *Venice, Maritime Republic*. Baltimore: Johns Hopkins University Press, 1973.

Laqueur, Thomas. *Making Sex: Body and Gender from the Greeks to Freud*. Cambridge, Mass.: Harvard University Press, 1990.

————. "Orgasm, Generation, and the Politics of Reproductive Biology." *Representations* 14 (spring 1986): 1–41.

Lattes, Laura. "Una letterata veneziana del secolo XVIII (Elisabetta Caminer Turra)." *Nuovo Archivio veneto*, n.s., 27 (1914): 158–90.

Legates, Marlene. "The Cult of Womanhood in Eighteenth-Century Thought." *Eighteenth-Century Studies*, vol. 10 (1976): 21–39.

Lerner, Gerda. *Women and History*. Vol. 2 of *The Creation of Feminist Consciousness: From the Middle Ages to Eighteen-seventy*. Oxford: Oxford University Press, 1993.

Levati, Ambrogio. *Dizionario biografico cronologico diviso per classi degli uomini illustri di tutti i tempi e di tutte le nazioni compilato dal Professore Ambrogio Levati: Classe V: Donne illustri*. Vol. 1. Milano: N. Bettoni, 1821–22.

Levi Malvano, Ettore. "La fortuna d'una teoria drammatica in Italia." *Giornale storico della letteratura italiana* 105 (1935): 60–103.

Logan, Oliver. *Culture and Society in Venice, 1470–1790*. London: B. T. Basford, 1972.

Lougee, Carolyn. *Le paradis des femmes: Women, Salons, and Social Stratification in Seventeenth Century France*. Princeton, N.J.: Princeton University Press, 1976.

Ligato, Maria Grazia. "Elisabetta Caminer, una giornalista veneziana del '700: La damina dello scandolo." Milano: Mondadori, 1987.

Luciani, Gerard. *Carlo Gozzi (1720–1806): L'homme et l'oeuvre*. 2 vols. Thesis, Université de Dijon, 1974. Lille: Atelier; Paris: Librairie Honoré Champion, 1977.

Lussano, Fiamma. "Misoginia e adulazione: Ambiguità dell'immagine femminile nel secolo dei lumi." *Studi storici* 25, no. 2 (1984): 547–58.

Malamani, Vittorio. "Una giornalista veneziana del secolo XVIII." *Nuovo archivio veneto* 2 (1891): 251–75.

Mangini, Nicolo. "Considerazioni sulla diffusione del teatro tragico francese in Italia nel Settecento." In *Problemi di lingua e letteratura italiana del Settecento*, proccedings of congress at Weisbaden, April–May 1962, 141–56. Weisbaden: Franz Steiner Verlag, 1965. Reprinted as chap. 1 of Mangini's *Drammaturgia e spettacolo tra settecento e ottocento* (Padova: Liviana Editrice, 1979)

———. *Drammaturgia e spettacolo tra settecento e ottocento*. Padova: Liviana Editrice, 1979.

———. *I teatri di Venezia*. Milano: Mursia, 1974.

Mantese, Giovanni. *Dal primo Settecento all'annessione del Veneto al regno d'Italia (1700–1866)*. Vol. 5, tomi 1–2, of *Memorie storiche della chiesa vicentina*. Vicenza: Accademia Olimpica, 1982.

Maschietto, Lodovico. *Elena Lucrezia Cornaro Piscopia (1646–1684:) Prima donna laureata nel mondo*. Padova: Antenore, 1978.

Masi, Ernesto. *La vita, i tempi, gli amici di Francesco Albergati: Commediografo del secolo XVIII*. Bologna: Zanichelli, 1878.

Mattioda, Enrico. *Il dilettante "per mestiere": Francesco Albergati Capacelli commediografo*. Bologna: Società editrice il Mulino, 1993.

Mazzolini, R. G., and S. A. Roe, *Science against the Unbelievers: The Correspondence of Bonnet and Needham, 1760–1780*. Oxford: Voltaire Foundation, 1986.

Melloni, Natalia. "Francesco Albergati e Carlo Gozzi." *L'Archiginnasio: Bullettino della Biblioteca comunale di Bologna* 16, nos. 1–3 (1921): 40–50.

Melzi, G. *Dizionario di opere anonime o pseudonime di scrittori italiani o come che sia aventi relazione all'Italia*. 3 vols. Milano: Pirola, 1848–59.

Memorie dell'I. R. Accademia di Scienze: Lettere ed Arti degli Agiati in Rovereto pubblicate per commemorare il suo 150esimo anno di vita. Rovereto: Stabilimento tipografico Grigoletti, 1901, 1903.

Menicucci, G. "Una letterata veneziana del Settecento." *Noi e il mondo* 16 (1926): 835–40.

Messbarger, Rebecca. *The Century of Women: Representations of Women in Eighteenth-Century Italian Public Discourse*. Toronto: University of Toronto Press, 2002.

———. "Voice of Dissent: A Woman's Response to the Eighteenth-Century Debate on the Education of Women." *Cincinatti Romance Review* 13 (1994): 69–80.

———. "Waxing Poetic: Anna Morandi Manzolini's Anatomical Sculptures," *Configurations* 91 (2001): 65–97.

Milano, Andrea, ed. *Misoginia: La donna vista e malvista nella cultura occidentale*. Roma, Edizioni Dehoniane, 1992.

Minuti, Rolando. "Giornali e opinione pubblica nell'Inghilterra del Settecento." *Studi storici* 25, no. 2 (1984): 319–31.

Molmenti, Pompeo G. *Epistolari veneziani del secolo XVIII*. Palermo: Remo Sandron Editore, 1914.

————. *La storia di Venezia nella vita privata*, vol. 3 of *Il decadimento*. 1927–29, reprint, Trieste: Edizioni Lint, 1973.

————. *Venice: Its Individual Growth from the Earliest Beginnings to the Fall of the Republic*. Vol. 2. Translated by Horatio Brown. Bergamo: Istituto italiano d'arti grafiche, 1908.

Monnier, Philippe. *Venise au XVIIIe siècle*. Lausanne: Bibliothèque romande, 1971.

Morelli Timpanaro, Maria Augusta. *Autori, stampatori, librai: Per una storia dell'editoria in Firenze nel secolo XVIII*. Firenze: Olschki, 1999.

————. *Lettere a Giuseppe Pelli Bencivenni, 1747–1808: Inventario e documenti*. Roma: Pubblicazioni degli Archivi di Stato, 1976.

Moschini, Giannantonio. *Della letteratura veneziana del secolo XVIII fino ai nostri giorni*. 4 vols. Venezia, 1806–8.

Motterle, Tullio. "Dal conte Azzolino ad Alberto Fortis: Cinque secoli di storia al monastero di San Pietro al Costo." In *Valle del Chiampo*, 225–53. Arzignano: Molin & Figli, 1974.

Muljačić, Žarko. "Le amicizie letterarie italiane di Miho Sorkočević." In *Problemi di lingua e letteratura italiana del Settecento*, proceedings of a congress at Weisbaden, April–May 1962, 164–69. Weisbaden: Franz Steiner Verlag, 1965.

Musatti, Eugenio. *La donna in Venezia*. Padova, 1892; reprint: Bologna?: Arnaldi Forni, 1975.

Natali, Giulio, ed. *Il Settecento*. Vol. 1 of *Storie letteraria d' Italia*. Milano: Vallardi, 1929–36; 6th ed., Milano: Vallardi, 1964.

Neppi Modona, Leo. "Per la storia della *Encyclopédie* in Italia: L'abate Giulio Perini collaboratore della *Encyclopédie Méthodique*." *Revue des études italiennes* 10 (1964): 81–91.

Norwich, John Julius. *A History of Venice*. 1982. New York: Vintage Books, 1989.

Odorisio, Ginevra Conti. *Donna e società nel '600: Lucrezia Marinelli e Archangela Tarabotti*. Roma: Bulzoni, 1979.

————. *Storia dell'idea femminista in Ialia*. Torino: Edizioni Rai radiotelevisione italiana, 1980.

Offen, Karen. "Defining Feminism: A Comparative Historical Approach." *Signs* 14, no. 1 (1988): 119–57.

Offen, Karen, Ruth Roach Pierson, and Jane Rendall, eds. *Writing Women's History: International Perspectives*. Bloomington: Indiana University Press, 1991.

Orestano, Francesco, ed. *Eroine, ispiratrici e donne di eccezione*. 7th ser. of *Enciclopedia biografica e bibliografica italiana*. Milano: Istituto Editoriale italiano, 1940.

Outram, Dorinda. *The Enlightenment*. Cambridge: Cambridge University Press, 1995.

Pachter, Marc, ed. *Telling Lives: The Biographer's Art*. York, Pa.: Maple Press, 1979.

Paladini Volterra, Angela. "Verso una moderna produzione teatrale." *Quaderni di Teatro* year 5, vol. 20 (1983): 87–126.

Pedrocco, Filippo. "Le illustrazioni della 'Donna galante ed erudita.'" In *La donna galante ed erudita: Giornale dedicato al bel sesso*, edited by Gioseffa Cornoldi Caminer, edited (1983) by Cesare De Michelis, 340–44. Venezia: Marsilio Editore, 1983.

Per il 150° anniversario 1900 dalla fondazione della I.R. Academia de scienze lettere ed arti degli Agiati in Rovereto. Rovereto: Tipografia Grigoletti, 1899.

Plebani, Tiziana. *Il "genere" dei libri: Storie e rappresentazioni della lettura al femminile e al maschile tra Medioevo e età moderna*. Milano: Franco Angeli, 2001.

Phillips, Patricia. *The Scientific Lady: A Social History of Woman's Scientific Interests, 1520–1918*. New York: St. Martin's Press, 1990.

Piva, Franco. "Contributo alla fortuna di Helvétius nel Veneto del secondo Sette-cento." Parts 1 and 2. *Aevum* 45 (1971): 234–87, 430–63.

———. "La cultura francese nelle biblioteche venete del Settecento: Vicenza." *Archivio Veneto*, 5th ser., 115 (1980): 33–83.

———. "Gli echi della morte di Voltaire e Rousseau nel *Giornale enciclopedico* di Venezia." *Aevum* 53 (1979): 498–518.

———. "Illuminismo e cultura francese nel Veneto del secondo Settecento." *Pubbli-cazioni dell'Università Cattolica del S. Cuore*, French ser., 8 (1972): 51–146.

Pomata, Gianna. "Storia particolare e storia universale: In margine ad alcuni manuali di storia delle donne." *Quaderni storici* 74 (1990): 341–85.

Postigliola, A., and N. Boccara, eds. *Periodici italiani d'antico regime*. Roma: Società Ital-iana di Studi sul secolo XVIII, 1986.

Preto, Paolo. "L'illuminismo veneto." In *Storia della cultura veneta*, edited by Girolamo Ar-naldi and M. Pastore Stocchi, vol. 5, bk. 1:1–45. Vicenza: Neri Pozza, 1985.

———. "I 'lumi' a Vicenza." In *Storia di Vicenza*, edited by F. Barbieri and P. Preto, vol. 3, bk. 2:379–87.. Vicenza: Neri Pozza Editore, 1990.

Pullini, Giorgio. "Il teatro fra polemica e costume." In *Storia della cultura veneta*, edited by Girolamo Arnaldi and M. Pastore Stocchi, vol. 5, bk. 1:277–307. Vicenza: Neri Pozza, 1985.

Rao, Anna Maria. "Il sapere velato. L'educazione delle donne nel dibattito italiano di fine Settecento." In *Misoginia: La donna vista e malvista nella cultura occidentale*, edited by Andrea Milano, 243–310. Roma: Edizioni Dehoniane, 1992.

Renzi, Orietta. "Elisabetta Caminer e la diffusione del dramma borghese nella sec-onda metà del Settecento." Directed by Nicola Mangini. Thesis, Università di Venezia, 1989–90.

Ribeiro, Aileen. *The Art of Dress: Fashion in England and France 1750 to 1820*. New Haven, Conn.: Yale University Press, 1995.

———. *Dress and Morality*. New York: Holmes and Meier Publishers, 1986.

———. *Dress in Eighteenth-Century Europe*. New York: Holmes and Meier Publishers, 1984.

Ricaldone, Luisa. *La scrittura nascosta: Donne di lettere e loro immagini tra Arcadia e Restau-razione*. Paris: Honoré Champion; Firenze: Edizioni Cadmo, 1996.

Ricuperati, Giuseppe. "I giornali italiani del XVIII secolo: Studi e ipotesi di ricerca." *Studi storici* 25, no. 2 (1984): 279–303.

———. "I giornalisti fra poteri e cultura dalle origini all'Unità." In *Storia d'Italia: Annali 4: Intellettuali e potere*, edited by Corrado Vivanti, 1085–1132. Torino: Einaudi, 1981.

———. "Periodici eruditi, riviste e giornali di varie umanità dalle origini a metà Ot-tocento." In *Il letterato e le istituzioni*, vol. 1 of *Letteratura italiana*, 921–43. Torino: Ein-audi, 1982.

Ricuperati, G., and Dino Carpanetto. *L'Italia del Settecento: Crisi trasformazioni lumi*. 1986. Roma: Editori Laterza, 1990.

Rimbauld, Caroline. "La presse féminine de langue française au XVIIIème siècle: Pro-duction e diffusion." In *Le journalisme d'Ancien Régime*, 199–216. Lyon: Presses Uni-versitaires de Lyon, 1982.

Roche, Daniel. *La culture des apparences: Une histoire du vêtement XVIIe au XVIIIe siècle*. Paris: Fayard, 1989.

Rogers, Katharine. *Feminism in Eighteenth-Century England.* Urbana: University of Illinois Press, 1982.

Rosa, Mario. "Encyclopédie, 'lumières' et tradition au 18e siècle en Italie." *Dix-huitième siecle* 4 (1972): 110–12.

Rosenthal, Margaret F. *The Honest Courtesan: Veronica Franco, Citizen and Writer in Sixteenth-Century Venice.* Chicago: University of Chicago Press, 1992.

Rumor, Sebastiano. *Antologia femminile vicentina: Biografia, bibliografia e saggi.* Vicenza: Luigi Fabris, 1907.

————. *Donne illustri vicentini: Per le nozze Ortolani-Fontana.* Vicenza: Paroni, 1881.

————. *Gli scrittori vicentini dei secoli decimottavo e decimonono.* Vol. 1. Venezia: Tipografia Emiliana, 1905.

Russell, Rinaldina, ed. *The Feminist Encyclopedia of Italian Literature.* Westport, Conn.: Greenwood Press, 1997.

————. *Italian Women Writers: A Bio-Bibliographical Sourcebook.* Westport, Conn.: Greenwood Press, 1994.

Saccardo, Rosanna. *La stampa periodica veneziana fino alla caduta della Repubblica.* 1942. Trieste: Lint, 1982.

Sama, Catherine M. "Becoming Visible: A Biography of Elisabetta Caminer Turra (1751–1796) during Her Formative Years." *Studi veneziani,* n.s., 43 (2002): 349–88.

————. "Elisabetta Caminer." In *Feminist Encyclopedia of Italian Literature,* edited by Rinaldina Russell, 37–39. Westport, Conn., Greenwood Press, 1997.

————. "Liberty, Equality, Frivolity! The *Nuovo giornale enciclopedico*'s Critique of Fashion Periodicals in Italy." *Eighteenth-Century Studies* 37, no. 3 (spring 2004).

————. "Women's History in Italian Studies: Elisabetta Caminer and 'The Woman Question.'" *La Fusta: Journal of Italian Literature and Culture* 10 (fall 93–spring 94): 119–36.

————. "Verso un teatro moderno: La polemica tra Elisabetta Caminer e Carlo Gozzi." In *Elisabetta Caminer Turra (1751–1796): Una letterata veneta verso l'Europa,* edited by Rita Unfer-Lukoschik, 63–79. Verona: Essedue Edizioni, 1998.

Sani, Bernardina. *Rosalba Carriera: Lettere, Diari, Frammenti.* Firenze: Olschki Editore, 1985.

Santangelo Giovanni Saverio, and Claudio Vinti. *Le traduzioni italiane del teatro comico francese dei secoli XVII e XVIII.* Roma: Edizioni di Storia e Letteratura, 1981.

Savoia, Francesca, ed. *La cantante e l'impresario e altri metamelodrammi.* Genova: Costa and Nolan, 1988.

Schiebinger, Londa. *The Mind Has No Sex? Women in the Origins of Modern Science.* Cambridge, Mass.: Harvard University Press, 1989.

Schor, Naomi. "Feminist and Gender Studies." In *Introduction to Scholarship in Modern Languages and Literatures,* edited by Joseph Gibaldi, 262–87. New York: MLA, 1992.

Scott, Joan W. *Gender and the Politics of History.* New York: Columbia University Press, 1988.

————. *Women, Work and Family.* New York: Holt, Rinehart and Winston, 1978.

Sheriff, Mary. *The Exceptional Woman: Elisabeth Vigée-Lebrun and the Cultural Politics of Art.* Chicago: University of Chicago Press, 1996.

Shevelow, Kathryn. *Women and Print Culture: The Construction of Femininity in the Early Periodical.* London: Routledge, 1989.

Showalter, Elaine. *A Literature of Their Own: English Women Novelists from Brontë to Lessing.* Princeton, N.J.: Princeton University Press, 1977.

Smith, Bonnie G. *Changing Lives: Women in European History Since 1700.* Lexington, Mass.: D.C. Heath and Co., 1989.

Soldini, Adriano, et al. *Il giornale letterario in Italia.* Bellinzona: La Scuola, 1960.

Soriga, R. "Giornalismo dipartimentale negli ultimi anni del Regno Italico." *Rassegna nazionale* 40 (1918): 150–54.

Lo spettacolo dell'Enciclopedia. 10 vols. Edited by Silvio D'Amico. Roma: Casa Editrice La Maschera, 1954–68.

Stewart, Pamela. "Eroine della dissimulazione: Il teatro di Lusia Bergalli Gozzi." *Quaderni veneti* 19 (1994): 73–92.

Stocchiero, Sebastiano. "La redazione di un giornale settecentesco." *Nuovo archivio veneto,* n.s., 40 (1920): 173–81.

Strenna veneziana pel 1865: Anno quarto: La letteratura e le sue donne passate e presenti. Venezia: Tipografia del Commercio Edit., 1864.

Strumia, Elisa. "Un giornale per le donne nel piemonte del 1799: 'La vera repubblicana.'" *Studi storici* 30, no. 4 (1989): 917–46.

Studi Storici 2 (1984). "I periodici d''Ancien Régime' come problema storiografico."

Targhetta, Renata. *La massoneria veneta dalle origini alla chiusura delle logge (1729–1785).* Udine: Del Bianco Editore, 1988.

Taricone, Fiorenza, and Susanna Bucci. *La condizione della donna nel XVII e XVIII secolo.* Roma: Carucci, 1983.

Torcellan, Gianfranco. "Alberto Fortis." In *Riformatori delle antiche repubbliche, dei ducati, dello stato pontificio e delle isole,* vol. 7 of *Illuministi italiani,* edited by Giuseppe Giarrizzo, Gianfranco Torcellan, and Franco Venturi, 281–390. Milano: Ricciardi, 1965.

———. "Andrea Memmo." In *Riformatori delle antiche repubbliche, dei ducati, dello stato pontificio e delle isole,* vol. 7 of *Illuministi italiani,* edited by Giuseppe Giarrizzo, Gianfranco Torcellan, and Franco Venturi, 195–277. Milano: Ricciardi, 1965.

———. "Francesco Griselini." In *Riformatori delle antiche repubbliche, dei ducati, dello stato pontificio e delle isole,* vol. 7 of *Illuministi italiani,* ed. Giuseppe Giarrizzo, Gianfranco Torcellan, and Franco Venturi, 93–192. Milano: Ricciardi, 1965.

———. "Giornalismo e cultura illuministica nel Settecento veneto." In *Settecento veneto e altri scritti storici,* 177–202. Torino: Giappichelli, 1969.

Turchi, Roberta, ed. *Il teatro italiano.* Vol. 4. Torino: Einaudi, 1987.

Ugoni, Camillo. *Della letteratura italiana nella seconda metà del secolo XVIII.* Milano: Bernardori, 1826.

"Una giornalista del '700." *Nazione della domenica* (Trieste) 3 April 1921.

Unfer-Lukoschik, Rita. "L'educatrice delle donne: Elisabetta Caminer Turra (1751–1796) e la 'Querelle des Femmes' negli spazi veneti di fine '700." *Memorie dell'Accademia delle scienze di Torino,* 5th ser., 24 (2000): 249–63.

———. "Das Familienunternehmen der Caminer: Zur Zirkulation europäischen Gedankengutes der Aufklärung im Italien des ausgehenden 18. Jahrhunderts." *Das Achtzehnte Jahrhundert,* Jahrgang 24, Heft 1 (2000): 25–36.

———. "Salomon Gesner fra Aurelio de' Giorgi Bertola ed Elisabetta Caminer Turra." In *Un europeo del Settecento: Aurelio de' Giorgi Bertola,* edited by A. Battastini, 401–24. Ravenna: Longo, 2000.

———, ed. *Elisabetta Caminer Turra (1751–1796): Una letterata veneta verso l'Europa.* Verona: Essedue Edizioni, 1998.

Ungherini, A. *Manuel de Bibliograhie biographique et d'iconographie des femmes célèbres contenant: Un dictionnaire des femmes qui se sont fait remarquer à un titre quelconque dans tous les siècles et dans tous les pays; les dates de leur naissance et de leur mort; la liste de toutes les monographies biographiques relatives à chaque femme, avec la mention des traductions; l'indication des portraits joints aux ouvrages cités et de ceux gravés séparement, avec les nomes des graveurs; les prix auxquels les livres, les portraits et les autographes ont eté portes dans les ventes ou dans les catalogues; suivi d'un répertoire de biographies generales, nationales et locales et d'ouvrages concernant les portraits et les autographes, par un vieux bibliophile.* Paris: Librairie Nilsson, 1892; supp. 1, Paris: Lib. Nilsson, 1900; supp. 2, Paris: Honoré Champion, 1905.

Vallini, Giulio. *Biografia universale antica e moderna, ossia storia per alfabeto della vita pubblica e privata di tutte le persone ch'ebbero fama per opere, azioni, ingegno, virtù, o delitti: Opera affatto nuova,compilata in Francia da una società di dotti e per la prima volta recata in italiano.* 1823; 2d ed., Venezia: Presso G.B. Missiaglia, dalla Tipografia F. Andreola, 1834–41.

Van Dijk, Suzanne. "'Journale des Dames' et journaux des hommes, la notion Femme." In *L'année 1768 à travers la presse traité par ordinateur*, 80–100. Paris: Editions du Centre national de la recherche scientifique, 1981.

Venturi, Franco. *L'Italia dei lumi: La Repubblica di Venezia.* Vol. 5, bk. 2, of *Settecento riformatore.* Torino: Einaudi, 1990.

———. *Venezia nel secondo Settecento.* Torino: Tirrenia Stampatori, 1980.

Vier, Jacques. *Histoire de la littérature française: XVIIIe siècle.* Vol. 1, Paris: Armand Colin, 1965; vol. 2, 1970.

Vincent-Buffault, Anne. *The History of Tears: Sensibility and Sentimentality in France.* Translated by Teresa Bridgeman. New York: St. Martin's Press, 1991. Originally published as *Histoire des larmes, XVIII–XIX siècles* (Paris: Rivages, 1986).

Vivien, Frances. *Il Console Smith, mercante e collezionista.* Vicenza: Neri Pozza, 1971.

Wolff, Larry. *Venice and the Slavs: The Discovery of Dalmatia in the Age of Enlightenment.* Stanford, Calif.: Stanford University Press, 2001.

Woodbridge, Linda. *Women and the English Renaissance: Literature and the Nature of Womankind, 1540–1620.* Urbana: University of Illinois Press, 1984.

Zinsser, Judith P. *History and Feminism: A Glass Half Full.* New York: Twayne Publishers, 1993.

Zironda, Renato. "Il teatro a Vicenza in età napoleonica." In *Il Vicentino tra rivoluzione giacobina ed età napoleonica, 1797–1813,* catalog of an exhibition at the Palazzo Costantini, edited by R. Zironda. Vicenza: Biblioteca Civica Bertoliana, 1989.

PART I
THE MAKING OF A WOMAN OF LETTERS
IN THE EIGHTEENTH-CENTURY VENETO

1. POEM ON AMBITION AND THE PASSING OF TIME (1763)[1]

Jealous old man, by whose perpetual flight
Beauty must end, and fame too is obscured,
Whence with your rapid course you fill with sorrow
Those who care only for frivolities and vanity.

For me your clock runs too slowly,
And my mind[2] is still too immature
To cut a presentable figure
Among the Apollonian company that I love.

I would nevertheless sing the worth of Paolina:
I would call her the great mother of the Gracchi,[3]
An august Matron of excellent customs.

Why do you despise, she was asked one day,
Jewels, the splendor of feminine ornaments?
My children are my jewels, replied she.

1. This sonnet is Caminer's first publication. The poem was published in the collection of poetry entitled *Poetici Componimenti per l'ingresso solenne alla dignità di Procurator di S. Marco per merito
dell'Eccellentissimo Signor Gian-Francesco Pisani* (Poetic compositions for the solemn entry to the dignified post of procurator of San Marco by the most excellent Gian-Francesco Pisani) (Venezia:
Guglielmo Zerletti, 1763), xv. Caminer dedicated her sonnet to Paolina Gambara Pisani, the
sister-in-law of the new procurator.
2. [Caminer's note.] The author of this sonnet is twelve years of age.
3. [Caminer's note.] Cornelia, illustrious Roman lady, daughter of Scipio Africanus and wife of
Consul Sempronius Gracchus, whose only care was to raise her own sons well, so as to instill in
their tender hearts all that could render them fit to serve the fatherland well.

2. POEM FOR ALBERTO FORTIS ON THEIR FRIENDSHIP
(11 OCTOBER 1768)[4]

Will this missive find you or not?
Perhaps in vain I must make this effort?
So much have I written thus far, that how I can move
This hand of mine I know not, nor what I say:
And yet I want to give you another proof,
That I am most worthy of your friendship,
That if you like to spout madness,
My wishes are no different.

Having the same taste is one thing
That renders friendship more constant:
It is true that I do not have your dose,
And that I lack many things;
But yet I try in verse and in prose
To follow always in your footsteps:
Already there is the will: I hope that one day
I will not disgrace my great teacher.

Then, to begin (we already understand
That everything I am writing is madness)
Know, friend, that I would fain have you near,
And far from you I live poorly:
At all hours I look for you, I call you;
Sighing, I wait for your arrival;
I tremble and suffer for a missive from you,
And I nearly faint away from the pain.

I shed tears over your memories, woe is me!
And I nearly scold anyone who takes you from me;
Of some beautiful person *passing by*
I silently ask *where is your wife:*
My mind, bereft of great common sense
Goes to the threshold of the judgment I do have;

---

4. *Per le faustissime nozze del Conte Pietro Dalle-Ore colla Marchesa Giulia Buzzaccarini* (For the most propitious wedding of Count Pietro Dalle-Ore with the marquise Giulia Buzzaccarini) (Padova: Cartallier e Sicca, 1839). Caminer undoubtedly did not intend for this poem to be published, having written it solely for her friend and mentor, the naturalist Alberto Fortis.

I would weep, I would cry out . . . but then I think
That there are others, if you are not here.

Here is a note: *Dear Mademoiselle,*
We poor Gazettes remind you that
More than one person emptied his purse
To read our little pieces of news:
Madness, we do not deny it, is well and good,
But it does not address us;
And all those who will not have us
Will send you madness, and your friend to the devil.

What do you make of this? And if the devil accepts,
Whatever will become of you? What will become of me?
And she is still among us; but what of sweet madness,
Our delightful common mother?
The wretched creature would remain in nothingness
Nor would there be any further memory of us!
Who will testify to our exploits,
If no authentic witness is left?

Oh! Let us make an effort worthy of ourselves:
May beautiful virtue crown our merits;
Let each of us dominate our own feelings,
And let us not obscure the splendor of so many ornaments.
I will cease writing: you cease
Lending me your noble ears:
Sing the required praises to my talents,
And to Madam a thousand compliments.

3. LETTER TO LAZZARO SPALLANZANI[5]

Venice, [2?] January 1769

Sir,

Although I am not able to read and appreciate the observations and discoveries of such a celebrated natural philosopher as yourself, because, despite myself, I lack the necessary knowledge, I do not consider myself exempt
from thanking you a thousand times over. The gift of one of your works is no

---

5. This letter is located at the Biblioteca Estense di Modena (hereafter BEM), Autografateca
Campori, Carte Paradisi.

less dear and honorable to me.[6] You are too great, sir; a sign of kindness from you is truly something flattering. You may be sure that I am very appreciative of this, although I blush a little knowing well my small merit.

I would very much like to offer you a present in return; but as yours is worthy of you, mine is but within my reach. What I dare to send you is two translations of two most worthy plays.[7] It is a small offering, sir, but it is all that I can give you to show you my esteem. Perhaps you will find some errors in my translations; I hope you will be so good as to accept them.

My father sends you his most humble compliments, and as for myself I am with the most sincere feeling of esteem and recognition, sir,

Your most humble and obliged servant,
Elisabetta Caminer

4. LETTER TO LAZZARO SPALLANZANI[8]

Venice, 4 February 1769

Sir,

I welcome the opportunity to write to you again as I must send you the short article by Schoeffer. Mr. Fortis's absence forces me to take the liberty of opening his letter, something I occasionally do. He will not have it in time to respond to your letter by this post, but I am very happy to be able to obey you, exactly as he would.

The goodwill which you display toward me and toward the trifling productions of my mind show that you are as courteous as you are knowledgeable. But you will be remiss if you continue in this manner. I know myself well enough, sir, and I am much put out by the fact that my situation will not permit me to aspire to the exercise of reason. I will have to limit myself to translation, or, at the most, to writing bits of poetry. The sciences, for which I might have some aptitude, will be forbidden to me forever. I shall not take the liberty that you grant to Mr. Fortis to include the *Extract* of Mr. Needham's reveries in the periodical currently being printed.[9] It seems to me that it would be necessary to make some small changes in order not to expose Mr.

---

6. Spallanzani had probably sent Caminer a copy of his *Saggio di osservazioni microscopiche* (1765).

7. Caminer is referring to her translations of two French dramas by Bernard Joseph Saurin and François Thomas Marie Baculard d'Arnaud, respectively, which she published in 1769: *Beverlei: Tragedia Urbana* (Beverley: An urban tragedy) (Venezia: 1769); and *Eufemia, ovvero il Trionfo della religione* (Euphemia; or, The triumph of religion) (Venezia: Colombani, 1769).

8. This letter is located at the BEM, Autografateca Campori, Carte Paradisi.

9. Caminer was writing to Spallanzani about the delicate issues involved in publishing a scathing review of John Turbeville Needham's critical version (in French; Paris, 1769) of Spallanzani's own *Saggio di osservazioni microscopiche* (1765) in the forthcoming issue of the *Europa letter-*

Bonnet, who would perhaps not want to break with a man *that he esteems and loves* despite his irrationalities and *his occult qualities.*[10] Without that [phrase] I would have translated this interesting piece and had it printed without delay.

Instead of wishing to approach a young woman without merit, pray, sir, that I might find myself in a position to devote myself to my mind, to appreciate your works as much as they deserve, and to have an incontestable right to testify that I am in effect, sir,

Your most humble and very obliged servant,

Elisabetta Caminer

The celebrated Mr. Schoeffer has just published a work entitled *First Essays on Snails, with three small engravings.*[11] These essays are dedicated to the society of patrons of the arts and commerce in London. In recognition of this dedication, the London society awarded the author a silver medal minted in his honor. Mr. Schoeffer describes eleven experiments he conducted on snails, which do not yet allow any final conclusions about the constant phenomena which occur with the mutilation of these unique animals.

5. LETTER TO GIUSEPPE GENNARI[12]

Venice, 4 October 1769

Most Illustrious, Revered, and Distinguished Sir,

Without the encouragement of Padre Fortis, who showed me some of your letters to him where you speak of me with particular good will, and without the kind expressions which fill the few lines with which you have favored me, I would not dare to ask a favor of you. Some information about the life of the late Mr. Facciolato would be very useful for my periodical. If you might be so generous as to favor me with some, and also anything you consider relevant about Mr. Brazuolo,[13] I would add the most sincere gratitude to the true and well-founded esteem that I harbor for you.

---

aria (March 1769, 33–38). For a detailed discussion of the complex debates of Lazzaro Spallanzani, Charles Bonnet, and John Turbeville Needham, see R. G. Mazzolini and S. A. Roe, *Science against the Unbelievers: The Correspondence of Bonnet and Needham, 1760–1780* (Oxford: Voltaire Foundation, 1986), esp. 7–52.

10. Caminer must be quoting from a letter or published text by Charles Bonnet.

11. Attempts to identify either Schoeffer or this publication were unsuccessful.

12. This letter is located at the Biblioteca del Seminario Vescovile di Padova (hereafter BSP), codice 620, vol. 10, carte 243 rv.

13. Both Jacopo Facciolati (1682–1769) and Paolo Brazolo Milizia (1709–69) were renowned classicists recently deceased at the time Caminer wrote this letter. The *Europa letteraria* published a eulogy of Facciolati in the October 1769 issue, 80–89.

Padre Fortis himself told me that you have honored me with one of your collections and that this evening it will be delivered to me by a certain Mr. Rizzi; therefore, I thank you a thousand times over in advance.

Please excuse the inconvenience that I cause you, and do not spare me when you know that I may be in a position to serve you. I pray that you offer my most sincere compliments to your learned circle of friends, and particularly to the countess Capodilista, my respectable and very dear friend, and to the learned and kind Madame Medici, whom I esteem infinitely though I have not met her.[14]

It is my infinite desire that you believe—and to do so justly, that you put to the test—her who testifies that she is with the most respectful esteem,

Your very humble and very obliged servant,
Elisabetta Caminer

6. POEM FOR A FRIEND ON LOVE'S DISILLUSIONMENTS (OCTOBER 1770)[15]

Tell me then, what do you mean
By writing certain things . . . certain things? . . .
By my faith, you are getting caught in the net.

And no comments or glosses are needed
To understand what you want to say
With those witty phrases of yours.

But if you did not want me to complete
My response in four lines at the most,
You would have been careful not to contradict yourself.

You offer me quite a pretty proposal!
That I *amuse myself*, that I *look to love*,
Even though I am hardly disposed to it,

14. Francesca Maria Capodilista (Alberto Fortis's mother) and Maria Medici were part of Gennari's circle of literary friends in Padua. Maria Medici (b. 1740) belonged to the Arcadian Academy with the name Nisa Antenorea. She was also known as Nisa Euganea.

15. This poem was published posthumously in the collection of poetry entitled *Per le faustissime nozze del Conte Pietro Dalle-Ore colla Marchesa Giulia Buzzaccarini.* As with the previous poem for Alberto Fortis, Caminer probably did not intend for this poem to be published, having written it solely for her friend Andrea Giulio Giuseppe Corner (b. 1727). Caminer may have met Corner through her father, since both men were impresarios at the S. Moisè Theater.

That I lend an ear to *more than one lover,*
And other similar nonsense
That perhaps your good humor suggested to you.

But then when I do neither these nor the others
You call my thinking *wise* and *honest,*
Although wary of beautiful things.

By my faith, a fine mode of persuasion this is!
If *error,* if *prejudice* is my custom,
Why *respect,* and not disdain do I inspire?

Eh, let us not fool ourselves!
Pure truth has its dwelling in our hearts,
And of dislodging it there is no hope.

Nor will it avail us to become angry with her
Or to keep her under lock and key;
For she will emerge in spite of us.

Although it may be a happy and fine counsel,
I'll bet that you do not approve of it,
And that you bring it up to me only to tease.

But oh! Do not speak to me of loving,
Whether in a wicked or good manner, not even in jest;
For I have lived enough among the damned souls,

And now I am enjoying purgatory as best I can.[16]

7. LETTER TO GIUSEPPE PELLI BENCIVENNI[17]

Venice, 20 October 1770

Sir,

Although the kindness with which you spoke about one of my translations in your *Novelle letterarie* obliges me to thank you—and I do so sincerely—I confess that this is not the only motive for which I am taking the liberty of writing to you, since I know that if one does not know someone, one speaks

16. This may be an oblique reference to Caminer's disillusionment at the outcome of her courtship with Francesco Albergati. See section 2 of "Volume Editor's Introduction."

17. This and all of Caminer's letters to Giuseppe Pelli are located at the Archivio di Stato di Firenze (hereafter ASF), Carteggi Pelli Bencivenni. This letter is contained in fascio 15 of the collection.

impartially about that person, relating what one's own honest soul tells one, and does not require thanks.[18] The civil and equally honest and courteous manner in which you spoke about me arouses in me an impartial esteem for you. Nor because prejudice would have women confined within unreasonable limits can I stop myself from assuring you of this and from begging you for a favor that you must absolutely grant me. I detest brutes and disdain barbarous satires and criticism, as much as I appreciate honest people and esteem civil and reasonable criticism. I use these as instruction, since a nearly innate inclination, I would say, drives me to make studying my only occupation. You found in my translation various *blemishes* to which, you say, one could have *alerted me in a friendly manner.*[19] I esteem you for this way of thinking, and I beg you to put into practice what you think, by *alerting me in a friendly manner* to my errors, so that I might avoid them in the future. This is the kind of docility that just criticism finds in me; I do not expect to be praised for this docility at all, but to oblige you not to disappoint it.

The abbé Perini, a good friend of my whole family and of mine, read me a portion of a letter of yours regarding my father. He would thank you if he were not away from the city [Venice], but I do it doubly, that is, for him and for myself.

Do not be amazed at this frankness of mine. I am not ashamed of it at all: and I would be wrong if I were. If I may be of service to you in any way, this same frankness of mine assures you that I will be pleased to do so, and that I am, sir,

> Your most devoted and obliged servant,
> Elisabetta Caminer

18. Caminer is thanking the Florentine journalist Pelli for having published a defense of her in his periodical, the *Novelle letterarie* (*Literary News*), earlier that month (12 October 1770). Pelli had written in response to a sustained—and sexually slanderous—attack against Caminer launched by Venetian journalist Cristoforo Venier two months earlier. Pelli's decision to defend Caminer was crucial at this early stage in her career, and this letter reveals that it occasioned the beginning of their correspondence. For the polemic with Venier and Pelli's role in defending Caminer, see section 2 of "Volume Editor's Introduction"; and Catherine M. Sama, "Becoming Visible: A Biography of Elisabetta Caminer Turra (1751–1796) during Her Formative Years," *Studi veneziani*, n.s., 43 (2002): 349–88.

19. Caminer is quoting from Pelli's published defense of her. Pelli had defended Caminer's translation, *L'onesto colpevole o sia l'Amore filiale: Dramma in cinque atti in prosa di Charles Georges Fenouillot de Falbaire de Quincey* (The honest criminal; or, Filial love) (Venezia: Fenzo, 1770), against Venier's scathing criticisms. After noting the successful performance of Caminer's translation in Florence, Pelli wrote: "A periodical found in it [her translation] some things to criticize, but it expressed itself in a way that makes one believe it was writing against this virtuous and honest girl not with the goal of instructing her, but with some other intention. We are not saying that her version [of the play] is without blemishes, rather [we are saying] that she did not deserve to be ill treated, that a decent man must pardon a girl for small errors, and that she could have been alerted in a friendly way instead of in the public eye" (*Novelle letterarie*, 20 October 1770, 651).

8. LETTER TO GIUSEPPE PELLI BENCIVENNI[20]

Venice, 17 November 1770

Sir,

I believe I would be committing an injustice to myself more than to you if, not following your frank and sincere expression, I showed myself to be a follower of that courtier's prejudice which I abhor, and to which, nevertheless, at times I cannot avoid acquiescing. You know that holding oneself above certain common prejudices is not always permitted to my sex, and almost never to my condition, so before declaring one's disdain for such things, it is necessary to discover what people think of them. The civil criticism that you made in your *Novelle*[21] about my translation was worthy of an honest man; the particular instructions that you were gracious enough to give me are worthy of a friend who from now on can claim my gratitude, and my friendship. You will surely not hold this friendship in disdain when one day I might be able to give you proof that I know it and feel it. I will be cautious from now on to avoid repeating the same linguistic errors that you have pointed out to me; I may make other, bigger errors in other equally small productions, especially in the periodical which you rightly call incorrect. But you know my style, and although I do not want you to take the trouble to point out all my shortcomings in regard to language, since it would be too laborious for you, still I trust in your friendship enough not to fear that you will keep silent about something which could by chance hurt me a great deal.

I will tell the abbé Perini all that you ask as soon as I see him. My father thanks you and sends you a thousand compliments. I do not send you any, so when I assure you that you can count on my friendship and that when you want to employ it in something that pleases you, you will give me to understand in the best way possible that you do not disdain that I am, kindest sir,

Your obliged servant and sincere friend,
Elisabetta Caminer

9. LETTER TO GIUSEPPE GENNARI[22]

Venice, 17 November 1770

Most Esteemed Friend,

It is with the greatest pleasure that I keep my word to you about the play *Antiope*. Venetians are extremely tolerant, and yet they were not enough so to

---

20. This letter is located at the ASF, Carteggi Pelli Bencivenni, fascio 15.

21. Pelli's *Novelle letterarie*. See "Making of a Woman," text 7.

22. This letter is located at the BSP, codice 620, vol. 13, carte 69 rv.

refrain from booing it. I was not at the theater, and I am glad of it; but my father was there, and he gave me this unpleasant news. I assure you, my most esteemed friend, that I feel terrible for the author. Even if he can maintain some kind of philosophical distance, he will not, I am sure, remain unaffected by this. The actors are complaining because they spent an immense sum in order to please him, and they rehearsed the play to the point of exhaustion; but in spite of the noble scenery and the excellent manner in which it was performed, it was a barbarous flop. Despite the negative reaction, they continue to perform it, come what may, but tomorrow they will throw it out with the wastepaper.

There, you are served, though in a way that does not correspond to my desire.

Preserve your friendship for me, make use of mine for you, send my greetings to your friends and believe me always

Your sincere friend,

Elisabetta Caminer

10. LETTER TO GIUSEPPE GENNARI[23]

Venice, 24 November 1770

Please consider me excused if I have not responded before now to your letter. You could not imagine how many annoyances, how many new encumbrances have prevented me from it. Here is an account of the tragedy [*Antiope*] for you from my father; from it better than from him or from me you will be able to judge for yourself when you read it.

I, too, am awaiting my boos; it is true that they will not belong entirely to me when *The Deserter*[24] and *The Two Friends*[25] are judged to deserve them, since, like an ambassador, a translator does not carry blame; but my choice of these plays might earn me my own portion.

---

23. This letter is located at the BSP, codice 620, vol. 13, carte 71.

24. Caminer published her translation of this play (*Le déserteur*) by Louis-Sébastien Mercier twice: in 1771 as a single publication (*Il disertore: Dramma in cinque atti in prosa di Louis-Sébastien Mercier* [Venezia: Colombani, 1771]) and again in 1772 in the first volume of her *Composizioni teatrali moderne tradotte da Elisabetta Caminer* (Modern theatrical compositions in translation) (Venezia: Savioni, ma si vende da Colombani, 1772). Her version of the play was performed in Venice during the carnival season of 1771.

25. Caminer published her transation of this play (*Les deux amis*) by Pierre-Augustin Caron de Beaumarchais (1732–99) in volume 3 of her *Composizioni teatrali moderne tradotte* (1772). Her version of the play—*I due amici ovvero il Negoziante di Lione*—was performed at the S. Angelo Theater during the carnival season of 1772.

I beg you to give my greetings to all your friends, especially to Madame Medici and to the amiable Madame Natalina Caldani.[26] Do not spare me in anything when I may serve you, and believe me forever

> Your most sincere friend,
> Elisabetta Caminer

11. LETTER TO GIUSEPPE PELLI BENCIVENNI[27]

Venice, 1 December 1770

Sir,

You can not give me a more precious gift than the promise of alerting me, however many times the occasion calls for it, to the errors that I might make, and of the best ways in which I could apply myself to my writing. I am at an age and in a situation that do not allow me to hope for mediocre knowledge, to say nothing of great learning, and yet I am full of desire to cultivate my mind. This is, if not the only, at least the most useful and constant inner disposition to which I have abandoned myself with joy. Therefore, think how disagreeable I find any obstacle to the fulfillment of your friendly intentions on my behalf. Insist as best you can, however, that I take advantage of them, and in the meantime accept my thanks for how much you would do for my periodical and for me. What can I possibly say, esteemed friend, in response to the question you ask, if I would like it if you directed some letters to me in the *Toelette*,[28] except that you do me too great an honor believing that I merit having my name mentioned there, especially by you? Whenever you wish, I will consider myself ever in debt to your kindness. But do tell me, I pray, what is the meaning of this *I will not do anything that might displease your Friends?*[29]

The same liberty with which you urge me to call upon you serves as a

---

26. Natalina Caldani was the wife of Leopoldo Marc'Antonio Caldani (1725–1813), a professor of anatomy and medicine at the University of Padua and part of Gennari's circle of friends. On Medici, see note 14 above.

27. This letter is located in the ASF, Carteggi Pelli Bencivenni, fascio 15.

28. Between 1771 and 1772 Giuseppe Pelli published a periodical entitled *Toelette o sia Raccolta galante di prose e versi toscani dedicata alle dame italiane* (Toilette; or, Gallant collection of Tuscan prose and verse dedicated to Italian ladies) (Firenze: si vende in Allegrini, Pisoni e Compagnia).

29. Caminer is quoting from Pelli's previous letter to her. Perhaps he had expressed concern that exuberant praise from him might arouse jealousy in some of Caminer's circle of colleagues and protectors (i.e., Giulio Perini, Francesco Albergati, Alberto Fortis, and her father, Domenico Caminer). See "Making of a Woman," text 12.

rule for you whenever you consider me able to make you understand that I
am truly

> Your very devoted servant and friend,
> [No signature]

P.S. My father sends his greetings. I will say hello to the abbé Perini when I
see him.

12. LETTER TO GIUSEPPE PELLI BENCIVENNI[30]

Venice, 15 December 1770
Sir,

    If you find expressed in my letters the sincerity that decorates my soul, I
find in yours, in addition to that [sincerity] which adorns you, the sincere
friendship you have for me; therefore, you may surmise whether I dutifully
return it to you in kind, and whether your letters are pleasing to me. Conserve that good disposition in which you find yourself in regard to me, and
believe as well that my very grateful heart wishes to have you share that disposition to please you in which I find myself. It consoles me to hear that my
latest translations seem less defective to you than the others, since the desire
I hold to become at least adequate makes me look with pleasure upon my
small advancements. You may be sure, my friend, that I will not desist from
my diligence, and that your encouragement will render me more attached to
you. You are correct about the errors with which the printing of the journal
is filled; I will always try to rid the final version of all errors: but if you knew!
I correct the drafts twice and as best I can, but in vain do I admonish the printers to execute my corrections and orders. I thank you with all my heart for
the honor that you want to offer me by addressing to me something you write
for the *Toelette*, which I will read with infinite pleasure. Your explanation of the
sentence I asked you about[31] could make me prideful, but I am discreet. I saw
in the fifth volume of this *Toelette* a dedication to a Miss E . . . C . . .[32] Who is
she? Your kind offers to favor me on occasion are obliging, and I promise you
with all the freedom of friendship that I will make use of them when neces-

---

30. This letter is located in the ASF, Carteggi Pelli Bencivenni, fascio 15.
31. See "Making of a Woman," text 11.
32. Pelli dedicated the fifth *tomo* of the *Toelette* to Caminer, identifying her only with the initials "E.C."

sary. As for myself, I do not make you any [offers], because you must well know the disposition of her who sincerely testifies herself to be, sir,

> Your very devoted, very obliged servant and good friend,
> Elisabetta Caminer

13. LETTER TO GIUSEPPE PELLI BENCIVENNI[33]

> Venice, 5 January 1771

I ask a thousand pardons of you if I, too, am forced to make use of another hand to write you; burdened on a Saturday with a great number of things to do, and given the undeniable need to go to the theater, it is necessary for me to dictate this letter to someone else while I am getting dressed. I thank you wholeheartedly for your letter, which is all the more precious to me in that it assures me once again of your friendship.

I will ask the abbé Perini for news of Madame Eleonora Cappelli, because all people of merit interest me, but you seem a little malicious with your *[Perini], who will revere her such as his temperament allows.*[34] My knowledge of his temperament does not in my opinion justify such a comment, but if I am to believe you, I do not know him well at all. But it is enough for me though to know that, apart from these shenanigans, he is a respectable man, and one who has great friendship for me.

You do not wish me a happy new year, and the reason you give me makes me very happy. I, who like you am an enemy of useless repetitions, imitate you; nor in this time of vow making do I wish for myself an opportunity to do something to favor you again, because you know that I am always and sincerely at your disposal. To give you proof of this I make liberal use of your kind expressions, and I pray that you will give me an exact account of the impression that the two comedies—one entitled *The Italian in Lapland,*[35] the other *The Sofa*[36]—make there [in Florence]; and I pray that you add to that your opinion of them. Conserve for me your kind sentiments, imitate me in my frank friendship, and always believe I am she who with profound esteem and high regard testifies to being, sir,

> Your very devoted and very obliged servant, and friend,
> Elisabetta Caminer

---

33. This letter is located in the ASF, Carteggi Pelli Bencivenni, fascio 16.

34. Caminer is quoting from Pelli's previous letter to her.

35. Efforts to locate information about this play have proved unsuccessful.

36. Caminer reviewed Francesco Albergati's comedy *Il Sofà* (Venezia: Luigi Pavini, 1770) in the November 1770 issue of the *Europa letteraria*, 79–81.

14. LETTER TO GIUSEPPE PELLI BENCIVENNI[37]

Venice, 19 January 1771

Sir,

I was not expecting anything less than courteous apologies from you, but know that I do not want so many, because I do not even grant myself so many. You grant me even the time for adorning myself; but in order to [have time to] write to my friends, I do not make it a necessity for myself. Whether I consider myself beautiful or ugly, if ugly, in vain would I hope to make up for nature's defects with art; if I am not ugly at all, I am pleased because even this can be an advantage, but I do not care about becoming less so. Do not think, however, that I have one of those philosophies that I call rude. No, one must live and embrace neatness, but not sacrifice to this the time owed to friendship.

As for the enigmas about the abbé Perini, I communicated the point of your letter to him, and I saw him laugh; I do not know what this laugh means. That he has esteem and friendship for me, I believe, because he has given me unequivocal proof of this: but in terms of what you tell me, that he keeps his distance from me because he esteems me too highly, you can spare me the jest.[38]

I will read with infinite pleasure the letter in the first volume of the *Toelette* with which you want to favor me, and I thank you again for it in advance; I have not yet received the sixth, so I cannot give you the justice you deserve for your letter.[39]

I know very well what *The Sofa*[40] is and I know that it will not be performed there [in Florence] until autumn; but *The Italian in Lapland* is probably being performed even now, and I pray that you will be able to tell me how that comedy is received, given however its genre, which I believe one can call shapeless. The other evening the periodical was mailed to you. Keep your friendship for me, and count on my [. . .][41] that I am always

Your very obliged servant and true friend,

Elisabetta Caminer

37. This letter is located in the ASF, Carteggi Pelli Bencivenni, fascio 16.

38. See "Making of a Woman," text 13. In fact, Perini was enamored of Caminer. See section 2 of "Volume Editor's Introduction."

39. This reference to "the sixth" volume is unclear. Pelli published two letters to Caminer in the seventh (1770) and twelfth (1771) *tomi* of the *Toelette*. The letters are essentially his discourses on the status of "the fair sex" in society. In the latter epistle, Pelli implores Caminer to "continue belying that women are inferior to men. Follow the path of virtue, make yourself an even greater name, and may this letter be an eternal document of my admiration and my esteem for you, not because you are just female, but because you are a singular female" (*Toelette* 12 [1771]: viii–ix).

40. Francesco Albergati's play, which Caminer reviewed in the *Europa letteraria* (November 1770).

41. Illegible word.

15. LETTER TO GIUSEPPE PELLI BENCIVENNI[42]

Venice, 2 February 1771

Sir,

A thousand annoyances kept me from writing to you last week, and I am writing to you with excessive haste in this letter as well. I received your beautiful letter, which I find very just, well written, and worthy of everyone's praises, if the praises that you direct at me be excluded, which, speaking frankly to one another, I have scarcely earned.[43] I thank you for them, though, my laudable friend, and I assure you that I will try to give you proof of my gratitude and my deference to your advice by striving to render myself worthy of such desirable praises. At least you treat our poor sex fairly! Yes, this fairness of yours has the effect of increasing my friendship for you. I gave your message to my father; he thanks you, and he sends you a thousand greetings. I know that you will appreciate this frank manner devoid of compliments. Preserve for me your honorable friendship, believe that I am very fond of you, write to me and keep me always as

Your very obliged and very cordial friend,
Elisabetta Caminer

16. LETTER TO GIUSEPPE PELLI BENCIVENNI[44]

Venice, 9 February 1771

Sir,

The news which you have given me about *The Italian in Lapland* is exactly that which I expected, and I congratulate myself on having been an astrologer.[45] You are mistaken, my good friend: the magic, the ghosts, the machines that are seen in this play were not added but introduced by the author [himself], whom I know, and who received a direct order to introduce them into the play by this impresario Campigli. He laughed, we laughed together at those insufferable madnesses, but it must be said that they are necessary for

42. This letter is located in the ASF, Carteggi Pelli Bencivenni, fascio 16.

43. This refers to one of the two letters that Pelli addressed to Caminer and published in his periodical, the *Toelette*. In *tomo* 5, Pelli had written: "The image of your true character that you have presented with your letters justifies that opinion of you which I had conceived from reading your translations and your writing for the journal entitled *Europa letteraria*. . . and [from] the accurate information I received about your amiable person from various friends. In essence, everything makes me esteem you sincerely and makes me regard you as one of those rare maidens who, overcoming their sex, cover a virile mind beneath a flattering female exterior."

44. This letter is located in the ASF, Carteggi Pelli Bencivenni, fascio 16.

45. Caminer prides herself on being an "astrologer" of public opinion.

the Florentine people. I do not know what possessed the Truffaldino of the Locomero Street troupe to write to Venice that that crazy comedy was mine.[46] May the heavens protect me from presenting a theatrical piece of my own without mature reflection, and from beginning with a shapeless comedy! I will choose another genre if by chance I set out to *venture*[47] to write something for the theater.

My father, who sends you a thousand compliments, charges me with telling you that he has not yet found the first volume, but he is looking for it and he hopes to serve you.

You are very curious with your surprise at my fashion for thinking about *curls* in terms of *distant friends!*[48] If you should view it as a fault, it would suffice to tell you in my defense that in thinking and acting like this I do not have the least merit, since I am made in such a way that curls have never made much of an impression on me, and friendship has made very much of an impression upon my heart.

I hope you will have ascertained from my last letter how much I like your letter, and how I am abashed by it. Do not amuse yourself by embarassing me if you do not want to impose obligation and circumspection upon my friendship, and check the exuberance with which I assure you I am

Your very devoted servant and very affectionate friend,
Elisabetta Caminer

17. LETTER TO GIUSEPPE PELLI BENCIVENNI[49]

Venice, 2 March 1771

Sir,

I believe I cannot better prove to you how sensitive I am to the goodness and the friendship with which you honor me than by providing you with the opportunity to give me another sign of it, and by procuring a pleasure for yourself as well. The person who will present you with this letter is Mr. de Blackford,[50] a German, a man full of merit and knowledge, whose talents have

---

46. This is another indication that Caminer might have written original theatrical works, although none have been found to date. See also "Making of a Woman," texts 32 and 33.

47. Caminer may have been quoting here from the person who had identified the comedy as hers.

48. Caminer is quoting from their previous letters. See "Making of a Woman," text 14.

49. This letter is located in the ASF, Carteggi Pelli Bencivenni, fascio 16.

50. Dominick de Blackford was an erudite man of letters, possibly from German-speaking Lorraine. He published novels and books describing his travels to Russia and to North America.

been made known by his works, and who, making a tour of Italy, was kind enough to grant my father as well as myself the honor of meeting him. Since he is coming to Florence to stay for some months, I believe I cannot present him to anyone better than yourself, whose politeness equals the talent and the reputation you have gained among literary people. I hope that you would enjoy procuring for him some acquaintances as desirable as your own, in order to make his stay in this city agreeable. Know that I would always bear in mind this pleasure which you would have granted me, and which will assuredly be a pleasure for you as well. I have the honor to be with the most respectful sentiments, sir,

> Your very humble and very obliged servant and friend,
> Elisabetta Caminer

P.S. My father thanks you for your obliging letter, and he will see that you have the volume you want in the next post.

18. LETTER TO GIUSEPPE PELLI BENCIVENNI[51]

Venice, 27 July 1771

Sir,

I do not have adequate words to express my gratitude for the beautiful letter you addressed to me in the *Toelette*; in any case, though, I thank you to the best of my ability, and one day I desire to earn the honor you are doing me. All women must be grateful for your just reflections, for the fairness with which you treat them. I then, who am chosen by you to communicate this, must certainly be one hundred times more obliged to you. My father thanks you for your letter, and he prays that you forgive him if he has not written to you because of his many occupations; but he does testify through me that he is very much obliged for Milord's[52] extract. This evening I will mail the periodicals to Allegrini;[53] in your packet you will find the letter of which I spoke

---

Domenico Caminer reviewed Blackford's *Essai sur la litterature Russe* (Livorno, 1771) and his *Précis de l'état actuel del colonies angloises dans l'Amérique Septentrionale* (Milan: Chez les Freres Reycends, 1771) in the *Europa letteraria* (August 1771, 72–76, and November 1771, 101, respectively). Domenico described Blackford a "good and learned friend," who wrote beautifully in French "despite the fact that it [was] not his native language" (*Europa letteraria*, August 1771, 76).

51. This letter is located in the ASF, Carteggi Pelli Bencivenni, fascio 16.

52. This may be a reference to Milord Cowper, a subscriber in Florence to Caminer's *Opere del Signor Salomone Gesnero tradotte con le due novelle morali de Signor D*** [Diderot] (Vicenza: Turra, 1781).

53. Pietro Allegrini was a bookseller who sold the *Europa letteraria* in Florence.

to you in my last [letter]. I am very eager to serve you in matters of greater importance, and in the meantime I pray that you believe I am with sincere esteem and cordiality, sir,

Your very devoted very obliged servant and true friend,

Elisabetta Caminer

19. LETTER TO GIUSEPPE GENNARI[54]

Venice, 17 August 1771

Most Esteemed Friend,

Do not worry about your extract; if dealing with scoundrels is of any use, I will certainly be able to prevent any errors.[55] Upon my faith, Padre Ringhieri[56] is right to rush into press again; I think my father will steal time away from his other occupations if he needs to, in order bring him justice. So my Lady Cattina is writing a little poem for the young abbé Beccalossi![57] Very

54. This letter is located at the BSP, codice 620, vol. 13, carta 106.

55. My interpretation of this rather oblique sentence is that Caminer is reassuring Gennari that since she already has experience as an editor in dealing with incapable printers, she knows what she needs to do in order to make absolutely sure that his extract will be printed without any errors. See "Making of a Woman," text 12. In his letter of 15 August 1771 Gennari had written: "I beg you to be careful with the correction of my extract, because with so many epochs it is easy to make errors in the numbers or in other areas, as I have seen in previous issues of the periodical. And this even more so, since I would be that much less worthy of pardon, if, in wanting to correct Mr. de la L.'s absurdities [about Padua], I fell into similar or worse errors." Gennari was referring to Joseph Jérôme de Lalande's very popular travel book *Voyage d'un français en Italie, fait dans les années 1765 et 1766* (Voyage of a Frenchman in Italy during 1765 and 1766) (Paris: Yverdon, 1769). In 1770 the Caminers published a series of reviews of de Lalande's multivolume work. Gennari provided them with the review of volume 8 of *Voyage* for the August issue (55–72), because it contained three chapters dedicated to his native city of Padua.

56. Francesco Ulisse Ringhieri da Imola (1721–87) was a theatrical poet whose works were reviewed in the *Europa letteraria.* I believe Caminer's comment here is a reference to a letter Ringhieri published in 1771 (*Lettera del Conte Rinieri Madassi ad un Cavaliere Napoletano*), in which he claimed that Cesare Beccaria planned to write a book on legislation. The *Europa letteraria* (September 1771, 47) condemned the letter as an imposture.

57. Catterina Ansaldi Gualtieri Boschi was a noblewoman from Messina and a member of the Accademia degli Agiati di Rovereto (an academy to which Caminer would later be admitted) and the Accademia de' Risorti di Capo d'Istria. The collection of poetry for the Brescian abbé Beccalossi was entitled *Poetici componimenti presentati all'Ill. S. Ab. Giuseppe Beccalossi per la Laurea da esso in ambe le Leggi riportata nel S. Coll. di Padova* (Padova: Conzatti, 1771). Caminer publicized the collection of poetry in the September 1771 issue of the *Europa letteraria* (99). For more on this collection, see note 69. Caminer continued to promote Boschi's reputation in the pages of her periodical: in 1777 she published a long poem by Boschi as proof that women were "no less capable of sound thinking than men." She chastised Boschi for her excessive modesty and for the

well; he will be able to boast proudly, and she will prove her friendship to him. I have no doubt that her verses should be good. But you are quite elegant, my great friend, with this preeminence that you grant me among the Corinnas of our day![58] As if one did not know oneself! In order for me to merit your praises, it would be opportune for you to actually evaluate me.[59] I know nothing sure about P. F. [Padre Fortis]; here, too, we heard strange discourses, which God forbid are true! But the prevailing voice says he is in Spalatro and that he will be in Venice shortly.[60] This is what some of his friends claim as well. The abbé Sibiliato[61] was here once again to favor me with a visit, but at the time I was at dinner with a lady. I hope, though, that before he leaves he will find a way to grant me the pleasure of seeing him, and that I will be able to tell him about your request. Send a thousand greetings to our great and learned Doctor Caldani,[62] to the amiable Madame Natalina, to the kind Patriarchi[63] and accept the assurances of my father and myself,

> Your most cordial servant and friend,
> Elisabetta Caminer

P.S. Here Professor Turinese claims only to have moved to a different house.

---

the way she did not promote herself enough, and she encouraged her to undertake the other "philosophical projects" which she had already begun thinking about, in order that Caminer might publish them in the periodical. See *Giornale enciclopedico*, May 1777, 81–86, esp. 81.

58. Gennari had written on 15 August 1771: "In truth I greatly rejoice at seeing that the gentle sex is applying itself to occupations other than those of the mirror and the toilette, and that every day the number of Corinnas grows, among whom you are the finest."

59. In other words, in order to for her to deserve Gennari's praises it would be necessary for him to truly consider what she has accomplished rather than just praise her.

60. The "strange discourses" Caminer is referring to are unclear. This was the year in which Fortis's break with the Augustinian order was officially recognized. As for his whereabouts, he had already returned from his first expedition to Dalmatia to the islands of Cres and Losinj (also known as Cherso and Osero). The inventory of his correspondence indicates that he was in Rome in June 1771 and back in Venice in September.

61. Clemente Sibiliato (1719–95) was professor of letters between 1760 and 1795 at the University of Padua.

62. On Leopoldo and Natalina Caldani see "Making of a Woman," text 10.

63. Gasparo Patriarchi (1709–80), a Paduan abbé of Florentine origin, was the author of various works in prose and poetry, a translator from the French, and the editor of a manual of rhetoric. Patriarchi collaborated with Gennari on editing the *Annales sive historia patavina ecclesiastica et prophana* of Giovanni Brunacci (1711–72) after the latter's death. Patriarchi was renowned for his *Vocabolario veneziano e padovano co' termini e modi corrispondenti toscani* (Padova: Conzattti, 1775).

20. LETTER TO GIUSEPPE GENNARI[64]

Venice, 5 September 1771

Most Esteemed Friend,

It would be useless for me to make excuses for my delay in responding to you: the package that accompanies this letter will show you that I wanted to serve you sooner than taking up your time with discourses would do. Not even one dissertation with the three engravings remains, thus only with great effort did my father obtain the one I am sending you. The origin of the Chinese descending from the Egyptians is so well confirmed that if we do not concede the proofs that exist, we can despair of ever knowing the truth. In the Chou-King,[65] a sacred Chinese book, Mr. de Guignes[66] speaks of it a lot, and he will speak of it a lot more in a work that he is now writing on this subject. After reading an essay of his on the ways to learn to read and understand Egyptian hieroglyphics, certain learned Chinese who traveled to France confessed that the perfect similarity between ancient Chinese characters and these hieroglyphics in particular plainly shows their origin, and they acknowledge Mr. de Guignes as the discoverer. This in fact is the greatest proof. Then in his *Universal History* Mr. Turpin[67] discovered many other proofs: for example, an infinite uniformity in the veneration of the name and the ashes of one's ancestors, in the horror of opening up cadavers, in the study of astronomy and of music, in some fundamental practices in government, etc. But you will read more about that in the next [issue of the] periodical, which will contain nothing less than the extract of the second volume of Turpin's *Universal History.* In any case the opinion is not new, and very positive things were said about it on the occasion of the question between Professor Turinese and Montagne [sic] on the Egyptian bust in the museum of His Sardinian Majesty.[68]

---

64. This letter is located at the BSP, codice 620, vol. 13, carta 109 rv.

65. *Le Chou-king, un des livres sacrés des Chinois, qui renferme les fondementsde leur ancienne hsitoire, les principes de leur gouvernement & de leur morale* (Paris: N. M. Tilliard, 1770). This is Joseph de Guignes's annotated edition in French of an ancient Chinese work (the *Shu King*) inspired by Confucian teaching. De Guignes also published *Mémoire dans lequel on prouve que les Chinois sont une colonie égyptienne* (Paris: Desaint & Saillant, 1759), which the Caminers reviewed in the *Europa letteraria*, February 1771, 48–53.

66. Josephe de Guignes (1721–1800) was a Sinologist and professor of the Siriac language at the Royal College of France.

67. François-Henri Turpin [Henriques Pangrapho, pseud.] (1709–99), *Histoire universelle imitée de l'anglois* (Paris: Bleuet, 1770–71). The *Europa letteraria*, September 1771, 31–39, published a review of volume 2 of this work (containing a history of Egypt and the peoples of Canaan), which Elisabetta signed.

68. Charles Emanuel III (1701–73).

I read Madame Boschi's verses, and I have great compassion for her. However, regarding what you attribute to my friends about the matter, I beg you not to move so quickly and to permit me to refuse your congratulations until a time when they are fully justified.[69] I ask that you give the little volumes you will find in the package to our great Caldani. Send my cordial greetings to him and to his kind consort equally, and to our other friends, and believe that I am sincerely and with all my soul

Your most cordial servant and friend,

E. Caminer

P.S. I am not responding to your queries about what is said of you in the periodical because I believe you know yourself and us well enough.[70]

21. LETTER TO GIUSEPPE PELLI BENCIVENNI[71]

Venice, 28 September 1771

Sir,

Your letter, which is for me a new proof of the friendship that you have for me, was extremely agreeable. Know, however, that I may fail to write to you because of too many necessary annoyances, but you will never, for that reason, have the right to become offended and suppose that I consider you to be *a scarcely useful and troublesome friend*. He who is a sincere friend is beneficent to me. A friend is not troublesome to me. I do not welcome other kinds of beneficences. Mr. Blackford[72] wrote to me from Milan: I will write to him at Deux-Ponts through Mr. Fontanelle, who is the author of the two gazettes.[73]

---

69. Gennari had written on on 31 August 1771: "I imagine that you will have seen Madame Boschi's tender verses along with others by her friends, and so I will say no more. But if she is right to complain because she is bereft of her beautiful young abbé, what will your Venetian friends say when you drop them barbarously, exchanging the lagoon waters [of Venice] for the Berici hills [of Vicenza]? Rather, what will Minerva say about you, when you abandon her militia to withdraw to the dewy fields of Venus? I have always loved Vicenza, but from now on I will bear her the fondest good wishes so that she will be happy and proud of you. I rejoice wholeheartedly in your every good fortune." In response to Caminer's cautious reaction to these congratulations, Gennari told her that he had heard the news from someone she had told directly. He had probably assumed that her engagement was common knowledge, but he reassured her that he would withhold his congratulations until she indicated a more appropriate time for them.

70. Gennari had complained that the Caminers had praised him too much in the *Europa letteraria*.

71. This letter is located in the ASF, Carteggi Pelli Bencivenni, fascio 16.

72. On Blackford, see "Making of a Woman," text 17.

73. Jean Gaspard Dubois-Fontanelle (1737–1812) was the editor of the *Gazette Universelle de littérature, aux Deux-Ponts* (1770–77). Caminer reviewed his play *Éricie* in the October 1768 issue of the *Europa letteraria*, 55–68. See also "Women and Society: Marriage or the Convent," text 1.

Here is the paper on medicine. I know Stratìo[?] by name. I do not know what to say about your opinion on *The Deserter*,[74] but I have the misfortune of not sharing your conviction. The conduct of that soul seems to me to be woven marvelously; although I am enamored of *Filial Love*,[75] it seems to me that there are many things besides the beautiful words [of the play]; its passion is extremely powerful, and the public of the Veneto has justified my conviction. No one in Venice remembers such a success; that drama [*The Deserter*] was repeated for twenty-three nights, and people were turned away right up until the last night because they could not fit inside the theater.[76] You could reproach the change I made in the ending by saving the deserter's life; but since I translated it and adapted it *for Venice*,[77] I would hope to justify myself: at least I will try to do so when I publish it in the edition of many of my translations that I am thinking of producing shortly. Command something of me always, and believe me

> Your very obliged servant and most cordial friend,
> E. Caminer

22. LETTER TO GIUSEPPE PELLI BENCIVENNI[78]

Venice, 19 October 1771

Sir,

I do not know what to say; we do not see eye to eye this time in judging *The Deserter*, and I am not at all inclined to assert my weak opinion over yours. However, the friendship I have for the author, the applause that the drama has generally received, and my intimate persuasion push me to respond to you so that you might see the light. The soldier, you say, did not place himself in that situation either out of a stroke of bad luck or out of excessive virtue: is it not perchance a stroke of bad luck [for a soldier] to fall under the command of a barbarous and ferocious colonel who puts his virtue to the test a thousand times and in the end causes him to forget himself for a moment?[79]

74. On this play by Mercier, see "Making of a Woman," text 22, note 79.

75. Caminer published her translation, *L'onesto colpevole o sia l'Amore filiale*, in 1769 (Venezia: Graziosi), again in 1770 (Venzia: Fenzo), and again in volume 2 of *Composizioni teatrali moderne tradotte* (1772). Caminer's translation was first performed during the carnival of 1769 at S. Salvatore Theater. The French original, *L'honnête criminel*, was published in 1767 but not performed until 1790 (at the Théatre italien).

76. Caminer's translation was peformed in Venice during the fall 1771 season.

77. Caminer's emphasis.

78. This letter is located in the ASF, Carteggi Pelli Bencivenni, fascio 16.

79. The play recounts the story of a young French soldier (Durimel) who is placed in a regiment with an abusive colonel. Eventually he flees the army. As a deserter, he is subject to the death penalty, so he leaves France and seeks refuge in a small town across the German border with a

Is it not a misfortune to find a rogue who exposes him and accuses him after he has spent seven years making reparations for his own error, if it can even be called that, with the most honest, the most virtuous, the most upright conduct? And out of what excessive virtue would you have had him place himself in that situation? The nature of his troubles excludes it. The father always speaks in the same tone, and this is appreciable, since the author sustained his character well; and the things he says are not the same, and many sound and moral maxims pass his lips, not just one. Why is it so surprising that a young, sensitive official who was [falsely] accused of turning in an unfortunate man [Durimel, the deserter] would be moved to compassion for him and take pity on the two virtuous women who adore him? Why is it surprising that he would see fit to save him [Durimel], since he knows very well that the often-cited example[80] would not be compromised by this one man's escape, and since he knows that Durimel's life was not odious to society, as is that of a thief or a murderer? The two *honored* women had not taken the deserter into their home as their patron, but as a clerk for their store; he revealed to them his real name, his native land; they took him in on a trial basis, they found him honest, and they kept him on. How often does one not take on servants about whom one cannot find precise information? Perhaps I do not comprehend all the force of your arguments, but this is certainly the way I see it.

I am extremely obliged to you for your offer to write me a letter for my little collection, and I thank you from the heart. But I would not like the world to think that I wanted to publish my own praises rather than a collection that might please the public.[81] Soon I will publish the manifesto for this collection, and I beg you, too, to find me some subscribers. Your friendship will pardon me for this trouble. The first volume will probably contain *Eufemia, Beverly, The Deserter,* and *The Interrupted Marriage.*[82]

---

widow (Madame Luzere) and her daughter (Clary), who take him in to help them tend their store. Durimel and Clary fall in love, and they are about to be married, when war erupts and Durimel's old regiment comes to the small town. He is recognized and exposed as a deserter and then sentenced to death. His father (the chevalier de Saint-Franc), long missing and presumed dead, turns out to be the very person assigned to oversee the execution. Under these emotionally charged circumstances, Durimel is put to death. Caminer changed the ending in her version by sparing the life of Durimel.

80. In other words, the deserter who is put to death serves as an example—and as a deterrent—to all potential deserters.

81. Ultimately, Caminer decided it was more politic to publish Pelli's letter in the *Europa letteraria* (June 1772, 47–50). See "Making of a Woman," text 30.

82. In fact, the first volume contains *Olindo e Sofronia, Eufemia, Disertore,* and *Matrimonio interrotto.* The last of these is Jean François Cailhava de l'Estandoux (1731–1813), *Le mariage interrompu: Comédie en trois actes, et en vers* (Paris : Merlin, 1769); translated as *Il Matrimonio interrotto: Dramma in 3 atti e in versi del Sig. Cailhava,* in Caminer, *Composizioni teatrali moderne tradotte,* vol. 1 (1772).

You owe me nothing for the paper on medicine. Command me always and believe me with sincerity

> Your very devoted very obliged servant and friend,
> E. Caminer

23. LETTER TO GIUSEPPE PELLI BENCIVENNI[83]

> Venice, 21 December 1771

Sir,

It has been a century since I have written to you, but do not blame me, since my numerous occupations were the cause of my silence. The abbé Perini is well and pays you his respects. If, however, you want more detailed news of him, write to him, and he will write to you. I have enclosed a manifesto for you;[84] in the package of the periodical that will be mailed to you next Saturday you will find some others. I pray that you take an interest in this edition by procuring subscribers for me; if you succeed in obtaining any, do favor me with their names so that I can make my calculations.

I believe it my duty to prove my friendship for you by announcing the conclusion of plans for my marriage to Doctor Turra[85] of Vicenza; the marriage will not take place, however, until the month of June.

If I may serve you, do not spare me, and believe I am eternally, sir,

> Your very obliged servant and very cordial friend,
> E. Caminer

24. LETTER TO GIUSEPPE GENNARI[86]

> Venice, 28 December 1771

Most Esteemed Friend,

I know you too well to doubt for a moment your friendship for me and the interest with which it will make you act on my behalf. I thank you wholeheartedly for your and Count Borromeo's[87] kindness, but allow me to say that

---

83. This letter is located in the ASF, Carteggi Pelli Bencivenni, fascio 16.

84. The manifesto of the first volume of her *Composizioni teatrali moderne tradotte*. A copy of this manifesto, dated December 21, 1771, is bound into the Biblioteca Bertoliana di Vicenza's copy of the *Composizioni teatrali moderne tradotte* (1772), vol. 3. It appears immediately prior to the "Dedication to Alberto Fortis," itself on pages 3–5.

85. On Antonio Turra, see section 2 of "Volume Editor's Introduction."

86. This letter is located at the BSP, codice 620, vol. 13, carta 122.

87. Anton Maria Borromeo (1724–1813), Paduan poet and dilettante man of letters whose circle of friends included Alberto Fortis, compiled and published a collection of Italian novellas

even without your name [on the list of subscribers] you would have received my volumes.[88] If, as you hope, you can procure even more subscribers for me, I will be extremely obliged to you. I thank you for your congratulations;[89] I would not be happy in my new state if it prevented me from forever maintaining an infinite friendship for you. I will do as you ask to acquire news about Morgagni, and I am very very grateful to you. It has been a long while since you have said anything of Madame Maria Medici, of our learned Nisa;[90] I hope she is well, and I beg you to pay her my respects, as I beg you to believe I am, eternally,

> Your most cordial friend,
> E. Caminer

25. PREFACE TO *COMPOSIZIONI TEATRALI MODERNE TRADOTTE (MODERN THEATRICAL COMPOSITIONS IN TRANSLATION)* (1772)[91]

All nations have their golden centuries, and in all nations this splendor unexpectedly fades, and shadows follow more or less densely according to circumstances. Our limited human comprehension does not understand why progress in the arts, the sciences, and letters suddenly comes to a standstill, or why it does not advance in proportion to the rapid growth that it usually enjoyed in the first years of its development. We are amazed by the Chinese, who, thousands of years before we were cultured, made use of the most important art of the printing press and never managed to make it easy to use by separating the individual characters.

As everyone knows, they [the Chinese] also had the harquebus,[92] they knew the properties of the magnet, and for long centuries they were profes-

---

(written by others), *Notizia de' novellieri italiani posseduti dal Conte Anton Maria Borromeo gentiluomo padovano con alcune novelle inedite* (Bassano: Remondini, 1794).

88. Caminer is thanking Gennari for procuring another subscriber to her new publication in Borromoeo, and she is assuring Gennari that she would have sent him copies of the book even if he had not become a subscriber. See "Making of a Woman," text 23.

89. Gennari had congratulated her on her engagement to Antonio Turra. See also "Making of a Woman," text 20.

90. In his next letter (7 January 1772) Gennari wrote: "In recent days your *Deserter* was performed for two evenings in this theater [i.e., in a Paduan theater], and the whole audience was very moved, as Madame Medici confirmed for me."

91. Elisabetta Caminer, "Prefazione della traduttrice," in *Composizioni teatrali moderne tradotte* (1772), 1:v–xix. Sections of this preface were published by Roberta Turchi in *Il teatro italiano* (1987) and by Angelo Colla in *Le stanze ritrovate* (1991).

92. The harquebus was an early type of portable gun, fired by a matchlock and trigger.

sors of astronomy. Yet despite this, they did not adopt mortars or cannons in wars, nor did they make use of magnetism in navigation, nor would their erudite Mandarins have been able to perfect the calendar without the aid of the Europeans, who were late to make discoveries but quick to make progress. Asia, having become our master, after the total decadence of the empire, either unexpectedly arrested midstream the course of almost every art and science, or returned to barbarism. But we who believe ourselves to be superior because of this fact,[93] what have we done with the dramatic art, one of the most useful arts for the education of the people? The commerce of the Italians, the spirit of peregrination that possessed them, the political situation in this beautiful part of Europe gave rise to and set into motion minds that in Spain, France, Germany, Poland, Russia, because of idleness and poverty, rusted away or became ferocious in the midst of their superstition and wars. Everything flourished at the same time here among us, and wealth, the arts, the sciences, and good literature settled in Italy. The most erudite men, the most industrious artisans, the most felicitous poets converged on the courts of the Carrara, della Scala, and Medici families in Florence, in Rome, and finally in Venice. Italy had pleasing comedies and regular tragedies almost before having theaters in which to perform them, even as other nations had in this genre monstrous and barbarous shows without appropriate scenery, without decency, without common sense. The Italians, who had all the necessary talents to justly appreciate and imitate ancient Greek tragic and comic writers, did not have the gift of rendering their own theatrical works moving and new. In matters of literature, the spirit of the sixteenth century was perhaps too *imitative* and servile. The tragedies of that period are more apt to inspire horror than tender pity. Those scenes that should have been full of passion were cold and languishing; the atrocity of catastrophe fell directly down upon the ill-prepared souls of the listeners and was more likely to make them break out in the cold sweat of horror than weep with commotion.[94] The dialogue in Tuscan comedies was full of finesse and Atticisms,[95] but the subjects were extremely similar to each other, always trivial, and frequently indecent. In Lombardy it was even worse. In any case, with all these defects, what remained was a sort of regularity in theatrical performances, more or less well sustained, which, truth be told, robbed the audience of the pleasure of sur-

---

93. In other words, the Chinese failure to make progress.

94. In the eighteenth century the term "commotion" was used to signify the state of being deeply moved or emotionally disquieted.

95. The term "Atticism" refers to anything typical of Attic Greek or to refined and elegant expressions.

prise but did not insult the public by taking up its time with eccentric concatenations and improbable events. This languishing propriety and the weak merit of style, which, in order to avoid bold rhetorical figures went to the opposite extreme of insufferable weariness, did not last long. Around the end of the century Tasso[96] began to take some liberties. He had a most lively imagination: from the very middle of his Jerusalem poem[97] sprang the first seeds of euphuism [*secentismo*].[98] The celebrated tragedy of *Torrismondo*[99] contains many of these; his *Aminta*,[100] as polished and harmonious as it is, conveys the turgidity that was already threatening to inundate the century. The desire to scatter posies and puns was, however, restrained by the universal timidity of imitators which had become the law of the land. But what can you do? The artificial shine of the antithesis, the boldness of the metaphors which had been sown sparingly in the works of that great man [Tasso] blinded the very individuals who had become accustomed to restraint. *Aminta* was extolled as a prodigy of the pastoral genre; *Pastor Fido*[101] followed close behind and was less elegant but more flowery. Marini,[102] a most fertile mind, enjoyed and had others enjoy the false beauties of a completely bombastic new style. He preserved vestiges of reasonableness; but after him, as the corruption became universal, there was no more good poetry in Italy for the course of a whole century, and the extravagances adopted in style spread to the structure of poems and plays. Lyric, epic, tragic, and comic poets of the seventeenth century competed to be the most extravagant in images, expressions, and architecture.

While the seeds of poetry that had been born again and had fallen again became more bastardized every day in Italy, they slowly sent down much deeper and healthier roots beyond the Alps. Almost at the same time, the great Corneille, Racine, Quinault, and Molière brought the tragedy, the drama, and the comedy to their highest perfection. Italian theaters were cluttered with extravagant monstrosities and insipid patchworks to which the name

96. Torquato Tasso (1544–95) was an epic poet of the Italian Renaissance.

97. *La Gerusalemme Liberata* (1581): Tasso's epic poem, set during the siege and liberation of Jerusalem by the crusaders in 1096–99.

98. The term "euphuism" refers to the baroque, often overblown or exaggerated style that was prevalent in seventeenth-century literature.

99. Tasso's *Re Torrismondo* (1587), a tragedy emulating Sophocles.

100. Tasso's *Aminta*, a pastoral drama first performed in 1573.

101. *Pastor Fido*, a pastoral drama by Giambattista Guarini (1538–1612), modeled on Tasso's *Aminta*, was first published in 1589.

102. Giovan Battista Marino (1569–1625) was most famous for his greatest work, *Adone* (1623), a poem of twenty cantos in octaves based on the eponymous myth in Ovid's *Metamorphoses* but written with Tasso's *Gerusalemme liberata* in mind.

Commedie dell'Arte was given. All the extravagances left in Spain by the Arabs, and grown happily there, arrived here along with the Spaniards. Contrived marvels invaded the prerogatives of the sensible comedy; the tedious monotony that had reigned for a long time was with little effort superseded by clamor, variety, and ornamentation. People no longer went to the theater to engage their minds, but only their eyes and their ears. Reason, common sense, regulation of the passions, delicacy, and the power of theatrical poetry established itself on the French stage and even now remain there. The century of Italian barbarities passed, or at least barbarities and extravagance no longer dominated our theaters absolutely and without opposition. At the beginning of this century, Lazzarini[103] revived the imitation of the Greeks. The marquis Maffei went much farther, but he wrote only one tragedy;[104] and our theaters were dedicated to translations, sometimes well and sometimes poorly done from the originals of Corneille and Racine, who had written a great number of them.

Goldoni[105] was more prolific; he was perhaps too much so. His comedies called the people back to reason, that same people that had flocked to other novelties and often deserted the theater offering the best performance to go and crowd the one where the actors' wit and jokes make every effort to embellish the carcass of an ill-proportioned and extravagant comedy.[106]

We were unable to rise again. Supported by a hundred favorable circumstances, the French—legislators of fashion and dictators of conversation who are consulted and followed faithfully from the parlor to the kitchen— did not allow themselves to be dislodged from the theater. They do not spare any diligence in order to take root even more deeply in their occupation [of our Italian stages]. After having brought the various known provinces of the dramatic art to the highest possible level, they are trying new avenues, and they are not attempting them in vain. Tired of being tied to ancient precepts

---

103. Domenico Lazzarini (1668–1734) was a playwright famous for his tragedy *Ulisse il giovane* (1720).

104. The marquis Scipione Maffei (1675–1755) was a journalist (cofounder of the *Giornale de' letterati d' Italia* in 1710), satirist, playwright, and literary critic. Maffei's tragedy *Merope* (performed in 1713 in Modena), written in blank verse, was received with international acclaim by contemporaries. *Merope* was considered the finest Italian tragedy before Alfieri, and it was translated by Voltaire.

105. Carlo Goldoni (1701–93) was a Venetian playwright who brought about the reform of the Italian theater (away from the commedia dell'arte tradition) through scripted comedies featuring believable characters from the middle and popular classes. On Goldoni, see note 11 in "Volume Editor's Introduction."

106. This is an allusion to the rivalry between Carlo Goldoni and Carlo Gozzi (1720–1806) over the status of the Italian theater. On Gozzi, see sections 2 and 4 of "Volume Editor's Introduction."

and to that rule which obliged authors to always employ the illustrious names of princes or heroes in tragedies and to bestow ridicule and hatred upon shortcomings or vices in comedies, they decided to profit from the immense resource of familiar situations.[107] The ancients did not believe that the tragic adventures of private individuals were capable of making a great impression on the audience. Those who attended Greek tragedies either were a free people, happy to see tyrants and violent men end badly, or they were a dominated people interested in the calamities of sovereigns. The misfortunes of private and unknown families would perhaps not have moved men who were completely occupied with public affairs or those who were hardened under the harsh yoke of slavery and accustomed to enduring affliction. Whatever the motive was (since it is not of great importance to guess at it), the ancient dramatists left all the merit of the attempt to the French of our time. Messieurs d'Arnaud, Beaumarchais, Mercier, Saurin, de Falbaire, and others[108] began to fashion with exquisite artistry for the stage many subjects for the theater. These cannot be called trivial at all, since virtue and noble passions cannot be trivial, but neither do they belong to the tragic that is commonly called sublime, because princes and heroes do not appear on the stage.

It was not peacefully permitted for the new species of drama to appear in theaters and to attract the curious people and engage them in the domestic details of unknown families. These details were ennobled by sentiments of refined virtue and rendered interesting sometimes by their very simplicity, sometimes by a confluence of fatal or threatening circumstances. The mere announcement of novelty raised eyebrows among all those who had already gained or who hoped to gain glory and advantage from tragedies or comedies of the usual kind. From a hundred sides biting criticisms flew, and many men of letters claimed that this third species was monstrous and unworthy of being multiplied. The uneducated multitude, guided solely by its own common sense, flocked to the theaters, was moved, called for repeat performances of the new dramas, returned to them often, and with the insistence of applause proved demonstratively to the disapproving scholars that sharpness of mind is fallacious whenever and however it wrongs the rectitude of the heart.

It does not at all behoove me at my age, and it is greatly superior to the

---

107. This is a reference to the new genre the bourgeois drama. See sections 2 and 4 of "Volume Editor's Introduction."

108. Caminer translated plays by all of these writers: François Thomas Marie de Baculard d'Arnaud (1718–1805), Pierre-Augustin Caron de Beaumarchais (1732–99), Louis-Sébastien Mercier (1740–1814), Bernard-Joseph Saurin (1706–81), and Charles Georges Fenouillot de Falbaire de Quincey (1727–1800).

tenuousness of my mind and my studies to—by stealing limited blocks of time from the more necessary occupations I have been able to assume so far—undertake an apology for this species of drama so bitterly criticized by the few and so well received by the many. The right that I might have acquired by transporting some of them from the French idiom into our own would not be sufficient to permit me to enter into discussions were it not for the fact that I have been rudely provoked by aggressors in spite of my sex and my young age, my weakness of mind, and the respect that I have forever shown and nurtured toward everyone.[109] Even Italy, which as we unfortunately know is lacking in good theatrical poets, is subjected to seeing them [good Italian theatrical poets] maligned by compatriots and snatched up by foreigners.[110] Even in Italy, unfortunately, there are those who inveigh against reasonable novelties. If, because of my misfortune and through no fault of my own, I were compelled to defend myself, and if, despite every regard for my weakness, I were directly and completely unjustly accused as the woman who is trying to change into gloominess and melancholy the comfort and entertainment that the Venetian people find in the theater, as the woman who is putting on stage the horrifying domestic cruelties of husbands, the desperation or the atrocious punishment of the wicked, the errors of seduced youth, loves, deceits, and even the galleys, I would conquer the repugnance and the aversion that I have and must have for disputes, and I would attempt to justify myself.

I would say, for example (but without making use of biting words that might lead people to suspect I was incensed), that inviting the people to a lugubrious play does not necessarily mean one is chasing them from cheerful ones. I would say that if the multitude wants to go and weep, one should not make a crime of it for the authors of tearful dramas, or for those who have translated them well or poorly. I would say that since, unfortunately, the effects of vice are well-known, the tears of honest families commonplace and the misfortunes of virtuous people frequent, it is difficult to know how one could believe pernicious that genre of play in which vice is held in abomination through its very comparison to afflicted virtue, through innocence betrayed by seduction, and loyalty sacrificed to false friendship, in order that the hearts of men might learn to soften. I would say that if one can draw examples of heroic virtue from the galleys, then one must perhaps prefer to take

109. This is an allusion to the criticism Caminer received from journalist Cristoforo Venier and especially from playwright Carlo Gozzi. On these polemics, see sections 2 and 4 of "Volume Editor's Introduction."

110. In other words, Italian poets such as Pietro Metastasio and Apostolo Zeno, who resided in foreign courts.

them from the galleys, which are more populated and closer to the common people than are thrones. Finally, I would dare to assert that the horrible death in *Beverley*[111] will not produce gamesters; that the seduction in *Jenneval*[112] will not invite youth to dangerous practices; that the anguishes in *The Deserter*[113] will never encourage people to neglect their own duties; and vice versa, that from the excessive generosity of Jean Fabre, living example in *Filial Love*,[114] children will absorb new amounts of tenderness for their fathers; from *The Two Friends*[115] they will learn how much is owed to friends and how far above the rest of humanity the person is raised who, when necessity requires it, goes beyond the limits of friendship that vulgar souls assign to it. I would beg the man who has begun a war against me to rid himself of every passionate prejudice for a moment and subject these dramas to an impartial examination.[116] For if the good morals of maxims taught to us through practice, [if] reasonableness of conduct, and [if] management of the most noble passions were able to instruct an audience perfectly persuaded by the verisimilitude of [a play's] events and disposed to receive impressions of virtue through the power of commotion, then who would ever want to wrong himself by inveighing with hostility against such theatrical performances? I would not adorn with sharp witticisms the simple reasons that I gently put forward. Nor

111. *Beverlei*, Caminer's translation of the play by Bernard-Joseph Saurin, which she first published in 1769. The protagonist of the play, Beverley, loses his entire family fortune to gambling. He commits suicide in prison, leaving behind a destitute wife and a six-year-old child.

112. *Jenneval ovvero Il Barnevelt francese*, Caminer's translation of the play by Mercier. Her version was performed in the S. Angelo Theater in Venice during the fall 1771 season. The protagonist of the play, Jenneval, is a young law student without money. He is desperately in love with Rosalia, a manipulative woman without scruples who is interested in Jenneval only for his eventual possible inheritance from a rich uncle. In order to purchase gifts for Rosalia and to submit to her whims, Jenneval steals money from his friends and lies to them. Rosalia nearly convinces him to kill his uncle before he comes to his senses and manages to save his uncle's life. On Caminer's translation of this play, see also "Making of a Woman," text 32.

113. See "Making of a Woman," texts 21 and 22 (and esp. n. 79) for the plot of this play.

114. *L'onesto colpevole o sia l'Amore filiale* (1769), Caminer's translation of Charles Georges Fenouillot de Falbaire de Quincey's *L'honnête criminel*. Caminer's version was performed at the S. Salvatore Theater in Venice during the carnival season of 1769. Fenouillot de Falbaire's play is based on events that occurred in France between 1756 and 1762, when the son (Jean Favre) of a Protestant father served a galley sentence in place of his father, who was a victim of political repression.

115. *I due amici ovvero il Negoziante di Lione*, Caminer's translation of the play by Pierre Augustin Caron de Beaumarchais. Her version was performed in Venice in the S. Angelo Theater during the carnival season of 1772. The play, which celebrates the values of the commercial class, recounts the story of Roberto, who goes to great lengths—risking his own reputation as an honest businessman—in order to preserve the honor and protect the financial stability of his merchant friend, Aurelio.

116. This is a direct appeal to Carlo Gozzi.

would I want to compare the effects that pathetic dramas can produce with those that are frequently produced by the often licentious tall tales and by the example of their unvirtuous characters which have the effect of corrupting young girls, brides, children, and servants. Perhaps emboldened by a great conviction, I would say to the detractors of the tearful drama: Oh, let us weep over the misfortunes that oppress virtue rather than constraining us to laugh at the happy successes of malice and vice! We love that suffering and virtuous imprisoned Fabre more than a sad servant who is rewarded and triumphant over the happy outcome of pleasing tricks: we are more satisfied by a series of moving familial events than by a forced turn of extravagances.[117] Leave us in peace, then, to make use of the power of our sensitive souls; and you go on to where there is laughter, for we will not be less good friends for this difference in inclination.

So as not to bore the lovers of the burlesque genre with tedious discourses, I would leave off saying a great deal of other things that would by chance provide a motive for new biting attacks, because it is too easy for a young girl, writing as best she knows how, to let slip some expression that might be deemed petty by men who are consumed by their studies.

But if in the very moment I was deciding to remain silent I heard someone persist in chastising me, Why did I not produce my own work instead of translating?[118] Why am I persuaded that the people are never wrong if they go to the theater where I call them to weep, and for other such crimes? then I would perhaps have the feminine weakness of not being able to keep from speaking, and I would say all in one breath, that out of the most profound persuasion, I am only too convinced of the weakness of my talents to succeed at writing a dramatic piece well; and, therefore, respecting myself and the public as one should, I will never have the temerity to have a work of mine performed if I think it bad or mediocre. I would add that perhaps translating good theatrical works can be instructive for creating some of one's own invention; that whoever wants to develop painterly talents sends a child to draw after the originals of good teachers; that in order to teach the art of oratory, sensible preceptors are needed to have their pupils translate the finest excerpts from Demosthenes and Cicero; that the Italian theater does not lose any of its dignity by receiving copies of a new species of drama; and that this is the manner in which to most easily enable our minds to become masters of the art that the French handle so well. To the cold regularity of our tragedies

117. A reference to commedia dell'arte stock characters (masks).
118. Pelli had encouraged Caminer to compose original works for the theater instead of dedicating herself to translation.

they unite passion, sentiment, and lively dialogue, and they profit from example: such is the charm of Corneille, of Racine, of Voltaire. The people love
to weep, and they listen to the same drama six, eight, fifteen, twenty nights
in a row: who is that powerful individual who can form a party so numerous
and constant, with total disregard for the inner sentiment of the people? Certainly not a young girl. I would finish speaking in my defense by repeating
the very wise phrase of a famous Italian writer: *Whoever tries with false zeal and
imposture to make his public become disgusted and nauseated by that which it enjoys is a traitor to it* [his public].[119]

While executing the translations that are included in this volume, I have
not always believed it necessary to remain servilely attached to the original.
Mr. Mercier, the author of *Olindo and Sofronia*,[120] had permitted me to shorten
some scenes which could have seemed too long to listeners, but for good reasons I was not able to have it performed on stage, and therefore I did not take
the liberty given to me. Virtuous readers will not be bored with the delica-
cies of sentiment that make the dialogue a tiny bit long in this drama.

The Deserter is deservedly one of the most successful theatrical compositions ever written. In Venice, where I had it performed last year, it was repeated for twenty-three nights in a row, and it enjoyed equal success in almost all of Italy. I did have to change the ending, however.[121] We are not
generally accustomed to the bloody harshness and the implacable penalty
of death for those unhappy individuals who desert the army; therefore, the
play's political goal did not make sense here in Italy, and the anguish that
the unhappy man suffers was enough to achieve the moral goal. There were
those who found fault with the change, and I myself was accused much more
caustically of having meddled with Mr. Mercier's work. I could not have the
town crier announce that the author had been pleased with the change.[122] I
tried to bring forth the happy ending in the best and most justifiable manner.

119. Here, Caminer is directly quoting Gozzi from his "Prefazione del Traduttare," in *Il fajel*
(Venezia: Colombani, 1772). Gozzi, in turn, would restate his original opinion from *Il fajel* in his
Il ragionamento ingenuo (originally published in the first volume of his *Opere* [1772])—and again in
the *Appendice al Ragionamento* (originally published in the fourth volume of his *Opere* [1772 or
1773])—making reference to Caminer's misuse of it in this preface.

120. Louis-Sébastien Mercier's *Olinde et Sophronie* was first performed in 1771.

121. See note 79 regarding this change. See also section 4 of "Volume Editor's Introduction."

122. [Caminer's note.] Here is what he wrote to me about this: "As in Italy, this death was not
well recieved in France. I wanted to make a political point with my play, to enlighten my nation
about the horror of this inhumane law which so coldly disposes of the life of a man who dares
to take recourse in natural law. I thought I would encourage her [France] to reject the law by offering her this tableau. She could not tolerate in painting that which she permits in reality. I owe
you renewed thanks for having changed this bloody catastrophe, etc. etc."

After twelve nights of performances of this drama, I was begged by the actors to make still one more change, to show in action what was previously recounted. I acceded to the entreaties of those valorous actors, who had helped ensure the success of *The Deserter* by playing their parts excellently. The two actresses who played the characters of mother and daughter outdid themselves; Valcour was an original, not a copy of the French official. I made this last change, however, more out of consideration than anything else, and I consider the first change more reasonable. I hope that objective people will not find it intolerable. I respect all the rest of my judges, but I will not tire the many with a preventive apology in order to save myself from the criticisms of the few. Perhaps in order to avoid one evil I would procure two of them, since there are *a few* individuals who will not be placated.[123]

Even in *The Interrupted Marriage,* which is of a different genre than the other dramas in this volume, I added something of my own, with the intention of adapting it for our [Italian] theater. Thinking better of it, I did not want to risk it. The French original went missing; I was unable, therefore, to retouch my translation on this point and make it more faithful to the original. I ask Mr. Cailhava or anyone who would be his champion to pardon me; and I am not asking for much, because the alterations to it should be of little importance.

26. LETTER TO GIUSEPPE PELLI BENCIVENNI[124]

Venice, 18 January 1772

Sir,

Do not accuse me of laziness, for goodness sake! I thank you from my heart for your good wishes for my marriage. Doctor Turra is in fact an expert botanist and a fine naturalist, but what must be most appreciated in him is his good soul. You may be certain, however, that my marriage will not interrupt our correspondence, and that whether you be near or far, there will be no cause for jealousy. Anyone who knows me cannot entertain that most vile sentiment. I told the abbé Perini that you are reading *The First Navigator,*[125] and

---

123. Caminer may have used italics here to stress her allusion to her two primary critics, Venier and Gozzi.

124. This letter is located in the ASF, Carteggi Pelli Bencivenni, fascio 17.

125. Giulio Perini's translation of two poems by Salomon Gessner and C. M. Wieland, *Il primo navigatore, e Selim e Selima: Poemi tradotti dal Tedesco dall'Abbate Giulio Perini Nobile Fiorentino* (Venezia: Palese, 1771), which the *Europa letteraria* had recently reviewed (October 1771, 69–77).

he responded that you are wasting your time. I asked him why, and he answered me, saying that certain things need to be felt.

Casanova should go to live on the world of the moon, because right now there is no longer a spot for him on earth.[126] I thank you for being willing to find subscribers for me. If you find any, do favor me with their names. The criticisms in the journal of Pisa were printed by Fenzo and had been given to him by the bookseller Bassaglia;[127] I do not know more than this. It seems to me that someone wants to create some mystery about this article. [Joseph] Smith had already sold his drawings, paintings, and library to the king [George III] of England for forty thousand *zecchini;* afterward, he took back almost everything, and now everything is in his house and owned by his widow.[128] I do not

126. Giacomo Casanova (1725–98) was a Venetian adventurer, novelist, translator, impresario, gambler, spy, and librarian. He is most famous for his memoirs, in which he recorded the details of his libertine lifestyle. First imprisoned by the Venetian State Inquisition on charges of impiety (1755) and then employed as a spy for the same inquisition some twenty years later (1776), Casanova had a contradictory relationship with his homeland and fled or was exiled from the Venetian Republic twice during his lifetime. His international notoriety was insured with the publication of his account of his remarkable escape (1756) from the Venetian state prison, the Piombi (*Histoire de ma fuite,* 1787). He wrote his memoir, *Histoire de ma vie,* during the last years of his life, and the twelve-volume work was published posthumously, first in translation (in German, 1822–28) and then in the original French (1826–38), but both versions were largely expurgated. Not until 1962 was the complete and unabridged manuscript published (in the original French). For a recent English translation of selected highlights from Casanova's memoir, see Giacomo Casanova, *The Story of My Life,* selected and introduced by Gilberto Pizzamiglio, trans. Stephen Sartarelli and Sophie Hawkes (New York: Penguin Books, 2000). At the time Caminer mentioned Casanova in this letter, he had not yet returned to Venice after his escape from the Piombi, and he was moving from one city to another across Europe, frequently fleeing because of financial debt, vendettas following duels, and other scandals.

127. Modesto Fenzo was the Venetian printer who published the *Europa letteraria* in this period, and Giammaria Bassaglia was a Venetian bookseller.

128. Joseph Smith (c. 1674–1770) was a merchant banker, investor, art collector, and agent for other British collectors. After attending Westminster School, Smith moved to Venice sometime around 1700 and never returned to England. He served as the British consul in Venice from 1744 to 1760 and again in 1766. Smith amassed a remarkable collection of books, manuscripts, engravings, paintings, drawings, prints, coins, gems, and medals. Caminer's letter may shed light on the mystery of what actually happened to Smith's collection. In a 1760 will he designated the bulk of his collection for his wife, Elizabeth Murray Smith, but in 1762—perhaps out of financial difficulties—he officially sold his collection to the young king of England, George III. Nevertheless, after Smith's death eight years later he still left an extensive collection to his widow. Scholars have speculated that somehow Smith had managed to amass a "second" collection, but Caminer's comment suggests that he may have taken back at least part of what he had officially sold to the king in order to leave it to his wife. On Smith and his collection, see the exhibition catalog *A King's Purchase: King George III and the Collection of Consul Smith,* catalog for an exhibition at the Queen's Gallery, March–December 1993 (London: The Queen's Gallery, 1993). See also Frances Vivien, *Il Console Smith, Mercante e collezionista* (Vicenza: Neri Pozza, 1971).

doubt that the letter[129] you want to write for me is beautiful and appropriate for my second volume. My father pays you his respects, and I am distinctly and truly, sir,

> Your most cordial friend and servant,
> E. Caminer

27. LETTER TO GIUSEPPE PELLI BENCIVENNI[130]

Venice, 1 February 1772

Sir,

I am greatly surprised that you have not received either the periodical or the manifestos. Pagani[131] is the person who should give you the package; I beg you to have him asked about it. Next Saturday, and just maybe even this evening, I will mail you the November issue.

I wrote to Perini what you asked me to tell him, since I have not seen him for several days. I owe you many thanks for the advantageous way in which you spoke of my edition in the *Novelle letterarie*:[132] you may be sure that I am most grateful for your kind friendship. I saw the project from Lucca, which is a kind of lottery; I saw it without wishing to, because it was sent to me by I know not whom with the extremely profane title of Excellency on the address. As for myself I doubt that few [*sic*] authors will want to subject themselves to that judgment under those conditions and with that prize.[133] You advise me to enjoy myself, but I assure you that being engaged will not change the way I live. I stay home almost every day, and every night I go to the theater, for which I have a true passion. Our carnival is even better than yours in terms of theaters: we have an opera seria, two opere buffe, three comedy playhouses, and one theater in which a mixture of comedies and musical intermezzi are offered. All of these theaters compete to entertain the public, so we get new things furiously—French translations, Italian originals, Spanish adaptations, and a thousand other kinds. Among these there are

---

129. On this letter, see "Making of a Woman," texts 22, 27, 28, 29, and 30.

130. This letter is located in the ASF, Carteggi Pelli Bencivenni, fascio 17.

131. Giuseppe Pagani was the bookseller in Florence who sold the *Europa letteraria*.

132. In the 17 January 1772 issue of his weekly literary periodical the *Novelle letterarie* Pelli had announced the forthcoming publication of Caminer's *Composizioni teatrali moderne tradotte*. He described Caminer as a "virtuous maiden well known . . . for her rare talents, and for her publications. . . . If the work itself is pleasantly useful, the fact that it was produced by a female must justly increase the number of those who will want to procure it for themselves. This is exactly what we desire to see happen" (41–42).

133. This is a reference to a literary prize awarded in Lucca whose criteria Caminer does not consider valid or serious: luck, rather than talent, will determine the winner.

many bad ones, but there are also many good ones. Not to mention the competition among the actors, the rivalries between authors, and the factions among the people: this is the most wonderful entertainment in the world. And there are those who write, those who complain, those who scorn, those who proclaim, those who criticize, and those who cover beneath the mantle of truth a fanaticism that then comes out after a long oration. I myself have done five things for the theater, either translated directly or translated and adapted; and I will do another one. All of them have enjoyed great success, and, content that I was not mistaken in my choice, I sit back tranquilly to see the things others have done and to laugh at the bites of those who wish to criticize wantonly. Spare me from having to tell you who Grisellini[134] is: I am not very good at making portraits. If you want to know about him in terms of literature, I will tell you that he has much talent, an embryo of infinite things, no profundity in any, a great deal of temerity, and the art of writing fashionable things. Jesuits one time, agriculture now, war during the period of the last war, and all in his own fashion. My father thanks you and sends you his respects. I am with the highest esteem, sir,

> Your most affectionate servant and friend,
> E. Caminer

28. LETTER TO GIUSEPPE PELLI BENCIVENNI[135]

[No place, no date][136]

Sir,

I cannot go on for weariness, but this will not keep me from thanking you hurriedly for the expense to which you are willing to go to favor me, for

---

134. Francesco Griselini (1717–87) was an agrarian economist and journalist of the Venetian Enlightenment who viewed the study of natural resources as a way to promote the economic advancement of nations and the well-being of their inhabitants. In 1764 he founded the most important agricultural periodical of eighteenth-century Italy, the *Giornale d'Italia spettante alla scienza naturale e principalmente all'agricoltura, alle arti ed al commercio*. Griselini's other major works include his dictionary of arts and trades, *Dizionario delle arti e de' Mestieri* (1768), and his provocative *Memorie spettanti alla vita ed agli studi del sommo filosofo e giureconsulto f. Paolo [Sarpi]* (1760), both a defense of Paolo Sarpi and an attack on the Jesuit order. Although Torcellan confirms Griselini's reputation (among contemporaries) as something of a dilettante and trend-conscious journalist ("pubblicista alla moda"), Caminer's description of him in this letter perhaps betrays some jealousy on her part of Griselini's ability to keep a finger on the pulse of public opinion. For Torcellan on Griselini, see "Francesco Griselini," in *Riformatori delle antiche repubbliche, dei ducati, dello stato pontificio e delle isole*, vol. 7 of *Illuministi italiani*, ed. Giuseppe Giarrizzo, Gianfranco Torcellan, and Franco Venturi (Milano: Ricciardi, 1965), 93–192.

135. This letter is located in the ASF, Carteggi Pelli Bencivenni, fascio 17.

136. Pelli responded to this letter on 30 May 1772.

the news that you want to give about my first volume in the *Novelle*,[137] and for the letter that you persist in wanting to write for me. Since my second volume is already published and I am waiting for the opportunity to mail it to you, and since the third volume is in print, the letter will have to go in the fourth volume. Also, I beg you to grant me this solicitude: be sure not to include anything that is inopportune for me to publish, even if it is inspired by your friendship and not justice. The bookseller who dispenses my translations is Mr. Paolo Colombani,[138] but it is better that whoever wants them write to my father or to me. Preserve your friendship for me, honor me with your commands, and believe I am with the most sincere sentiment

> Your most obligated servant and friend,
> E. Caminer

P.S. My father sends you his compliments.

29. LETTER TO GIUSEPPE PELLI BENCIVENNI[139]

Venice, 20 June 1772

Sir,

Forgive me if I do not answer you at length. I thank you for your letter, and I have some things to tell you, but I am married as of this morning, I leave this evening for Padua and Vicenza, and lack of time does not permit me to go on at length. I will write you from my new home; preserve your friendship for

> Your very obliged and very cordial friend,
> Elisabetta Caminer Turra

30. LETTER TO GIUSEPPE PELLI BENCIVENNI[140]

Vicenza, 3 July 1772

Sir,

I am stealing a moment from the manifold variety of my occupations to remind you of your friendship for me and to honor my duty to you. The letter with which you have favored me is very beautiful, so much so that I must consider it an honor; but pardon me, you are too kind, and I am too exposed to the indiscretion of malicious or envious people who want to believe me

---

137. In Pelli's periodical, the *Novelle letterarie*. See "Making of a Woman," texts 22, 26, 27, 29, and 30.

138. Paolo Colombani was the bookseller in Venice who sold Caminer's theatrical translations as well as the *Europa letteraria*.

139. This letter is located in the ASF, Carteggi Pelli Bencivenni, fascio 17.

140. This letter is located in the ASF, Carteggi Pelli Bencivenni, fascio 17.

culpable for even the most innocent actions.[141] If you have read the preface to *Fayel*, which occasioned the one in my first volume, you will be convinced of this truth.[142] Therefore, if I myself published my own praises in one of my volumes, I would be laying myself open to my persecutors, so your erudite letter will be published by my father in our periodical. In the meantime, please receive my sincere thanks.

I have not seen your gazette[143] where you have done me the favor of speaking about my first volume, but I will have my father send it to me.

You will want some news from your friend: here it is. My situation would be completely happy if I were not so far from my family, my friends, and my home. My husband is the most respectable man, the most adorned with solid qualities, and the most affectionate I could possibly find. I have in him a tender spouse and a sincere and admirable friend whose company is the only recompense I have for my losses, at least up to a certain point. My parents-in-law love me a great deal, and I am lacking nothing in terms of the comforts of a civil and tranquil life. I cannot, however, become accustomed so quickly to being far away from so many dear persons, or to the shift from a free, relaxed, and good city [Venice] to a silly, malicious one full of prejudices [Vicenza]. Fortunately for me, I meet with various people, but with none of them intimately. I keep very much to myself, and I forget that I am in the beautiful and delightful but lazy and stolid Vicenza, whose very kind but deep down evil inhabitants would render it hateful to me if I paid much attention to them!

I hope that here in my new home I will not lack in letters from you. If I can do anything for you, call on her who is always equally, sir,

> Your very obliged servant and very cordial friend,
> Elisabetta Caminer Turra

P.S. I beg you urgently to tell me for sure if an introduction to the *Flora italica*[144] by my husband, whose name is already known to you, has been pub-

---

141. On this letter see "Making of a Woman," texts 22, 26, 27, 28, and 29.

142. Carlo Gozzi's preface ("Prefazione del Traduttore") to *Il fajel*, his translation of Baculard d'Arnaud's tragedy. For the polemic between Gozzi and Caminer, see sections 2 and 4 of "Volume Editor's Introduction."

143. Pelli had published a very positive review of the first volume of Caminer's *Composizioni teatrali moderne tradotte* in the 26 June 1772 issue of his *Novelle letterarie*, 415–16. He cited other periodicals' favorable reviews of her work and expressed his hope that Caminer's example would inspire more Italian women to "occasionally set aside their soft luxuries [*piume*], their toilette and their frivolous idleness to aspire to be something more than delicate, beautiful, and agreeable" creatures.

144. Antonio Turra was a founding member of Vicenza's Agrarian Academy and was its lifetime secretary from 1773 until his death in 1797. *Florae italicae prodromus*, a catalog of seventeen hundred species of Italian plants, was his most famous publication. In 1780 he published this catalog with the printing press he and Caminer had recently opened in their home.

lished or is about to be published in the proceedings of the Academy of Siena. This introduction was accepted and read in the above academy; you could find out something about it from Professor Baldassari. I pray that you answer me immediately, send the letter to me in Venice, and include a cover letter to my father. I beg you to give this matter your immediate attention.

31. LETTER TO GIUSEPPE GENNARI[145]

Venice, 3 August 1772

Most Esteemed Friend,

Having desired in vain to see you in Padua when I passed through, I need to write to you so that you will know that my change in status and in home must not interrupt our correspondence, and to offer you all that I can do for you in my new home here. I rely so much on your friendship that I beg you frankly to continue favoring with articles my father's periodical, which will continue to be mine as well, given that I will never stop working on it. Pay my respects many times to all our friends, and believe I am with all my soul

Your most cordial friend,

El. Caminer Turra

32. REVIEW OF THE FINAL VOLUME OF *COMPOSIZIONI TEATRALI MODERNE TRADOTTE* (1772–73)[146]

So at last, thank heavens, this collection of theatrical translations is finished. Some will have praised it; others will have found fault with it; the greatest number will not have done one or the other thing. The literary periodicals and gazettes of our transalpine neighbors, to tell the truth, have said good things about it;[147] but we, good Italians, who are not gallant like the French, we do not have to do so, assuming that the collection was not unworthy of it at all. These women are too quick to become impertinent; furthermore, if they aimed to obtain some honor through the cultivation of their talent, they would perhaps become something contrary to the good rules somewhat generally established in polite society. Whether these translations are good or bad, therefore, we will content ourselves by observing

---

145. This letter is located at the BSP, codice 620, vol. 13, carte 165.

146. This review of the fourth volume of Caminer's *Composizioni teatrali moderne tradotte* (1772) was published in the *Europa letteraria*, September 1772–January 1773, 37–39, signed ECT.

147. Both the *Journal encyclopédique de Bouillon* (1772) and the *Mercure de France* (1773) had published flattering comments about Caminer and her theatrical translations. See section 1 of "Volume Editor's Introduction."

that the present volume has a few too many typographical errors, and that the translator did not take our past warnings seriously in this regard. She excuses herself, in truth, in a foreword, citing her distance from Venice as the reason for such an inconvenience, but the effect is no less displeasing to us, even though it will be necessary to have patience and consult the errata found at the end of each comedy.

This fourth volume contains five theatrical works instead of four. The first is *Clarice*,[148] a drama in prose by Mr. I. A. P. preceded by a humorous dialogue in the preface, where the author cites the reason why he wrote one of these contested dramas instead of a tragedy. *Clarice* is simple and has an uncomplicated plot, but it is pathetic, moving, and, sadly, taken from real examples. *Janie; or, Disinterest*[149] by the chevalier D. S. V. V. is preceded by the French editor's foreword. It is a society drama in two acts, in prose, very simple, but scattered with refined and genteel phrases. *Jenneval*,[150] a drama in prose by Mr. Mercier, very much applauded last year on the stages of the Veneto, written with force by the author and representing the dangers of the seduction of naive youth, is the third composition in this volume; preceding it is appended a preface by the eloquent Mr. Mercier. After a passage from a letter by Voltaire about the work it precedes is *The Peloponnesians; or, Atreus and Thyestes*,[151] a brand-new tragedy in verse by this immortal author, to whom this translator has dedicated her version of the play; it is the latest of all that he published, and it was not even performed in France or anywhere else. *The Triumph of Good Wives*,[152] a character comedy in prose by the German Mr. Elia Schlegel, brings this collection to a close and completes the author's obligation to it. Now we shall see what she can do. We have treated her in different ways: we have wished for her the charity of her neighbor; then we criticized her a bit, since literati must behave according to the tenor of literary circumstances; then we took care what we said; but in general we treated her kindly and we did not look for those defects that perhaps abound in her translations, because in the end we do not dislike her. If she adopts a good disposition she will profit from this kind of moderate education and will apply herself to doing something entirely her own that will make her worthy of our full compassion.

---

148. *Clarice,* Caminer's translation of the play by Jean André Perreau.

149. *Giannina ovvero Disinteresse,* Caminer's translation of the society drama by Benoît Joseph Marsollier des Vivetières.

150. On this play, see "Making of a Woman," text 25, note 112.

151. *I Pelopidi ovvero Atreo e Tieste,* Caminer's translation of the tragedy by Voltaire.

152. *Il trionfo delle buone moglie,* Caminer's translation of the comedy by Johann Elias Schlegal.

33. LETTER TO GIUSEPPE PELLI BENCIVENNI[153]

Vicenza, 20 August 1773

Sir,

Why are you so amazed and why do you want to credit me with merit because of the interest that your Elisa inspired in me when she was alive and the sadness which she causes me now that she is deceased? We are not masters over the impressions that events and people make upon us, nor do we have any merit or fault in that regard; both one and the other belong at the most to a certain formation that has occurred [within ourselves] without our will. We cry at a comedy and upon reading a novel, we fall in love with someone who is completely unworthy, and we are sometimes insensitive to real misfortunes and to visible worthiness. I pride myself on not being so, for good and virtuous traits have always inspired esteem and sympathy in me, and the misfortunes of others and the destruction of human beings have inspired compassion in me at every moment. I am quite far, however, from boasting about something I could not change even if I wanted to. Tell me, what is happening with that friend of yours who was once more than a friend to Elisa? Does he live far from her daughter? And this girl, how is she faring after the loss of her mother?

Ghelina[154] is still here; I think she has reconciled with her father, and that he gives her something instead of giving her, as she wished, her dowry. They tell me that now she is looking for a house in the most remote quarter of the city in order to be away from society; in fact, she lives a very isolated life.

I am more than persuaded by the effect that the plays performed by the French comic actors have here. As mediocre as this company is, its artistry and rules are such that it undoubtedly surpasses the best of our Italian companies.

You ask me for news of myself: I am healthy, nor is there any appearance that I am about to give my spouse the testimony of which you speak, even though my marriage is fourteen months old today. As far as letters are concerned, whether it is for better or for worse that I occupy myself with them, and despite my small success, I will certainly never abandon them. I now have it in mind to write a comedy; we shall see what will come of it. Speaking of comedies, have you seen the terrible one that won second prize in Parma? What devil of a play is that?[155] The coronations made last year and this (ex-

153. This letter is located in the ASF, Carteggi Pelli Bencivenni, fascio 18.

154. Although it has been impossible to identify "Ghelina" (or "Ghellina," as Caminer sometimes spells it) precisely, Caminer's correspondence reveals that she was a noblewoman from Vicenza who created a scandal by marrying a man from a lower class.

155. Francesco Marucchi's comedy *La Marcia* (Parma: Stamperia reale, 1773) won second prize in the competition of the Royal Academy of Parma (no prize having been deemed worthy of first

cept for the marquis Albergati's comedy)[156] are highly suspicious. The bad play *Zelinda*[157] won first prize over *Corrado*,[158] which deserved the award; the play *The March* [*La Marcia*] obtained second prize this year. Could there possibly be some swindling afoot?

The *Europa letteraria* continues. I am waiting very impatiently for your promised news about your book on political economy. Is it at an advanced stage? Will you publish it immediately? What is your system?

You see, what I had told you about Grisellini has come to pass; but what need is there of verification? His character is too well known.

The abbé Perini was in Vicenza, but many, many days have passed since he left; therefore, I was unable to give him your greetings.

My spouse thanks you and sends you many compliments. Rely on me and believe I am always

> Your very obliged servant and very cordial friend,
> El. Caminer Turra

34. POEM FOR A FRIEND ON INFINITE TEDIUM (OCTOBER 1773)[159]

Where are you, my friend, that you do not come
And so far from me you stay?
Do you not think of how bored I must be?
Or rather, do you not know how angry I am?
Oh! If in your breast you have a kind and pious heart,
Return soon, or return no more;
For if you stay away much longer,
I shall die of consumption a few days hence.

---

prize that year). Caminer had published a scathing review of Marucchi's play in the *Europa letteraria*, March 1773, 86–90. See also "Making of a Woman," text 35.

156. *Il Prigioniero commedia del signor marchese Francesco Albergati Capacelli* (Parma: Stamperia reale, 1773). Domenico Caminer reviewed Albergati's play—which the Albergati scholar Enrico Mattioda has called "the first Italian tearful comedy"—in the *Europa letteraria*, May 1773, 54–62. See E. Mattioda, *Il dilettante "per mestiere": Francesco Albergati Capacelli commediografo* (Bologna: Il Mulino, 1993), 70–82. See also "Making of a Woman," text 35.

157. Orazio Calini's tragedy *La Zelinda* (Parma: Stamperia reale, 1772).

158. *Corrado, marchese di Monferrato: Tragedia*, by Francesco Ottavio Magnocavallo, conte di Varengo di Casal-Monserrato (Parma: Stamperia reale, 1772).

159. This poem was published posthumously in a collection of poetry entitled *Per le faustissime nozze del Conte Pietro Dalle-Ore colla Marchesa Giulia Buzzaccarini*. Caminer probably did not intend for this poem to be published, having written it solely for her friend Giuseppe Giupponi (1733–1809), a lawyer and author of legal texts.

The clock tolls three and I am dying of sleepiness,
Nor can I keep these eyes open any longer;
My books cannot give me pleasure,
My writing brings me displeasure:
An ancient devout old man and grandfather
Invites me to say the Miserere with him,
Because in fact the holy days are upon us,
And all but the rogues do good.

But God forgive me (for I am a Christian,
And my soul is not wicked and depraved)
How strange you see! I can find no way
On heaven or on earth to do pious works.
So much does fury tear and pull me apart,
So much does the devil come across my path,
That I could nearly grab you by the throat,
For having left me here alone.

But you, invoking the Lord and Mary,
Do not even listen to me and will not return.
Oh, pious soul, at least do not forget
My miserable self in your prayers!
If perchance you do not find me at home
When you return, you may be sure
That I am truly dead and buried
Of infinite and arch-infinite tedium.

35. LETTER TO GIUSPPE PELLI BENCIVENNI[160]

Vicenza, 8 October 1773

Sir,

I am a little peeved with you about the two comedies crowned at Parma: resign yourself to it. I will not begin to justify the marquis Albergati; I am quite sure that you are rather mistaken about *The Prisoner*, which one cannot possibly call a bad comedy. In any case I do not require that you think as I do about this; but that you could compare it with that abomination, *The March*, seems impossible to me.[161] Furthermore, you find both of them bad, you cannot finish reading them, and then you allow someone to speak of them or you

160. This letter is located in the ASF, Carteggi Pelli Bencivenni, fascio 18.
161. On the plays *The Prisoner* and *The March*, see "Making of a Woman," text 33.

speak in that way about the second one in the *Novelle letterarie?* Why are you so inconsistent? Why such excessive praise, and why so detailed? In the spirit of our openness as friends, allow me to disapprove of you this time.

As far as my comedy is concerned, the subject I have chosen is pathetic without being tragic; I cannot tell you what it will turn out to be.

I very much desire to see published the book you speak to me about, which will certainly do you honor; thank you for giving me news of it.[162]

Ghellina[163] lives very quietly, and is so withdrawn that she is not even mentioned in prattling Vicenza.

My husband thanks you very much for your greetings and returns them to you. I beg you to consider me always, sir,

> Your very obliged servant and very cordial friend,
> El. Caminer Turra

36. LETTER TO GIUSPPE PELLI BENCIVENNI[164]

Vicenza, 1 April 1774

Sir,

I owe you and offer you a thousand thanks for the fabric swatches with which you have favored me. However, these lustring silks[165] do not seem either as fine or as beautiful as those a [. . .][166] makes. You are bit lazy about this and it is impossible to know to what extent. If the book you wanted to publish requires more work than you had imagined, your merit will be all the greater, and its usefulness more universal. Get moving, then, and finish it. It would be a shame to let it go. I would not have considered republishing and expanding my translated comedies were it not for the entreaties of a printer to whom I yielded.[167] The second collection will consist of six volumes of

---

162. See "Making of a Woman," text 33.

163. On Ghellina, see "Making of a Woman," text 33.

164. This letter is located in the ASF, Carteggi Pelli Bencivenni, fascio 19.

165. Lustring silk was a type of shimmering silk popular in the eighteenth century. I extend my thanks to costume historians Doretta Davanzo Poli and Patricia Ward for their assistance with the translation of this term.

166. Illegible word.

167. Caminer is refering to the publisher Pietro Savioni, who published the second edition (1774) of her first collection of theatrical translations as well as the four volumes of her second collection, *Nuova raccolta di composizioni teatrali tradotte da Elisabetta Caminer Turra* (New collection of theatrical compositions translated by Elisabetta Caminer Turra) (Venezia: Savioni, 1774–76). Publicly "transferring" such ambition onto male contemporaries was a common strategy used by women intellectuals as a way to cloak their own ambition and thus protect their good reputations.

four comedies each and will offer a general idea of European theater. If you could find anyone interested in buying these new volumes, or better yet, this set along with the four republished volumes, I would be indebted to you a thousand times over.

My husband, grateful for your kind greetings, sends you his own, and I am with the most perfect esteem, sir,

> Your very obliged and very cordial servant and friend,
> El. C. T.

37. LETTER TO LAZZARO SPALLANZANI[168]

Vicenza, 23 January 1777

Most Illustrious Renowned and Revered Sir,

What will you say when you see a letter from me after such a long time? I trust that you will deign to welcome it with your usual goodness. If, for some reason, after a long silence you were to write to me, I am sure that I would esteem it to be my good fortune and I would thank you for it. Without desiring an equal sentiment which I cannot demand from you, I dare to promise myself that you will kindly welcome a request of mine nevertheless.

The *Giornale enciclopedico*, which was once entitled *Europa letteraria*, is moving from Venice to Vicenza. Because my father's many affairs do not allow him to make it his principal occupation, he has agreed to allow me to take on the responsibility, whereby this periodical might perchance become more refined and more exact than the many objects to which he applies himself have allowed. Shall I dare to beg you to honor this paper and its author with some sign, some small piece of news, be it an extract or something else which, coming from you, will always bring the paper credit and advantage? You may be certain of all my gratitude if you deign to grant me this favor. Your recommendation and your approbation can help with subscriptions as well. Permit me to multiply your troubles and at the same time beg you to put to the test the sincere sentiment of gratitude and of indelible esteem with which I am always

> Your very devoted, very obliged servant,
> Elisabetta Caminer Turra

---

168. This letter is located at the BEM, Autografateca Campori, Carte Paradisi.

38. FLY SHEET FOR THE *GIORNALE ENCICLOPEDICO*
IN VICENZA (C. JANUARY 1777)[169]

The newspaper at hand carries its explanation in the title. The word *Encyclopedia* means *concatenation of cognitions*, and the goal of this periodical is precisely to gather and present together diverse cognitions which, remaining scattered, would be largely unknown.[170] This is due to the limited commerce between the booksellers of Italy and those of our transalpine neighbors, the contempt in which some nations hold others, political reasons, and the neglect on the part of many people. The author of this paper, which was published for several years in Venice, certainly does not wish to adopt a bombastic air about her undertaking, or insist that it is necessary to humanity, that the educated world cannot do without it, that its successors will be interested in it, and that something better does not exist in nature: these commonplaces of venality or self-love are not sufficient to inspire appreciation of a work. But if it is true that the cognitions of the intellect, owing to a certain concatenation of causes and effects, both physical and moral, are useful to the heart, and that knowledge contributes to happiness, a repertory of such cognitions, an exact and consistent account of their status and of their progress, a means by which to know those works that various amateurs can then procure for themselves, a union of the diverse thoughts of cultured peoples, will not perchance be at all useless. And if, prescinding from these goals of usefulness, one wants to consider an encyclopedic journal in terms of pleasure, the curiosity which finds its nourishment in learning all that happens in a day, the pleasure that tries to gently suck upon flowers and follows the maxim of not meddling with the fruits, the idleness that weighs upon others and upon itself for not knowing how to pass the time, together all of these [curiosity, pleasure, idleness] might draw advantages from it.[171] With such explanations, the author intends less to procure the sale of the paper than to justify herself before a public, to whom any writer is accountable for her own goal. She is too convinced that encomiums bestowed upon authors do not help their

169. Caminer published and distributed this fly sheet (*foglio volante*) both independently and bound into volumes of her periodical. A copy of it is bound in the Marciana Library's copy of the February 1777 issue of the *Giornale enciclopedico*. It was published by Marino Berengo in *Giornali veneziani del Settecento: Linea di sviluppo della stampa periodica veneta* (Milano: Feltrinelli, 1962), 385–87.

170. Throughout this manifesto, Caminer consciously echoes the principles (and sometimes exact phrases) of d'Alembert in his *Preliminary discourse* (1751) to the *Encyclopédie*.

171. An allusion to the classical and humanist trope of the industrious bee taking nectar from many plants and producing a single, sweet result. The motto of the *Europa letteraria*—Floriferis ut apes in saltibus omnia libant (Lucretius, *De rerum natura*, bk. 3 line 11)—had also employed this trope.

books, and that whoever slavishly recommends books in order to please authors does a very poor job of recommending them. With this premise, here is the system and the content of the journal.

Literature: Extracts of books from all the nations of Europe. They will be done by several persons, since an encyclopedic journal can be produced, but an encyclopedic head cannot be found; and, in addition, the author knows too well her weak powers and the meagerness of her talent.[172] Whoever is not knowledgeable about the subject of a book will not point out new things and notice cases of plagiarism or errors. About mathematics only a geometer will speak justly, about philosophy only a philosopher, about medicine only a physician, about poetry only someone who crafts it or enjoys it, just as about gallantry and clothing only a Ganymede and a flirt could hold profound discourse, about fortune a beautiful young woman and about misfortunes an ugly one, about slander an idle person, about pleasures the Great Turk, about delicate sensibility those souls who are good at their own great cost. Therefore, we will often implore the assistance of the naturalist, the jurisconsult, the astronomer, the chemist, etc., and for those books which do not reach us here, extracts will be translated from the *Journal encyclopédique de Bouillon,* from the *Gazzette littéraire* at Deux-Ponts, from the *Mercure de France,* etc., etc.[173] Praises will not be spared for good authors, since the praise of a virtuous man is the recompense of another. A reasoned and civil criticism will be adopted as needed, whatever impetuous partisans might claim. Adulations that are debasing, and malicious satires, and hateful personalities will always be avoided; unfortunately, these are pleasing to many, and could contribute to the sale of the *Journal,* but they would not be praiseworthy of the person writing it.

Original passages, Capricious or Serious Thoughts, Tales, etc., written in prose and in verse by Italians, since one does not always wish to restrict oneself to accounts of others' thoughts.

Academies: Problems proposed and resolved, worthy men's admission into them [academies], their new establishments, and everything that relates to them as well as to the universities of every country.

Theater: Unpublished theatrical compositions, since when they are published they will be spoken of the way other books are, since drama is a part of literature.

172. As she had done in the 1772 preface to her collection of theatrical translations ("Making of a Woman," text 25), Caminer used this fly sheet both to advertise her periodical and to make preemptive strikes at possible criticisms that might be directed at her.

173. These three periodicals, the *Journal Encyclopédique de Bouillon* (1760–94), the *Gazette Universelle de littérature, aux Deux-Ponts* (1770–77), and the *Mercure de France* (1724–78, 1778–91), were among the most important in France during the eighteenth century.

Anecdotes, Remarkable Facts, Eulogies of Illustrious Men and Women, Discoveries in the Sciences and the Arts, Inventions, Fashions . . . and why not fashions? Oh, how many times do fashions reveal the character of heads! And how much honor could the antiquaries of future centuries earn with an article from a journal of this century if, however, it could happen that one century knew about a Journal from the preceding one!

Literary News. This [section] will contain succinct notices either of those books which cannot be had immediately for the writing of an extract, or of those which do not merit it: what becomes of an extract, in fact, when the book is bad?

Historical Events. The news about daily political events can, in part, be of service to the history of nations. In addition, when humans see actions that are considered so different [from their own] they experience a kind of consolation in perceiving that they are [not different but] equal.

Passages from the Best Italian Journals given either in their entirety or in extract form, so that whoever does not purchase them can be informed about their content.

Other articles will be determined as the occasion demands. The initials of the person who wrote each article will be appended to it, or, for whoever does not wish to be known, the letters N. N.[174] will appear; and this so that no one will earn merit or demerit with the things of others. These initials will almost always be omitted in the literary news, even when original, in the historical events, in the simple relations of academies, etc., and principally in the translated extracts, in order to avoid equivocations, since the author of the *Journal* does not wish to attribute to herself anything other than a translation whenever she is translating. Praise for work that is not one's own must make a person of sentiment blush.

One hundred four issues of this *Journal* will be published each year, numbered in such a way that, at every eighth or ninth issue, a volume may be formed. The issues will come out twice a week, or once a month in volume form, as subscribers prefer. In Vicenza twenty-two Venetian *lire* a year or eleven *lire* a semester will be paid in advance for this. Postage in other cities is the responsibility of subscribers, and the money will be sent without expense to the *Journal*.

Men of letters [*Gli uomini di Lettere*] will do me the pleasure of continuing to direct their opuscules, extracts, discoveries, compositions, etc., to Madame

---

174. The Caminers used "N. N." or *nullo nomine* to indicate that a review published in the periodical was anonymous (or that the author peferred not to have his initials published with his or her review). For issues of authorship in the Caminer periodicals, see section 4 ("Journalistic Writing") of "Volume Editor's Introduction."

Elisabetta Caminer Turra in Vicenza or to Mr. Domenico Caminer in Venice, from whom they can obtain the *Journal,* as well as from the booksellers Mr. Paolo Colombani in Venice and Mr. Antonio Veronese in Vicenza, in addition to the others in the various cities named on the masthead each month.

39. POLEMIC WITH A READER FROM VICENZA (1777)[175]

A. *Review of* Compendium of the History and the Moral of the Old Testament, with Explanations and Reflections[176]

But for how long will the Holy Scripture, that book which was dictated by a divine legislator as the source of our faith, as a guide for our conduct, as the origin our salvation, have need of reflections, and new explanations? Or, better yet, how long will men insist on renewing discussions about a work which is superior to reason, and which should simply be revered in silence? When will a more simple and straightforward argument convince them of the necessity of keeping quiet?

We do not intend to condemn or to consider less than respectable those comments and explanations of this divine book that the church has thus far believed necessary in order to make it accessible to simpletons, idiots, in short, the common people. We shall leave without response the reflections of those unbelieving rationalists [*Ragionatori*] who are trying to spoil our century, by claiming among other things that they can decide that the necessary explanations mentioned above are palliatives, offspring of either an excessive or apparent zeal, almost as if a book, just because it is necessary for everyone, should have been naturally made to suit everyone's abilities. God in his distributive justice made penetrating minds and simpletons; the church has consecrated the decisions of the former, and we good Catholics venerate them. We hope, though, that we will not be mistakenly blamed for claiming that this is enough, that the Scripture must be believed and followed blindly, and

175. I have grouped together the following texts which make up this polemic: (a) Caminer's review of a book (*Giornale enciclopedico,* January 1777, 76–80) and (b) a reader's response to the review, which Caminer published together with her response to the letter (*Giornale enciclopedico,* February 1777, 17–20). Giovanni Mantese published the reader's response and most of Caminer's response to the reader in *Memorie Storiche della Chiesa Vicentina* (1700–1816) (Vicenza: Accademia Olimpica, 1982), 16–17. For a discussion of these texts, see Angelo Colla et al., "Tipografi, editori e librai," in *L'età della Repubblica veneta (1404–1797),* vol. 3 of *Storia di Vicenza,* edited by Franco Barbieri and Paolo Preto (Vicenza: Neri Pozza Editore, 1990), bk. 2:150–51.

176. *Giornale enciclopedico,* January 1777. Caminer is reviewing the first volume of the *Compendio della Storia e della Morale dell'antico Testamento, con Spiegazioni e Riflessi* (Vicenza: Veronese, 1777), an Italian translation of the original work by François Philippe Mezanguy. The article is signed E.C.T.

that paper and ink should be better employed than in commenting on it [the Scripture] and explaining it again.

It is necessary, however, to confess that there are certain particular cases in which this maxim does not apply, and the countenance of the affair changes. That which gave rise to the work we are announcing is one of these, since the author says he undertook his compendium with explanations and reflections *by order of God, as he has reason to believe.* Inspirations often decide the destiny of men, and even more so of women. This is especially true of orders from Heaven, which are the most clear [of all], as must be the one [order] had by our author, who must have obtained his information from a good source. Such inspirations must be very highly respected in order that a work made according to this principle will not become an exception to the general rule.[177] We will limit ourselves, therefore, to praising the zeal and the submission of the author, and to giving a little taste of his *Reflections, etc.,* so that our readers, forming for themselves an idea of the work, will be able to decide whether to acquire it or leave it at the bookseller's.

The Sacred Scripture, adequately simplified in a new compendium which is similar to others, is elucidated by our author in every chapter. Here is one of his explanations. "*God saw that the light was good.* This word does not at all signify that this light pleased God after having created it, as if he had not known it before; but only that after having made it, he approved of it, finding it in accordance with the rules of his divine knowledge. Perhaps some would like to know what the luminous body that lit the world was, since the sun, the moon and the stars were not yet formed. But the silence of the Holy Spirit on this point teaches us to suppress our curiosity."

Truly, were it not too bold to permit oneself to offer a *reflection* on these explanations and reflections, we could perchance observe that every Christian knows very well that he must suppress his curiosity when things are unintelligible to him, and that it is no great novelty to conclude that we know nothing because we are supposed to know nothing. In terms of the *approbation* God made of the light, one could reflect that the explanation says nothing more than the text does. For what purpose does our author want, as it were, to justify the words of God? That omnipotent Being, the Eternal Knower of things already foreseen by him and dependent upon him, knew very well the light before making it, as the author himself grants. He did not need to *approve of it* after *having seen it to be in accordance with the rules of his divine knowledge,*

177. In other words, although most commentaries on the Scripture are not necessary or praiseworthy, this *Compendium* must be an exception to this rule, since it was—according to its author—directly inspired by God. Caminer is being ironic here.

almost as if he had not known beforehand that it would have come out that way, as if he could have doubted it. The Holy Scripture says that God saw that the light was good: we must believe it without extrapolating, and we must let our self-love and our inadequacy take pleasure in having done something we were supposed to do.

This first volume contains the holy story of the Creation until the sacrifice of Abraham. The explanations and the reflections of the author are, truth be told, infinitely longer than the material itself [i.e., the Old Testament], as often happens with those who transform texts [*Commutatori*]. But he promises us that the subjects will not always require such extensive explanations, or *reflections as profound* as the ones we have quoted. We will content ourselves in the future, therefore, with only announcing the publication of the other volumes of this work, hoping that our review of the first volume has made it sufficiently known.

However much the public wants to esteem this work, it will always be a consolation to us to have reason to speak about a book translated and printed in Vicenza, where books are so uncommon. It will be even more of a consolation, for a woman especially, to be able to speak about a translation done by a member of that sex, which, [while] courting men's injustice, seems to willingly renounce its own portion of talent and common sense in order to receive a frivolous exchange of apparent homages, ill-founded praises, dangerous adulations, and futile bonds, which keep us ever more bound in slavery even as we believe ourselves to be receiving tributes and as we go along proud of our empire. The Vicentine translator,[178] whom we do not believe we are allowed to name, since she modestly hides herself, is certainly not among this number. She has learned a foreign language, knows how to wield a pen, and knows how to sit at a writing table rather than at her toilette. As a result, she inspires the desire that is rare in women, that of seeing her make herself useful to her nation by translating works that can bring her real advantages or pleasures, which is perhaps the same thing.

B. Response of a Reader, Followed by a Response from the Journalist

To the Author of the *Giornale Enciclopedico*
A Letter Deemed Opportune to Print

Madam,

A person who for good reasons does not name himself believes it opportune to alert you to an error in which, to your disgrace, you have fallen.

---

178. The catalog of the Marciana Library indicates that the translator was Terenzia Ghellini (1736–1810).

Because of this error you are being universally excommunicated in your new home, and you run the risk of being regarded as a person with whom only traitors to their very home can associate. How come? You say in your extract of the *New Compendium, etc.* that books are uncommon in Vicenza! Do you know that this truly excessive statement has turned against you all those who possess books and all those who are thinking of possessing some? that it has stirred up patriotic love in everyone's souls, provided inexhaustible material for discussion for at least eight days, and changed our customary greetings into a *What do you think of the periodical's statement? Did you hear what airs the lady who composes it puts on?* Forgive me, you are wrong. We have great men, we have those who deserve to be so, and it does not behoove you to excite against yourself the furor of everyone by doing injustice to everyone. This is what I think, I believe I am permitted to tell you so, I wait for your justification, and I am, in the meantime,

> Your, etc.,
> Anonymous

Sir,

Decency requires that one respond to letters: this duty which I fulfill— despite being convinced that both of our letters are of little interest to the readers of this periodical—will prove to you at least that I understand courteous behavior, and will serve as the first part of my response. You will understand easily from this tone, sir, that you should not expect justifications of some words to which you have given your own interpretation. I would not forgive myself if I had lived in a shell in Vicenza over the course of almost five years to the point of not knowing that the magnificent library of our learned and equally humane and courteous monsignor is one of its principal adornments, that there is a public library, and that very many private citizens possess many books and some good books. I am not so completely from another world as to be ignorant of all this. Since I have had many books belonging to many people pass through my very own hands, and since I have had the good fortune to be surrounded by a number of learned friends who possess the best of these, I would believe I was obliged to justify myself to myelf, not to others, if I had betrayed my character enough to publish an ignorant, insufficient[179] impertinence against an entire town out of malice, or in order to put on airs that would make me ridiculous. But forgive me, you do a real injustice to your home by condemning an imaginary one: you would have it believed that in Vicenza people do not know how to read, when, believe me, they know how to read very well. Since I found it consoling to be able to speak of a book that

179. The original is "insuffistente" [*sic*].

was *translated and published in Vicenza,* it is clear enough that that *where books are uncommon* means *where few are published,* and this is a very great truth. Wanting to argue captiously, one could understand differently; but why do so? If the vexations that you mention were true, I could, in order to quiet them, publish in my periodical a catalog of all the libraries in town, beginning with the public one and ending with that of a poor friend of mine who, for lack of a better place to put them, keeps his sole twenty-four books locked in a trunk. If these vexations were true, your town would be extremely frivolous, which it is certainly not; this *new home* of mine would grant me little hospitality, which would do it wrong. No, sir; you have taken the prattle of some idle persons for the complaints of an entire town. Believe me, your town does not bother so much with this foolishness; do not do it this injustice.

Permit me to end this long letter with a conclusion that I believe I owe to myself. I am too profoundly convinced of the tenuousness of my mind and of the few studies[180] I was able to undertake following my inclination [for study]—reasonable or extravagant as it may be—to ever have the ridiculous vanity of believing myself to be something serious, to raise myself up in criticism of a town, or to consider anyone beneath me. If an excess of self-love blinded me to the point of not allowing me to know these truths, I would respect myself at least enough as behooves a young woman in order not to draw derision upon herself. This reason and the duty prescribed to every person not to offend anyone at all no matter how poorly educated they may be have been and will always be the rule of my conduct. If someone who, like yourself, misunderstands my words will do me the honor of believing me, there will no longer be anyone who interprets me badly. Should preconception not want to lose its own rights, and should there be someone who obstinately resolves to believe as he pleases, I believe I am permitted to assure you that, as tranquil and indifferent as I have been on other occasions when I heard similar indiscreet insipidities attributed to myself by some elegant compatriot of yours, I will be compiling my periodical without worry. For if, because of the scarcity of my knowledge, my periodical does not come out well, as I nonetheless would like to be capable of making it, at least it will not occupy itself with material like this, which, not being of interest to the public, would perchance cause some of my subscribers to laugh, and would be tiresome to the majority of them.

I am your, etc.,

El. Caminer Turra

180. Caminer employed a nearly identical phrase in the preface to her *Composizioni teatrali moderne tradotte* (1772), vol. 1. See "Making of a Woman," text 25.

40. LETTER TO CLEMENTE VANNETTI[181]

Vicenza, 8 April 1779

Kindest Chevalier, Sir,

I have two of your letters in front of me to which I must respond, and I will do it point by point.

You always give me bad news: why do you allow our subscribers to desert? And as for them, why do they desert? All joking aside: I beg you not to miss an opportunity should it ever present itself to find substitutes for them.

By this time you will have received the thirty copies of the epistle. I received the three payments for a year of the periodical, and the money for the epistle and the sermon.

I am greatly pleased that the latter has come out to your liking both in terms of the printing and my decisions. I corrected it myself, both because I am your *manager* and because I am certain of taking more care than a hireling would do. In terms of the printing, since it pleases you, know that it is done in a new publishing house opened with the financial investment of my husband with the idea of printing the periodical, although he does not interfere [in running it], because it would not be proper for him to do so, since all the profits are his.[182] Therefore, if you need to print something, write to me when necessary, and I will give you a better price than you will find elsewhere. Returning to the sermon, have no doubt that my friend and I liked it, and do not doubt generally about anything of yours.

We are friends, and we can speak to each other freely. I state beforehand and I repeat that all your things are beautiful, that I like all of them, and that I am very willing to serve you in everything and for everything that I can. But allow me to beg you to spare me from printing the manuscripts that I am sending back to you. Your epistle is beautiful, elegant, happy, full of sense, but it is too particular to be adapted to a periodical meant to contain general materials of interest to everyone. It excites my admiration anew, but some-

181. This letter is located in the Biblioteca Civica di Rovereto (hereafter BCR), MS.7.3 (81, 81 bis, 82).

182. Antonio Turra was the *capitalista*, or financier, of the publishing house. The bookseller Antonio Veronese probably oversaw the printing process, and Elisabetta Caminer made the primary editorial decisions of the press. In the eighteenth century the relationship between printer, bookseller, and *capitalista* was complex; sometimes one person filled all three roles, or, more typically, two or more individuals assumed different roles in collaboration with each other and split costs and profits among themselves. See Mario Infelise, *L'editoria veneziana nel Settecento* (Milano: Franco Angeli, 1989), chap. 2. For details on the Turra publishing house (opened in 1779 and called the Stamperia Turra from 1780 to 1794), see section 2 of "Volume Editor's Introduction." See also "Making of a Woman," text 41.

times it behooves me to regard myself as a simple journalist. Also, tell the truth, are you speaking sincerely when you praise the sonnet sent to you? I think you have a generous soul, and a certain goodness of heart prejudices you a little too much when it comes to your friends. Nevertheless, where in this sonnet do you find a thought that is in the least manner observable; where do you find anything that is not extremely common? You who write so harmoniously, how do you tolerate a *Therefore if I have gay eyes, a laughing mouth?* How can you like *if I am as merry as the way he painted me from life?*[183] And then what need is there to say that the painter painted him *with a brush,* or rather, *with his brush?* And since when can *crying and poison* in the heart of those who love have become a commonplace these days, when lovers experience paradises, and a little difference between them serves only to heighten their senses? In short, I find this sonnet extremely bad, and I confess to you that I believe I would be doing myself a wrong by printing it as something good. As for your verses, I have no other difficulty than the one I mentioned to you, and I beg you to forgive me for that. But why do you never write for me those beautiful little pieces for the *Lazzaretto*[184] that suit me best of all, and that were so well liked? You promised me an extract, and I am waiting for it.

In the meantime, here are the fifty copies of the bells [*campane*][185] with the volumes for March. For these, you will be kind enough to pay Baldassarini 2.10 *lire,* and forty-eight *lire* for the Bible.

I have no idea if the abbé Denina[186] is the author of the legislation[187] but whoever it is, he is a very great man.

The judgments you are communicating to me about the volumes of the periodical are infinitely agreeable to me, and I beg you to continue them, one after another. Know that I am at your disposal and believe me, etc. etc.,

[No signature]

---

183. Caminer is quoting from the sonnet Vannetti would like her to publish.

184. The *Lazzaretto letterario* was a semiregular column in the Caminer periodical that was written by Clemente Vannetti and his friends in the late 1770s. Its "reviews" of imaginary books were humorous or sarcastic critiques of contemporary society. The column was provocative enough that it was eventually discontinued.

185. Caminer's meaning here is unclear.

186. Carlo Denina (1731–1813) was a Piedmontese Enlightenment intellectual of many and varied interests ranging from theology, history, and politics to literary history and linguistics. One of his major works was a general history of the Italian Peninsula, *Delle Rivoluzioni d'Italia* (1769–70).

187. This is a reference to Giovanni Scola's review (in four parts, between October and December 1778) of a work entitled *Principi della Legislazione universale* (Principles of universal law) (Parigi: la Vedova, [1777]) and available in Siena at the bookshop of Pazzini and Carli. Scola claimed that, although the book was attributed to (Georg Ludwig) Schmidt d'Avenstein (1720–

41. LETTER TO MICHELE SORGO (MIHO SORKOČEVIĆ) [188]

27 September 1779

My Dear Friend,

I write to you from a place that the [. . .][189] could call sad, and the lovers of happiness narcotic, but that to me is delightful, and you may believe it since I am writing to you from there. At the foot of Mount Berico, slightly above the Palace of Count Volpe, whom you know, Scola, Thiene, Trissino, and my husband, and the sweet *half*[190] that is myself, we have taken a small house that is not brilliant, not magnificent, but that seems to me made for study and for the sentiments. It is too beautiful here not to exalt that sentiment of friendship. I am convening here with you, then; come and join us if you want to put my judgment to the test.

Let us not discuss the insolence of the postal services; it is a given, and I am sure I will be obliged to them if they get this letter to you. How very kind you are! But are you only kind? I do not know the reason why, but a certain fatality has always led me to be unsatisfied with appearances and to want sentiment rather than words. This kind of indiscretion has always hurt me, yet I believe I am allowed it, at least in terms of friendship, and in the end I desire nothing more than that which I give. Rest assured, then, that nothing interests me more than believing that at such a distance and over such a stretch of time the man of whom I will always have a sweet memory conserves for me a friendship in the strictest sense of the word. I have met an infinite number of foreigners: none but you has made a strong impression upon me; I have made none of them the frequent subject of my conversations. Allow me to compare you a bit with one of them: Count Greppi of Milan. He is a man

---

1805) and was supposedly written originally in French, it was actually written in Italian by an anonymous Italian author. Our searches indicate, however, that the work was published by Schmidt in French as *Principes de la législation universelle* in Amsterdam (Chez M. M. Rey) in 1776.

188. The letter is located in the Archivio Storico dell'Ist. Acc. Iugoslavia di Zagabria, fondo Kaznacic, XV 21/A IV/45. For this letter I rely directly on the transcription of it by Lorenza Farina in "Carteggi di Elisabetta Caminer Turra," directed by Marco Pecoraro (thesis, Università di Padova, 1978–79), 251–54. No signature is indicated by Farina. Part of this letter was published in Žarko Muljačić, "Le amicizie letterarie italiane di Miho Sorkočević," in *Problemi di lingua e letteratura italiana del Settecento* (Wiesbaden: F. Steiner GMBH, 1965), 163. Michele Sorgo (Miho Sorkočević) (1739–90) was an aristocratic man of letters from Ragusa (modern day Dubrovnik), friend of Alberto Fortis, and contributor to Caminer's *Nuovo giornale enciclopedico*. Between 1775 and 1777 Sorgo was in Italy, where he spent a great deal of time in Bologna and Venice. He also traveled to Modena, Padua, and Vicenza, where he undoubtedly met Caminer.

189. Illegible word.

190. Caminer's emphasis.

gifted with all the qualities of the mind (I am not familiar with those of his heart), an enlightened traveler, and a man with such manners that they make up for his immense wealth and the source through which his father obtained it, finance. He would be the second foreigner whom I recall with pleasure, but I do not have a friendship with him: you may deduce the difference between him and you in my soul.

Why ever do I speak to you so often of my soul? It seems that I believe it is of interest to you. Self-love! Not even in simple solitude and in deep reflection does it leave us. My friends are marvelously well, and they love you as much as you are dear to me.

The translation of Gessner[191] you ask about will soon be published at my own expense, in a very beautiful edition which I am supervising, since my husband has spent money to open a printing house of which he is the financial sponsor [*capitalista*] and which goes by the name of Veronese, a bookseller from Vicenza.[192] I hope the year will not end before the publication of the first volume of this work: it is more dear to me than any other of my making, because it makes me shed tears often. I would also like to give you news from a town whose most notable people you know, but there is nothing interesting to report. The poor countess Poiana is in a deplorable state. Death is upon her with all its horrors; atrocious pain and the terrible progress of her cruel illness have not managed to destroy her hope at all, and one hopes that she will persevere. We will never be able to distinguish which of these two impulses [i.e., hope or perseverance] will prevail in such cases. Count Caldogno lost his other son, the last offspring of his family, and as lovable as he was unlucky. His mother's ill-fated bloodline, the carelessness of youth disdainful of necessary treatments for fatal illnesses, the imprudence caused by affairs of the soul, and a courage superior to nature caused a boy of nineteen to die of consumption,[193] [a boy] who added culture, talent, and the gifts of chance to graceful manners, and who inspired the hope that he would resemble his father only in external features. You would not have met him, because he was at the court of Bavaria when you left Vicenza. It is rumored that Count Caldogno, already separated from his wife by divorce, might try to free himself and take a new wife in order to secure a male heir for his family; this would be bad for his daughter.

We do not have any other interesting news: nuns, *dimesse*,[194] weddings,

---

191. *Opere del Signor Salomone Gesnero* (1781).

192. See "Making of a Woman," text 40.

193. Consumption was the term used for pulmonary tuberculosis.

194. The Italian term *dimesse* refers to pious women who lived secluded lives and were devoted to charitible works and to teaching catechism. These women "originally intended to follow 'a

theaters, [all] are too commonplace to be worth mentioning. They will always exist as long as we are able, and we will be able as long as . . . hush! I wanted to say as long as there is material. Let us leave pedantries aside: they will always exist as long as we are alive. Farewell, honorable and dear friend. Write to me often, and remember me even more often.

[No signature]

42. LETTER TO CLEMENTE VANNETTI[195]

Vicenza, 3 January 1780

Dearest Chevalier, Sir,

I must respond to two of your letters. Let us speak first about business. I saw the project for the work on painting, and I showed it around. Those in the know and the artists deemed one part of it to be practically useless: this is the poem. Painters do not read verse to understand their art, and others have very little interest in it.[196] In fact, Dolfin's book about sculpture and etching, published in free verse in 1777 in Milan, had very little success. Du Fresnoy's poem on the art of painting with annotations in Latin, translated and published in Rome and elsewhere in 1750, also enjoyed little success.[197] And yet it also offers an idea of the lives of excellent painters, which, nevertheless, can be found more extensively in various works on painting.

The second part, then, that is, the itinerary and the other things, may be good and useful if well executed, and thanks to these things a printer is willing to publish the other part as well, but here is the catch: he would like to see the manuscript.

I anticipate difficulties, but without the manuscript you will not find anyone to publish it at his own expense. If your friend wants to entrust it to me, I give you my sacred word that no use whatsoever will be made of it, and that the printer will undertake its publication, and that you will have it back without anyone's knowing. I have no other interest in this affair than to serve you. You decide.

I become endlessly angry when I receive a letter from you and hear about

---

third way' (other than marriage or the convent) of serving God in the world" (Anne Jacobson Schutte, "Glossary," in *Autobiography of an Aspiring Saint*, by Cecilia Ferrazzi (Chicago: University of Chicago Press, 1996), 89.

195. This letter is located in the BCR, MS.7.26 (113, 113b, 114, 114b).

196. On Caminer's perception of poetry's general lack of popularity see "Women and Society: Marriage or the Convent," text 8.

197. Charles Alphonese Du Fresnoy's *Art of Painting*, originally written in Latin, and subsequently translated into modern languages. The many translations of this work include one by the British painter Joshua Reynolds.

the extreme tardiness of these damned couriers in delivering packages to you. Of what use is the diligence?[198] Here is the one for December;[199] when will it reach you?

Our accounts about which you speak can be settled easily. You owe me six *lire* for the rest of the Bible, four for the three copies of the booklets, six for the issues printed specifically for you, and then there will now be the subscriptions. I owe you fifteen *soldi* for a *Lazzaretto*.

I wait impatiently for the eulogy of Zorzi; the sad subject that would seem uninteresting to your friend and to some of my friends occupies my soul more than any other. I am not suited for writing eulogies, or circumstances do not allow me to do so; but fatal losses have immersed my soul in sadness on more than one occasion, and some of my wounds are bleeding even now and will bleed for a long time to come.

Only a few days ago an amiable woman, the countess Teresa Poiana, to whom I was very attached, made me desire to write a eulogy. But it is too difficult to make private virtues appear truly worthy in the eyes of the public, without becoming overly enthusiastic or pedantic; [it is too difficult] to convey certain delicate contrasts that are of infinite merit to those who are perspicacious and sensitive. Oh, my friend, this lady's life was a series of misfortunes and an example of greatness; her death, without exaggerating, an object of shock and deep reflection, and, one could say, an inimitable model. Furthermore, this lady would merit a eulogy much more than do many so-called heroes; those illustrious names that we venerate in histories, if we go back to the sources of their virtues without relying upon emotions, are by far inferior to a woman. Your Baron Malfatti, who was here the day of her death, heard a great deal of talk about this rare woman; you could get details about it from him.

Your grotesque portrait appears before my eyes to distract me from these dark thoughts a little bit. How very curious you are! Eh! It does not matter; your frock, your pose do not interest me. Come very very often.[200]

Thank you for your canzone; everything you do is beautiful.

You like foccaccia that much! Wait until Easter arrives; here during that period they make some that passes for good; I will send you one, little one.

I have Pompei's book;[201] if you do not want to have anything to do with

198. The diligence was a kind of stagecoach used for delivering mail.

199. The December issue of the *Giornale enciclopedico*.

200. In the original, "Venite tanto e tanto."

201. This may be a reference to Girolamo Pompei (1731–88), poet and translator of ancient Greek authors, whose works include *Canzoni pastorali* (Verona: A. Carattoni, 1764), *Le Vite di*

it, I will say a few words about it; I do not think one can say much about that sort of thing. Farewell; conserve your friendship for me and make use of mine.

[No signature]

43. LETTER TO CLEMENTE VANNETTI[202]

[Vicenza, 1780]

Dearest Chevalier,

Here is the package with four copies of the periodical, three of the *Aeneid*, and fifteen copies of the abbé Monti's article. The article about Pompei, for which I also thank you, did not fit on one sheet and was printed on two. You will have it at the earliest opportunity.

How obliged I am to you for the trouble you have to suffer because of the boxes.[203] You will hear from me about these in another letter. In the meantime, accept my apologies and my thanks. When I have your friend's manuscript I will write to you about it more diligently and more precisely.

It is to your detriment that you wrote the eulogy of Zorzi in Latin; so I will not speak of it myself, but I will have it spoken about. It is the great delirium of all you Latinists that you do not want to do a little honor to your own language, and that you prefer to it a dead language that very few people consider anymore.

In terms of the book about the fine privilege of staying in the *sancto sanctorum*, do you regard it to be well done? I am holding my tongue and listening.

I revere you many many times, and I am, etc.,

[No signature]

44. LETTER TO ALBERTO FORTIS[204]

Vicenza, 2 March 1780

You Damned Madman,

How in the world do you expect me to keep my arms from going limp when I sit down to write to you? What is left of me after I have read one of

---

Plutarco (Verona: Moroni, 1772–73), and *Nuove canzoni pastorali ed altre rime diverse* (Verona: Moroni, 1779). Perhaps in this letter Caminer is referring to the latter work, since it had been recently published.

202. This letter is located in the BCR, MS.7.26 (120).

203. In the original, "cassette."

204. This letter is located in the Biblioteca Bertoliana di Vicenza, Carteggio Trissino, G.1.1.3 (E.105). Angelo Colla published this letter in his essay "Elisabetta Caminer Turra e il giornalismo 'enciclopedico,'" in *Varietà settecentesche: Saggi di cultura veneta tra rivoluzione e restaurazione*, vol. 3 of

your letters? It feels like there is nothing more insipid than myself. But how, how the devil can you jumble together such eccentric ideas, distant as they are from each other, and make sense of them with your unique train of thought? And what can compare to this, except your own mind? Keep sending me these brilliant caprices; they form the delight of our conversation as well as of your friends. Send them to me more often; we can practically hear you speaking, and your letters will never be taken the wrong way. In other words, if you want me to beg your mind with my heart, know that only the most interesting expressions issue from my heart for you. Know that my heart tells you much more than my mind can ever suggest, but I will never match your flights of fancy.

I have Lorgna's[205] orders regarding the books. All send you their greetings. Everyone is laughing and crying at the same time; you are made to inspire such contradictions. Farewell. At the risk of seeming immodest, I send you an embrace. Is it possible to do any less for someone who, in order to please me, had the goodness not to die?

[No signature]

45. LETTER TO AURELIO DE' GIORGI BERTÒLA[206]

19 August 1780

My Dear Sir,

I have waited to respond to your letter—the most obliging letter a gentleman could write to someone who aspires to be worthy—because I was hoping the book you had promised me would arrive at any minute and that I would have been able to tell you how much pleasure I had taken in reading it. But since it has been delayed, I cannot let more time pass without assuring

---

Filologia Veneta (Padova: Editoriale Programma, 1991), 97–98. Fortis was away from Venice during this period, traveling between Spalatro (or Spalato, modern Split), Ragusa (modern Dubrovnik), and southern Italy.

205. Anton Maria Lorgna (1735–96) was a mathematician at the Military College of Verona and the founder of a scientific society in Verona, Società italiana delle scienze.

206. This letter is located in the Biblioteca Comunale Di Bassano Del Grappa, Epistolario B. Gamba, XVI–A.12, 2475. Aurelio di Giorgi Bertòla (1753–98) was a poet, literary critic, translator, and historian. One of Bertòla's most important literary contributions was his effort to popularize German literature in Italy through his critical essays on the subject and with his Italian translations of poetry from German. Bertòla's knowledge of the German language singled him out among other Italian translators of German literature (including Caminer) who worked from French versions of the original works. Bertòla's publications include *L'idea della poesia alemanna* (1779), *Idea della bella letteratura alemanna* (1784), and his translation of a selection of the Swiss poet Gessner's idylls, *Scelta d'Idillj di Gessner tradotti dal Tedesco* (Napoli: Raimondi, 1777).

you that I now add a feeling of gratitude to the high esteem I have had for you, and the correspondence which at first seemed honorable to me has now become even more dear to me. And in fact, what could be greater than the cultivation of such a sentiment?

You do me too much honor in taking the trouble to criticize an opinion of mine, and yet I cannot think what it might be. I would have thought my opinions too inconsequential to be disputed by someone like you. I hasten to take advantage of your correction, and I could not have a better guide for improving my ideas.

What apprehension you inspire in me with your advantageous prejudice regarding my Gessner translation! How much I risk losing! I am not immune to self-love, although I do not have much, and I feel that your esteem is overly flattering. In any case, I will soon make my prejudices known to you; as the enclosed manifesto indicates, this favorite work of mine will soon be published, this work to which I have surely given all my best efforts and which has cost me tears from my heart, since I cannot defend myself from the sweet commotion that occurs when I am translating what is in my opinion the most noble, the most tender, and the most delicate of things. You who with such goodness have offered to introduce my periodical in these towns—so unlike those who do nothing even after prodding from me—will you deign to take on the introduction of my Gessner translation as well? In a city, in a kingdom[207] where I do not have any contacts, the book might sell very well, but I would never dare to inconvenience you if I did not feel you were favorably inclined to help me. How fortunate for me if you were to find that in my translation I had not failed to follow in your footsteps![208]

As for my periodical, I am enclosing a manifesto with all the details. I will be eternally grateful if you carry out your obliging plan. I have never had a subscriber in this kingdom.

Please forgive me if I am lacking in etiquette regarding the paper for this

207. Bertòla was in Naples at this time, as professor of history and geography at the Accademia di Marina.

208. Bertòla had already published his selection of Gessner's idylls in 1777. Thus Caminer was "following in Bertòla's footsteps"—not to say his shadow—when in 1781 she published her more ambitious project, the three-volume translation of Gessner's complete works, *Le opere di Salomone Gesnero* (1781). In 1787 Caminer published two other versions of her translations of Gessner, *Idilli del Signor Salomone Gessner Tradotti*, in two volumes (Livorno: C. Giorgi), and *Il primo navigatore: Poemetto del sig. Salomone Gessner, tradotto dalla signora Elisabetta Caminer Turra* (Livorno: C. Giorgi). For the competitive relationship between Caminer and Bertòla regarding their roles as translators and promoters of Gessner's work and for their differing aesthetics of translation, see Rita Unfer-Lukoschik, "Salomon Gessner fra Aurelio de' Giorgi Bertola ed Elisabetta Caminer Turra," in *Un europeo del Settecento: Aurelio de' Giorgi Bertola*, ed. by A. Battistini (Ravenna: Longo 2000), 401–24, where part of this letter is published.

letter, as I do not want to make it too heavy,[209] and honoring myself with your commands consider me always

> Your very devoted very obliged servant,
> El. Caminer Turra

46. LETTER TO CLEMENTE VANNETTI[210]

Vicenza, 13 September 1781

Dearest Chevalier,

I thought I had already thanked you, and I do so now profusely for Baroni's biography,[211] which will be discussed soon. Scola also sends infinite thanks. I sent Count Barbieri his copy and mailed the others to you. I hope you have received them.

I am enclosing the August issue of the periodical.

There will be no portrait of me in my translation of Gessner because no painter has yet been able to create a fair likeness of me; I do not know why, and I especially wonder why everyone paints me looking ten years younger than I am.

Mr. Tranquillini had already written to someone else about the books you mention, but I cannot help him. I am unacquainted with Goldoni's new comedies, I do not know where *The Secret Marriage* was published—I have only seen it performed on stage—and as far as *Beverley* is concerned, since my translation of it is published and bound with the other comedies, it is not worthwhile for me to break up two to extract that one play.[212] If he wants the whole volume, I will sell it to him for ten *lire* a copy, though it is worth sixteen.

I have not mentioned the Zorzi matter,[213] not out of disregard for something which must be good, since it pertains to you, but because I do not understand Latin as well as you believe I do and it is too much work for me on top of my endless, unbearable responsibilities. Send me the extract, and it will be published immediately. That is everything. I am with greatest distinction

> Your very devoted, very obliged servant,
> El. Caminer Turra

209. Caminer probably used a lightweight, inexpensive paper for this letter.

210. This letter is located in the BCR, MS.7.7 (100, 100b).

211. Baroni (1682–?) was a painter from Vannetti's hometown (Rovereto). Caminer reviewed Vannetti's *Notizie intorno al Pittore Gasparantonio Baroni Cavalcabò di Sacco* (Verona: Eredi di Marco Moroni, 1781) in the *Giornale enciclopedico*, December 1781, 69–71.

212. Caminer's translation *Beverlei*, published in her 1772 *Composizioni teatrali moderne tradotte*.

213. On the eulogy of Zorzi written in Latin by Vannetti, see "Making of a Woman," texts 42 and 43.

47. LETTER TO LAZZARO SPALLANZANI[214]

Vicenza, 6 July 1789

What must my respectable friend be thinking of me? What must he be thinking, this man whose friendship and goodness are so precious to me, when it seems that I would endanger his good disposition toward me? Oh! May he know that appearances are deceiving, but my heart is blameless! I do have faults, and I would confess them to my incomparable friend rather than disguise them, but they are not the kind that would put me among the most extreme prejudices.[215]

Your letter actually arrived nineteen days late, but that is nothing: extremely serious revolutions occurred in my home, because of which for a long time I have been close to taking the most decisive steps possible in a woman's life. The situation has just recently been happily resolved, but it kept me so agitated that not only my dearest friends and my most pressing work had to suffer, but I did not even know who I was any more. My health suffered repeatedly, I was oppressed by ill humor; and when a decisive change in circumstances finally allowed me to recover, I found myself enveloped in the chaos of neglected work and a thousand embarrassments. All of this prevented me from tending to matters, for which I was constantly admonishing myself. I confess this much in order to absolve myself of any appearance of ingratitude and incivility. I hope you will accept these truths, and assure me of your continued friendship for me!

Before discussing business, I will speak to you about that which interests me more than anything else. You are planning a trip to this area next autumn; the news has cheered my friends and me, since we hope to obtain a pleasure from it that you will perhaps not want to refuse us. At the foot of delightful hills and mountains, repositories for observations and objects of pleasure for the eyes and for the soul, Count Fracanzan,[216] one of my two best friends, has a noble country house where he takes the greatest pleasure in gathering his friends. The master of the house and his guests warmly beg you to spend some days here, in Orgian[o], twenty miles from Vicenza, where you will be able to satisfy the objective of your trip and also find yourself among five or six people who are full of admiration and sentiment for you, where it is not unlikely to find Fortis, and where I would be thrilled to see you. From the end

214. This letter is located at the BEM, Autografateca Campori, Carte Paradisi.

215. In the original, "ma non sono di quelli che debbano farmi l'ultimo dei pregiudizj."

216. Giovanni Battista Fracanzan (1732–1816) was a close friend of Caminer's in the last decade of her life and a witness for her final will and testament. She often visited him at his villa in Orgiano.

of October until about the twenty-second of November you will find here
the person who most desires your arrival. Shall I give my friend the good
news that you accept our sincere invitation?

Months and months ago I sent a parcel to Padre Harasti da Buda[217] in Milan to be forwarded to you. It contained two of the three volumes of my Gessner translation,[218] one of them for you, since you did me the honor of enjoying the others, and the other for Professor Bertòla, from whom I asked you to
obtain seven *lire*. Then on the occasion of the departure of the incomparable
Gritti, our representative, I mailed in the same fashion two copies of a collection [of poetry], for which I confess a bit of pride,[219] again one copy for
you and the other for Bertòla, who was owed one as a coauthor. The loss of
these volumes pains me because it will be hard for me to find more of the latest ones stolen from me, but I will look for them and I will send them again
with the first journal, if in the meantime you do not tell me that you have received them.

The *Giornale* has suffered because of the wretched circumstances I mentioned above. You will have received the January and February issues of the
current year, but not the December issue which [. . .]220 in the next post. I am
working furiously to catch up to the current month.[221]

For last year's issues and for those to come, please be kind enough to
send them to the abbé Amoretti[222] in Milan.

217. Gaetano Harasti di Buda was a member of the Accademia de' Georgofili in Florence and
of the Accademia Agraria of Vicenza. He published essays on corn, flax, and wheat harvest-
ing and on beekeeping. The Agrarian Academy of Vicenza—where Antonio Turra was lifetime
secretary—awarded prizes to his essays on corn, wheat, and flax, the Stamperia Turra published
them, and the *Nuovo giornale enciclopedico* reviewed them. His works include *Della più utile coltivazione
e manipolazione del lino: Memoria coronata dalla pubblica Accademia agraria di Vicenza nel di 19 settembre 1782*
(Vicenza: Turra, 1783), *Dalla più utile coltivazione del frumento: Memoria che reportò il premio dalla pubblica
Accademia agraria di Vicenza il di 22 settembre 1783* (Vicenza: Turra, 1784), *Dalla coltivazione del maiz: Memoria che riportò il premio [dell' accessit] dalla pubblica Accademia Agraria di Vicenza nel di 2 ottobre 1786* (Vicenza: Turra, 1788), and *Catechismo sulla più utile educazione delle api nel Gran-Ducato di Toscana, presen-
tato al Concorso dell'anno 1784* (Firenze: G. Cambiagi, 1785).

218. The first and second volumes of her translation. I presume here she is speaking of *Le opere
del Sig. Salomone Gesnero* (1781). A third edition of this work was published in two volumes in Vicenza, c. 1790.

219. *Tributo alla verità* (Vicenza: Turra, 1788), the collection of poetry Caminer organized and
published in honor of Camillo Gritti. Included in this collection are verses by Giuseppe Parini,
who dedicated a few stanzas to Caminer herself (see n. 131 of "Volume Editor's Introduction").

220. Blank space.

221. Caminer had yet to publish the March, April, May, or June 1789 issues of the *Nuovo giornale enciclopedico*.

222. Carlo Amoretti (1741–1816) was an erudite man of varied interests ranging from theology
to the arts to agriculture. Between 1767 and 1769 he was a professor of theology and canonical

How obliged I am to you for what the good Talassi[223] writes to me of your kindness!

I close here so as not to increase the mass of this letter; and in true agitation until I receive one from you [. . .][224] I declare that I am with the most respectful devotion

Your very devoted and obliged servant and friend,

El. Caminer Turra

48. LETTER TO LAZZARO SPALLANZANI[225]

[July 1792][226]

Most Illustrious and Esteemed Patron and Friend,

Full of blame in your regard, but even more full of faith in your indulgent friendship, which will not suppose that I have willfully or capriciously fallen into this state, I will get right to a subject that is worrying me.

Two weeks ago Doctor Turra was secretly advised that searches of his publishing house would be conducted to determine whether or not he had published letters by Spallanzani under a pseudonym and with the imprint of Zoopoli, in which the government of Milan and even particular individuals were criticized.[227] A second warning informed him that someone in Vicenza had been authorized to spend as much as twenty-four *zecchini* to bribe a former employee of Turra's, so that he would act as a spy and an informant in this matter. Someone persuaded this person not to participate in this evil venture, and he did in fact desist. But last Sunday two abbés arrived in Vicenza, one of them fat and wearing a wig, the other tall and with long hair, both rumored to be from Milan but whose names are not known. As soon as they

law at the University of Pavia. In 1783 he was named secretary of the Agrarian Society of Milan ("Società Patriottica"), where he pursued agrarian and economic studies. His works include *Coltivazione delle api* (1784) and *Della ricerca del carbone fossile, suoi vantaggi e suo uso nel Regno d'Italia* (1811).

223. Perhaps this is a reference to Angelo Talassi, author of *La piuma recisa* (Venezia: Storti, 1778) and *L'olmo abbattuto: Poema* (Lisbona: Nella Stamperia di Antonio Rodrigues Galhardo, 1795).

224. Blank space.

225. This letter is located at the BEM, Autografateca Campori, Carte Paradisi.

226. Colla et al. published part of this letter in "Tipografi, editori, librai," 157; Colla presumes the date of the letter to be 14 July because of the short note from Fortis dated as such which opens Caminer's letter. This was not the first or the last of Caminer's conflicts with censors. Two years later, in January 1794, a package of more than fifty books and pamphlets directed to her from the bookseller Lorenzo Manini of Cremona was stopped by censors in Vicenza (ASV, Inquisitori di Stato, busta 372).

227. The term "imprint" refers to the indication of the place where a work was published, often included on its title page. "Zoopoli" was one of several ficticious city names often listed as the place of publication in an attempt to avoid censorship.

arrived, they inquired about the publishing house and they mentioned Turra as the one who had married Caminer, at which point they looked for Bardella's shop.[228] In fact, they came immediately, found the publishing house closed, and passed by Turra's house, where they spoke with him at length about publications, about Fortis, about the Bozza Museum now called the Gazola (Count Gazola is a very good friend of Volta's) without ever identifying themselves, thereby obliging Turra to assume a guarded attitude and finally to dismiss them. They said nothing of the business about you, and they might be innocent people, but we believe they are spies. I was not able to speak with Bardella, who left the city, but today I will find out if they went to his place. That is everthing. Even good people have to fear wicked individuals, so I felt obliged to warn you. In extreme haste, I fervently beg you to answer our Fortis's prayers, and, awaiting news from you, I am forever

> Your very obliged very devoted servant and friend,
> El. Caminer Turra

49. LETTER TO AN UNIDENTIFIED RECIPIENT[229]

21 February 1796

My Dear Friend,

To hold a conversation, to make your mind sing! As long as I do not make the priest sing. For nearly two months now I have been unable to get out of bed. Daily fever, pains, etc. But I will write about my infirmities a little better another time; at least I am answering only one of your many letters, so do not believe me to be the most ill-mannered person in the world. The person who delivered your letter left it at my house, where he was told that I was ill and not seeing anyone. If he had returned or if I had known where he was I would have had my friends help him. I will write to you, about everything; in the meantime, for goodness sake, [send me] the extract of the book you promised me. Think well of your friend,

> El. Caminer Turra

228. Domenico Bardella was a Vicentine bookseller in whose shop Caminer and her colleagues often met. See Colla et al., "Tipografi, editori, librai," 148.

229. This letter is located at the Biblioteca Comunale di Forlì, Piancastelli. It appears to have been written in another hand—probably dictated by Caminer, who was so ill that she was unable to write—and by someone who had difficulty with spelling. In this case, it is plausible that the person wrote "Ingegnere" for "ingegno" and "prette" for "prete" in these sentences: "Tener conversazione, far cantare il vostro Ingegnere! Basta ch'io non faccia cantare il Prette." I have translated these lines according to this hypothesis.

PART II
WOMEN AND SOCIETY

❀ THE INTELLECTUAL LIFE ❀

1. ON WHY WOMEN WRITE DIFFERENTLY FROM MEN (1769)[1]

The debates over the thesis that serves as the epigraph to this book have long been settled.[2] What cultured nation does not know that the mind, or the ability to think, to understand, to imagine does not depend on one's sex? It is no different for this faculty than for the metals that are used to fabricate the most essential tools: that is, everything depends on its tempering. Education, or a certain practice that often serves in its place, is what tempers minds. Evidence of women's capabilities was dispersed everywhere, but no one had gathered it together: it required a gallant people to take up this concern. It seems that a more delicate organization, more subtle and more sensitive fibers, more abundant and more subtle blood, and a purer nervous fluid render women more apt to succeed in matters of delight, taste, and finesse than in certain works of the mind; and it is up to the metaphysicians, who know how to apply the knowledge of our structure to that of the human mind, to decide on such an obscure point. It is a simpler matter to agree upon the advantages that women have in expressing themselves better and even more easily than men. A wise woman [*donna di spirito*] says in certain letters of hers, that *their* [women's] *ignorance makes their style beautiful, because the expressions of their hearts are precisely those that present themselves to their pens.* Men, who are ordinarily more educated, who pursue regulated courses of study, and who read continually,

---

1. In *Europa letteraria*, May 1769, 20–22, signed EC. Caminer is reviewing Jean François De Lacroix and Joseph de La Porte's *Histoire littéraire des femmes françoises* (Literary history of French women) (Paris: Lacombe, 1769). Except for the passage beginning with "This is why deception" and ending with "for a woman to write ten," she is translating the French review of this work published in the 5 April 1769 issue of *Affiches, annonces et avis divers*, ed. Jean Louis Aubert (Paris: Bureau des Affiches).

2. In the heading to the review, Caminer indicates that the epigraph to the book is "What women can do!" (Quid femina possit!), from Virgil's *Aeneid*.

have only those expressions that their memories dictate to them, or those which the mind's toil and contention provide. Therefore, the first expressions are not their own and the others are purely factitious and too effortful to be as simple, natural, and lively as those of women. They [men] don't have that artlessness which increases the value of things so much. They portray the ideas of the mind and rarely the emotions of the soul. *This is why deception comes more easily to men. They work with their heads; women with their hearts; and on certain occasions, for the very same reason, it requires greater effort for a man to write one page than it does for a woman to write ten.*[3] But let us get to the design of this book: here is its outline. It is a series of letters presumably written to a woman in which one finds first a compendium of the lives of all the women authors [in the book], with anecdotes that were gathered about them. This is followed by an analysis or an extract of their works in prose or in verse, letters, novellas, novels, moral works, poems of every type, etc.

It begins with the twelfth century, so that Eloisa [Heloise] opens the scene. But since she wrote in Latin, the entry on her contains only various translations of her letters and the famous epistle by Pope.[4] After this, the first woman whose original writing is provided is the queen of Navarre, author of *One Hundred New Tales*,[5] and after this princess, all women, whose works exist in every genre, are arranged in this copious library according to their cate-

3. I have placed these two original sentences in italics to distinguish them from the rest of the review, which is a translation. Caminer's suitor Francesco Albergati Capacelli reacted hotly—if playfully—to this part of the review. In a 6 June 1769 letter to Caminer, he wrote: "Oppressed and tormented by remorse for having lavished praises on a man, such as myself, who does not merit them, you wanted to make up for it at the expense of the rest of the male sex, humiliating it and devaluing its merits. . . . Oh, God, my poor Bettina, into what abyss of errors have you fallen? What blasphemies have you pronounced? What heresies have you published? And the wise censors do not oppose you? And the Holy Tribunal of the most Holy Inquisition is silent? And the whole world is not rising up in protest and in war against you? But if everyone is tolerating this, I will be the one to speak up. 'This is why deception comes easier to men.' I have never read a blacker, more horrible, more heretical line than this" ("Lettere di Francesco Albergati Capacelli alla Bettina (Nov. 1768–Nov. 1771)," ed. Roberto Trovato, *Studi e Problemi di Critica Testuale* 28 [1984]: 147).

4. The correspondence arising from the ill-fated amorous relationship between the medieval scholar and canon Pierre Abélard (1079–1142) and his pupil, the learned Héloïse (dates unknown), was first published in 1616 and gave rise to many editions over the centuries. In 1717 Alexander Pope published a long poem entitled "Eloïsa to Abelard"—essentially his reconstruction of the story of the two lovers—which enjoyed great popularity during the eighteenth century.

5. Marguerite d'Angoulême (1492–1549), duchesse d'Alençon and queen of Navarre, was the author of contes, plays, and verse. The reference to a work entitled *One Hundred New Tales* must refer to her *L'heptaméron des Nouvelles* (Paris: J. Cavellier 1559), a collection of tales modeled after Boccaccio's *Decameron*. For a modern edition in English, see *The Heptameron*, trans. P. A. Chilton (New York: Penguin Books, 1984).

gory. As far as one can tell, if some of them [women] were omitted, luck was with those who wrote only ascetic works, like, for example, Madame de la Vallière, author of *Christian Reflections on the Historical Books of the Old Testament*, etc.[6] This work is almost always unusual and interesting. One learns various things in it; those who have read a lot will happily revisit many works about which they had only a vague idea; and a good number of people will find it completely new.

2. ON EXCEPTIONAL WOMEN (1769)[7]

Unfortunately, because of delays in mail delivery and because commerce among our booksellers and our transalpine neighbors is not yet extensive enough, it too often happens that we are forced to base our judgment of new books on the opinions of foreign journalists, necessarily making use of their labors, with the inevitable result that we sometimes adopt some of their superficiality.[8] The French journalist who wrote the review of the *Dictionary of Celebrated Women* seems to have written it with very little friendliness toward our sex, because his essay consisted of a mere two or three passages. One describes a young girl who allowed herself to be seduced by her lover because of his flattering promises. He then abandoned her, and she followed him in vain to England hoping to force him to support her. The other passages describe two women who had the lowly merit of making witty remarks about the situation. The person writing this review finds that it is a solemn injustice to dwell upon these examples while passing over that respectable number of women who distinguished themselves in the virtues, in letters, in the sciences, in the arts, and even in arms, many of whom deserve to be better known to

6. Caminer seems to have confused two women authors here. Louise Françoise de la Baume Le Blanc, duchesse de La Vallière (1644–1710), former mistress of Louis XIV of France, published a work entitled *Réflexions sur la misericorde de Dieu par une dame pénitente* (Reflections on the mercy of God by a penitant woman) (Paris: A. Dezallier 1680) after quitting the court and dedicating herself to a devout life. The author of the work Caminer refers to here, *Réflexions chrétiennes sur les livres historiques de l'Ancien Testament* (Paris: Veuve de N. Desaint, 1773) was written by Marie-Madeleine d'Aguesseau Madame Le Guerchois (dates unknown).

7. In *Europa letteraria*, November 1769, 79–94, signed EC. Caminer is reviewing Jean François De Lacroix's *Dictionnaire historique portatif des femmes célèbres* (Portable historical dictionary of celebrated women) (Paris: L. Cellot, 1769).

8. In an earlier issue of the *Europa letteraria* (April 1769, 42–45) Caminer's father had published a translation of a French journalist's review of the *Dictionnaire historique portatif* (itself published in the March 1769 issue of the *Mercure de France*). With this opening sentence Caminer attempts to excuse her father's negligence, even as she essentially disregards journalistic custom by publishing a second review of the dictionary in order to correct both the French journalist's original review and her father's uncritical translation of it.

the world than they are presently. Moved by this blameless affection for her sex, a woman must think to speak up for all the others in this voluminous work, choosing the names most deserving of celebrity, and most capable of exciting a praiseworthy emulation. Should any wily individual wish to believe that self-interest and gratification motivate on this occasion a pen which should be perfectly impartial, let him keep it to himself; there is no reason for us to hide ourselves, and in any case it is most reasonable that women find satisfaction in seeing themselves as good as men at everything.

So as to avoid jumping from one subject to another, as the alphabetic order of dictionaries tends to do, it seemed appropriate to separate the illustrious women who are found in the first volume into classes of a sort, according to various kinds of merits, virtues, or graces.[9]

We will speak first about the women who became famous for their love of chastity or for their conjugal loyalty, which they embodied to the highest degree. Among the others, Arnalda di Rocas,[10] a young Cypriot girl, deserves distinguished mention. After the capture of Nicosia, while on board a boat bound for Constantinople, she feared she was destined for a harem. In order to prevent that, she had the courage to meet death by setting fire to the gunpowder on board. The ship and the entire crew exploded into the air. The Levant saw not only this example of chastity and strength. The death of the famous Venetian maiden Erizzo[11] was even more heroic and tragic. In vain did Mohammed II flatter and threaten her to make her cede to his brutality. She resisted so valiantly that the tyrant killed her himself, as he had done to Irene, another young Christian maiden, for the same reason. These two heroines' deaths were not marred by the stain of suicide, as was Arnalda's, and much before her that of the Etruscan Clusia,[12] who leapt from a tower to avoid falling into the hands of Valerius Torquatus, who had asked for her from her father, whom he held under siege. Coupling an equal love of chastity with a

---

9. De Lacroix's dictionary itself is organized alphabetically, and the set of "classes" is Caminer's.

10. I was unable to locate information on Arnalda di Rocas, either in De Lacroix's dictionary or elsewhere.

11. Erizzo (or Erici) was the daughter of Paolo Erizzo, governor of Negroponte. When Mehmet II conquered the island, he had her father put to death and claimed her for his own. When she resisted him, he had her decapitated.

12. Clusia was the daughter of King Thuscus. When Valerius Torquatus asked for her hand and was refused, he attacked their castle. Clusia leapt from the tower, preferring death, and according to Plutarch, the wind filled her dress, allowing her to land safely. However, in Plutarch's account, Valerius violated her after her safe landing and for that act was banished by the Romans to the island of Corsica. See Plutarch, *Moralia: Greek and Roman Parallel Stories*, trans. Frank C. Babbitt (Cambridge, Mass.: Harvard University Press), 4:277–79.

deep tenderness for her dead husband, the Paduan Bianca della Porta[13] was able to earn even greater fame. Enslaved in Bassano, where she was fighting against the tyrant Azzolino, she threw herself from a window to avoid submitting to his dishonest intentions, and once healed, seeing that she had no other options for defending her honor, she asked permission to visit her husband's grave; granted permission, with supernatural effort she pulled the tombstone down upon herself and was crushed. There is no need of a tragic play to demonstrate the tender love Artemisia II, queen of Caria,[14] felt for her husband, Mausolus. She was even more commendable than the warrior Artemisia I,[15] who united with Xerxes when he launched the war against the Greeks, and who distinguished herself above all the Persian generals [whom she accompanied into battle]. Taking the peoples of Latmus by surprise, she gained control of their city in only a few hours. Artemisia II, who was no less valorous, likewise loved her husband. After his death she had erected in his honor a mausoleum that became one of the seven wonders of the world. And not satisfied with this, every day she mixed a little of Mausolus's ashes in her own drink and served as his sepulcher herself. Equally laudable, although different in nature, is the love that [Lady] Godiva, wife of Count Leofri[c],[16] had for her subjects, the inhabitants of Coventry. To relieve them from burdensome taxes she accepted the condition her husband set for her—to ride naked across the city on a horse, right in the middle of the day. Before carrying this out, she ordered all the people to shut themselves in their homes and not look out their windows, and so the generous woman obtained a considerable favor for her people without sacrificing the laws of the most exacting modesty.[17]

Although of a different nature, the second class [of women] does equal honor to our sex. These are the women whose natural and acquired qualities

13. I was unable to locate della Porta in De Lacroix's dictionary or elsewhere.

14. Artemisia II, queen of Caria (c. 395–351 B.C.E.), daughter of Hekatomnus, was a devoted wife and coruler. Together with her husband Mausolus (who was her full brother), she resisted Athenian imperial aims.

15. Artemisia I (c. 520–? B.C.E.) was the daughter of Lygdamis and queen of Halicarnassus. Caminer merges the two battles described in De Lacroix's dictionary in which Artemisia I participated: the first (c. 480 B.C.E.) in which she accompanied the Persians in alliance with Xerxes against the Greeks, and the other (no date is recorded) in which she entered Latmus under the ruse of celebrating the festival of Cybele.

16. Leofric was the earl of Mercia and lord of Coventry.

17. Lady Godiva (c. 1040–80) is a legendary Anglo-Saxon hero whose story may be partly true. According to legend only one person disobeyed her request that all town inhabitants close their shutters and not look out when she rode by. "Peeping Tom," as this individual came to be called, looked through a hole in his shutters and was immediately struck blind.

were worthy of completely ruling powerful empires, and who were the first in-
stigators of laudable actions or clamorous events. One of these was the learned
and eloquent Aspasia of Miletus,[18] who directed a school of oratory in Athens
which distinguished subjects attended, including Socrates himself, to whom
she taught rhetoric and gave various lessons in politics. Pericles, who was his
disciple, married her, and she enlisted his aid in helping her homeland against
the Samian people, who where defeated because of the help that the people
of Miletus received from Athens. Even the war of Megaris, where the famous
Peloponnesian War originated, was the result of Aspasia's words, she being an-
noyed with the people of Megaris. So respectable and famous was her name
that Cyrus [the younger] wanted his favorite [concubine] Milto,[19] a Phocaean
by birth, to adopt it, as she was worthy of it in every way. Milto passed from
the hands of Cyrus to those of Artaxerxes,[20] and the latter had to give her over
to Darius one day, when he had to grant Darius whatever he wished. But upset with her concession to this arrangement, he [Artaxerxes] made her the
priestess of the Sun, obliging her in this way to chastity. Both she and Darius
were irritated by this; and their indignation gave rise to a conspiracy, which,
when discovered, cost the lives of fifty brothers of that prince. Just as the first
of the two Aspasias caused a revolution in Greece, and the second played a big
role in the politics of Persia, so another Greek woman in later times became a
celebrated figure in Constantinople. Athenais, daughter of Leontios, sophist
of Athens,[21] beautiful, educated, and amiable, favored by Pulcheria,[22] rose to
the throne, becoming the wife of Theodosius [II]. However, she was a woman,

18. Aspasia of Miletus (c. 464–c. 420 B.C.E.), daughter of Axiochus, was born in Miletus in Ionia.
She was one of the most famous ancient Greek women, renowned for her political influence and
for her philosophical education. On the following account of her, see Plutarch, *Lives*, trans.
Bernadotte Perrin (1916; reprint, Cambridge, Mass.: Harvard University Press, 1996), vol. 3, *Pericles*, 24.

19. Aspasia the Younger (Aspasia the Wise; surname Milto) (fl. 415–370 B.C.E.) was the favorite
concubine and adviser of Cyrus, who had her change her surname Milto to Miletus, after the earlier Aspasia.

20. Artaxerxes (c. 451–360 B.C.E.) murdered his brother Cyrus the Younger, became king of Persia, and, as spoils of war, took Aspasia as part of his harem. He, in turn, was forced to cede her to
his son Darius.

21. Athenais (Eudoxia) (c. 400–460) was the empress of the Eastern Roman Empire, the wife of
Theodosius II, and the mother of Licinia Eudoxia. Her father named her Athenais after her birth-
place, Athens, but she took the name Eudoxia when she converted to Christianity. Her husband,
Theodosius II, was the emperor of the Eastern Roman Empire, 408–50.

22. Pulcheria (409–53), a highly popular empress of the Eastern Roman Empire, was the first
woman to earn this title (in 414) by her own merit and not by being the wife or mother of a man
who had become emperor or by producing heirs for the dynasty. She was the elder sister of the
weak ruler Theodosius II, whom she dominated. She adopted the young Athenais and groomed
her for marriage to her brother. However, when Athenais married Theodosius, she too was

despite the qualities that distinguished her from other women; a joke of Pulcheria's made her forget every favor received, so that she convinced Theodosius to send Pulcheria away from the court, and she then governed the empire as she pleased. As is usually the case, a lie that seemed inconsequential necessarily led to other lies which, arousing the suspicions of the jealous and weak Theodosius, ruined her and led to the decapitation of the emperor's minister Paulinus.[23] Imprudence ruined more than one woman who was close to holding or already in possession of a distinguished rank. Icasia, an educated and beautiful young girl, lost the hand and the throne of the emperor Theophilus for having answered him with too spirited a response.[24] He feared a woman who knew more than he did. But Atheneis's lack of sincerity deserved reproach much more than did Icasia's boldness. She was removed from the court and she suffered this upset patiently; she lived on books and pious works for the rest of her days. Among the great women rulers are the celebrated Queen Elizabeth of England[25] about whom so much has been written that it would be useless to go over it again, and her mother, Anne Boleyn.[26] The schism in that reign and the death of the most enlightened subjects are such that the wedding of Henry VIII forms a memorable era.[27] Anne Boleyn had a tragic end, but she was not so generally pitied as was Amalasuntha, daughter of Theo-

---

named empress, and the ensuing power struggle between the two women led to Pulcheria's temporary withdrawal from the court.

23. Since Theodosius was in the habit of signing things without reading them—giving too much power, in Pulcheria's opinion, to his ministers—Pulcheria decided to teach him the importance of assuming more responsibility. She prepared an edict stating that Theodosius had agreed to sell his wife—Athenais—to her. He signed the document without looking at it, and when he next called for his wife, Pulcheria refused to release her, claiming that he had sold Athenais to her. Angered by this charade, Athenais convinced Theodosius to deprive Pulcheria of her power. Pulcheria discovered what was about to happen and left Constantinople on her own. Athenais assumed the position of empress but was forced to abandon the court a year later, after her lie about an apple given to her by her husband led him to suspect adulterous relations between her and his friend Paulinus, whom he then had killed.

24. Theophilus I, Byzantine emperor, ruled 829–42. De Lacroix's dictionary does not specify what Icasia said, but it indicates that she eventually retired to a convent, where she wrote many works.

25. Queen Elizabeth reigned 1558–1603.

26. Anne Boleyn married Henry VIII in 1527, and he had her beheaded in 1536 on unsubstantiated charges of adultery.

27. Henry VIII governed 1509–47. The schism here must refer to his break with the Roman Catholic Church after it refused to sanction his divorce from Queen Catherine so that he could marry Anne Boleyn. The death of the most enlightened subjects may refer to those like Cardinal Wolsey who lost their lives because they could not work Henry's will with the church or to those like Thomas More who died because they refused to sanction Henry as the supreme head of the Church of England.

doric, king of the Ostrogoths, during the barbarous age in Italy.[28] She was famous for her learning, for science, for the various languages she knew, and much more for her prudence and for the wise leadership with which she governed her own father's realm after the death of her husband Eutharic until her son Athalaric would come of age. She was deprived even of this when her cousin Theodahad took the throne and with an excess of ingratitude cruelly sentenced her to death. She deserved to be avenged, and her death was the reason behind the expedition of Belisarius, who defeated the Goths, and the war that was waged by Narses after the disgrace of that celebrated captain. Among the many other women celebrated for their involvement in governments and for the advantages they brought to their nations one must mention Bianca de Castile, very well known in the history of France, and mother of the holy King Louis;[29] one must mention Agnèse Sorel[30] who knew how to use love in the service of the revival of the French monarchy, and Gabrielle d'Estrées,[31] who, far from weakening or distracting him, inspired valor in the great king Henri IV. All the people grieved the death of this woman, who was so adored by the monarch. She had a much more tranquil death than that of the unfortunate Françoise de Foix[32] a decade earlier. Her love of François I made her the victim of a cruel husband, who had her killed with all the lugubriousness of a horrid tragedy by forcing her to bleed to death in her own castle. The fantasy and the pen of Mr. d'Arnaud would recount this dismal story very well![33]

Since the prescribed limitations of an extract do not allow us to transcribe the very lengthy entry on the Amazons, who in any case are very well known,

---

28. Amalasuntha (c. 495–535) was the queen of the Ostrogoths. She was the niece of King Clovis and the daughter of King Theodoric (b. c. 455), who founded the Ostrogothic kingdom in Italy and ruled it from 489 to 526.

29. Bianca de Castile (b. 1169) was the daughter of Alfonso IX, king of Leon (r. 1188–1230), and Eleanor, daughter of Henry II, king of England. Educated by her mother, Bianca de Castile married King Louis of France (Louis VIII, r. 1223–26), oldest son of Philippe-Auguste.

30. According to De Lacroix's dictionary, Agnès Sorel (1409–49) threatened to leave King Charles VII of France (r. 1422–61) if he did not desist from his idea of leaving the French throne to foreigners, that is, to the English king.

31. Gabrielle d'Estrées (1573–99), duchess of Beaufort, was the daughter of Jean d'Estrées. She was the mistress of King Henri IV (de Navarre) (1553–1610) and bore him two sons. Her sudden death led to suspicions that she may have been poisoned in order to prevent a marriage between herself and Henri IV. Other rumors indicated that Henri himself may have poisoned her.

32. Françoise de Foix, comtesse de Châteaubriand (c. 1490–1537), was the wife of the count of Châteaubriand and mistress of King Francis I of France (1494–1547, r. 1515–47). According to De Lacroix's dictionary, her husband locked her in a castle room, and after six months he had two surgeons bleed her from all four limbs and watched as she bled to death.

33. This is Caminer the translator speaking: this very year she published her translation of François Thomas Marie Baculard d'Arnaud's *Euphème*.

we will content ourselves with gathering facts about these valorous warriors, who formed and succeeded in the difficult task of "building the foundation of a monarchy that established the glory of their sex by showing that women are capable of doing honor to the scepter, and the crown as well, by the manner in which they wear it."[34] They conquered the areas of the Cimmerian Bosporus, a great part of Sarmatia, [and] the inhabitants of the Caucasus; they made subjects of Iberia, Colchis, and Albania; they entered Asia Minor along the Black Sea, and, taking control of the vast valleys irrigated by the Thermodon and the Iris, they built Themiscyra, the seat of their empire; they extended along the coasts of the Aegean, and they built cities there, which are eternal monuments to their victories. The Amazons united themselves with Priam, king of Troy, against the Greeks after the death of Hector, and they fought valiantly; Penthesilea, their queen, died in battle at the hands of the great Achilles. And if they lost a lot in the two battles they fought against Theseus—one to exact revenge for the girdle that Queen Antiope was forced to cede to Heracles, who had accompanied Theseus in this endeavor, and for Hippolyte, whom he had abducted,[35] and the other for the Temple of Achilles that they tried in vain to destroy—if they lost a lot in these two battles, those who survived withdrew to Cappadocia and continued to make a name for themselves in arms even though they were unable to keep all of their conquests. Although they did not enjoy fame equal to that of the Asian Amazons, those who were discovered in Africa three hundred years ago nevertheless deserve equal praise. They followed in the steps of the earlier ones, and foreign princes claim glory to be allied with them. Equally valorous are the Amazons in America, who were often seen armed at the head of entire battalions fighting against their enemies, and emboldening the Indians. One of them, still a young girl, did not allow herself to fall until she had killed five Spaniards with poisoned arrows. The spirit of the Asiatic Amazons inspired many many other famous women, among them the distinguished Aldrude, countess of Bertinoro,[36] in Romagna. She united with Guglielmo degli Aleardi[37] to help the people of Ancona, who were under siege by the archbishop of

---

34. Caminer is reproducing the quotation in De Lacroix's dictionary from the abbé Guyon in his *Histoire des Amazones anciennes et modernes*, pt. 2, chap. 4, art. 1 (*Dictionnaire historique portatif*, 1:105).

35. As was common in ancient accounts, Caminer's version of this story seems to conflate or confuse the Amazon queens Antiope and Hippolyte. For the various and conflicting versions of this story, see Robert Graves, *The Greek Myths* (1955; reprint, New York: Penguin Books, 1986), 2:124–26.

36. I was unable to find information about Aldrude, countess of Bertinoro, in De Lacroix's dictionary or elsewhere.

37. According to De Lacroix's dictionary, Guglielmo degli Adelardi was one of the most powerful and noble citizens of Ferrara, and he forced the troops of the emperor Frederick I and the Venetians to retreat from Ancona, which they had besieged for about seven months in 1167.

Mainz and the Venetians. She forced the bishop and his troops to flee, and as a result she forced the Venetians, who had been tricked by the bishop into lending him a great number of arms, to withdraw as well. While returning home at the head of her army, she encountered enemy troops and wreaked such carnage upon them that they were obliged to take refuge in Sinigaglia to save themselves. Romagna was not a witness to only this example of valor. Cia, wife of the tyrant Ordelassi,[38] and equally valorous as he, governed Cesena while her husband commanded Forlì, and she defended it bravely; and if the four Guelfs, whose lives she wanted to save despite the orders of her husband, had not forced her to shut herself in the Cittadella, which was then mined by Cardinal d'Alborna, Cesena would never have been taken. She would have been a formidable challenge to the pope, just as Jeanne de Belleville[39] was to the French. She wanted to take a strange revenge for the death of Olivier III, Monsieur de Clisson, her husband, whom the King of France had decapitated. Having sent her own twelve-year-old son away from the kingdom, she armed three ships, which she used to lay siege to all the French she encountered. She made landings in Normandy, and there she launched assaults on many castles. Equally valorous, although not equally famous because not as favored by fate in terms of an illustrious birth, was Maria d'Estrada, the wife of a soldier of [Fernand] Cortes, the conquistador of Mexico. In all the battles that her side waged, she showed extraordinary valor. Unmindful of being a woman, she vied with the most valorous men in that endeavor, amazing the Spaniards as well as the defeated Americans.

Many other examples are found in this *Dictionary* of courageous women about whom we will remain silent for the sake of brevity, and so that we may speak about some of them who distinguished themselves in the fine arts.[40] Diana Mantovana[41] of Volterra made remarkable copper engravings; with her *Baccante* after Giulio Romano, she left one of the most beautiful monuments

38. Cia was the wife of tyrant Ordelassi of Forlì during the fourteenth century.

39. Jeanne de Belleville Clisson was the wife of Olivier III, lord of Clisson. She was renowned during the reign of Philippe VI de Valois, king of France. After the king had her husband decapitated in 1343, she sold her jewels, purchased warships, and became a leader of a band of royal knights, avenging her husband's death by massacring any loyal subjects of the king whom she encountered upon her extensive travels.

40. It is striking that a host of renowned Italian women artists were not mentioned in De Lacroix's dictionary—Lavinia Fontana (1522–1614), Sofonisba Anguissola (c. 1535–1625), Artemisia Gentileschi (1593–c. 1652), Giovanna Garzoni (1600–1670), Rosalba Carriera (1675–1757), and Giulia Lama (1681–1747), to name but a handful—and that Caminer did not attempt to vindicate the reputations of these women in her review (especially those from the Veneto), as she had done for Italian women of letters and science excluded from the dictionary.

41. Diana Scultori Ghisi (a.k.a. Diana Mantuana or Mantovana; 1547–1612) was the only sixteenth-century female engraver to sign her prints with her own name. In Rome, Mantovana pub-

ever produced by the burin.[42] Aristarete of Sicyon[43] became famous among ancient Greek women for her paintings on canvas; Catterina Canton[i] of Milan[44] among modern Italian women; among the French, Elisabeth[-Sophie] Cheron,[45] who, in addition to music, mastered the learned languages and poetry to an excellent degree. Among the cultivators of drawing, one cannot deny a certain place to Johanna Koerten of Amsterdam.[46] With scissors, she cut up white paper the way painters work with the brush; and she executed among other things the portrait of the emperor Leopold, which he kept in his own museum as a truly rare object.

But the women who cultivated the sciences in ancient times were not rare. They were almost as common then as are those women today who pretend to become cultivated, to study, and who spout pretensions and unfortunately serve as fodder for the wits' laughter.[47] The following are but the scarcest portion of the number of ancient learned women: Abrotelia and Bio Pythagoreans,[48] of whom Iamblichus makes honored mention; Axiothea,[49] who used to dress as a man in order to take part in Plato's classes; Arete, daughter and disciple of Aristippus,[50] the old founder of the Cyrenaic sect, who was

---

lished her own plates and engravings after drawings by her artist father, Giovanni Battista Scultori, and by her architect husband, Francesco da Volterra.

42. The burin is a tool used for engraving.

43. According to Pliny the Elder, Aristarete was the daughter and pupil of the sixth-century-B.C.E. potter and vase painter Nearchus. See Pliny, *Natural History* 35.147, trans. H. Rackham (1952; reprint, Cambridge, Mass.: Harvard University Press, 1995), 9:369.

44. Catterina Cantoni (or Cantona) (d. 1605) was a printmaker and portraitist admired by King Philip II of Spain. In 1559 she traveled to Spain with her compatriot and newly appointed court painter Sofonisba Anguissola (c. 1535–1625).

45. Elisabeth-Sophie Chéron (1648–1711) was a French painter and printmaker and one of the first women to be admitted to the Académie Royale de Peinture et de Sculpture (in 1672). An acclaimed portraitist, history painter, and engraver, Chéron exhibited some of her works at the Salon in Paris.

46. Johanna Koerten (or Koorten) (1650–1715), from Amsterdam, was a painter, silhouette cutter, embroiderer, and wax modeler. Her pioneering cut-paper works were commissioned by royalty from across Europe and Russia.

47. Caminer incorporates this commonplace eighteenth-century stereotype of the dilettante female intellectual in order to distinguish truly accomplished female intellectuals from superficially cultured women. More precisely, she employs it here to protect women's accomplishments from the negative, sexist stereotype of false or ignorant women. See section 3 of "Volume Editor's Introduction."

48. Abrotelia (fifth century B.C.E.), ancient Greek Pythagorean philosopher, was the daughter of Abroteles of Tarentum.

49. Axiotha of Philesia (fl. 350s B.C.E.), ancient Greek Platonist, was a student of Plato and reputedly dressed as a man in order to attend his lectures. See Diogenes Laertius 3.46.

50. Arete of Cyrene (fl. 370–340 B.C.E.), ancient Greek philosopher, was the daughter of Aristippus, a pupil of Socrates who founded the hedonistic Cyrenaic school of philosophy. Arete

the mother of Aristippus Metrodidactus,[51] and who gave public lessons in philosophy; Argia, Theognida, Artemisia, and Pantaclea, daughters and disciples of the dialectician Diodorus;[52] and, along with many others, Agnodice, a young girl from Athens.[53] After a decree was passed by the Areopagus[54] prohibiting women from practicing medicine and as a result obstetrics, this praiseworthy young girl [Agnodice] went dressed as a male to study medicine and obstetrics, especially under Herophilos. She did so because she saw that the women of Athens, who ordinarily had difficult deliveries, preferred to die rather than be helped by men. Once she finished her studies she revealed to the pregnant women of Athens that she was a woman and she became the most popular doctor. The other professors were so jealous they accused her of adultery. She defended herself by baring her chest before the judges. The decree was revoked and women were permitted to practice obstetrics. Only one reservation might arise from this fact: is it possible that so many women kept this secret? We know ourselves! Our sex's desire for knowledge seems to be equally as strong as the desire to talk.

However much it necessarily arouses wonder to hear that a young woman became an excellent doctor, it fades in comparison with a new surprise, the entry on Aganice [Aglaonice] of Thessaly.[55] She succeeded so well that, despite the lack of help that ancient astronomers had, she predicted the eclipse with precision. As a result she mastered those areas of knowledge that remained unknown for a little while after her time. No one duplicated Aglaonice's choice and her success in studies over the course of many centuries. The unfortunate Hypatia[56] flourished many years after her, and the direction of the famous University of Alexandria was entrusted to her profound knowl-

---

succeeded her father as head of the school and is believed to have taught natural science, moral philosophy, and ethics for thirty-five years. Scholars believe she wrote at least forty books, including treatises on education and agriculture and on Socrates himself.

51. Arete's son Aristippus was a pupil of his mother, nicknamed "Metrodidactus" ("mother-taught").

52. According to Ménage, these dialectician philosophers (fl. 300s–200s B.C.E.) were sisters (daughters of Diodorus Cronus). See Gilles Ménage, *The History of Women Philosophers*, trans. Beatrice H. Zedler (Lanham, Md.: University Press of America, 1984), 53.

53. Agnodice lived in the fourth century B.C.E.

54. An ancient council to the king.

55. Although Caminer (and De Lacroix's dictionary) call her "Aganice," she is referring to Aglaonice of Thessaly (fl. fifth century B.C.E.), whose ability to predict solar and lunar eclipses led many to believe she was a sorceress.

56. Hypatia (370–415), ancient Greek philosopher, astronomer, and mathemetician, taught geometry, algebra, and astronomy in Alexandria, where she was the head of the Neoplatonist school. She was murdered by a Christian mob opposed to her scientific rationalism.

edge of philosophical and mathematical subjects. She died there, torn to shreds by an enraged populace, the victim of the far-from-phlegmatic zeal of Saint Cyril, who had accused her of impeding the reconciliation of the governor Orestes with him.[57] Perhaps in those dangerous times she had pointed out the boundaries of the two powers,[58] which are today clearly drawn. Our Italy boasts among the ancient cultivators of mathematics Teodora Dante of Perugia;[59] but her fame bows before the glory of the our contemporary, Madame [Maria Gaetana] Agnesi.[60] Our transalpine neighbors were even richer than we were in this category. In the last century, the celebrated astronomer Maria Cunitz[61] flourished in Silesia and Jeanne Dumée[62] in Paris. While she was alive, the former awakened the admiration of the most educated men for having mastered many living languages—Latin, Greek, and Hebrew. She was full of information about history and physics, she knew theoretical and applied music, and she left behind astronomic tables, a splendid and lasting proof of her genius and distinguished knowledge. Dumée penned a work entitled "Conversations on Copernicus' Opinion on the Movement of the Earth." In this book she explains very clearly the doctrine of the three movements attributed to our globe, weighing favorable and unfavorable positions in relation to the Copernican system.

And, because men in their injustice are convinced by some facts that, along with the many other prerogatives [they enjoy], they would like to claim exclusively for themselves the right to teach in universities, the worthy author of our *Dictionary* mentions a good number of women who held posts and taught classes at the most celebrated universities. The city of Bologna alone can boast of Dorotea Bucca [Bocchi], professor of philosophy, Elisabetta Gozzadini [Bitisia Gozzadina], who held a chair in law there, and Elisabetta

57. Saint Cyril was the Christian bishop of Alexandria, and Governor Orestes was prefect of the city of Alexandria.

58. Christian and pagan powers.

59. Teodora Dante of Perugia was a sixteenth-century mathematician. According to De Lacroix's dictionary, she learned mathematics from her father and in turn taught the subject to a nephew, who became an able mathematician himself.

60. Maria Gaetana Agnesi (1718–99), Italian mathematician and philosopher from Milan, was appointed in 1749 to occupy a chair of mathematics at the University of Bologna, which she refused. Her major work, *Analytical Institutions* (1748), was one of the first and most complete works on finite and infinitesimal analysis.

61. Maria Cunitz (1601–64) was the first woman to attempt to correct Kepler's Rudolphine Tables. Her major publication was *Urania Propitia* (Frankfurt, 1650).

62. Jeanne Dumée (b. 1680) was a French astronomer of the seventeenth century. Her manuscript "Entretiens sur l'opinion de Copernic touchant la mobilité de la terre" (Conversations on Copernicus's opinion regarding the motion of the earth) supported Copernican and Galilean theories on the earth's movement.

Calderini [Novella Caldarini], who, married to Giovanni di S. Giorgio, professor of law at the University of Padua, substituted for her husband whenever illness or pressing business prevented him from giving public lectures.[63] To these three Bolognese women who prospered in barbarous times our century adds one who surpasses them by far, and whose name need no longer fear the offenses of time: the most celebrated Madame Laura Bassi,[64] who counts among her disciples many of the most renowned professors, who came out of her school and joined the ranks of the most illustrious academies of Italy.[65]

One must concede, however, that it would not be a useful thing if a great number of women were to succeed so well, because then we would see things turn upside down, and men who are fit for something better would be reduced to spinning in order to survive. What must not be neglected in the education of women, and which can go hand in hand with the management of families, and with the other functions that are prescribed to women, is a sufficient cultivation of the mind, which, if it became less rare, would bring no small number of advantages to civil society. It would shape character, and it would spare those women who in an affected manner try to pull themselves out of the ordinary embarrassment of making fools of themselves with their efforts to make it known, whether it is true or not, that they are not completely foolish. And it would prevent us from having to blush upon hearing the wonderment people express when a woman is a little less uneducated than usual.

Many many Italian women of the sixteenth century who were worthy of

63. There is little information available about these three women, all of whom lived between the twelfth and fifteenth centuries. Bocchi (fl. 1390s–1440s) was the daughter of a professor of medicine and moral philosophy at the University of Bologna who succeeded her father (c. 1436) after his death and taught philosophy for nearly forty years. According to De Lacroix's dictionary, Gozzadini (c. 1209–49) received a chair as professor of law in 1239. See also Ethel M. Kersey, *Women Philosophers: A Bio-Critical Source Book* (Westport, Conn.: Greenwood Press, 1989), 8; and Marta Cavazza, "Dottrici e lettrici dell'Università di Bologna nel Settecento," in *Annali di storia delle università italiane* (Bologna: Clueb, 1997), 1:109–25.

64. Laura Maria Caterina Bassi (1711–78) was an experimental philosopher and an important influence in the shift from Cartesianism to Newtonianism in Italy. Bassi was a lecturer at the University of Bologna, and she also held a chair in experimental physics at Bologna's Academy of the Institute for Sciences. Very few of her lectures or her annual dissertations in physics and mathematics have survived. Her major works on mechanics and hydrolics include *De problemate quodam mechanico* (1757) and *De problemate quodam hydrometrico* (1757).

65. As Caminer knew, the naturalist Lazzaro Spallanzani had studied under Laura Bassi. Despite Caminer's conviction that Bassi's reputation "need not fear the offenses of time," in fact the experimental philosopher was quite forgotten for centuries, and her accomplishments have only recently been brought to light again. See Paula Findlen, "Science as a Career in Enlightenment Italy: The Strategies of Laura Bassi," *Isis* 84 (1993): 441–69; and Marta Cavazza, "Laura Bassi 'maestra' di Spallanzani," in *Il cerchio della vita: Materiali di ricerca del Centro Studi Lazzaro Spallanzani di Scandiano sulla storia della Scienza del Settecento*, ed. W. Bernardi and P. Manzini (Firenze: Olschki, 1999), 185–202.

esteem are found in this dictionary, and among the others we find Maddalena
Acciaiuoli of Florence,[66] Francesca Basso of Venice,[67] Tullia d'Aragona of
Naples,[68] Lucia Avogadro of Bergamo,[69] elegant poets praised by the celebrated men of their day. This latter woman especially enjoyed the honor of
seeing Torquato Tasso comment on many of her own poems. No less than
these were Catterina de Badajoz[70] of Spain, who distinguished herself in Latin
poetry; Ann de Bins of Antwerp,[71] who was compared by Svezio[72] in Flemish
to the Greek Sappho; and among the English Aphra Behn, employed by
Charles II in political strategies, who, applying herself to mathematics, chro-
nology, and theology, became learned in every one of these sciences. Her
beautiful translation into English of Fontenelle's [*Conversation on the Plurality of*]
Worlds survives.[73] Long before these women, that is in the fifteenth century,
Laura Cereti of Brescia[74] and Cassandra Fedele of Venice,[75] who defended

66. Maddalena Salvetti Acciajuoli (d. 1610), was a Florentine poet who was included in Luisa
Bergalli's anthology of Italian women poets, *Componimenti Poetici delle più illustri Rimatrici d'ogni secolo*
(Poetic compositions by the most illustrious female poets from every century) (Venezia: Marino
Rossetti, 1726). According to De Lacroix's dictionary, Salvetti Acciajuoli published a volume of
poetry in Florence in 1590.

67. Perhaps this is a reference to the sixteenth-century poet Francesca Baffa, included in Luisa
Bergalli's 1726 anthology of Italian women poets, *Componimenti Poetici delle più illustri Rimatrici*.

68. Tullia d'Aragona (c. 1510–56) was a celebrated courtesan and poet, originally from Rome.
She was perhaps the first woman to enter into the discussion of the ethics of love by casting herself as the protagonist in her *Dialogo dell'infinità dell'amore* (Venice: Giolito de' Gerrari, 1547). See,
in this series, Tullia d'Aragona, *Dialogue on the Infinity of Love*, ed. and trans. Rinaldina Russell and
Bruce Merry (Chicago: University of Chicago Press, 1997).

69. Lucia Albani Avogadri, a sixteenth-century poet acclaimed by contemporaries, was the
daughter of Cardinal Albani. Luisa Bergalli included Avogardi in her 1726 anthology of Italian
women poets, *Componimenti Poetici delle più illustri Rimatrici*.

70. Catterina de Badajoz (d. 1553) was a composer of Latin verse.

71. Ann de Bins of Antwerp, sixteenth-century poet, was known as "the Sappho of Antwerp."
According to De Lacroix's dictionary, de Bins refused to marry, in order that she might dedicate
herself to letters.

72. De Lacroix's dictionary refers to him as François Swertius; Caminer calls him Svezio.

73. Aphra Behn (1640–89) was an English poet, dramatist, and fiction writer. In 1688 she published *Theory of the System of Several New Inhabited Worlds*, an annotated translation of Bernard de
Fontenelle's *Entretiens sur la pluralité des mondes* (1686), which popularized the mechanistic theories
of Descartes through a dialogue between a philosopher and a "lady of quality." For a modern edition, see Bernard Le Bovier de Fontenelle, *Conversations on the Plurality of Worlds*, trans. H. A. Har-
greaves (Berkeley: University of California Press, 1990).

74. Laura Cereti (or Cereta) (1469–99) was an erudite author of epistolary essays in Latin on
both traditional humanist themes and on the condition of women in society. Her autobio-
graphical letter book, *Epistolae familiares*, was first published posthumously, in 1640. See, in this
series, Laura Cereta, *Collected Letters of a Renaissance Feminist*, ed. and trans. Diana Robin (Chicago:
University of Chicago Press, 1997).

75. Cassandra Fedele (1465–1558) was a Venetian woman of letters whose Latin orations and
correspondence with European monarchs made her the most famous woman writer and scholar

public theses in philosophy, became famous in different areas of knowledge. For her profound knowledge and for the eloquence of her Latin orations, the latter especially earned the praises of the celebrated men of her day and many demonstrations of esteem from powerful monarchs, particularly from Popes Julius II and Leo X.

But if we want to get to our own times, how many just praises did the famous marquise du Châtelet of France[76] earn, she who cultivated her own talents so well! We are indebted to this lady, who was extremely well versed in letters, for an explanation of Leibniz's philosophy entitled *The Institutions of Physics*, a *Treatise on the Nature and Propagation of Fire*, and an annotated translation of Newton's work, *Mathematical Principles of Natural Philosophy*, known under the title of *Newton's Physics*. The learned author garnered celebrity and well-deserved honor because of these praiseworthy labors, but she was neither the first nor the only woman in France to masterfully treat the most abstruse subjects in physics. Anne Henriette de Colombières[77] made a great name for herself in that kingdom by publishing her *Reflections on the Causes of Earthquakes*. Among the learned French women about whom this *Dictionary* speaks, significant space is given to Madame Dacier,[78] whose works and whose life are very well known to all men of letters. No less deserving of praise, even though she dedicated herself to less lofty subjects, was the countess de La Fayette,[79] author of the novels *Zayde* [*Zaïde*], *The Princess of Clèves* [*La princesse de Clèves*] and *The Princess of Montpensier* [*La Princesse de Montpensier*], nor should one confuse with the crowd of erotic writers the young Hélisenne de

in Europe. See, in this series, Cassandra Fedele, *Letters and Orations*, ed. and trans. Diana Robin (Chicago: University of Chicago Press, 2000).

76. Gabrielle Emilie de Breteuil, marquise du Châtelet (1706–49), was a French noblewoman, courtier, and companion of Voltaire who frequented the foremost mathematicians and scientists of Paris and was a renowned physicist and interpreter of Leibniz and Newton. Like Bassi in Italy, Châtelet was instrumental in the shift from Cartesianism to Newtonianism in France. Châtelet published her controversial *Institutions de Physique* anonymously in 1740; her *Dissertation sur la nature et la propagation du feu* was published four years later, in 1744. Her translation of Newton's *Principia Mathematica*, the *Principes mathématiques de la philosophie naturelle*, although completed in 1747, was not published until 1759 (posthumously). Her works will appear in translation in this series.

77. Anne Henriette de Briqueville de Colombières was renowned in eighteenth-century France for her *Reflexions sur les causes de la tremblment de terre*.

78. A scholar of ancient Greek and Latin, Anne Dacier (d. 1720) published many works, including a translation of comedies by Terence (*Les comedies de Terence, avec la traduction et les remarques, de Madame Dacier* [Rotterdam : G. Fritsch, 1717]) and a critique of La Motte's opinion of Homer and his translation of the *Iliad* (*Des causes de la corruption du goût* [Paris, 1714]).

79. Marie-Madeleine Pioche de la Vergne, comtesse de Lafayette (1634–93), published *La Princesse de Montpensier* in 1662, *Zayde* in 1669–70, and *La princesse de Clèves* in 1678. The latter work is frequently identified in French literary histories as the first modern novel. For a modern English version, see Marie-Madeleine Pioche de la Vergne Lafayette, *The Princess of Clèves*, trans. Terence Cave (Oxford: Oxford University Press, 1992).

Crenne de Picardie,[80] who published a book entitled *The Torments of Love*, with a *Discourse on Love* [*Les Angoysses douloureuses qui procedent d'amores*]. Oh! How many things this sensitive young woman—who perhaps not without some reason chose this argument—could have said in her book! How many readers will this book interest! And how many more could perhaps add appendices to it![81]

Not only famous women who have died but many who are still living are named in this *Dictionary*, and they receive well-deserved praise from the author: Madame Bellot,[82] author of *Reflections on Nobility and the Third Estate: Reflections of a Provincial Woman on the Discourse of Mr. Rousseau*,[83] and many other learned works; Madame du Bocage;[84] Madame Le Prince de Beaumont,[85] author of excellent books on the education of girls; Madame Denis, Voltaire's niece;[86] Marie-Antoinette-Marie Fagnan,[87] a famous woman of letters; and

80. Marguerite Briet, known as Hélisenne de Crenne (c. 1510–c. 1552), published *Les Angoysses douloureuses qui procedent d'amores*—one of the earliest novels in French—in 1538; it was very popular in its time, going through eight editions by 1560. For a modern English version, see Hélisenne de Crenne, *The Torments of Love*, trans. Lisa Neal and Steven Rendall (Minneapolis: University of Minnesota Press, 1996).

81. This sounds like a personal note on Caminer's part; she published this review the year of her failed courtship with Albergati (1769). Her tone here also echoes that in her 1770 poem on love's disillusionments. See section 2 of "Volume Editor's Introduction" and "Making of a Woman," text 6.

82. Madame Bellot was the author of *Observations sur la Noblesse e le tiers-état: Réflexions d'une Provinciale sur le discours de M. Rousseau* and other works.

83. Jean-Jacques Rousseau (1712–78) wrote two influential discourses: *Discourse on the Origin of Inequality* and *Discourse on the Arts and Sciences*. There are numerous editions of both.

84. Marie-Anne Du Boccage (1710–1802) was the author of *Les amazones: Tragedie en cinq actes* (Paris: F. Merigot, 1749) and *Lettres, contenant ses voyages en France, en Angleterre, en Hollande, et en Italie, faits pendant les années 1750, 1757, & 1758* (Dresden, G. C. Walther, 1771).

85. Jeanne-Marie Le Prince de Beaumont (1711–80) was an extremely popular French novelist and prolific author of moral tales and educational works for children. Her books were quickly translated into every major European language. Caminer's translation of Le Prince de Beaumont's twelve-volume series of pedagogical works for girls, young women, and new brides was the first in Italian: *Il magazzino delle fanciulle, ovvero dialoghi tra una savia direttrice e parecchie sue allieve di grado illustre: Opera di Madama di Beaumont: Prima traduzione italiana* (Vicenza: Francesco Vendramini Mosca, 1774), *Il magazzino delle adulte, ovvero dialoghi tra una savia direttrice e parecchie sue allieve di grado illustre che serve di continuazione al Magazzino delle fanciulle: Opera di Madama Le Prince de Beaumont: Prima traduzione italiana* (Vicenza: Francesco Vendramini Mosca, 1781); *Istruzioni per le giovani dame ch'entrano nel mondo, e si maritano; loro doveri in questo stato, e verso i loro figlioli; per servire di continuazione e di compimento al Magazzino delle fanciulle, e a quello delle adulte: Opera di Madama di Beaumont: Prima traduzione italiana* (Vicenza: Francesco Vendramini Mosca, 1782).

86. Born Marie-Louise Mignot Arouet (c. 1710–90), Madame Denis was the daughter of Voltaire's oldest brother. She married a man of the middle class, Jean-Baptiste Denis, and after his death in 1744 she went to live with her uncle (Voltaire) and stayed with him until his death. She wrote several works, including a play, *La coquette punie*.

87. Marie-Antoinette-Marie Fagnan was an eighteenth-century woman of letters. According to De Lacroix's dictionary, she was the author of *Le miroir des princesses orientales* and other works.

numerous others. But since France now looks down on our Italy, almost with an eye of pity, the French author did not deign to mention in the midst of his living compatriots even the famous Madame Agnesi of Milan, or the deservingly celebrated Madame Laura Bassi, whom we mentioned above, or the learned and most notable Venetian countess [Luisa] Bergalli Gozzi,[88] who honors letters, and particularly fine poetry, with her excellent compositions, and by the way she cultivated her own mind from the time she was a young girl. If our author wanted to improve his *Dictionary* greatly, he should have made sure it was complete, and not overlooked many others among our Italian women, such as Maddalena Campiglia,[89] valorous Vicentine poet of the sixteenth century, whose name is only one of many we could mention.

We will close this review, which has perhaps become too lengthy. One cannot really deny praise to the author of our *Dictionary*, both for the effort it must have taken to gather the articles that form two volumes as large as these and for the clarity and the impartiality with which they are written. Women, and especially those who have some merit, will no doubt be obliged to him, but they would have been much more so if, among the women celebrated for their merit, he had not mixed in so many women unworthy of being mentioned. He included, for example, the courtesans Acmè and Agna, the glutton Aglaide, the wicked Violante de Bats, who with her talent for indecency had her own husband assassinated, the venomous Brinvilliers, the unjust Constantin, the incestuous Cratea, the debauched Clodia,[90] and many oth-

---

88. Luisa Bergalli Gozzi (1703–79) was a student of the poet Apostolo Zeno and of the painter Rosalba Carriera, a member of the Arcadian Academy, and the most renowned female poet, playwright, and translator of eighteenth-century Venice. Bergalli translated the works of Terence, Racine, and Molière, and she composed original works for the theater, including *Agide, re di Sparta* (1725), a drama set to music by Giovanni Porta; *Le avventure del poeta* (1730), a comedy satirizing the nobility and writers' dependence on them for patronage; and *Elenia* (1730), a melodrama set to music by Albinoni. Bergalli also compiled and edited two collections of poetry by Italian women: an edition of Gaspara Stampa's poetry (*Rime di Gaspara Stampa* [1738]) that was instrumental in reviving Stampa's reputation as a poet, and the ambitious two-volume collection of poetry by Italian women poets from the thirteenth century up to and including Bergalli's contemporaries (herself among them), *Componimenti Poetici delle più illustri Rimatrici*.

89. Maddalena Campiglia (1553–95), of Vicenza, authored various works in prose and in verse, among them *Discorso della signora Maddalena Campiglia sopra l'Annonciatione della Beata Vergine e la Incarnazione del S. N. Giesù Cristo* (1585) and *Flori: Favola boscareccia* (1588). The latter will appear in this series.

90. According to De Lacroix's dictionary, Acme was a confidante and servant of Empress Livia (wife of Augustus) who wrote a counterfeit letter in the empress's name and was put to death in the first year C.E.; Agna was a famous courtesan in Rome, remembered by Horace for the polyp in her nose; Aglaide ate ten pounds of meat and bread in one meal and drank in equal quantities; Violante de Bats was a seventeenth-century Spanish woman who had her husband assassinated in 1608 by her lover; Marie-Marguerite d'Aubray, marquise de Brinvilliers, was remembered by

ers. These women do not deserve celebrity or a place among illustrious women for their vices and defects, but rather infamy or eternal oblivion. It must be mortifying for virtuous women to see themselves lumped together with those who possess shameful and atrocious qualities, and to witness such a confusing mixture of virtue and vice in a book whose purpose would seem to be solely that of paying them tribute.

3. POEM IN HONOR OF CATERINA DOLFIN TRON (1773)[91]

That one adorned with civic honors
And a select multitude of virtues,
Whose noble labors and illustrious fame
Are told from Pole to Pole,
Who has won the hearts of the Veneto people,
The only suitable applause and prize
For which he can be seen as noble and glorious,
Tell me, gentle LADY, is that not your Spouse?

And are you not she to whom the Poets'
Happy God of the Ascrean Hills responds,
Whose sweet songs he blends with noble vein
Special gifts, blessed with which you bless;
Who are the highest glory of the
Adriatic shores in this age, clear
Example of how much noble intelligence
And knowledge nature has bestowed upon our sex?

If you are those two, ah! It is useless
To sing of YOUR noble endowments.

Madame de Sévigny for her involvement in various political intrigues in which she poisoned innocent people; Constantin was a seventeenth-century woman who performed abortions for women who were trying to avoid the dishonor of pregnancy and was sentenced to death by hanging in 1660; Cratea was a Corinthian tyrant who had an incestuous relationship with her son; and Clodia was a Roman courtesan believed to be the woman celebrated by Catullus in his verse as "Lesbia.".

91. This poem is contained in the collection of poetry organized by Luisa Bergalli Gozzi entitled *Rime di donne illustri a sua eccellenza Caterina Dolfina cavaliera e procuratessa Tron nel gloriosissimo ingresso alla dignità di procurator per merito di San Marco di sua eccellenza cavaliere Andrea Tron* (Rhymes of illustrious women to Her Excellency Caterina Dolfin Chevalière and Procuratess Tron on the occasion of His Excellency Chevalier Andrea Tron's most glorious entrance to the post of meritorious procurator of San Marco) (Venezia: Pietro Valvasense, 1773), 20–21. I would like to acknowledge the generous assistance of Paschal Viglionese in the translation of this poem.

Europe and Asia know that among the
High heroes for whom famous Venice is known
ANDREA shines distinctly, that you make
His days joyful as his happy wife,
And that your virtues' only task
Is to be bound to the destiny of that great soul.

Live, lovely LADY, and for a long time
May he live with you, he who will
Ever be the pride and glory of these noble lands,
And an immortal name in future history.
For this may his memory live forever
Where the sun sets and where it rises.
This is all that is fitting to sing
And tell you on this happy day.

4. ON A CRITIQUE OF *THE SCOURGE OF HUMANITY*
(1786)[92]

A friar published an indecent satire against the gentle sex in rhymed octo-
syllabic verse. In the same meter, a Tuscan lady responds to him. All women
whose defense she has taken up must be grateful to her, even though in nam-
ing some of those who have distinguished themselves above all others in the
present day, she limited herself to Tuscany and Geneva alone, while in all the
other parts of Italy there are women who are very well educated and worthy
of standing alongside great men.

The printer Savioni of Venice is about to republish this defense of the
fair sex.

---

92. In *Nuovo giornale enciclopedico*, May 1786, 109. There is no signature, because announcements
in the section of the periodical announcing new books were never signed. Caminer is announcing the publication of *La difesa delle Donne, o sia Risposta Apologetica al libro detto lo Scoglio dell'umanità di
Duinilgo Valdecio fatta dalla Marchesa di Sanival* (The defense of women; or, An apologetic response
to the book called *The Scourge of Humanity* by Duinilgo Valdecio [Carlo Maria Chiaraviglio])
(Siena: Bindi, 1786). The defense of women was written by Fausto Salvani under the pseudonym
the marquise of Sanival. Apparently, the male identity of the author was not known to Caminer;
and she did not comment on some of the parodic moments in the text. *The Scourge of Humanity*
was a "best-seller" during the eighteenth century, with multiple editions and published responses
to it. See Luciano Guerci, *La discussione sulla donna nell'Italia del Settecento: Aspetti e problemi* (Torino: Tirrenia Stampatori, 1987), 25, 73; and Rebecca Messbarger, *The Century of Women: Representations of
Women in Eighteenth-Century Italian Public Discourse* (Toronto: University of Toronto Press, 2002), 6,
69, 161.

5. ON THE ERROR OF EXALTING SOME WOMEN
BY INSULTING OTHERS (1790)⁹³

What does it matter if a book has not been published recently, when for one or another reason it is good? We were not able to speak earlier about the one we are announcing now, but its singularity is new enough so that after two years it can still pass for new among its readers.

The author of this work, Mr. Domenicandrea Barbieri, has a merit that is rare among authors: that of regretting having written it, at least according to what the editor claims in a foreword to the book. God forgive him if, whatever his motive, an *officious* lie is involved in such a declaration! Whatever it may be, one must suppose that Mr. D. B. has a timid soul and that he is rather thin-skinned, since in giving preference to the women of Venice he keeps the city of the runners-up incognito; perhaps he fears a very natural explosion of bites and scratches, or a form of wrath that is even more fatal.

There are people, however, who are so wretched that, in defending a cause, they have the ability to offend their champions as well as their adversaries; and it is perhaps the case with Mr. B. He exalts the women of one city over those of another, and then he claims that in the vast, praised city one woman has earned his *highest regard* as the one who shines among the many for her physical and moral qualities, to the point that she is the *beautiful Moon* among the *beautiful Stars who crown her with the brightness of their rays.* Is this not, in fact, the same as displeasing the majority of women, who, according to the current fashion, cannot find it gratifying to be regarded as the courting *Stars* rather than the courted *Moons?* Who knows if Venetian women might not be inclined to send the author's praises back to him for some other reason altogether? Let *intelligent* readers draw their own conclusions from the following thought. According to Mr. B., the female sex of the Veneto is the delight of everyone with her sweet ways, *fluid* tongue, moving and noble manners, liveliness, charms, "and more and much more with those tender *sentiments* of their *sensitive* and HUMAN hearts, that capture and prey upon *every* good little sweet-natured *Christian man.*" Oh! You see what odd and particularly delicate praise this is! After these premises the author thinks he must prove that the women

---

93. In *Nuovo giornale enciclopedico d'Italia,* September 1790, 64–69, with no signature. Caminer is reviewing Domenico Barbieri's *Paragone delle Donne di due città* (Comparison of the women of two cities) (Venezia: Domenico Fracasso, 1788). Barbieri does not name the city he is comparing with Venice. Since the author's surname is typical of the Veneto region, the city is almost certainly from the same region—perhaps Belluno or, given Caminer's particular interest in the book, even Vicenza.

of his city are inferior to Venetian women; and here, in succinct form, is the brilliant portrait he paints of them.

Mr. B.'s compatriots are, generally speaking, *small, awkward,* and *coarse, although* strong and robust. (Perhaps Mr. B. is from a mountain somewhere?) Everything in them tends to be *big* and *large:* hands, feet, chest, neck, ears, etc. The author does not like that they walk slowly and with a show of modesty, *so that the sweet zephyr and the light breeze that delicately flaps around them cannot make the pompous andrienne*[94] *rustle and the sash of their fancily trimmed bodice flutter.* What a shame! And what happy Gessnerian[95] images the author employs! Let us continue. The almost total inelegance of those poor wretches even makes their clothing nauseating. As far as their minds are concerned, *they are slow, cold, insipid précieuses.* In their behavior they resemble the *Longobards* or the *Burgundians;* their manners are *hard, coarse, a bit primitive, and lacking in gentility, polish, or gracious urbanity.* Their talents are *few;* their minds are *sterile* and *empty* of all *social, civic, and patriotic* ideas, full of ineptitude and every sort of prejudice. Their conversation is *tedious, boring,* and slanderous; and they show themselves to be *picky* and *nauseating* to anyone wanting to *deftly* introduce serious subjects. In the *matter of flirtation, in which* they really should be as expert as the *other* women from *other* cities that are less remarkable in this matter (so Mr. D. B.'s city is more remarkable than Venice! The argument is very simple, since he finds that Venetian women are the exact opposites of . . .),[96] the simpletons have not even learned the basic elements of that lovable art: and thus they are so boorish, coarse, and uneducated that they could not be more so. "I will not go so far as to say," continues the author, "that as women gifted with human sensitivity they do not feel the itch of voluptuousness (what a delicate declaration!), or that they do not acquiesce to the sweet invitations of the pleasing Goddess in whose obscure temple EVEN THEY *frequent* rites and secret mysteries. But the sweet, blithesome, delicate *sentiments* of a *sensitive,* tender, and passionate heart still seem *in* their hearts obtuse and enveloped *in* their internal shell, not *polished,* or honed *on the lathe,* so to speak, of *modern* gentility and French *delicacy.*"[97] Married women counsel maidens not to marry beneath themselves, so as to preserve the nobility of their family name (here the author forgets that he was speaking of *common* women as much as of ladies).

94. The "andrienne" was a style of dress popular earlier in the century; with this comment, the author was implying that the women of his city were dreadfully out of style.

95. Caminer is referring to the imagery employed by Salomon Gessner in his idyllic poetry, which she had translated and published in 1781.

96. In other words, the exact opposites of the women from the unnamed city.

97. Opening quotation marks are missing in Caminer's piece; I added them here.

They have the same scruple about cavalieri serventi,[98] except when they happen upon some *young dissolute rascal*, etc., who seems like a *dandy straight out of a novel*, or else some wealthy man who is ready to *provide for the daily necessities of the very hungry stomachs of the illustrious ladies*. The person writing here owes the author of this very delicate letter[99] the consolation of knowing that her city, well examined by him, is completely exempt from these disgusting defects.

Readers might believe the portrait of the women of . . . to be finally completed. Anything but: now we come to the negative tinges. Those unhappy women are, says the author, so poorly educated that they understand nothing about managing a household, they do not know *arithmetic*, they do not know how to weave *green, blood-red, dark, or blue woollen cloth* the way a strong woman or the relatives of Augustus and Tanaquil used to do.[100] They do not know how to draw, they do not know how to paint (tsk, tsk!), they do not know how to sing, they do not know how to play [musical instruments], they do not know the Italian language, *logic, geography, physics, natural history, astronomy, sacred and secular history*, they do not know, etc., etc., etc. Oh, blessed are Venetian women, repositories of science, models of serious occupation, etc., etc., etc.! Those poor devils among whom the author was born read at the very most Metastasio and Goldoni, *masters*, as everyone knows, *of depraved customs*. But it is to be hoped that they will cast off these depraved writers and give themselves to the sciences, now that Mr. D. B. would have them hope for the greatest good fortune of *becoming*, in that case, *very dear and praiseworthy in his eyes*. And one hopes for this even more, since he is also discreet, and with *judgment and foresight* he dispenses them from having to study *anatomy, metaphysics, medicine, mathematics, politics, and jurisprudence*. See how easy it is to satisfy Mr. D. B.!

We will dispense with following him in his examination of the variety of climates relative to the effects they produce on the *living* human bodies who

---

98. Literally, "servant-knight." Descending from the medieval tradition of courtly love, the "cavaliere servente" was an aristocratic man designated to be a companion for a married woman (also of the aristocracy). Sometimes the woman chose her "cavaliere servente" and sometimes he was selected by her husband. In theory, the "cavaliere servente" was a platonic friend whose responsibility it was to accompany his mistress on social outings and to provide amusement at her toilette, but often the relationship was also sexual. Thus, the "servant-knight" could serve two purposes, seemingly at odds with each other: he acted as a monitor of a wife's behavior and as a vehicle for her to seek erotic satisfaction outside of matrimony. The "cavaliere servente" was frequently a subject of ridicule during the eighteenth century and was most famously satirized in Giuseppe Parini's mock-epic poem *Il Giorno*.

99. Perhaps this publication was written as a letter dedicated to an illustrious Venetian woman.

100. In other words, the way biblical or ancient Roman heroines did.

inhabit them, and in his notes on a certain *pasta* or *sperm* whose details we believe it does not behoove us to discuss.[101] After having given his opinion, he leaves it to the naturalists and natural philosophers *of greater leisure* and wisdom than himself to investigate the matter; and we will imitate him by leaving it to journalists *of greater leisure* and wisdom than ourselves to write a longer and more profound extract of this good book.

Having arrived near the end of the book, we find that the author mentions some women of his city as exceptions to the miserable rule he has established, so that, becoming the key to the enigma, we are forced to let go of the idea that we had formed of his lack of courage, and, on the contrary, we must admire his intrepidity no less than his happy acumen, thanks to which he so easily apprehends the correlations between the actions of the strong woman and the science of fluttering the andrienne, of flirting, etc., etc., etc.

6. ON MARY WOLLSTONECRAFT'S *VINDICATION OF THE RIGHTS OF WOMAN* (1792–93)[102]

This woman is the champion of her sex. But what will she gain? Revolutions are not so easy or frequent in all genres.

༂

In his national education project the bishop of Autun focused almost entirely on men, and, in accordance with the gentility that is typical of such men, he almost completely neglected that which pertains to women. Chastising him for this, the author of the work we are announcing is attempting to make up for his omission by extensively addressing everything that concerns her sex, which she is trying to bring up out of the void in which some would leave it. It is true that in Europe educated women are praised and adored, and they have a tremendous and perhaps the principal influence in the most serious of matters: but at what price? All their power depends upon

---

101. This is undoubtedly a reference to the human reproductive system, which Caminer could not have discussed directly without appearing immodest.

102. Caminer's first comment is from the *Nuovo giornale enciclopedico d'Italia*, October 1792, 125–26, when she is announcing the publication of a 1792 London edition (she does not mention the publisher) of Mary Wollstonecraft's *Vindication of the Rights of Woman*. The second review is from the *Nuovo giornale enciclopedico d'Italia*, August 1793, 117–18, in which Caminer is announcing the publicaton of a French translation of Wollstonecraft's work published in 1792 in Paris (by Buisson) and Lyons (by Bruyset). The review has no signature, because announcements in the section of the periodical announcing new books were never signed.

youth and beauty, rather than stemming from that distributive justice which should base their power on a better education, on the development of their intellectual abilities, on the cultivation of their reason, and on the knowledge of their own purpose and their own duties. This is the source from which Madame Wollstonecraft would like female power to spring, and this is the system on which her book turns. Her book proves for the millionth time that women might deserve the honor of being considered part of the human race.

7. ON AN ENCOMIUM OF ISABELLA TEOTOCHI MARINI: *THE ORIGINAL AND THE PORTRAIT* (1793)[103]

The original is the noblewoman Isabella Teotochi Marini; her portrait was painted by the famous Madame [Elisabeth Vigée] Le Brun. Valorous poets celebrate both one and the other [woman]. We saw the original; we did not see the portrait or read the illustrations;[104] but for the two latter things we rely upon the illustrious names who produced them, and for the former, we repeat what we have said other times about the amiable, very learned, beautiful, genteel countess Teotochi Marini, the bane of many women and the object of admiration of many men, that is, of those men who love graces united with good manners, and knowledge that is free from pedantic affectation. The noblewoman Marini, celebrated by the Pindemontes, the Bertòlas, the Cesarottis of the world, etc., etc., may not pay any great attention to our praises,

---

103. In *Nuovo giornale enciclopedico d'Italia*, August 1793, 105–6, with no signature, because announcements in the section of the periodical announcing new books were never signed. Caminer is reviewing a collecton of poetry entitled *L'Originale e il ritratto* (The original and the portrait) (Bassano: Remondini, 1792), which was published in honor of Isabella Teotochi, a Venetian patrician and *salonnière*, and Elisabeth Vigée Le Brun, the celebrated French court painter who painted Teotochi's portrait in 1792. Although Teotochi edited this work, it should not be confused with her celebrated collection of original "written portraits" of writers and artists, *Ritratti scritti da Isabella Teotochi Albrizzi* (Portraits written by Isabella Teotochi Albrizzi) (Brescia: Bettoni, 1807). The collection of poetry being reviewed here was organized by Teotochi's friend Constantino Zacco and contains poetry by many of the men who frequented Teotochi's Venetian salon (many of whom were also friends and colleagues of Caminer's), including Bertòla, Cesarotti, Lamberti, Pagani Cesa, Sibiliato, and both Giovanni and Ippolito Pindemonte.

104. In other words, Caminer had met Teotochi but had not seen the portrait by Vigée Le Brun or read the poems dedicated to the two women. Upon meeting Caminer in the fall of 1788, Teotochi penned the following description of her in a letter to a mutual friend, Michele Sorgo (Miho Sorkočević): "Since last week the celebrated Elisabetta Caminer Turra has been here, and she kindly allowed me the opportunity to meet her in person. Truly, one may apply that beautiful verse to her: 'she lives among books and keeps herself wise' (cited from Žarko Muljačić, "Le amicizie letterarie italiane di Miho Sorkočević," in *Problemi di lingua e letteratura italiana del Settecento*, proceedings of a congress at Weisbaden, April–May 1962 [Weisbaden: Franz Steiner Verlag, 1965], 164–69).

but she should hold in some regard those souls who express themselves with sincerity. They are so few! And we have such an eminent place among them!

8. ON THE EXCESSIVE MODESTY OF A LEARNED WOMAN (1794)[105]

Essay on the health of unmarried daughters, with some reflections on marriage, by Mr. Virard, supplemented with an essay on hysterical affections[106] by Mr. E. [Henry] Manning, edited and translated into Italian by Miss "Anonymous." Why in the world does the praiseworthy young woman "Anonymous" hide herself? Might she be of the opinion, humiliating to her sex, that in cultivating her talent she brings dishonor to women? It might not become a woman to parade herself as a professional expert, but must she blush for having played so useful a role [as translator], and for having directed her own studies toward the good of her peers? It is certainly doing them a great favor to speak about the true state of their health, and to try to explain what might be imagined or studied in their illnesses. After all, we respect the modesty of Miss "Anonymous," and we would only like to know who she is so that we might know to whom we should direct our praises.

❀   FASHION   ❀

1. LETTER TO AGOSTINO VIVORIO[107]

Vicenza, 1 November 1776

Here, my friend, are the papers you wanted, and I am sending you the originals because I was not able to copy them. I hope you will grant me the

---

105. In *Nuovo giornale enciclopedico d'Italia*, September 1794, 114, with no signature, because announcements in the section of the periodical announcing new books were never signed. Caminer is reviewing *Saggio sulla salute delle figlie nubili, con alcune reflessioni sul matrimonio, del Signor Virard, aggiuntovi un saggio delle affezioni isteriche del Signor E. Manning, traduzioni italiane di Madamigella N. N. Corredate di Note* (Essay on the health of unmarried daughters, with some reflections on marriage, by Mr. Virard, supplemented with an essay on hysterical affections by Mr. E. [Henry] Manning, edited and translated into Italian by Miss "Anonymous") (Pavia: Pietro Galeazzi, 1794).

106. The term "affections" is synonymous with "disease" or "a diseased state."

107. Agostino (Francesco) Vivorio (1743–1822), a Vicentine by birth, joined the Augustinian order in 1762 and moved to Verona, where he studied theology, philosophy, and (under Anton Maria Lorgna) mathematics. In 1771 Vivorio returned to Vicenza and dedicated himself to teaching young nobles. In 1782 he returned to Verona and became secretary of the scientific academy Lorgna founded, the Società Italiana delle Scienze, and professor of letters in the Collegio Militare there. Vivorio probably became acquainted with Caminer and her periodical

pleasure of sending the one on fashion[108] back to me as soon as possible, that is, before Saint Martin's Day. It is designed to provoke laughter and to demonstrate ever more clearly that everything in the world is a contradiction, since France offers us more striking examples of futility at the same time as it makes us envy its great men. Who knows if I might not be able to oblige myself to some lady by letting her know that, if she does not have sustained attention or sentiment within her heart, she can at least apply them to her clothing and hair, that she can show her desires without too much embarrassment, and that she can form sweet smiles even if she has an enormous and ugly mouth? You can either send the satires back to me when you want or throw them out. Vile indignities that are either unjust or indiscreet and that make themselves more abhorrent than the objects of their derision are not important to me.[109] Show these trifles, especially the first one, to our dear Bonogurio, beautiful as he is with his bandage around his head: he must look like the blindfolded God [*il Dio bendato*]. Tell him that, even though he left me very brusquely, I am sorry to hear of his illness, although I believe it to be minor, and that I love him in spite of himself. Yesterday we were in the excellent company of the best of men. You and your friend, whom you are fortunate to have near you, were missed, and we felt your absence very much. Farewell my very dear friend: preserve your friendship for me, but sweeten it a little, because bitterness frightens me. Remember me often,

Elisabetta Caminer Turra

2. REVIEW OF THE NEW FASHION SUPPLEMENT TO THE *TUSCAN GAZETTE* (1777)[110]

Victory, happiness for our sex, and for that part of the other sex which knows its own interests well enough not to put on excessive airs by disparaging lov-

---

through his friend Alberto Fortis. Vivorio contributed articles to the Caminer periodicals over the years, and his friendship with Elisabetta lasted for the rest of her life. Caminer's letter to Vivorio is to be read in conjunction with the subsequent text in the anthology. Paired together, the two texts grant us the rare opportunity to see Caminer's critique (in a private letter) of her own review of a Florentine fashion supplement (before she publishes it in her periodical several months later). The letter (a copy) is located in the Biblioteca della Bertoliana in Vicenza, MS.G.4.4.12 (coll. Le 1).

108. I.e., her review of a Florentine fashion supplement. See below, text 2.

109. In the original, "A me non preme di vili indegnità, che sono o ingiuste, o indiscrete, e che si fanno disprezzare molto più del difetto, che accusano."

110. In *Giornale enciclopedico*, April 1777, 90–92, signed ECT. Caminer did not identify the periodical she was reviewing here. I am indebted to Doretta Davanzo Poli for identifying it as a new fashion supplement being introduced by the editors of *Gazzetta Toscana* (Tuscan gazette).

able, womanish futilities. The lords of creation, in fact, have descended toward their most humble handmaids so that, almost universally having become elegant baubles along with the women, they do not leave them in the dregs, not even in matters of appearance.[111] And now, as a reward for their kindness and as a reward to women for their gracious example, Italy's genius is shaking itself from the sleep that was making it sluggish, sharpening its wits and employing the fine arts to make both sexes happy. Mr. Anton Giuseppe Pagani and Mr. Antonio Fabrini of Florence have formed an association through which they propose to supply small engravings of male and female figures every two weeks. The colored figures in miniature will appear in everyday dress or in court dress with all the most exact accessories, from the hair at its roots all the way to the tips of the shoes inclusively, according to the various styles that the dictators of the century pass as law every quarter of an hour. Already everyone easily understands the French, who, in a strange contradiction, offer a bizarre contrast of solidity and superficiality: they perfect the sciences, expand the arts, torment themselves over fashion, and produce—if not with equal merit, with equal fortune—great men and foppish dandies. They inspire undiscerning admiration on the part of ecstatic Italians, who, while copying the latter [dandies] and expressing admiration for the former [great men], console themselves as they ape gestures and movements in front of the mirror for being in the final end their masters from the beginning.[112] Colors, galloons,[113] bonnets, embroidery, mantillas,[114] cravats, laces, little purses, fans, small hats, big hats, hoops, no hoops, feathers, no feathers, wide and narrow dresses, low waistlines and high waistlines, hairstyles of every kind—all will be expressed, elucidated with proper explanations and opportune notes. And men will know if they should attend to their affairs with collars of many or few layers,[115] with a minuet step, or with an English

111. In other words, men, who impose the lastest fashions upon women, have decided to particpate along with women in following fashion trends—even at the cost of becoming frivolous themselves. They have done so, Caminer writes, to make sure that women will not reign over men in any area—not even in the ridiculous area of fashion.

112. In other words, as Italians stand before their mirrors aping the latest French gestures and movements, they console themselves for having been masters of the French in the past in all things concerning grace and style. Thoughts of their own supposed historical preeminence, Caminer suggests, are what allows her compatriots to accept that the French are the model to follow now.

113. Trimmings of various kinds used to decorate dresses.

114. Long veils for women that descended from the top of the head to just below the shoulders and were attached to the head with a hair comb.

115. Depending on the length of the shirt collar, it could be wrapped around the neck once or many times, thus altering its thickness.

air.[116] Women will know if they can manage their families better with great or small circumference in their dress, and to what *braccio italiano*[117] the height of their coiffure should correspond. All this will be known and seen for the sum of thirty *paoli* a year or, for nonsubscribers, three *lire* for each figure, a sum which would be considerable perhaps in other cases, but which is very small for the matter at hand. This happy enterprise will begin in May; it will distract men and give them relief from ponderous thoughts and administer new means for women to continue their open or secret rule over men. It will make the Florentine booksellers rich, and it will be good for our newspaper as well, whose merit will be indisputable if it can often report such important news.

3. REVIEW OF CLEMENTE BONDI'S POEM ON FASHION
(1778)[118]

The abbé Bondi's interesting Laments,[119] presented some time ago in the most vibrant way, earned for him most strongly the applause of sentiment, which is the best judge in matters of poetry. His many other diverse works have earned him a respectable name among poets, and he leaves nothing to be desired in this poem except that he might have extended and developed somewhat his plan and his research. Fashion, a futile matter in itself, but which is an essential part of luxury and of interest to commerce, takes on various modifications according to nations and to individuals. It is impressive because of the number of its devotees. It occupies the mind and distracts the heart, it affects customs no less than clothes, and it increases the means of our

116. In other words, with an affected, perhaps overly gracious air or with a more sober, formal tone. The implication behind this phrase is the contrast between French and English fashions.

117. An Italian *braccio* was a wooden measuring tool for cloth, which was about fifty to seventy centimeters long, depending on the type of cloth and the city (Doretta Davanzo Poli, "The Fashion Trades in Venice," in *I Mestieri della Moda a Venezia: The Arts and Crafts of Fashion in Venice, from the Thirteenth to the Eighteenth Century*, ed. Davanzo Poli [London: European Academy and Accademia Italiana, 1997], 15).

118. In *Giornale enciclopedico*, January 1778, 65–69, signed ECT. Caminer is reviewing Clemente Bondi's long poem entitled *La Moda Poemetto* (Fashion) (Padova: Penada, 1777). Clemente Bondi (1742–1821) was a satirical poet and a librarian first for the aristocratic Zannardo family in Mantua and then for the Archduke Ferdinand of Milan, whom Bondi followed to Vienna. Bondi published a series of satirical poetic works, including the one on fashion which Caminer reviewed (*La Moda*, 1777), and *Le Conversazioni* (1778), a portrait of aristocratic society which was modeled on Giuseppe Parini's *Giorno*.

119. [Caminer's note.] It is very well known to many, and we take the liberty of mentioning to everyone his much-praised *canzone* that begins as follows: "Gozzi, you urge me in vain," etc., addressed to the late abbé Gozzi and written on the occasion of the destruction of the Jesuit order, of which the author was a member.

subservience to the French.[120] Thus, it could perhaps have been subjected to a slightly more detailed examination and criticism in a greater quantity of lines. Then we would have gained a greater number of beautiful verses, since everything written by this well-mannered and learned writer bears the mark of elegance and philosophy. He is one of the very few [poets] who are worthy of reviving the ages of the Virgils, the Dantes, and the Ariostos with one of those great works that make an author's name eternally famous. Some individual pieces of poetry, if they have have interesting subjects and a polished style, can without a doubt bring fame to a writer. But a poem in which an orderly mind and a radiant soul must match the correctness of writing to the scope of the project, [and must match] the multiplicity of ideas and the knowledge of things, opinions, and men to the force and truth of sentiment, [and must] bring together the tranquil order and the great flights of a genius, which, by subjecting itself, so to speak, to sky and earth and abyss, embraces what is real, launches itself into what is possible, and in presenting the truth, renders artifice convincingly and pleasantly—this is one of those undertakings that places the poet among the number of the chosen few who create an era in letters. Philosophies have changed, new worlds have been discovered, clamorous events have happened—all the fruit of the inconstant genius and the constant nature of men: how many do not offer fertile ground to a mind that is capable of raising itself to render these events even more memorable and interesting thanks to the spell that poetry casts? Mr. Bondi's talent and his felicitous essays give us hope that someday he might want to set himself such a goal. In the meantime, we will offer an idea of the present poem, which takes aim at the caricature—which has become a passion—of the new styles in dress and hair, a reflectable object that usually rules the souls of women and the minds of the many female-men with whom we are inundated.

Speaking with Fashion, *daughter of the Seine*, about the fashion doll that arrives among us from those happy river banks, gives so many who are lazy something to do, and provides a happy pastime for so many who are bored with themselves, the poet says:

> Tell me which peoples
> Must the new Archetype correct,
> And whose ornaments do you first
> Deign to copy, O Goddess?
> Certainly not the people of Asia,

120. I have taken the liberty of translating the word *Oltramontani* that Caminer used here as "French," rather than as "transalpine neighbors" since it is clear from the rest of the review that she was speaking specifically of France.

Who in priestly cloaks
Wrap twisted strips
Around their shaved heads,
Nor that of the American savage,
Not yet corrupted enough,
Not the one of nude Ethiopia,
And not the one who lives at the pole,
Belted, with rough furs.
Peoples unknown to you, always the same,
Who, consulting nature and the climate
And the never changing use of time,
Have not yet learned from their ancestors
To derisively change the earliest clothing,
And the ancient ways,
Only to be then mocked themselves
One day by their grandchildren, etc.

Speaking of the many followers of fashion, the author, most felicitous in his descriptions, says among other things:

You penetrate the cloisters, and you assist
The solitary young Virgin
Who secretly takes and hides
Her faithful mirror,
And in the meantime,
Remembering the Parlatory[121]
Arranges the soft monastic veil
Into the latest fashions and folds.
You artfully shave ample tonsures
Around the monkish heads,
And you surround the white cranium
With a just and equal crown of hair,
And you send the elegant little abbé to the altar
With his hair arranged and with bizarre emblems[122]
Once unknown to the Sanctuary.

---

121. The parlatory, or *parlatorio,* was the area of the convent where eighteenth-century nuns could receive visitors. The young nun in this poem is recalling the fashions worn by women from the outside world which she had seen through the grilled windows of the parlatory and is attempting to mimic them with her own monastic clothing, the veil.

122. In other words, his tonsure *alla moda* is like a billboard announcing his fashionable look.

Who will want to recognize himself in the following portrait? No one. But if by chance there is a person of good faith who cannot hide from himself, will it be a new fault of ours—as we have been blamed so many other times—that a character has been delineated that does not find originals if only because it exists in nature?[123] Whatever the case may be, we will run the risk of quoting it.

> In the heart of every City a select new species
> Of insects is evolving, a strange order
> Of Nymphs and Ganymedes, to whom Nature
> Has granted the seeming exterior of a woman or of a man,
> A movement, a voice, and a something or other,
> That resembles a soul.
> Nothing more, except a fatal instinct
> To study new ways to dress and to create or copy new forms
> Of clothes, habits, and manners that are ever more strange,
> And more ridiculous: the prized virtue
> Of competing to be the one who best knows
> How to elegantly deform himself.

After a most natural description of the hairstyles and ornaments for women's heads, the following image seems to us sublime. Let us say it for truth's sake, even though we are women ourselves and may find ourselves mortified by it:

> And so the lofty machine (the toupee)
> Is completely realized by growing under your auspices,
> So that feminine heads, ornate at least on the outside,
> Triumphantly show it off like a pyramid on the forehead.
> In similar guise, they erect in churches
> The marble mass of proud mausoleums
> Adorned with images and trophies,
> Rare work of the industrious chisel,
> While in the meantime these tombs hold within their empty hearts
> Only a handful of ashes, silence, and shade.

We believe these excerpts suffice to introduce and recommend this poem, and we hope to have the opportunity to quote many others by this elegant author.

123. In other words, despite the fact that no one would want to recognize himself in the following portrait, and that only someone who is completely honest with himself will admit to seeing himself in it, Caminer asks if it is her fault if the character in this portrait is not original, but commonplace, if only because it is found in nature.

4. REVIEW OF THE MILANESE *JOURNAL OF THE LADIES AND FASHIONS OF FRANCE* (1786)[124]

The manifesto for a *Journal of the Ladies and Fashions of France* was published in Milan, objects [ladies and fashions] that go together naturally, as everyone can see. This publication will embrace moral and delightful novellas, *sensitive little novels*, *gracious* short stories in translation and in the original, and these lovely things in order to procure *the moral well-being of women*. There is more. Instructions for the fair sex, in which matters of *virtue* will be linked together with matters of the *toilette*. One would think that these two things clashed with each other, but it must not be so. Also: poems, which the person who wrote the manifesto defines as *the poetic part*, in order to begin educating the fair sex. These are supposed to *enliven* the hearts of women, as in those [poems] that will be *amorous, humorous, and bizarre*, and in order that they might enliven women's hearts in a healthy way, the *sacred*, the *philosophical*, and the *tedious*—which as we know are all one thing—will be eliminated. Also: gallant varieties, which is to say literature, music, painting, anecdotes, and witty puns that will be *delineated* in a *bizarre* way. Also: current French fashions, an article that is declared *the most interesting*; and here there will be engravings, descriptions, and all that can contribute to straightening out women's heads. We were complaining, poor women, that our education was neglected: the Heavens have provided for us, too! Good parents, in what a happy age our daughters are born! With twenty-four *lire* a year you will protect them from boredom and from awkwardness, and you will shape their minds and hearts. We were able to jest until this point; but upon reaching the following passage from the incredible manifesto, we cannot hide our reasonable indignation. Glance at it, readers, and whoever wants this wise periodical afterward, grab it. "In this way, this periodical *being to be the triumph of Italian ladies*, one does not despair of a gracious welcome from them and from the friends of this most respectable sex. In a work consecrated to women's pastimes, it will be easy for another woman to find a way to distinguish herself: she desires to mask what is useful with what is pleasing, and it must be a truly good fortune to be able to say she is preparing an idleness for them that could *enchant* their minds,

---

124. In *Nuovo giornale enciclopedico*, May 1786, 121–24. Caminer took the unusual step of creating a special column for this review, entitled simply "Fashion" (*moda*) and bearing no signature. She is reviewing the new fashion periodical, published in Milan, entitled *Giornale delle Dame e delle Mode di Francia* (*Journal of the ladies and fashions of France*), which was essentially an Italian translation of the French periodical *Cabinet des modes* but designed specifically for Italian readers. Grazietta Butazzi published a modern (abridged) edition of the Milanese periodical entitled *Giornale delle nuove mode di Francia e d'Inghilterra* (Torino: Umberto Allemandi, 1988).

leave some trace in the depth of their hearts, and likewise give real value to a momentary distraction. Dedicated to the Graces, this work will not even be deprived of *that tone of indulgence* that characterizes it. This way, any criticisms that arise will be disarmed: their suggestions will be embraced, however, as will the means to continually improve the periodical and to reconcile *self-love* with truth. And the principal goal of this work will always be to instruct the fair sex with pleasantness and with *gallantry.*"

To top it all off, it seems that the author of this periodical is a woman. Were we not treated with enough disdain by men without reducing ourselves to the humiliation of showing ourselves to be contemptible?

5. REVIEW OF THE VENETIAN FASHION PERIODICAL
THE GALLANT AND LEARNED WOMAN (1786)[125]

A capricious manifesto published in Venice by the Albrizzi bookshop at San Benedetto promises for the first week of September the first issue of a new periodical entitled *The Gallant and Learned Woman*, written à la mode, that is to say, without the chaff [*crusca*],[126] and with the glorious liberty that reigns among writers of bon ton.[127] To entice women, who are meant to be the principal owners of this periodical, the female editor lists the articles in the first four issues, and they are "Tales" that are not moral. The first is "What to Do?" "A

125. In *Nuovo giornale enciclopedico*, July 1786, 114–15, with no signature, because announcements in the section of the periodical announcing new books were never signed. *La donna galante ed erudita: Giornale dedicato al bel sesso* (The gallant and learned woman: Journal dedicated to the fair sex), edited by Gioseffa Cornoldi Caminer, is another Italian version of the French *Cabinet des Modes* (see also "Women and Society: Fashion," text 4). Caminer had a delicate task in reviewing this periodical, because—as scholar Cesare De Michelis has surmised—it was edited by her sister-in-law, Gioseffa Cornoldi Caminer. See section 3 of "Volume Editor's Introduction." For a modern (abridged) edition of the *Donna galante*, see De Michelis, ed., *La donna galante ed erudita: Giornale dedicato al bel sesso* (Venezia: Marsilio, 1983). See also chapter 5 of Messbarger, *Century of Women*, which is dedicated to a discussion of the *Donna galante*.

126. The expression "la crusca" refers to the conservative Florentine Accademia della Crusca, founded in 1582, which was dedicated to defending the "purity" of the Italian language—the hegemony of the Florentine dialect and the literary models of Dante, Petrarch, and Boccaccio—against "invasion" by other dialectal or foreign words (thereby separating the seed from the chaff). In the context of the Enlightenment linguistic debate, Elisabetta Caminer and her father rejected the traditional, Crusca-oriented approach and favored clarity and simplicity of style over scholastic formality, especially for the language of periodicals. They joined other progressive thinkers in favor of expanding the Italian language through the use of other dialects and especially through the adoption of foreign words or neologisms and thereby giving it the elasticity to clearly and accurately express new ideas. See Colla, "Elisabetta Caminer Turra e il giornalismo 'enciclopedico,'" 100–108.

127. The expression "bon ton" is synonymous with grace and ease in cultured, élite society. Caminer is making direct reference to Cornoldi's words in her "Author's Justification."

Sweeping Criticism of Cavalieri Serventi."[128] "Ways to Conserve Women's Beauty." "Thirty Things (*Preferably Joined Together*) That Make a Woman Perfect." "What Is the Most Likely Quality to Make a Marriage Happy?" "An Unusual Event That Happened to a Lawyer from the Veneto While in the Countryside This Summer of 1786." "Another at a Ball in the . . . Theater on the Occasion of the Fair." "Article on Brooches." "An Accident, Not Very Unusual, That Happened to a Beautiful Young Lady." "French Canzone." "Erudition: Weddings of the Ancient Romans." "Apology of Modern Marriages." "New Books That Are Suitable for the Female Sex." Theatrical events will form an important section. Every fifteen days a small volume and two prints of miniature figures will be published. Subscribers will pay sixteen *lire* a year, and nonsubscribers twenty *soldi* for each issue containing figures. Ladies will so easily find what they need in this periodical that it will be hard for them not to compete at increasing the number of its subscribers.

❀ MARRIAGE OR THE CONVENT ❀

1. AGAINST FORCED MONACHIZATION OR FORCED MARRIAGE: A REVIEW OF DUBOIS-FONTANELLE'S *ÉRICIE, OR, THE VESTAL* (TRANSLATED INTO ITALIAN BY F. ALBERGATI) (1769)[129]

The excellent translation of this famous drama, of which we already provided an extract in the October 1768 issue of our periodical,[130] is worthy of greater applause. *Bialgerat, the Arab poet* who has learned the Italian language and who has learned to write Italian verse so well that he has been able to lend great

---

128. Caminer's use of italics, roman type, and dashes in this review is somewhat inconsistent. In some cases—after consulting the *Donna galante ed erudita* itself—I have separated titles that Caminer appears to have merged together in her review. "What to Do? (a tale)" and "A Sweeping Criticism of Cavalieri Serventi," for example, were set together as a single title here in the review but were actually published separately, in the second and first issues of *The Gallant and Learned Woman*, respectively.

129. In *Europa letteraria*, May 1769, 45–46, signed EC. Caminer is reviewing Francesco Albergati Capacelli's Italian translation of Dubois-Fontanelle's *Éricie ou la Vestale* (Éricie; or, the Vestal), which was first published in 1768, forbidden to be performed on stage, and burned as irreligious. Caminer had introduced Albergati to the play and encouraged him to translate it. Albergati published his translation—*Ericia, o la Vestale: Dramma francese* (Amsterdam: 1769)—under the pseudonym "Bialgerat, Arab Poet." Editions of his translation were also published the same year in Venice (by Colombani) and Verona (by Moroni) ("Lettere di Francesco Albergati Capacelli alla Bettina," 102).

130. Caminer had published a review of the French original in the October 1768 issue of the *Europa letteraria*, 55–68.

elegance to his translation, while at the same time keeping it extremely faithful to the original, is greatly mistaken if he flatters himself that he can always remain hidden as he would like. It is not always time to don a mask, and he will grant us the favor of raising his.[131] He will thus allow everyone to do well-earned justice to the senator marquis Albergati, who is very well known to the Republic of Letters for his beautiful translations of Racine, Crébillon, and Voltaire, for his own productions, and for his particular love of letters, which makes him a friend of whoever cultivates them. The tragedy he has most recently translated, and of which we now speak, was publicly burned in Paris, perhaps for political reasons rather than out of piety. He defends it with a discourse that is found at the end of the tragedy itself, and he clearly demonstrates how absurd it is to call it contrary to religion and to the monastic state. In fact, as he reflects, anyone can be happy in the state that she has chosen for herself, and that of the cloister is not excluded. But Mr. Fontanelle speaks through the mouth of Éricie against those fathers who force their own children to embrace a state that is repugnant to their nature. If Éricie had been forced into marriage, would she not have been equally unhappy? Would she not have declaimed equally against her condition? All of the translator's reflections are extremely just. When we revealed the name of this learned chevalier, we offered the highest praise possible to both him and his translation. Whatever may be the reason that motivated him to hide it, we had our own for revealing it, and we are very sure that justice, readers, and booksellers will be obliged to us for it.

2. ON THE CONVENT: TRANQUIL HAVEN OR PAINFUL PRISON? (1773)[132]

In announcing this book (the printing of which is magnificent, and the editing done by the learned and erudite Mr. D. Baldarini of Vicenza is very precise) we cannot deny the canon Fardinello, episcopal vicar, just praise for his zeal and for the wise idea he had of publishing these sermons of his. They will be useful to those who, like him, were destined to the mournful duty of com-

---

131. In fact, Albergati had given Caminer permission to reveal his identity ("Lettere di Francesco Albergati Capacelli alla Bettina," 126, 131).

132. In *Europa letteraria*, April 1773, 68–70, signed ECT. Caminer is reviewing Fardinello's *Sermoni alle Monache nelle loro Vestizioni e Professioni, coll'aggiunta di alcune Riflessioni sopra lo Stato Religioso, consecrati al Sua E. Reverendissima Monsignor Marco Cornaro Vescovo di Vicenza* (Sermons to nuns on their veil taking and on their profession, supplemented with reflections on the religious state, dedicated to the Most Holy Monsignor Marco Cornaro, bishop of Venice) (Vicenza: Vendramini Mosca, 1773).

forting those women who leave society, and they could be even more useful to many female members of religious orders. We will leave aside those [women] who are inspired by Heaven, who are guided and fortified by the grace of God. But if we exclude these, whose holy resolve we silently respect, a number of unhappy women unfortunately need external help: those who are not firm in their resolve, or those who are unfortunate victims sometimes of politics, sometimes of coercion, and even more often of the imagination, who drag themselves through their bitter and languishing days, and who can hope for a change in circumstances only at the end of a life spent between desires and boredom. Unfortunately, an inopportune spirit, which in these circumstances might therefore be called a tempter, suggests to these unlucky women who do not figure among the number of those who live in seclusion because of holy inspiration, that God did not give us freedom so that we would deprive ourselves of it, or a will so that we would negate it. It suggests that the most efficacious manner in which to please this Maker of men is to render oneself useful to the human race, as these women are not, in any possible way. And it suggests that one cannot compare the fulfillment of a wise and virtuous mother's august duties with the merit of chanting the requisite canticles in a cloister, which is a tranquil place of repose for those inspired by Heaven, but a painful prison for those who are nothing except women sent away from society. These sermons could actually comfort them, placing before their eyes those advantages to be drawn from the inconveniences their situation might have, since all situations are likely to have some. As for ourselves, we wholeheartedly renew our praises for the author of this work, but we sincerely desire that the number of women so very poorly favored by grace as to need it will not grow.

3. POEM OFFERING ADVICE TO A BRIDE AND GROOM UPON THEIR MARRIAGE (1774)[133]

Sweet care of Love, fair DAMSEL,
And you, YOUNG LAD, ornament and pride of BERGA,
For you I unwillingly loosen my tongue
And raise my voice in this humble song of mine:
For nothing in common with the holy name

---

133. Caminer's poem was published in the collection of poetry entitled *Poesie per le faustissime nozze del Signor Conte Niccolò Nievo con la Signora Contessa Bernardina Ghellini nobili vicentini* (Poems for the most propitious wedding of Count Niccolò Nievo with Countess Bernardina Ghellini, Vicentine nobles) (Vicenza: Vendramini Mosca, 1774), xix–xxii.

Of beautiful Pure Truth have the poetic exertions,
Or the many insipid collections
By now no longer read.[134]

I who follow what is true, I who am not unaware
Of the qualities that Nature has placed in you,
I to whom are known the famous deeds
Of both your lofty and illustrious families,
I who honor you in my heart and who have always been
Sparing with mean and odious adulation,
I would not have destined my verses
To narrate that which everyone knows.

But since ancient social custom
Now binds Man, who is no longer free,
Since those who try to follow their own will
Are now seen as crude, or enemies of mankind,
Since everyone, friend to his own deceit,
Pretends that only those who agree with him are his friends,
I am constrained to offer you my song,
Illustrious COUPLE, which you have not asked for.

I sing of your union, and of your noble endowments,
In which happy BERGA glories;
I sing of the illustrious memory of your ancestors,
The eternal pride of centuries far in the past;
I sing of the honors of future history
In their desired latecoming grandchildren,
And first of all of the children who will be born to you,
Heroic Citizens dear to the Fatherland.

You will render them glorious children
Ever superior to Jealousy and Time;
Because of you, they will not fall into the cruel clutches
Of prejudice and of common error;
From you they will learn that to give wise counsel
To the Fatherland or to be worthy of the laurel crown,

---

134. Caminer is referring to the custom of publishing collections of occasional poetry—such as the one for which she wrote this poem. It was a common practice during the eighteenth century to produce such collections for celebrating important social or governmental events. On occasional poetry, see section 4 of "Volume Editor's Introduction."

It is vain to seek out every arcane record of other peoples' achievements,
Every saying attributed to others.

From your example, forming a deity for themselves,
Happy SPOUSES, honor of this land,
They will know that the practice of slander
Always leads to blame, contempt, and sorrow;
Nor in the gloomy light of idleness will they see
That which is only hidden or imaginary,
But, always following a wise moral system,
They will be willing to believe that others follow it also.

They will learn from you, lofty hearts,
That merit must be admired wherever it shines,
Because all men are equal, though not all descend
From the Blood of Heroes favored in Heaven;
That Virtue alone which kindles our souls
Can establish difference among us,
Not chariots of gold or distinguished titles,
Or vast estates off limits to common folk.

From you, cherished BRIDE of a beloved groom
Your illustrious and beautiful daughters will learn
That Fate allows women, too,
To rise up glorious beyond the stars.
But that we create for ourselves a lowly position,
By becoming slaves to the latest fashions,
And by being intent only upon changing them often,
It is we who make of ourselves a weak sex.

Gods, you who have in your care
Souls alight with with honor and glory,
Watching over them for the ultimate good of the Berico town,
If my predictions you will render correct,
If on this amiable and affable COUPLE,
As you always have, you will always keep your eye
So that they offer fine examples in the end,
Worthy you will be, oh Gods, of new Temples.

And if you, COUPLE, living image of Virtue,
With whom Love resides,
Ever read these poems, and if it should happen

That you do not appear embarrassed by them and by my wishes for you,
I will no longer have sad thoughts on the banks of the Bacchiglione
On the happy shores of my native Sea,
Nor will I envy the laurels
Of the Etruscan Corilla, Irminda, Dori.[135]

4. REVIEW OF LETTERS ON THE DUTIES OF NUNS' SUPERIORS (1778)[136]

If, by renouncing the vanities of our century, nuns aspire to a more perfect state, which is to say that of a redeeming God's spouses, at the same time they take on the obligation of doing nothing for the whole course of their lives, as much as is possible given human weakness, which is unworthy of the examples they have received from their divine spouse. In order to keep them on this narrow road of spiritual health, and in order to continuously instruct them in their duties, they need, in addition the mother [abbess] who supervises them inside the cloisters, an enlightened [male] superior to guide them in the practices of religion, in the observance of the canon they have embraced, and in difficult situations when they seem to be threatened by some danger. But these superiors do not always have the enlightenment and the zeal that their task demands. This book was written for them no less than for nuns.

5. POEM FOR A YOUNG WOMAN AS SHE TAKES THE VEIL (1781)[137]

I am not struck with amazement if unknown loves
With fearless heart you flee, oh maiden,
And on the threshold of a lonely cell
You trample the deceitful flowers of the world.

For to overcome vulgar errors
Every beautiful soul has sufficient strength from Heaven,

135. This is a reference to female poets of the Arcadian Academy: Corilla Olimpica (Maddalena Morelli of Pistoia), Irminda Partenide (Luisa Bergalli Gozzi), and Dori (perhaps a reference to Dorotea Del Bono, known as Dori Delfense in Arcadia).

136. In *Giornale enciclopedico*, January 1778, 103–4, with no signature. Caminer is reviewing a work entitled *Lettres sur les devoirs d'un supérieur de religieuses, par M. L. D. M.* (Letters on the duties of a superior to nuns, by M. L. D. M.) (Paris : Humblot, 1777) written by the abbé Paul de Montis.

137. Caminer's sonnet was published in a collection of poetry entitled *Poesie nell'occasione che veste l'abito di S. Benedetto nel Nobilissimo monastero di S. Zaccaria di Venezia la nobil donna Foscarina Garzoni che prende il nome di Maria Pisana* (Poems on the occasion that the noblewoman Foscarina Garzoni dons

And she who knows she is following a benign star
Happily abandons the storms of love.

I admire only that, endowed with virtue,
You renounce sweet and respected affections,
And the sacred duties of the useful life;

That your tender heart is not swayed and influenced
By the tears of a sick and stunned Mother:
Oh what mighty strength is given to the chosen ones![138]

6. REVIEW OF A BOOK OFFERING ADVICE TO NEW WIVES AND MOTHERS (1783)[139]

No other subject is discussed or written about so much as is education; and if ever the number of poorly educated men and women was great, it is precisely so in our age. Books are well and good, but example, which contradicts the most wisely dictated books, corrupts everything, and leaves only the outer shell of a good education, if that, which it often does not do. The recognized need to put order into such an important affair has led many philosophers and many decent people who are mediocre in philosophy to propose very different systems of moral instruction, some more and some less commendable, because they are all produced out of love for the public and the private good. There are some who want to utilize the beautiful and naked truth in this endeavor, and some who prefer the enchantment of the fable. But example, ah! good example continuously presented, and bad example continually hidden from the eyes of youth, is perhaps the great agent that, to the exclusion of all else, should be employed whenever possible.[140] If the example set by your family or your town does not measure up to their lessons, send the son or daughter you wish to educate very far away, and keep them there until they have absorbed good principles into their blood by the kilo. This is

---

the habit of San Benedetto in the most noble Monastery of San Zaccaria of Venice and takes the name of Maria Pisana) (Venezia: Stamperia Fenzo, 1781), xxviii.

138. Here, Caminer is commenting ironically on the young girl's indifference to her mother's grief at the prospect of her daughter's withdrawal from the world.

139. In *Nuovo giornale enciclopedico*, September 1783, 38–45, with no signature. Caminer is reviewing *Letters addressed to two young married ladies, on the most interesting subjects* (London: J. Dodsley, 1782). The author is anonymous.

140. This seems to contradict Caminer's general philosophy of openly showing both virtue and vice—at least on stage in bourgeois dramas—as an educational device. Perhaps she distinguishes between real life and the theater or between adults and youths in this matter.

the advice that should be given to all fathers and mothers who desire to have well-educated descendants. But the problem is that fathers and mothers are usually blind to their own defects and therefore are not in a position to avail themselves of good advice.

The author of the letters that we are announcing, who appears to be a woman, is presumably speaking to two young women who are already well educated, and she tends more than anything else to train them to apply the good principles they have absorbed to their new status as wives and mothers of families. The subjects about which she attempts to give them wise counsel are religious and moral duties, pleasing talents, public diversions, the tenderness owed to husbands, the education of children, the management of the household. . . . If this book had issued from one of our [Italian] pens, truly, it would pass for a kind of satire. By now women of fashionable society believe they have free rein to be irreligious, barely delicate in matters of integrity, extremely rude at the slightest whim, frenetic and extravagant when going to shows, indifferent and perhaps worse toward their husbands, negligent about the education of their children, and habitually ruinous to their own families. They prefer to every need or advantage of their families the vanities and the extravagances that make their own heads spin in all directions of the compass.

The education of children is treated more pointedly than the other issues by the author, who has devoted many letters to the topic. In these [letters] she shows most dissuasively[141] what an important thing it is to cultivate their intellectual faculties, to give them healthy and precise notions about religion, truth, benevolence, humanity, compassion, effort, work or application, the works of nature, and the Creator of the world. There is more fervor and eagerness to do a good deed than there is order in all of this, but the subjects are always well chosen and written with energy.

Despite the great man's fame, the lady author means to refute the Genevan philosopher's system of education, which demands that the first part of it [education] must be purely negative and circumscribed to protect the heart from vices and the soul from error.[142] According to Mr. Rousseau, if it were possible to raise a young child until the age of twelve without his knowing how to tell his right hand from his left, as long as he was healthy and robust, his intellect would open to his first lessons, and his reason, devoid of all

141. In other words, as we shall see, the British author argues effectively against Rousseau's system of education as outlined in his influential book on the subject, *Emile ou de l'Education* (Emile; or, On education), originally published in 1762. For a modern English translation, see Jean-Jacques Rousseau, *Emile; or, On Education*, ed. and trans. Allan Bloom (New York: Basic Books, 1979).

142. Here the British author is critiquing (in her letter 13, vol. 2) key passages from book 2 of *Emile*. See Rousseau, *Emile*, ed. Bloom, 93–94.

habits and preconceptions, would not work against the endeavors of the instructor. By attempting nothing, one would obtain prodigies.[143] He proposes that the exercise of the body be increased at that age, but that the intellectual side be left idle. The anonymous lady reflects quite rightly that such a passive education is not feasible. Natural curiosity will continually push children to ask questions, to procure information from whoever appears before them, and even from the most foolish servants. Therefore, while acquiring useful knowledge, their unoccupied souls will imbibe base, absurd, and trivial ideas. Indolence and laziness will become habitual for them, and consequently out of this will come boredom and abhorrence for every application.

Without being an enemy of feminine clothing and ornaments, the author draws attention to the foolishness of mothers who regard these as a primary part of the instructions they give or have others give to their daughters. "Lord Halifax in his excellent *Advice to a Young Girl*[144] says that the person who does not know how to dance well is excellent in one defect. I do not claim to decide whether in this proposition that wise man who lived in the previous century had an opinion well founded in every aspect, but it is certain that in our day dance is held to be one of the principal points of female education in all systems. Some time ago I saw a letter written to an *elegant* woman who had three daughters, and she spoke about them in this way: *About Caroline, my eldest, I have the satisfaction of being able to tell you that she consecrates exactly every hour of her day to her dance and singing lessons. She is beginning to show great taste in dress. She already knows how to arrange her beautiful hair to the best advantage, and to use false hairpieces well; it often happens that she gives good advice to her hairdresser.*[145] *I flatter myself that she will become a very beautiful person. . . I have never seen such skin. . . such a delightful complexion. Her industry [spirito] would surprise you. . . . She has recently invented a water for washing the neck that I have tried and that is superior by far to Warren's milk of roses; she has also discovered an excellent hand paste. She makes the most beautiful lace*[146] *you could ever see. I have not seen my two younger daughters for some time now. I have placed*

---

143. Rousseau believed that at this early stage of a child's education, it was through the very lack of input on the part of a teacher that extraordinary results would be achieved.

144. Caminer's rendition of the title is *Avvertimenti a una fanciulla* and refers to George Halifax's *The Lady's New years gift, or, Advice to a daughter: Under these following heads: Viz. religion, husband, house and family, servants, behavior and conversation, friendship, censure, vanity and affectation, pride, diversion, dancing,* 3d ed. (London: Gillyflower and Partridge, 1688).

145. "Sa di già disporre i suoi bei capelli con massimo vantaggio, e metter a profitto i capelli finti." But the English original says: "She begins to discover a *pretty taste* for *dress,* and knows how to manage her fine hair to the best advantage, with very little help of a *false,* or of a *frizeur."*

146. Caminer used the term *rete* (in this context, *lace),* although in the original text the word is "card purses": "She makes the very prettiest *card purses* you ever saw" (2:144). Perhaps in order to adapt the text for her readers, Caminer substituted a Venetian object of women's handiwork (lace) for the original British one (card purses).

*them in another boarding school, since that stupid Mistress Strietlan [Mistress Strictland]
was only teaching them to read English and to do plain-work.*[147] *So I removed those two poor
creatures from such a foolish education and placed them with Madame della Motte [Madame
Delamot], a famous French teacher. The principal reason that decided me is that she has the
best dancing master in England, etc.* Alas, this vain and ridiculous mother was in
too much of a hurry to congratulate herself about the talents and perfections
of her favorite Caroline. This unfortunate girl, educated in coquetry, barely
reached the age of eighteen when she fell prey to a married rogue, and she fled
with him to France, where she died shortly afterward in misery and disgrace."

Speaking about clothing, the author advises her two female friends to
persist in preferring elegant simplicity to all the overwrought, superfluous ornaments, which are seen as ridiculous not only by educated people, but by
entire populations. "Few women," she says, "imagine the extent to which their
clothes expose their character. Tell me how a woman dresses, and I will tell
you exactly what she is. Dress is a sure way to read her heart," and her mind.
It is pitiful to see to see how gallant women torture themselves to invent fan-
tastic decorations and to look like frauds or something worse. Their misguided delight in making themselves seen blinds them to the point that they
cannot read the derision, the disdain on the physiognomies of all who look
at them attentively, and who unfortunately often judge their customs by
those appearances which place them at the level of the most vile creatures.
To those among the coquettes who have some residue of common sense, one
cannot repeat often enough the authors's maxim "that a beautiful woman
never shows her beauty to such advantage as when she tries to hide it."

The following lines would sound like Arabic to young women of fashionable society in Italy or France. "A woman can never strive enough to please
her husband. She must make a special effort to excel in the things he prefers.
Apply yourselves to this important point in all aspects. Does he love books,
music, etc.? Remember that every talent, however common it may be, becomes interesting when it serves to amuse your husband. Your beautiful friend
Mistress P. . . . never seemed more lovable than when, having sung an Italian
arietta to please her guests, she added that she had taken great care to learn
it because she knew that her husband liked it very much. He was present, and
he gave her a look full of tenderness and the most express satisfaction."

The lady author says very many other beautiful and good things about

147. I rely on the original English text (2:145) here for the terms "boarding house" (*pensione*) and
"plain-work" (*lavorare*) as well as for the surnames mentioned in this paragraph: "I have changed
their *boarding school,* for that stupid Mistress Strictland taught them nothing in this world but
reading English and plain-work": The term "plain-work" refers to simple needlework, as distinguished from embroidery.

this subject that we shall not refer to our readers, because in some circumstances it is quite desirable to exercise moderation even when administering
good doctrines. England has a breed of marriages that are both categorized
and maintained in a very different way from that which we generally adopt
[in Italy].

The anonymous author greatly and unreservedly disapproves of the
game of cards, as something that is always accompanied either by interest or
by intemperance, which renders it fatal to domestic cares, etc. In general, it
will be found that the author is tediously pedantic, and no capable [*brava*]
woman will be curious about her book.[148]

7. FROM A POEM OFFERING ADVICE TO A FRIEND UPON HER MARRIAGE (1785)[149]

[. . .]
I do not ask of you [men] that in a servile way
You should bend to every feminine caprice,
Or that the true thought in your mind
Should be masked or hidden by a flattering style,
Or that you should speak ill of people,
Or that you should hold every other woman in low esteem,
And much less do I ask to have you around me
Like adoring and restless lovers.

I do not wish to believe that right-thinking women
Find pleasing these dangerous ways
That are often wont to conceal hurtful
Reprehensible plans and poisonous subterfuges
On account of which minds are led astray, and hearts, blameless,
Humiliated slaves in hateful chains,
Drip blood, and suffer in vain
Under the oppression of your sex.

---

148. This is a strangely critical ending for a reasonably favorable review on the whole. Perhaps
Caminer was sensitive about this book's competing with her recent translation of a similar manual for new wives and mothers by Jeanne-Marie Le Prince du Beaumont, *Instruzioni per le giovani
dame* (1782).

149. Caminer organized and personally published this collection of poetry for the wedding of
her young friend Francesca Ceroni (1770–1826), who was a poet and friend of Giovanni Pindemonte: *Ottave per le felici nozze de' Signori Francesca Ceroni e Giuseppe Dottor Disconzi (Octaves for the happy
wedding of Francesca Ceroni and Doctor Giuseppe Disconzi)* (Vicenza: Turra, 1785). I have translated for
this anthology a selection of stanzas (2, 3, 14, 15, 16, and 17) from Caminer's lengthy poem.

[. . .]

Oh, you light-hearted, gentle young woman,
Who in the tenderest flower of youth
Venture out into the world, in which there awaits,
Mixed in with the good, an immense army of deceits,
May Honesty, Reason, perfect Virtue
Be guides for you in avoiding the harm that may follow;
But may they be led by Fortune, on which depends
The ofttimes strange order of events.

Oh, how many unfortunate women, how many
With wise hearts, incorruptible minds,
Hear themselves slandered at every instant
For a fault at times imaginary, at times apparent!
Oh, how many women reputed to be saintly and honest
By people who are seduced or blinded
Hide abject souls and perverse horrors
Under the veil of Fortune and honors!

Ah, may the charms of seduction stay far from you
That bring in their wake suffering and humiliation;
Far from you fatal, untrustworthy friends,
Whom you would necessarily despise one day;
Far, the insidious flattering tongues,
That forever surround a young woman,
And all the other vices and defects unknown to you
Which spoil peoples' hearts in different guises!

Far from the empty, boring frivolousness
That loves and refines only fashions and caprices;
Far from the cultured lunacy that appreciates only
Those who have books in their hands and glib maxims on their lips;
Far from the haughtiness that despises everyone
Only to find itself despised and wretched in the end;
From stupid, humiliated baseness
May destiny protect your life!

[. . .]

8. FROM A REVIEW OF A SATIRICAL POEM OFFERING
ADVICE TO NEW NUNS (1786)[150]

Finally, we have here in our hands those *Capitoli*[151] that we merely announced in the May issue, because we had not yet seen them. If, independently of these, we did not already hold in high esteem the learned and noble Milanese chevalier[152] who is their *Hidden Author,* and if the desire to pay homage to truth did not influence us to speak well of them, we would find ourselves confounded, but so it goes. A bizarre and new caprice put it into the poet's head to address a prologue to those who receive a copy of his book as a gift, believing that to be a better idea than seeking a patron among great personages armed with a *string of resounding titles,* who in general cannot only bestow little or no authority at all, but most of the time either do not know how to read or do not even want to repay the *rotten lies* included in the Dedication by reading the work. Now, we repeat, what would we do if, having *received the Capitoli as a gift,* we were not naturally persuaded by them upon reading the first phrases of the author's prologue? Since, says he, one cannot look a gift horse in the mouth, he flatters himself that those discreet persons who have received his book as a gift will not be concerned to look at it too closely, or wish to find fault at any cost. From these persons, whom he must certainly number among his friends, *he hopes to obtain pity if not pardon,*[153] that pardon and that pity, he adds in jest, that "I will never be able to justly claim from anyone who will have had to spend his pennies [*baiocchi*] on it." [. . .]

If we followed our usual rule that does not permit us in a periodical of few pages to concede much space to poetry, which is not universally loved these days, we would have concluded after transcribing . . . [one] sonnet, which gives an idea of the author's brilliant style. If we listened to the pleasure we de-

---

150. In *Nuovo giornale enciclopedico,* July 1786, 65–75, signed ECT. Caminer is reviewing *Capitoli piacevoli d'Autore occulto per la prima volta pubblicati* (Pleasant capitoli by a hidden author published for the first time) ([Milan, with false imprint of Utrecht], 1785). The author is Francesco Sforzino da Carcano, a friend and colleague of Caminer's. I have translated selected passages from her lengthy review of this book.

151. *Capitolo* is a technical term indicating a satirical poem in terza rima, a verse form (adopted by Dante in the *Divine Comedy*) consisting of a continuous series of tercets in which the second line of each tercet rhymes with first and third lines of the following one (aba, bcb, cdc, etc.).

152. Francesco Sforzino da Carcano (1735–94) was an aristocratic Milanese poet and a member of the Accademia dei Trasformati in Milan. Carcano's home was frequented by many intellectuals of his day, including Giuseppe Baretti, who was a close friend. In addition to his collection of poetry reviewed here, Carcano published at least two other works: *Sogno del premuroso Fuggi Fatica* (1789) and *Sermone intorno ad alcune false opinioni tenute da varii nello scrivere poeticamente* (1790).

153. A quotation from the introductory sonnet of Petrarch's *Canzoniere.*

rived from reading his verses, which display the stamp of a fine author, although perhaps marred sometimes by the severity of the Crusca, [then] desirous of procuring this same pleasure for others, we would dwell longer in order to refer numerous passages from them to our readers. But we will not do one or the other thing, and, only in order to concede something both to our rule and to our pleasure, we will choose here and there from some of his verses that will certainly inspire the *individuals who did not receive copies of the book as a gift* to spend their *pennies* to procure this elegant collection for themselves. [. . .]

Utterly brilliant is a *Capitolo* dedicated to a nun on the occasion when she takes the veil. In these tercets, the poet says:

> There will not be elaborate imagery
> Or beautiful style, or Petrarchan phrases
> Or the usual praises of blond tresses.
> . . . .
> For it is not fitting to praise too highly the face
> And the pomps of the world to a maiden
> Who has completely segregated her heart from society.

Instead he gives solid advice to his young nun and reminds her that even in that holy state she must be on her guard against temptations.

> For you did not believe marriage to be a danger
> Only for evil lay people.
> The infernal clawed monster lands there
> Like a vulture in the Church and in the Refectory,
> In the Cloisters, in the Cell, and it sinks its claws into veils,
> For, if he tempts the Hermits in the Hermitage,
> Would it perhaps seem surprising to you
> That he should tempt the sisters in the convent parlatory?

In fact, having carefully examined the whole matter, the author, who does not wish to pay court to his young nun, or trust her more than he should, concludes:

> And that they are real women I do declare
> In their dress and further in their speech, and I conclude
> That they are the same in all things as other women.
> They too will have to oppose the flesh
> With a strong shield with all their might;
> Nor with this do I allude to impure things;
> Heaven forbid that because of me
> This or that virgin should blush, who sees herself,
> Just like us, to be made of flesh, skin, and blood.

The poet does not distrust chastity or the other important virtues of nuns, but he fears just a little bit, if nothing else, the self-love, the vanity, and the taste for supremacy that an abbess can have in common with a queen. . . .

> That commanding pleases you so much,
> Because it is a natural temptation
> That is only displeasing to saints,
> And it is an incentive to vanity, to say the least,
> And a direct occasion I would call it.
> Am I evil to reason in this way?
> My beloved sisters, I know that we are not speaking
> About people who belong to the corrupt secular world
> But about Virgins . . . yes, daughters of Adam.

To this vanity against which the poet wishes to forewarn the new nun he believes he must also attribute the excessive tolling of bells, and he gives good reasons for this: that if, among the other excuses, they indicated that the bells are rung in order to urge people to goodness,

> I respond: while the sun is shining on everyone,
> It could help, but not when the faithful
> Are resting their tired limbs upon their beds.
> The Anchorites clad in their shaggy pelts
> In their deserts and in their mountain grottos,
> Their minds turned toward the King of the Heavens,
> Arose with the dawn, and at midnight
> Prayed with streaming tears to God
> To pardon them for their sins;
> But they certainly did not toll bells,
> Disturbing with such inconsiderateness
> Weary people at all hours.

It cannot be denied that one reads few compositions for nuns that are written in this tenor. We will not print the much more risqué things that the author included, since our periodical does not provide the authentic publishing place of the book.[154] Readers will have to procure it for themselves and will admire as we do a writer who knows how to combine the graces of poetry with the strength of a philosopher and the palliatives of a prudent man. [. . .]

154. The book was published with a false imprint of Utrecht, and the *Nuovo giornale enciclopedico* lists it this way, when in fact the book was published in Milan. With this phrase, and with her revelation that the anonymous author is from Milan, Caminer thus alerts her readers where they should look if they want to procure the book for themselves.

It must be said that the noble author is more modest than he wishes to appear in his *Notes*, because we know from a reliable source that he has another collection of poems ready, and the fear that the first ones will not be acceptable to readers prevents him from publishing them. But we hope that the applause which readers will not fail to give his *Capitoli* will convince him to multiply their [the readers'] pleasures.

SERIES EDITORS'
BIBLIOGRAPHY

Note: Items listed in the volume editor's bibliography are omitted here.

PRIMARY SOURCES

Alberti, Leon Battista (1404–72). *The Family in Renaissance Florence.* Translated by Renée Neu Watkins. Columbia: University of South Carolina Press, 1969.

Arenal, Electa, and Stacey Schlau, eds. *Untold Sisters: Hispanic Nuns in Their Own Works.* Translated by Amanda Powell. Albuquerque: University of New Mexico Press, 1989.

Astell, Mary (1666–1731). *The First English Feminist: "Reflections on Marriage" and Other Writings.* Edited by Bridget Hill. New York: St. Martin's Press, 1986.

Atherton, Margaret, ed. *Women Philosophers of the Early Modern Period.* Indianapolis: Hackett Publishing Co., 1994.

Aughterson, Kate, ed. *Renaissance Woman: Constructions of Femininity in England: A Source Book.* London: Routledge, 1995.

Barbaro, Francesco (1390–1454). Preface and book 2 of *On Wifely Duties.* Translated by Benjamin Kohl. In *The Earthly Republic,* edited by Benjamin Kohl and R. G. Witt, 179–228. Philadelphia: University of Pennsylvania Press, 1978.

Behn, Aphra. *The Works of Aphra Behn.* 7 vols. Edited by Janet Todd. Columbus: Ohio State University Press, 1992–96.

Boccaccio, Giovanni (1313–75). *Famous Women.* Edited and translated by Virginia Brown. The I Tatti Renaissance Library. Cambridge, Mass.: Harvard University Press, 2001.

———. *Corbaccio; or, The Labyrinth of Love.* Translated by Anthony K. Cassell. 2d rev. ed. Binghamton, N.Y.: Medieval and Renaissance Texts and Studies, 1993.

Bruni, Leonardo (1370–1444). "On the Study of Literature (1405) to Lady Battista Malatesta of Moltefeltro." In *The Humanism of Leonardo Bruni: Selected Texts,* translated by Gordon Griffiths, James Hankins, and David Thompson, 240–51. Binghamton, N.Y.: Medieval and Renaissance Studies and Texts, 1987.

Castiglione, Baldassare (1478–1529). *The Book of the Courtier.* Translated by George Bull. New York: Penguin, 1967.

Cerasano, S. P., and Marion Wynne-Davies, eds. *Readings in Renaissance Women's Drama: Criticism, History, and Performance, 1594–1998.* London: Routledge, 1998.

Christine de Pizan (1365–1431). *The Book of the City of Ladies.* Translated by Earl Jeffrey Richards. Foreword Marina Warner. New York: Persea Books, 1982.

———. *The Treasure of the City of Ladies.* Translated by Sarah Lawson. New York: Viking Penguin, 1985.

————. *The Treasure of the City of Ladies*. Translated by Charity Cannon Willard. Edited by Madeleine P. Cosman. New York: Persea Books, 1989.

Clarke, Danielle, ed. *Isabella Whitney, Mary Sidney and Aemilia Lanyer: Renaissance Women Poets*. New York: Penguin Books, 2000.

Crawford, Patricia, and Laura Gowing, eds. *Women's Worlds in Seventeenth-Century England: A Source Book*. London: Routledge, 2000.

Daybell, James, ed. *Early Modern Women's Letter Writing, 1450–1700*. Houndmills: Palgrave, 2001.

Elizabeth I: Collected Works. Edited by Leah S. Marcus, Janel Mueller, and Mary Beth Rose. Chicago: University of Chicago Press, 2000.

Elyot, Thomas (1490–1546). *Defence of Good Women: The Feminist Controversy of the Renaissance*. Edited by Diane Bornstein. New York: Delmar, 1980.

Erasmus, Desiderius (1467–1536). *Erasmus on Women*. Edited by Erika Rummel. Toronto: University of Toronto Press, 1996.

Female and Male Voices in Early Modern England: An Anthology of Renaissance Writing. Edited by Betty S. Travitsky and Anne Lake Prescott. New York: Columbia University Press, 2000.

Ferguson, Moira, ed. *First Feminists: British Women Writers, 1578–1799*. Bloomington: Indiana University Press, 1985.

Galilei, Maria Celeste. *Sister Maria Celeste's Letters to Her Father, Galileo*. Edited by and translated by Rinaldina Russell. Lincoln, Nebr.: Writers Club Press of Universe.com, 2000.

Gethner, Perry, ed. *"The Lunatic Lover" and Other Plays by French Women of the Seventeenth and Eighteenth Centuries*. Portsmouth, N.H.: Heinemann, 1994.

Glückel of Hameln (1646–1724). *The Memoirs of Glückel of Hameln*. Translated by Marvin Lowenthal. New York: Schocken Books, 1977.

Henderson, Katherine Usher, and Barbara F. McManus, eds. *Half Humankind: Contexts and Texts of the Controversy about Women in England, 1540–1640*. Urbana: University of Illinois Press, 1985.

Humanist Educational Treatises. Edited and translated by Craig W. Kallendorf. The I Tatti Renaissance Library. Cambridge, Mass.: Harvard University Press, 2002.

Joscelin, Elizabeth. *The Mothers Legacy to her Unborn Childe*. Edited by Jean leDrew Metcalfe. Toronto: University of Toronto Press, 2000.

Kaminsky, Amy Katz, ed. *Water Lilies, Flores del Agua: An Anthology of Spanish Women Writers from the Fifteenth through the Nineteenth Century*. Minneapolis: University of Minnesota Press, 1996.

Kempe, Margery (1373–1439). *The Book of Margery Kempe*. Translated and edited by Lynn Staley. New York: W. W. Norton, 2001.

King, Margaret L., and Albert Rabil, Jr., eds. *Her Immaculate Hand: Selected Works by and about the Women Humanists of Quattrocento Italy*. Binghamton, N.Y.: Medieval and Renaissance Texts and Studies, 1983; 2d rev. paperback ed., 1991.

Klein, Joan Larsen, ed. *Daughters, Wives, and Widows: Writings by Men about Women and Marriage in England, 1500–1640*. Urbana: University of Illinois Press, 1992.

Knox, John (1505–72). *The Political Writings of John Knox: "The First Blast of the Trumpet against the Monstrous Regiment of Women" and Other Selected Works*. Edited by Marvin A. Breslow. Washington, D.C.: Folger Shakespeare Library, 1985.

Kors, Alan C., and Edward Peters, eds. *Witchcraft in Europe, 400–1700: A Documentary History*. Philadelphia: University of Pennsylvania Press, 2000.

Krämer, Heinrich, and Jacob Sprenger. *Malleus Maleficarum* (ca. 1487). Translated by Montague Summers. London: Pushkin Press, 1928; reprint, New York: Dover, 1971.

Larsen, Anne R., and Colette H. Winn, eds. *Writings by Pre-revolutionary French Women: From Marie de France to Elizabeth Vigée-Le Brun.* New York: Garland Publishing Co., 2000.

de Lorris, William, and Jean de Meun. *The Romance of the Rose.* Translated by Charles Dahlbert. Princeton, N.J.: Princeton University Press, 1971; reprint, Hanover, N.H.: University Press of New England, 1983.

Marguerite d'Angoulême, Queen of Navarre (1492–1549). *The Heptameron.* Translated by P. A. Chilton. New York: Penguin, Viking, 1984.

Mary of Agreda. *The Divine Life of the Most Holy Virgin.* Abridged from *The Mystical City of God* by Fr. Bonaventure Amedeo de Caesarea, M.C. Translated by Abbé Joseph A. Boullan. Rockford, Ill.: TAN Books, 1997.

Myers, Kathleen A., and Amanda Powell, eds. *A Wild Country Out in the Garden: The Spiritual Journals of a Colonial Mexican Nun.* Bloomington: Indiana University Press, 1999.

Teresa of Avila, Saint (1515–82). *The Life of Saint Teresa of Avila by Herself.* Translated by J. M. Cohen. New York: Penguin, Viking, 1957.

Weyer, Johann (1515–88). *Witches, Devils, and Doctors in the Renaissance: Johann Weyer, "De praestigiis daemonum."* Edited by George Mora with Benjamin G. Kohl, Erik Midelfort, and Helen Bacon. Translated by John Shea. Binghamton, N.Y.: Medieval and Renaissance Texts and Studies, 1991.

Wilson, Katharina M., ed. *Medieval Women Writers.* Athens: University of Georgia Press, 1984.

————, ed. *Women Writers of the Renaissance and Reformation.* Athens: University of Georgia Press, 1987.

Wilson, Katharina, and Frank J. Warnke, eds. *Women Writers of the Seventeenth Century.* Athens: University of Georgia Press, 1989.

Women Critics 1660–1820: An Anthology. Edited by the Folger Collective on Early Women Critics. Bloomington: Indiana University Press, 1995.

Women Writers in English, 1350–1850. Series of 30 vols. projected, suspended after publication of 15 vols. Oxford: Oxford University Press, 1993–94.

Wroth, Lady Mary. *The Countess of Montgomery's "Urania."* 2 pts. Edited by Josephine A. Roberts. Tempe, Ariz.: MRTS, 1995, 1999.

————. *Lady Mary Wroth's "Love's Victory": The Penshurst Manuscript.* Edited by Michael G. Brennan. London: Roxburghe Club, 1988.

————. *The Poems of Lady Mary Wroth.* Edited by Josephine A. Roberts. Baton Rouge: Louisiana State University Press, 1983.

de Zayas, Maria. *The Disenchantments of Love.* Translated by H. Patsy Boyer. Albany: State University of New York Press, 1997.

————. *The Enchantments of Love: Amorous and Exemplary Novels.* Translated by H. Patsy Boyer. Berkeley: University of California Press, 1990.

SECONDARY SOURCES

Akkerman, Tjitske, and Siep Sturman, eds. *Feminist Thought in European History, 1400–2000.* London: Routledge, 1997.

Backer, Dorothy Anne Liot. *Precious Women*. New York: Basic Books, 1974.

Barash, Carol. *English Women's Poetry, 1649–1714: Politics, Community, and Linguistic Authority*. New York: Oxford University Press, 1996.

Battigelli, Anna. *Margaret Cavendish and the Exiles of the Mind*. Lexington: University of Kentucky Press, 1998.

Beasley, Faith. *Revising Memory: Women's Fiction and Memoirs in Seventeenth-Century France*. New Brunswick, N.J.: Rutgers University Press, 1990.

Beilin, Elaine V. *Redeeming Eve: Women Writers of the English Renaissance*. Princeton, N.J.: Princeton University Press, 1987.

Benson, Pamela Joseph. *The Invention of Renaissance Woman: The Challenge of Female Independence in the Literature and Thought of Italy and England*. University Park: Pennsylvania State University Press, 1992.

Bissell, R. Ward. *Artemisia Gentileschi and the Authority of Art*. University Park: Pennsylvania State University Press, 2000.

Blain, Virginia, Isobel Grundy, and Patricia Clements, eds. *The Feminist Companion to Literature in English: Women Writers from the Middle Ages to the Present*. New Haven, Conn.: Yale University Press, 1990.

Bloch, R. Howard. *Medieval Misogyny and the Invention of Western Romantic Love*. Chicago: University of Chicago Press, 1991.

Bornstein, Daniel, and Roberto Rusconi, eds. *Women and Religion in Medieval and Renaissance Italy*. Translated by Margery J. Schneider. Chicago: University of Chicago Press, 1996.

Brant, Clare, and Diane Purkiss, eds. *Women, Texts and Histories, 1575–1760*. London: Routledge, 1992.

Briggs, Robin. *Witches and Neighbours: The Social and Cultural Context of European Witchcraft*. New York: HarperCollins, 1995; New York: Penguin, Viking, 1996.

Brink, Jean R., ed. *Female Scholars: A Traditioin of Learned Women before 1800*. Montréal: Eden Press Women's Publications, 1980.

Brown, Judith C. *Immodest Acts: The Life of a Lesbian Nun in Renaissance Italy*. New York: Oxford University Press, 1986.

Bynum, Carolyn Walker. *Holy Feast and Holy Fast: The Religious Significance of Food to Medieval Women*. Berkeley: University of California Press, 1987.

Cervigni, Dino S., ed. *Women Mystic Writers*. Special issue of *Annali d'Italianistica*, no. 13 (1995).

Cervigni, Dino S., and Rebecca West, eds. *Women's Voices in Italian Literature*. Special issue of *Annali d'Italianistica*, no. 7 (1989).

Charlton, Kenneth. *Women, Religion and Education in Early Modern England*. London: Routledge, 1999.

Chojnacka, Monica. *Working Women in Early Modern Venice*. Baltimore: Johns Hopkins University Press, 2001.

Chojnacki, Stanley. *Women and Men in Renaissance Venice: Twelve Essays on Patrician Society*. Baltimore: Johns Hopkins University Press, 2000.

Cholakian, Patricia Francis. *Rape and Writing in the "Heptameron" of Marguerite de Navarre*. Carbondale: Southern Illinois University Press, 1991.

———. *Women and the Politics of Self-Representation in Seventeenth-Century France*. Newark: University of Delaware Press, 2000.

Clogan, Paul Maruice, ed. *Medievali et Humanistica: Literacy and the Lay Reader.* Lanham, Md.: Rowman and Littlefield, 2000.

Crabb, Ann. *The Strozzi of Florence: Widowhood and Family Solidarity in the Renaissance.* Ann Arbor: University of Michigan Press, 2000.

Davis, Natalie Zemon. *Society and Culture in Early Modern France.* Stanford, Calif.: Stanford University Press, 1975. Especially chaps. 3 and 5.

————. *Women on the Margins: Three Seventeenth-Century Lives.* Cambridge, Mass.: Harvard University Press, 1995.

DeJean, Joan. *Ancients against Moderns: Culture Wars and the Making of a Fin de Siècle.* Chicago: University of Chicago Press, 1997.

————. *Tender Geographies: Women and the Origins of the Novel in France.* New York: Columbia University Press, 1991.

Dixon, Laurinda S. *Perilous Chastity: Women and Illness in Pre-Enlightenment Art and Medicine.* Ithaca, N.Y.: Cornell Universitiy Press, 1995.

Dolan, Frances, E. *Whores of Babylon: Catholicism, Gender and Seventeenth-Century Print Culture.* Ithaca, N.Y.: Cornell University Press, 1999.

Donovan, Josephine. *Women and the Rise of the Novel, 1405–1726.* New York: St. Martin's Press, 1999.

De Erauso, Catalina. *Lieutenant Nun: Memoir of a Basque Transvestite in the New World.* Translated by Michele Ttepto and Gabriel Stepto. Boston: Beacon Press, 1995.

Erickson, Amy Louise. *Women and Property in Early Modern England.* London: Routledge, 1993.

Ezell, Margaret J. M. *The Patriarch's Wife: Literary Evidence and the History of the Family.* Chapel Hill: University of North Carolina Press, 1987.

————. *Social Authorship and the Advent of Print.* Baltimore: Johns Hopkins University Press, 1999.

Ferguson, Margaret W., Maureen Quilligan, and Nancy J. Vickers, eds. *Rewriting the Renaissance: The Discourses of Sexual Difference in Early Modern Europe.* Chicago: University of Chicago Press, 1987.

Fletcher, Anthony. *Gender, Sex and Subordination in England, 1500–1800.* New Haven, Conn.: Yale University Press, 1995.

Frye, Susan, and Karen Robertson, eds. *Maids and Mistresses, Cousins and Queens: Women's Alliances in Early Modern England.* Oxford: Oxford University Press, 1999.

Gallagher, Catherine. *Nobody's Story: The Vanishing Acts of Women Writers in the Marketplace, 1670–1820.* Berkeley: University of California Press, 1994.

Garrard, Mary D. *Artemisia Gentileschi: The Image of the Female Hero in Italian Baroque Art.* Princeton, N.J.: Princeton University Press, 1989.

Gelbart, Nina Rattner. *The King's Midwife: A History and Mystery of Madame du Coudray.* Berkeley: University of California Press, 1998.

Goldberg, Jonathan. *Desiring Women Writing: English Renaissance Examples.* Stanford, Calif.: Stanford University Press, 1997.

Goldsmith, Elizabeth C. *Exclusive Conversations: The Art of Interaction in Seventeenth-Century France.* Philadelphia: University of Pennsylvania Press, 1988.

————, ed. *Writing the Female Voice.* Boston: Northeastern University Press, 1989.

Greer, Margaret Rich. *Maria de Zayas Tells Baroque Tales of Love and the Cruelty of Men.* University Park: Pennsylvania State University Press, 2000.

Hackett, Helen. *Women and Romance Fiction in the English Renaissance.* Cambridge: Cambridge University Press, 2000.

Hall, Kim F. *Things of Darkness: Economies of Race and Gender in Early Modern England.* Ithaca, N.Y.: Cornell University Press, 1995.

Hampton, Timothy. *Literature and the Nation in the Sixteenth Century: Inventing Renaissance France.* Ithaca, N.Y.: Cornell University Press, 2001.

Hardwick, Julie. *The Practice of Patriarchy: Gender and the Politics of Household Authority in Early Modern France.* University Park: Pennsylvania State University Press, 1998.

Harth, Erica. *Ideology and Culture in Seventeenth-Century France.* Ithaca, N.Y.: Cornell University Press, 1983.

———. *Cartesian Women: Versions and Subversions of Rational Discourse in theOld Regime.* Ithaca, N.Y.: Cornell University Press, 1992.

Haselkorn, Anne M., and Betty Travitsky, eds. *The Renaissance Englishwoman in Print: Counterbalancing the Canon.* Amherst: University of Massachusetts Press, 1990.

Herlihy, David. "Did Women Have a Renaissance? A Reconsideration." *Medievalia et Humanistica,* n.s., 13 (1985): 1–22.

Hill, Bridget. *The Republican Virago: The Life and Times of Catharine Macaulay, Historian.* New York: Oxford University Press, 1992.

A History of Women in the West. Vol. 1 *From Ancient Goddesses to Christian Saints,* edited by Pauline Schmitt Pantel. Cambridge, Mass.: Harvard University Press, 1992. Vol. 2, *Silences of the Middle Ages,* edited by Christiane Klapisch-Zuber. Cambridge, Mass.: Harvard University Press, 1992. Vol. 3, *Renaissance and Enlightenment Paradoxes,* edited by Natalie Zemon Davis and Arlette Farge. Cambridge, Mass.: Harvard University Press, 1993.

Hobby, Elaine. *Virtue of Necessity: English Women's Writing, 1646–1688.* London: Virago Press, 1988.

Horowitz, Maryanne Cline. "Aristotle and Women." *Journal of the History of Biology* 9 (1976): 183–213.

Hufton, Olwen H. *The Prospect before Her: A History of Women in Western Europe.* Vol. 1, *1500–1800.* New York: HarperCollins, 1996.

Hull, Suzanne W. *Chaste, Silent, and Obedient: English Books for Women, 1475–1640.* San Marino, Calif.: Huntington Library, 1982.

Hunt, Lynn, ed. *The Invention of Pornography: Obscenity and the Origins of Modernity, 1500–1800.* New York: Zone Books, 1996.

Hutner, Heidi, ed. *Rereading Aphra Behn: History, Theory, and Criticism.* Charlottesville: University Press of Virginia, 1993.

Hutson, Lorna, ed. *Feminism and Renaissance Studies.* New York: Oxford University Press, 1999.

James, Susan E. *Kateryn Parr: The Making of a Queen.* Aldershot: Ashgate Publishing Co., 1999.

Jankowski, Theodora A. *Women in Power in the Early Modern Drama.* Urbana: University of Illinois Press, 1992.

Jansen, Katherine Ludwig. *The Making of the Magdalen: Preaching and Popular Devotion in the Later Middle Ages.* Princeton, N.J.: Princeton University Press, 2000.

Jed, Stephanie H. *Chaste Thinking: The Rape of Lucretia and the Birth of Humanism.* Bloomington: Indiana University Press, 1989.

Jordan, Constance. *Renaissance Feminism: Literary Texts and Political Models*. Ithaca, N.Y.: Cornell University Press, 1990.

Kelly, Joan. "Did Women Have a Renaissance?" In *Women, History, and Theory*. Chicago: University of Chicago Press, 1984. Also in *Becoming Visible: Women in European History*, edited by Renate Bridenthal, Claudia Koonz, and Susan M. Stuard. 3d ed. Boston: Houghton Mifflin, 1998.

———. "Early Feminist Theory and the *Querelle des Femmes*." In *Women, History, and Theory*. Chicago: University of Chicago Press, 1984.

Kelso, Ruth. *Doctrine for the Lady of the Renaissance*. Urbana: University of Illinois Press, 1956, 1978.

King, Carole. *Renaissance Women Patrons: Wives and Widows in Italy, c. 1300–1550*. Manchester: Manchester University Press 1998; distributed in U.S. by St. Martin's Press.

Krontiris, Tina. *Oppositional Voices: Women as Writers and Translators of Literature in the English Renaissance*. London: Routledge, 1992.

Kuehn, Thomas. *Law, Family, and Women: Toward a Legal Anthropology of Renaissance Italy*. Chicago: University of Chicago Press, 1991.

Kunze, Bonnelyn Young. *Margaret Fell and the Rise of Quakerism*. Stanford, Calif.: Stanford University Press, 1994.

Laqueur, Thomas. *Making Sex: Body and Gender from the Greeks to Freud*. Cambridge, Mass.: Harvard University Press, 1990.

Larsen, Anne R., and Colette H. Winn, eds. *Renaissance Women Writers: French Texts/American Contexts*. Detroit: Wayne State University Press, 1994.

Lerner, Gerda. *The Creation of Patriarchy and Creation of Feminist Consciousness, 1000–1870*. New York: Oxford University Press, 1986, 1994.

Levin, Carole, and Jeanie Watson, eds. *Ambiguous Realities: Women in the Middle Ages and Renaissance*. Detroit: Wayne State University Press, 1987.

Levin, Carole, et al. *Extraordinary Women of the Medieval and Renaissance World: A Biographical Dictionary*. Westport, Conn.: Greenwood Press, 2000.

Lindsey, Karen. *Divorced Beheaded Survived: A Feminist Reinterpretation of the Wives of Henry VIII*. Reading, Mass.: Addison-Wesley Publishing Co., 1995.

Lochrie, Karma. *Margery Kempe and Translations of the Flesh*. Philadelphia: University of Pennsylvania Press, 1992.

Love, Harold. *The Culture and Commerce of Texts: Scribal Publication in Seventeenth-Century England*. Amherst: University of Massachusetts Press, 1993.

MacCarthy, Bridget G. *The Female Pen: Women Writers and Novelists, 1621–1818*. Cork: Cork University Press, 1946–47; New York: New York University Press, 1994.

Maclean, Ian. *Woman Triumphant: Feminism in French Literature, 1610–1652*. Oxford: Clarendon Press, 1977.

———. *The Renaissance Notion of Woman: A Study of the Fortunes of Scholasticism and Medical Science in European Intellectual Life*. Cambridge: Cambridge University Press, 1980.

Matter, E. Ann, and John Coakley, eds. *Creative Women in Medieval and Early Modern Italy*. Philadelphia: University of Pennsylvania Press, 1994.

McLeod, Glenda. *Virtue and Venom: Catalogs of Women from Antiquity to the Renaissance*. Ann Arbor: University of Michigan Press, 1991.

Meek, Christine, ed. *Women in Renaissance and Early Modern Europe*. Dublin: Four Courts Press, 2000.

Mendelson, Sara, and Patricia Crawford. *Women in Early Modern England, 1550–1720.* Oxford: Clarendon Press, 1998.

Merrim, Stephanie. *Early Modern Women's Writing and Sor Juana Inés de la Cruz.* Nashville, Tenn.: Vanderbilt University Press, 1999.

Miller, Nancy K. *The Heroine's Text: Readings in the French and English Novel, 1722–1782.* New York: Columbia University Press, 1980.

Miller, Naomi J. *Changing the Subject: Mary Wroth and Figurations of Gender in Early Modern England.* Lexington: University Press of Kentucky, 1996.

Miller, Naomi J., and Gary Waller, eds. *Reading Mary Wroth: Representing Alternatives in Early Modern England.* Knoxville: University of Tennessee Press, 1991.

Monson, Craig A., ed. *The Crannied Wall: Women, Religion, and the Arts in Early Modern Europe.* Ann Arbor: University of Michigan Press, 1992.

Newman, Karen. *Fashioning Femininity and English Renaissance Drama.* Chicago: University of Chicago Press, 1991.

Okin, Susan Moller. *Women in Western Political Thought.* Princeton, N.J.: Princeton University Press, 1979.

Ozment, Steven. *The Bürgermeister's Daughter: Scandal in a Sixteenth-Century German Town.* New York: St. Martin's Press, 1995.

Pacheco, Anita, ed. *Early Women Writers, 1600–1720.* London: Longman, 1998.

Pagels, Elaine. *Adam, Eve, and the Serpent.* New York: Harper Collins, 1988.

Panizza, Letizia, ed. *Women in Italian Renaissance Culture and Society.* Oxford: European Humanities Research Centre, 2000.

Panizza, Letizia, and Sharon Wood, eds. *A History of Women's Writing in Italy.* Cambridge: Cambridge University Press, 2000.

Perry, Ruth. *The Celebrated Mary Astell: An Early English Feminist.* Chicago: University of Chicago Press, 1986.

Rabil, Albert. *Laura Cereta: Quattrocento Humanist.* Binghamton, N.Y.: MRTS, 1981.

Rapley, Elizabeth. *A Social History of the Cloister: Daily Life in the Teaching Monasteries of the Old Regime.* Montreal: McGill-Queen's University Press, 2001.

Raven, James, Helen Small, and Naomi Tadmor, eds. *The Practice and Representation of Reading in England.* Cambridge: Cambridge University Press, 1996.

Reardon, Colleen. *Holy Concord within Sacred Walls: Nuns and Music in Siena, 1575–1700.* Oxford: Oxford University Press, 2001.

Reiss, Sheryl E., and David G. Wilkins, ed. *Beyond Isabella: Secular Women Patrons of Art in Renaissance Italy.* Kirksville, Mo.: Turman State University Press, 2001.

Rheubottom, David. *Age, Marriage, and Politics in Fifteenth-Century Ragusa.* Oxford: Oxford University Press, 2000.

Richardson, Brian. *Printing, Writers and Readers in Renaissance Italy.* Cambridge: Cambridge University Press, 1999.

Riddle, John M. *Contraception and Abortion from the Ancient World to the Renaissance.* Cambridge, Mass.: Harvard University Press, 1992.

———. *Eve's Herbs: A History of Contraception and Abortion in the West.* Cambridge, Mass.: Harvard University Press, 1997.

Rose, Mary Beth. *The Expense of Spirit: Love and Sexuality in English Renaissance Drama.* Ithaca, N.Y.: Cornell University Press, 1988.

———. *Gender and Heroism in Early Modern English Literature.* Chicago: University of Chicago Press, 2002.

————, ed. *Women in the Middle Ages and the Renaissance: Literary and Historical Perspectives.* Syracuse, N.Y.: Syracuse University Press, 1986.

Sackville-West, Vita. *Daughter of France: The Life of La Grande Mademoiselle.* Garden City, N.Y.: Doubleday, 1959.

Schiebinger, Londa. *Nature's Body: Gender in the Making of Modern Science.* Boston: Beacon Press, 1993.

Schutte, Anne Jacobson, Thomas Kuehn, and Silvana Seidel Menchi, eds. *Time, Space, and Women's Lives in Early Modern Europe.* Kirksville, Mo.: Truman State University Press, 2001.

Shannon, Laurie. *Sovereign Amity: Figures of Friendship in Shakespearean Contexts.* Chicago: University of Chicago Press, 2002.

Shemek, Deanna. *Ladies Errant: Wayward Women and Social Order in Early Modern Italy.* Durham, N.C.: Duke University Press, 1998.

Sobel, Dava. *Galileo's Daughter: A Historical Memoir of Science, Faith, and Love.* New York: Penguin Books, 2000.

Sommerville, Margaret R. *Sex and Subjection: Attitudes to Women in Early-Modern Society.* London: Arnold, 1995.

Spencer, Jane. *The Rise of the Woman Novelist: From Aphra Behn to Jane Austen.* Oxford: Basil Blackwell, 1986.

Spender, Dale. *Mothers of the Novel: 100 Good Women Writers before Jane Austen.* London: Routledge, 1986.

Sperling, Jutta Gisela. *Convents and the Body Politic in Late Renaissance Venice.* Chicago: University of Chicago Press, 1999.

Steinbrügge, Lieselotte. *The Moral Sex: Woman's Nature in the French Enlightenment.* Translated by Pamela E. Selwyn. New York: Oxford University Press, 1995.

Stephens, Sonya, ed. *A History of Women's Writing in France.* Cambridge: Cambridge University Press, 2000.

Stuard, Susan M. "The Dominion of Gender: Women's Fortunes in the High Middle Ages." In *Becoming Visible: Women in European History,* edited by Renate Bridenthal, Claudia Koonz, and Susan M. Stuard. 3d ed. Boston: Houghton Mifflin, 1998.

Summit, Jennifer. *Lost Property: The Woman Writer and English Literary History, 1380–1589.* Chicago: University of Chicago Press, 2000.

Teague, Frances. *Bathsua Makin, Woman of Learning.* Lewisburg, Pa.: Bucknell University Press, 1999.

Todd, Janet. *The Secret Life of Aphra Behn.* London: Pandora, 2000.

————. *The Sign of Angelica: Women, Writing and Fiction, 1660–1800.* New York: Columbia University Press, 1989.

Van Dijk, Susan, Lia van Gemert, and Sheila Ottway, eds. *Writing the History of Women's Writing: Toward an International Approach: Proceedings of the Colloquium, Amsterdam, 9–11 September 1998.* Amsterdam: Royal Netherlands Academy of Arts and Sciences, 2001.

Wall, Wendy. *The Imprint of Gender: Authorship and Publication in the English Renaissance.* Ithaca, N.Y.: Cornell University Press, 1993.

Walsh, William T. *St. Teresa of Avila: A Biography.* Rockford, Ill.: TAN Books and Publications, 1987.

Warner, Marina. *Alone of All Her Sex: The Myth and Cult of the Virgin Mary.* New York: Knopf, 1976.

Warnicke, Retha M. *The Marrying of Anne of Cleves: Royal Protocol in Tudor England.* Cambridge: Cambridge University Press, 2000.

Watt, Diane. *Secretaries of God: Women Prophets in Late Medieval and Early Modern England.* Cambridge: D. S. Brewer, 1997.

Welles, Marcia L. *Persephone's Girdle: Narratives of Rape in Seventeenth-Century Spanish Literature.* Nashville, Tenn.: Vanderbilt University Press, 2000.

Whitehead, Barbara J., ed. *Women's Education in Early Modern Europe: A History, 1500–1800.* New York: Garland Publishing Co., 1999.

Wiesner, Merry E. *Women and Gender in Early Modern Europe.* Cambridge: Cambridge University Press, 1993.

———. *Working Women in Renaissance Germany.* New Brunswick, N.J.: Rutgers University Press, 1986.

Willard, Charity Cannon. *Christine de Pizan: Her Life and Works.* New York: Persea Books, 1984.

Wilson, Katharina, ed. *An Encyclopedia of Continental Women Writers.* New York: Garland, 1991.

Woods, Susanne. *Lanyer: A Renaissance Woman Poet.* New York: Oxford University Press, 1999.

Woods, Susanne, and Margaret P. Hannay, eds. *Teaching Tudor and Stuart Women Writers.* New York: MLA, 2000.

INDEX